Russia's Wars of Emergence, 1460–1730

MODERN WARS IN PERSPECTIVE

General Editors: H. M. Scott and B. W. Collins

This ambitious series offers wide-ranging studies of specific wars, and distinct phases of warfare, from the close of the Middle Ages to the present day. It aims to advance the current integration of military history into the academic mainstream. To that end, the books are not merely traditional campaign narratives, but examine the causes, course and consequences of major conflicts, in their full international political, social and ideological contexts.

ALSO IN THIS SERIES

Russia's Wars of Emergence, 1460–1730

Carol B. Stevens

PEARSON
Longman

Harlow, England • London • New York • Boston • San Francisco • Toronto
Sydney • Tokyo • Singapore • Hong Kong • Seoul • Taipei • New Delhi
Cape Town • Madrid • Mexico City • Amsterdam • Munich • Paris • Milan

PEARSON EDUCATION LIMITED

Edinburgh Gate
Harlow CM20 2JE
United Kingdom
Tel: +44 (0)1279 623623
Fax: +44 (0)1279 431059
Website: www.pearsoned.co.uk

First edition published in Great Britain in 2007

© Pearson Education Limited 2007

The right of Carol B. Stevens to be identified as author of this work has been
asserted by her in accordance with the Copyright, Designs and Patents Act 1988.

ISBN: 978-0-582-21891-8

British Library Cataloguing in Publication Data
A CIP catalogue record for this book can be obtained from the British Library

Library of Congress Cataloging in Publication Data
Stevens, Carol Belkin.
    Russia's wars of emergence : 1460–1730 / Carol B. Stevens.
        p. cm.
    Includes bibliographical references and index.
    ISBN-13: 978-0-582-21891-8
    ISBN-10: 0-582-21891-8
    1. Russia—History, Military.   I. Title.

    DK51.S65 2007
    947'.04—dc22
                                        2006052477

10 9 8 7 6 5 4 3 2 1
10 09 08 07

Set by 35 in 10/13.5pt Sabon
Printed in Malaysia (CTP-VVP)

The Publisher's policy is to use paper manufactured from sustainable forests.

Contents

Maps

Acknowledgements

We are grateful to the following for permission to reproduce copyright material:

Map 1 adapted from www.euratlas.com; maps 4 and 6 adapted from Gilbert, Martin, *Atlas of Russian History* (Marboro Books, 1989), by permission of Wiedenfeld and Nicolson, a division of the Orion Publishing Group; maps 5 and 9 adapted from Frost, Robert I., *The Northern Wars, 1558–1721* (Pearson Education, 2000), by permission of Pearson Education Limited; map 7 adapted from Stevens, Carol Belkin, *Soldiers on the Steppe: Army Reform and Social Change In Early Modern Russia* (Northern Illinois University Press, 1995), by permission of Northern Illinois University Press; map 10 adapted from Konstam, Angus, *Poltava, 1709: Russia Comes of Age* (Osprey, 1994) © Osprey Publishing Ltd.

In some instances we have been unable to trace copyright holders and would appreciate any information that would enable us to do so.

Abbreviations

AAASS	American Association for the Advancement of Slavic Studies
AAE	Akty sobrannye v bibliotekakh i arkhivakh Rossiskoi Imperii Arkheograficheskoiu ekspeditsieiu
AI	Akty istoricheskie
AIIuZR	Akty, otnosiashchiesia k istorii iuzhnoi i zapdnoi Rossii
AMG	Akty Moskovskago gosudarstva
AN SSSR II	Institut istorii, Akademiia Nauk Sovietskikh Sotsialisticheskikh Respublik
CASS	Canadian-American Slavic Studies
ChOIDR	Chteniia v Imperatorskom obshchestvie istorii i drevnostei rossiskikh pri Moskovskom universitetie
CMRS	Cahiers du monde russe et soviétique
CSSH	Comparative Studies in Society and History
DAI	Dopolnenie k aktam istoricheskim
FzOG	Forschungen zur Osteuropäischen Geschichte
IZ	Istoricheskie zapiski
JfGO	Jahrbücher für Geschichte Osteuropas
PSRL	Polnoe sobranie russkikh lietopisei
PSZ	Polnoe sobranie zakonov
RGADA	Rossiiskii gosudarstvennyi arkhiv drevnikh aktov
RGVIA	Rossiiskii gosudarstvennyi voenno-istoricheskii arkhiv
RIB	Russkaia istoricheskaia biblioteka
SEER	Slavonic and East European Review
SR	Slavic Review
VIO	Voennaia istoriia otechestva
ZhMNP	Zhurnal Ministerstva Narodnago Prosveshcheniia

Chronology

Part I: 1450–1598

1420	Golden Horde breaking apart
	Khanates of Crimea and Kazan, steppe successors
1425–62	Reign of Vasilii II in Moscow
	Intermittent civil war
1453	Constantinople falls to the Ottoman Turks
1456	Vasilii's campaign against Novgorod ends with Treaty of Iazelbitsy and Moscow's claim of suzerainty
1462	**Ivan III** ascends Muscovite throne
	Muscovy begins period of rapid expansion; for example:
1462	Muscovite raids to the northeast
1463	Absorption of Iaroslavl
1465	Muscovy raids the Iugra tribes
1470–8	Final absorption of Novgorod, although shows of force, confiscations continued thereafter
1470s–1480s	Raids on Lithuanian borderlands
1485	Absorption of Tver
1466 or 1468	Tver merchant Afanasii Nikitin begins his journey to India
1467–78	Muscovy involved in Kazan's succession struggles
1472	Tatar attack on Muscovy halted at Aleksin and Serpukhov
1480	Muscovy joins Khanate of Crimea in military alliance
	The Stand on the Ugra (Great Horde and Lithuania v. Moscow and allies)
1480–93	Tensions among Pskov, Novgorod, Livonian Order, Moscow
1485	Construction begins on Moscow Kremlin
1486–7	Muscovy involved in Kazan's dynastic disputes

1490s	Moldavia joins Crimean–Muscovite alliance against Lithuania
1492–4	Hostilities between Lithuania and Muscovy
	Livonian tensions:
1492	Construction of Ivangorod
1494	Twenty-year hiatus in Hanseatic trade in Novgorod begins
1500–3	Muscovite war with Lithuania; Livonian Order supports Lithuania
1500	Growing use of *pomest'e* or service landholding
1500	Muscovite victory on the Vedrosha River against Poland and Lithuania
1505	**Vasilii III** comes to the throne of Moscow
1508	Muscovite–Lithuanian tension leads to hostilities
1510	Muscovy annexes Pskov
1510s	Crimean–Muscovite alliance breaking down
1510s–1520s	Dynastic quarrels in Kazan and Muscovite intervention
1512–22	Moscow at war with Lithuania, ending in five-year truce
1513–14	Sieges of Smolensk, capture of the city by Muscovy
1514	Muscovite defeat on the Orsha
	Crimea allies itself with Lithuania
1521	Crimean attack reaches the city of Moscow
1522	Appearance of *guliai gorod*
1523	Construction of Vasil'sursk to ease attacks on Kazan
	Relations between Muscovy and Kazan relax in late 1520s
1527	String of fortresses completed guarding southern Muscovy
	Muscovite Lithuanian truce extended to 1534
1533	Young **Ivan IV** comes to Muscovite throne (regency)
1547	**Ivan IV** is crowned Moscow's first tsar
1550–1	Construction of Sviazhsk outside Kazan
1550s	Important reforms, including:
	Introduction of the *streltsy* or musketeer troops
	Law Code of 1550
	Regularization of service-land (*pomest'e*) requirements
1546–52	Successive attacks on Kazan leading to its conquest, October 1552
1554, 1556	Conquest of Astrakhan by Moscow
late 1550s	Southern fortresses built to protect expanding southern frontier

1557–8	Unsuccessful Muscovite attack on Crimea
1558–83	Livonian War: Sweden, Poland–Lithuania, Muscovy
1558–63	Muscovites largely successful in Livonia
1559–60	Failed Muscovite campaigns against Crimea
1562–3	Muscovy's campaign against Polotsk captures the city, but thereafter Muscovite successes begin to stall
1563–70	Seven Years' War (Denmark v. Sweden)
1565	*Oprichnina* begins in Muscovy
1569	Ottoman campaign against Muscovite Astrakhan fails
	Union of Lublin joins Poland and Lithuania in Commonwealth
1571	Crimean troops reach the city of Moscow
1572	*Oprichnina* dissolved
	Second Crimean attack turned back
	Southern defences reorganized in following years
1577–82	Muscovite exhaustion; flight and poverty in the heartland
1580–1	Forbidden Years limit peasant movement
1582	The Peace of Iam Zapolskii
1583	Treaty ends War with Sweden; Narva and Ivangorod become Swedish possessions
1582	Ermak briefly captures capital of Khanate of Sibir
1584	**Tsar Fedor** inherits the throne; Boris Godunov dominates regency
1591	Death of Dmitrii (non-canonical son of Ivan IV) in Uglich
1590–5	Resumed fighting in eastern Baltic
	Continued fortress construction on the southern frontier
1595	Treaty of Teusino ends fighting with Sweden
1595–1602	New walls, fortifications added to Smolensk fortress by Muscovy
1598	Death of Tsar Fedor; succession unclear
	Godunov elected after nine-month hiatus

Part II: 1598–1697

1598	**Tsar Boris** crowned
	Expansion into southern borderlands as heartlands depopulate
1601–3	Famine in central Muscovy

1604	Claimant to throne, Dmitrii, gains support in Muscovite southwest
1605	Brief reign of **Tsar Fedor Godunov**
	Dmitrii and his army advance on Moscow
	Battle of Dobrynichi; mercenary Captain Jacques Margeret
1605–6	**Tsar Dmitrii**
1606	**Tsar Vasilii Shuiskii** enthroned after Dmitrii's assassination
	Shuiskii's rule challenged by Bolotnikov, Riazan forces, Pretender Peter, and a second Dmitrii
1608–9	Tushino functions as a rival to Moscow, the rebel capital
	Shuiskii negotiates with Sweden, Poland, as latter's army advances
1610–11	Shuiskii's abdication
	Selection of Wladyslaw of Poland as successor
	Polish troops occupy Moscow; military resistance organizes
1612	Moscow reconquered from Polish forces (Minin and Pozharskii)
1613	**Tsar Michael Romanov** crowned
1617	Peace of Stolbovo marks end of fighting with Sweden
1618–48	Thirty Years' War
1619	Truce of Deulino marks end of fighting with Commonwealth
1632–4	Smolensk War
	Moscow's siege of the city fails
	Use of new formation troops
	Peace of Polianovka
1635–53	Construction and garrisoning of Belgorod defensive wall across south
	Formation of Belgorod military administrative district
1645	**Tsar Aleksei Mikhailovich** inherits the throne
1640s–1650s	Building of Simbirsk defensive line
1648	Khmelnytsky rebellion in Ukraine against Royal Poland
1649	Ulozhenie; Law Code enserfs Muscovite peasantry
1654	Pereiaslav Agreement (Muscovy and Ukraine under Khmelnytsky)
1654–67	Thirteen Years' War: Muscovy v. Commonwealth
1656–61	Muscovy v. Sweden

1657	Bodgan Khmelnytsky's death
1659	Muscovy's fighting with Commonwealth intensifies
	Battle of Konotop ends in Muscovite defeat, large manpower losses
1660–	Muscovite army steps up use of new formation troops
Late 1660s– late 1680s	Continued fighting especially devastating in Right Bank Ukraine
1667–71	Cossack Stenka Razin's activity turns to rebellion in Muscovite south
1676	**Tsar Fedor** inherits the throne
1678–81	Russo-Ottoman War ending in Treaty of Bakhchisarai
1679	Izium defensive line construction begins; Ukrainain resettlement
1678–82	Military reform culminating in abolition of precedence ranking
1682	On Tsar Fedor's death, co-tsar's **Peter** and **Ivan** rule jointly after rebellion in the capital; **Sophia**, their sister, acts as their regent
1686	Treaty of 'Eternal Peace' with Poland
	Russia joins Holy League
1687	Muscovy's campaign against Crimea fails
1689	Treaty of Nerchinsk sets Sino-Muscovite border in Amur valley
1689	Second Muscovite campaign against Crimea also fails
	Overturning of Sophia's government
	Tsars Peter and **Ivan** begin their joint personal reign
1695	Peter's first campaign against Ottoman Azov fails
1696	Peter's second campaign on the Black Sea littoral succeeds

Part III: 1698–1730

1696	Ivan, Peter's half-brother, dies; **Peter** rules alone
1697–8	Peter's Grand Embassy to Europe
	Strelets rebellion in the Russian capital
1699	Preparations for war against Sweden
1700	Great Northern War begins
1700	Charles XII of Sweden defeats Russian siege of Narva
1701–6	Swedish troops fighting in Poland; Russian troops winning near Baltic

1705	National conscription supports Russian troops
1705–8	Astrakhan rebellion; Bulavin rebellion
1707–9	Poltava campaign – Swedes move against Russia
1708	Battle of Lesnaia; Swedish army baggage train lost
	Cossack Hetman Mazeppa shifts his support to
	Charles XII
1709	Battle of Poltava; Swedish defeat
	Defeated Swedes retreat into Ottoman Empire
	War continues near the Baltic
1710–11	Russo-Ottoman War
	Pruth campaign – Russian forces defeated
1711	Senate created; institutionalization of power accelerates
1713, 1723	Russian *landmilitsiia* regiments take shape
1721	Peace of Nystadt concludes the Great Northern War
1722–4	Russo-Persian War
	Creation of Nizovoi Corps
1725	Peter's death; **Catherine I** succeeds to the throne
1727	Catherine dies, succeeded by **Peter II**, whose rule lasts till
	1730
1732	Russian forces withdraw from Caspian ports

Introduction

This book examines the development of Russian military power and its interaction with social, administrative and ideological change in Russian society. It covers a period of nearly 300 years, from the reign of Ivan III in the fifteenth century beyond that of Peter I in the early eighteenth century. It begins as the principality of Moscow emerged as an important military contender in western Eurasia, among those states left after the collapse of the Mongol Empire. Since the 1240s, Moscow and its neighbours had been adjuncts to that vast steppe conglomeration, which connected eastern Europe with China and Persia. The Mongols had conquered and maintained their empire with fast-moving, rapidly mobilized armies of cavalry archers, whose native turf was the open and sparsely populated steppe. Muscovy, like other societies on the steppe periphery, adopted some of the Mongol Empire's successful military strategies and structures. Its armies too were dominated by troops of cavalry archers. Guns and gunpowder, which by the early fifteenth century were contributing to major transformations of armies and their tactics further west, were of less obvious value to such steppe forces. Guns and artillery could slow the pace of fast-moving cavalry units. So, although both Muscovy and the Tatar Khanates knew and used some gunpowder weapons, these weapons were of relatively minor military importance to them.

From the time of Ivan III, however, the direction of Muscovy's military concerns underwent first subtle and then increasingly rapid change. For many years, steppe-style warfare, with its far-reaching raids, the capture of prisoners and the devastating property damage that accompanied it, remained an important military format for Muscovy, and the cavalryman-archer the dominant military figure. However, Muscovy underwent rapid territorial expansion in the late fifteenth and throughout much of the sixteenth century. It came into increasingly frequent military contact with the

Baltic and Scandinavian powers, with Poland and Lithuania and with the Ottoman Empire, and it defended long and lengthening steppe frontiers. In this context, fortress defence and gunpowder warfare were of growing interest, despite the existing military framework. At the same time, confrontations with its new, larger neighbours also required more numerous, more reliable and better-supplied armies. Through the persistent wars in the seventeenth century, Muscovy aspired to a quite different kind of army that was very large, and yet still included trained gunpowder troops (both infantry and cavalry) supported by a state bureaucracy.

By 1730 Russia had in many respects achieved its new military aims. It had attained parity with contemporary European states, without abandoning the military demands of its still important steppe frontiers. The many reform projects of the seventeenth century had proved important precursors to Peter I's reorganization of the Russian military (and much else). The changes were vindicated, in part, by the Russian victory in a protracted and gruelling war against Sweden, the Baltic's dominant military power. In territorial terms, the gains of the Great Northern War (1700–21) were not impressive by comparison with Russia's dramatic acquisitions of the preceding century in Ukraine and Siberia. Symbolically, however, its newly achieved access to the Baltic seacoast was taken to represent a turn away from the steppe and its emergence into a European (and Ottoman) community of major powers. The army and navy with which these results were achieved shared a variety of key characteristics with other members of that community: its government identified and claimed the necessary men and resources, and it commanded not only the technology and organization, but also the social and political will to deploy large, trained, permanent, and (largely) state-supported armed forces. Notwithstanding its successes, the Russian military of the early eighteenth century had some unusual characteristics by comparison with early modern European armies (and navies). The defence needs of Russia's still open steppe resulted in a deployment of residential militia, for example. Its army maintained an unusually high proportion of cavalry, and its navy acted more as a support for the army than as an independent military arm. Nonetheless, according to the understanding of military historians, it had achieved the creation of a 'modern' military, which over the coming century would rival the achievements of other European powers. The reigns of Peter's consort and son in the years following his death demonstrated the degree to which Petrine changes had become the fundamental standard for Russian military activity.

This remarkable three-century-long transition was not easily achieved by the Muscovite state or by the socially, ethnically and religiously diverse population that made up the Russian Empire. Individual elements of the transformation (such as Peter I's military reforms) and its broader questions (what was the nature of Muscovite rebellion?) are hotly debated by historians and military theoreticians. For others, the answers to such questions have current political, patriotic and cultural implications. This book offers a synthesis for students of the many interpretations and sources illuminated by a lively, ongoing exchange of ideas. At the same time, it is hoped that the particular synthesis offered here will also contribute to the advancement of debate. Several important themes in that synthesis deserve to be clearly stated at the outset.

First, the broad similarities of military change in central and western Europe and in the Ottoman Empire during the early modern period have not escaped the notice of historians. Since the mid-1950s much of the discussion of those similarities has revolved around the concept of 'military revolution'. Michael Roberts then suggested that a series of important changes in warfare took place, largely between 1550 and 1650, as gunpowder and firearms were generally adopted, and, as infantry armament, became important elements of armies and navies. First, tactics changed: individual knights and archers were gradually replaced by trained men bearing firearms; since these latter were organized in troops with a hierarchy of commanding officers their battlefield abilities changed. Second, army size grew dramatically, as governments proved themselves capable of mustering more and more men and resources. Large armies brought changes in strategic manoeuvres, as so many men could be moved across significant distances, albeit with great cost and complexity. Finally and perhaps most significantly, Roberts stressed the ways in which social and political structures interacted with military change. A society politically dominated by an independent nobility that prided itself on its role as knights and cavalrymen, for example, might resist supporting the growth of infantry forces commanded by a king. Alternatively, states developed sophisticated administrative methods and ready funding sources to support large trained armies year-round. Intangibles such as social discipline (would soldiers obey their officers?) were also important factors. Since Roberts initially voiced the interpretation, Geoffrey Parker and others have extended and refined definitions of military revolution. Jeremy Black, among others, has countered with the idea of key periods of military change rather than revolutionary change confined to a particular period.

All schools agree, however, that a dramatic alteration had taken place in European and Ottoman military capabilities by the eighteenth century.[1]

It is clear that the Russian transition shared many elements with the kind of changes described in the preceding paragraph. By the Petrine era, the Russian Empire mustered regiments of trained, tactically responsive infantry and cavalry, a supporting navy, and the kinds of administrative structures that could reliably put such units in the field.

However, Russian military change is not entirely described by the European military transition. Muscovy was not a part of the first military changes of the early modern period, led by the Spanish Habsburgs; Russia's army was then a mobile steppe cavalry. Indeed, it was not an integral part of the competitive Euro-Ottoman military nexus at all until the second half of the seventeenth century at the earliest. Even after Peter I, the Russian military force retained some quite atypical features, including its defensive landmilitia and its high percentage of cavalry. One interpretation of these distinctions, vocally shared by individual Russian leaders including Peter I himself, sees Russia emerging from backwardness and stagnation to adopt, as well as it was able, western or European military standards. Another version, no doubt generated in part in response to the preceding, argues the case for Muscovite exceptionalism; the unusual, often conflicting demands upon the Russian armed forces in the early modern era resulted in uniquely Russian military successes and solutions.

This text urges a rather different interpretation. Muscovy's military transformation was a geopolitical one as well. Russia's primary military and diplomatic concerns moved away from its steppe neighbours and its southern frontiers by the eighteenth century; its rivals in Constantinople and in Europe occupied the foreground of its foreign policy as the Empire itself expanded. In military terms, such a change certainly included a deliberate effort to import and replicate important elements of its new rivals' military styles. If Russia's geopolitical focus shifted, however, its environment and some of its immediate military foes did not. Not only Russia, but also the Habsburgs, the Ottomans, the Polish-Lithuanian armies and the Swedes often fought on the edges of what we now think of as eastern Europe. This characteristically included tracts of enormous size and a relatively sparse population; a land of open grassy steppe in the south, punctuated by marshy wetlands like the Pripet marshes in the north. In a pre-industrial world, this made quite different demands on armies and on the arrangements that supported them – very different from fighting in western Europe, for example. Defensive garrisons and a high proportion of cavalry were military responses to such conditions not only by Russia, but also by other military forces operating in the area. Their replication along the eastern frontier of Europe suggests a different path of military development, and is not best understood by reference to backwardness or modernization. In the Russian case (as in others) this 'military revolution in [north]eastern Europe'[2] carried political, administrative and social implications.

Military change is neither simply and starkly military, nor technological. The second particular emphasis of this volume is its focus on the military changes, as much as military innovation *sensu stricto*. Thus, this book focuses on the ways in which political organization, the political will of elites, environment, economics and social structure interacted with Russia's military efforts in the early modern era. To offer but a few related examples:

Changing Russian political structures are particularly important for understanding its military perspectives. European Russia was quite sparsely populated in the early modern period; it had a self-sustaining but hardly thriving agricultural economy. For this reason, an important problem for a Muscovite military was how its government could mobilize and use effectively resources that were both limited and scattered. The development of the service landholding system is an oft-cited example of how Muscovite political and administrative institutions dealt with one element of this problem. Thus, by the early 1500s members of the elite were being offered land for their own use if they served loyally in the Muscovite army. This arrangement helped to wean men away from private armies and consolidate Russian political and military power in the early part of the sixteenth century. The gradual regularization of such military service put a large army at Moscow's disposal in return for minimal cash investment.

Military position and court status were closely linked indicators of social standing for the Muscovite elite. Beginning in the seventeenth century, however, it became necessary to abandon a noble cavalry army in the sixteenth-century mode for a mass army with infantry and cavalry regiments. The ability to accomplish that required a very cautious renegotiation of social and political expectations among the elite. Among other things, that process spurred the legal codification of serfdom.

Finally, economic and administrative questions – how to conscript, pay and supply an army – interacted delicately with developing state structures and a changing society. Contextual questions such as these are an important element in understanding the constraints and successes of Russian military change in the early modern period.

The nature of Russian military innovation is another theme of this volume. Although Muscovy and then the Russian Empire certainly had expansionist modes, these were by no means persistent or uniform efforts. Like most other governments, however, when it put troops in the field, Muscovy usually wanted to win. Its ability to do so depended on continuing, often innovative, domestic responses to developing military problems. As the Empire grew and its armies came into contact with different opponents and differing military styles, it also adapted or borrowed outright military techniques and organizational forms being used by its enemies. When the Russian military did make use of foreign military practices, insofar as such things can be documented, it did so in an eminently practical and experiential way. Adopting the military usages of a successful enemy was (and is) a common phenomenon. In the early modern era, the Ottoman, French and Venetian armies and navies borrowed techniques from one another, often after experiencing their successful application in battle. Thus, Muscovy adapted cavalry techniques from its steppe neighbours in the fourteenth century, and Peter I deliberately borrowed Swedish organizational principles early in the eighteenth century.

While this seems both predictable and unsurprising, a few more words deserve to be said, lest its implications pass unrecognized. First, this emphasis on practical experience implies a relative absence of discussion about the theoretical 'arts of war'. To a certain extent, this was characteristic of the period, rather than a Muscovite peculiarity. In the Netherlands, for example, where there was a printed literature about military theory and behaviour, military innovation still tended to develop as much from battlefield confrontation as from written exposition.[3] Muscovy however remained aloof from any (printed) debate about military theory and behaviour until the time of Peter I and after. Thus it was concrete exposure and awareness – more information, the techniques of mercenaries, battlefield experience and diplomatic contact – that helped direct Russian military innovation. Although ideology, religious and political affinity helped or hindered Russia's acquisition of such information, they themselves were not the governing factors. Practical experience was. When Russia borrowed military techniques, therefore, it did not usually reproduce 'European' or 'steppe' techniques. Rather, it borrowed specific techniques from particular armies, most frequently from its immediate adversaries – typically the Swedes or the Poles. Adapting new techniques often required adjustment with domestic political and social institutions, as mentioned above, but it also encouraged the development of regional military characteristics.

Just as Russia's military experience was far from uniformly European, some of its characteristics (and some of Russia's military borrowings) came from non-European sources. The European emphasis of much military history obscures the impact on the Russian military and society of its southern neighbours. These ranged from the highly organized, militarily formidable Ottoman Empire, through the Ottoman's Crimean ally, to nomadic peoples on the steppe whose raiding attacks were a persistent and debilitating problem both to Muscovy and to its successor, the growing Russian Empire. The nature of the military (and socio-political) impact of its southern neighbours on Russia is less intensively studied, although there seems little doubt that the impact was wide-ranging and significant. The defensive 'walls' of the Muscovite south, for example, represented an innovative use of military resources for defence; the frontier zones also created an anomalous social space, which helped Muscovy to negotiate the transition to a mass army.

One should certainly not, however, envision Muscovy as fighting two different kinds of war – one against the south and another in the west. In Muscovy-Russia's most successful moments, military innovations taken on by Moscow's socio-political institutions were applied with some uniformity across Moscow's army. If arquebuses were used in the annexation of Pskov, Muscovites also brought them to the stand on the Ugra. Rapid cavalry raids and the *guliai gorod* were a staple of war against Lithuania as well as in the east. The standing units that defended the southern frontier by the 1720s were equally prepared to launch a cavalry response and to march westward to battle. In short, the Muscovite army used military and technological innovation to develop a coordinated, unified response along all its frontiers.

Russia's military efforts across the early modern period thus emerge as a particularly close interplay of domestic concerns and adjustments with European military technologies and innovations filtered by the requirements of military life in western Eurasia. By the mid-eighteenth century, this proved a potent combination indeed.

The numerous political changes and linguistic diversity in eastern Europe and western Eurasia lay complex pitfalls for those writing about the area. This book strives to combine familiar spellings and names with historical accuracy where possible, although the results may not strike individual readers as felicitous. Existing English-language conventions have been generally observed. Thus, Moscow and Kiev, not Moskva and Kyiv; by the same token, Fedor not Theodore and Aleksei not Alexis. Muscovy refers to the pre-Petrine government; Russia to an ethno-geographic area and the Petrine state. When writing Ukrainian names, I preferred –sky to –skyi, while for Russian names such endings are written –skii. Place names are particularly difficult, since individual locations in the Baltic area have quite different names in three or more languages/political arenas. I have attempted to indicate variations on the first use and thereafter consistently use one version – often the Russian one, since it is the principal research language of this book. A glossary of terminology used in the book is included for the readers' convenience. Transliteration uses Library of Congress conventions.

In writing books, authors incur debts, intellectual and otherwise. I am very grateful for the generous help and advice offered by so many individuals, without whom this book could not have been written. Any historical work depends on the written work of predecessors and contemporaries, only some of whom appear in the citations. I should like further to thank Brian Davies, Paul Bushkovich, Janet Martin, Robert Frost, Viktor Ostapchuk, Marshall Poe, Evgenii Anisimov, Lindsey Hughes, Aleksander Kamenskii, Charles Halperin, Elise Kimmerling-Wirschafter, Ben Barker-Benfield and many others variously for illuminating comments and conversations, helpful suggestions, and the careful reading of parts of the manuscript. A number of conferences have listened and commented helpfully on relevant essays, and I am most grateful to all those who participated: 'Muscovy, identity and cultural diversity' (University of California, Los Angeles, 1993); 'Peter the Great' (Gargnano, Italy, 1997); 'The Russian army and society' (Cambridge, Mass., 2000); 'Modernizing Muscovy' (Cambridge, Mass., 2001); 'Writing military history' (Hamilton, NY, 2002); and 'Lives of old Muscovy' (Cambridge, Mass., 2003). Colgate University has offered me generous leaves, support and travel funds. IREX funding permitted me to finish work on the Petrine transition. Friends and family have been generous with their time and moral support. My thanks to them all.

I owe some particular thanks beyond those above. Andrew MacLennan, late of Longman, commissioned and encouraged this book in its early stages. Professor Hamish Scott of St Andrews suggested the book to me; he has been a model editor since the beginning. His patience during the book's long gestation, his care in editing and suggesting improvements, and his encouragement and interested good humour throughout have been much appreciated. Finally, my spouse, Philip Uninsky, has contributed immeasurably to this book in myriad ways.

For its shortcomings, I am alone responsible.

Notes

1 The essays in Clifford Rogers, ed., *The Military Revolution Debate* (Boulder, Col., 1995) articulate a number of the perspectives still being debated.

2 Robert I. Frost, *The Northern Wars, 1558–1721* (Harlow, 2000), 310.

3 Geoffrey Parker, *The Military Revolution. Military Innovation and the Rise of the West, 1500–1800* (Cambridge, 1988), 21–2.

PART I

1450–1598

CHAPTER 1

The constituents of Muscovite power, *c*.1450

Prelude

In the first half of the fifteenth century Muscovy was still a principality of quite modest size by comparison with some of its Eurasian neighbours. The territory it claimed enveloped the principalities of Rostov, Tver, and Iaroslavl in a huge westward-facing C, without yet absorbing them. At its widest, in the south, Moscow's easternmost and westernmost territories were separated by about 800 kilometres (500 miles). In the east its greatest extent from north to south was perhaps a bit larger. These territories in the north-central section of European Russia shared some harsh environmental realities that would play an important role in shaping and limiting Muscovite capabilities in the early modern period (fifteenth–eighteenth centuries). In the north, Muscovy was covered by cold expanses of evergreen forest, *taiga*, where fur hunting and other forest extraction provided a more reliable living than agriculture alone. Further south, most of the major cities and most of the population was in a mixed forest zone. Here, despite the northern climate and short growing season, agricultural lands were passable and, in one area near the city of Vladimir, even excellent. The forests also served as a protective barrier against the open steppe whose rich lands, trade routes and raiding nomads Muscovy regarded with ambivalence.

The population of Muscovy was sparse and widely dispersed in the first part of the fifteenth century. Even in the southernmost regions, it probably had not yet attained seven people per square kilometre.[1] Peasants lived in isolated villages, raising rye and oats, gathering forest products and raising livestock. Small and distant villages simply moved to a new location when soil and other local resources gave out. For those closer to the

Muscovite capital, a growing and somewhat denser population encouraged different agricultural techniques in more permanent settlements. In addition to agriculture and extraction, Muscovites also lived from trade, largely but not exclusively in furs, salt, artisanal and forest goods; trade routes led southward across the open steppe to Crimea and to southeastern Europe. In the early fifteenth century the landscape was dominated by those who taxed these fundamental economic activities: Orthodox Christian monasteries and elite landholders who claimed payments from peasants (who could move away if demands became too onerous); trade fairs and transit taxes supported towns and principalities. The Muscovite prince was the ideological and political centre of the system: an overlord who had absorbed nearby principalities and claimed the fealty of those within them.

The lands of northwestern Eurasia in this era had very limited economic, bureaucratic and demographic resources. As a result, military power was not a matter of competitive margins in technology or strategy. A prince's ability to exercise political authority, despite geographic and institutional limitations, was a key element; although basic, this was not easily achieved. In particular, it depended upon social stability and cohesion from a loyal political elite.

The basic economic and political arrangements of Muscovy had suffered two significant shocks shortly before 1450. First, there was the international demographic catastrophe of the Black Death. In the 1350s and in repeated waves into the 1400s epidemic disease devastated Muscovy's population and that of its neighbours. Particularly important among these, the Golden Horde was Muscovy's overlord, guardian of the steppe trade routes, and heir to the western end of the Mongol Empire. Combined with political infighting and economic disruption, demographic shock helped to undermine the Horde's stability. Early in the fifteenth century the Horde divided into three or four entities, and its control and protection over the steppe trade routes dissolved. Second, between 1430 and 1450, Muscovy erupted into civil war. From 1380 until the start of these hostilities, Muscovy had been on a bumpy but surprisingly successful path of expansion. It had claimed the political heritage of the Grand Prince of Vladimir, attached itself to the moral and institutional power of the eastern Orthodox church, and had grown in wealth and population as it took over neighbouring principalities. But the civil war proved a political vortex, shattering clan and dynastic relationships, and drawing in Moscow's neighbours. As Muscovy recovered, the victorious prince, Vasilii II, began to re-establish the political authority of his throne.

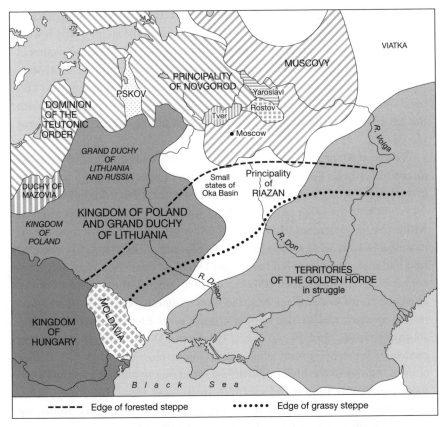

MAP 1   *Western Eurasia, c.1400* (adapted from map on www.euratlas.com)

The accession of Ivan III to the Muscovite throne in 1462 was a pivotal moment in Moscow's political and military development. Most dramatic of all was its uneasy international situation. For Moscow, the uncertainties that followed the collapse of Mongol control were nearly as intimidating as they were liberating. Several potential heirs to the Horde's power were poised competitively on the steppe. To the south and east of Moscow were three rival khans, all members of the Mongol royal family. A senior khan led the Greater Horde near the mouth of the Volga, north of the future Khanate of Astrakhan. Another member of the royal family ruled the Khanate of Crimea, across the steppe to Muscovy's south. The last, the Khanate of Kazan, was on the northern Volga directly east of Moscow. Southeast of the khanates were the Nogai; this nomadic people laid no claim to the Mongol heritage, but often proved a vital ally for those who did. Muscovy's attitude toward the three khanates was ambivalent. Any re-creation of the Golden Horde's former all-encompassing control under the Great Horde was not in its interest. At the same time, Moscow's commerce depended upon trade routes that crossed the steppe, which were less well protected under the Horde's successors and Moscow's current rivals. From 1450 to 1520 such geopolitical considerations motivated Muscovite policies towards the khanates more than its religious and cultural dissimilarities with them.[2] That is, Muscovy often cooperated with the Khanates of Crimea and Kazan to prevent any resurgence of the Great Horde.

To the west of Muscovy, the Grand Duchy of Lithuania, since 1385 linked to Catholic Poland by a dual monarchy under the Jagellonians, had grown significantly more powerful in the aftermath of Mongol collapse. As recently as the reign of Vitovt (d. 1430), Lithuania had annexed lands within 240 kilometres (150 miles) of Moscow, adding to the number of its subjects who were Orthodox Slavs. The size of its Orthodox population had more than once led the Grand Duchy to challenge Moscow's pre-eminence in the Russian Orthodox church. Since Lithuania and Poland stretched south to the Black Sea, the dual monarchy also controlled lands on the western end of the steppe, crucial parts of trade routes running southwest from Moscow. In short, the Grand Duchy was itself a strong contender for steppe prominence as the Golden Horde divided into smaller entities. Earlier in the fifteenth century, Lithuania might have seemed even more formidable than it did in 1450. In the mid fifteenth-century, however, interruptions in the Baltic trade and political disarray following Vitovt's death had somewhat diminished its influence.

As it recovered from civil war, Moscow had little difficulty in seeing itself as the only remaining north Russian contender for power on the steppe.[3] By the early 1400s Muscovy controlled not only Moscow and its hinterland, but had absorbed Vladimir and other territories as well. In the middle of the fifteenth century a number of independent principalities still coexisted with Moscow in the north, some more autonomously than others: Rostov, Iaroslavl, Tver, Riazan, as well as the prosperous commercial centres of Pskov and Novgorod. Despite the impressive territorial dimensions of Novgorod in particular, these principalities were militarily no match for Muscovy. If they were not contenders with Moscow for the role of the Horde, these northeast Russian principalities were concerned with protecting themselves from Muscovite encroachment. Lithuania's proximity and size encouraged them to appeal to the Grand Duchy for aid and support to balance Muscovite expansion. Relations among these close Russian Orthodox neighbours were thus frequently tense, if not precisely over the future of the steppe.

Muscovy by 1460 was thus a regional power naturally concerned with the international power shifts left by the collapse of the Golden Horde. Its neighbours, both Islamic khanates on the steppe and contentious east European states, shared this international orientation. Nearly all of them had become embroiled in the Muscovite dynastic wars under Vasilii II. Ivan III's activities, which signalled a newly aggressive Muscovite foreign policy, initiated a new round of international tensions.

A new political consensus

Muscovy's ability to negotiate this demanding situation depended particularly on two closely linked domestic arrangements. One was the transformation of its political structure; the other, the military organization to which politics was so closely linked. In the aftermath of civil war and reconstruction, neither political nor military structures were formal or institutionalized. Political power was patrimonial and unregulated. It was measured by personal relationships at the royal court in Moscow, where the reigning Grand Prince ruled in conjunction with the heads of major clans or families. By the 1460s, these powerful figures included *boiars* from up to 15 Moscow-based clans, as well as allies, service princes and men of the Muscovite royal family – specifically, Ivan's four younger brothers. In addition, the court included a less powerful but more numerous population of courtiers (*dvoriane*) and other serving men (*deti boiarskie*) who might owe allegiance directly to the Grand Prince or to another of the elite figures just mentioned.[4] These men served the Muscovite Grand Prince at court and on the field of battle for a variety of reasons. Some princes had been vanquished by Moscow's army, while others were no doubt both intimidated and attracted by Moscow's growing might. Less exalted, but still wealthy and important, families were also drawn to the Muscovite court by its superior military and political power as well as sheer wealth in land, servants and trade goods. Loyal service to Moscow thus held the promise of rich rewards. If only one could be noticed amidst the cut-throat competition at the court, status and riches greater than those available in most nearby principalities might be won by nobles and courtiers. For the Grand Prince, maintaining stability and a ruling consensus among these competing figures was a necessary precursor to any international or military success.

Boiars were leading men, representing powerful clans and associated webs of personal alliance, clients and servants. By the middle of the fifteenth century Moscow's *boiars* consistently came from a fairly stable group of families. *Boiar* families supported themselves in large part from lands, purchased or bestowed on them within or near the Principality of Moscow. Acquiring new lands allowed a clan to expand support to its family members and clients. Although these formidable clan groupings competed with one another for high status at the Grand Prince's court in Moscow, *boiar* families after the civil war conceded the need to cooperate with the ruler's assertion of power. Clan feuds and rivalries served only to tear the court apart, destroying the source of the wealth and power that each clan hoped to attain. The dynasty, for its part, solicited advice from its chief courtiers and resolved matters with their consent.[5]

These *boiars* were, above all, a warrior elite. Military prowess won them prominence in their clans and at the Muscovite court. When they attained exalted rank, they attended the court and acted as political advisers. At the same time, they continued to serve in military capacities, leading their retinues into battle and commanding their sovereign's troops.[6] *Boiars'* retinues, made up of free men and slaves and drawn from their relatives, clients and servants, were declining in size and importance by the 1460s.[7] Instead *boiar* advancement was reflected in positions of correspondingly higher trust and authority in the sovereign's forces. *Boiars* and their associates might also be appointed viceregents (*namestniki*), temporarily governing lands in the name of their prince in return for 'feeding' (*kormlenie*) by the local taxpayers.

By contrast with the *boiar* clans, most service princes were recent arrivals at the Muscovite court. Royalty and recently independent rulers in their own right, these princes were forced into Moscow's sphere because their lands had been conquered; because they had been intimidated by Moscow's growing power; and because war had impoverished them. Others were attracted by opportunities for advancement; although loyal service to Moscow meant a loss of independence, in return it offered access to wealth and power that only Moscow commanded.[8] Service princes did not all join Moscow in the same way. Some of them attended court in Moscow but still essentially presided over their former subjects; others did not leave their lands. Still others were allies rather than vassals, some more truculent and jealous of their positions than others. The relative standing of these men at court in Moscow depended on individual circumstances, although their royal blood and recent independent status inclined them to expect particular consideration in their competition with *boiar* families for position, status and advancement.

Members of the royal family, such as Ivan's four younger brothers, were a political issue unto themselves. Prior to Vasilii II (r. 1425–62), the Muscovite throne had for several generations passed according to male primogeniture, from father to eldest surviving son in vertical succession. This was contrary to prevailing usage elsewhere in European Russia, which was lateral male succession, from brother to brother. At first the Muscovite anomaly was a genealogical accident – there were no lateral heirs in the grand princely family, no surviving royal brothers or uncles. However, Ivan's father, Vasilii II, did have surviving uncles, and in 1430 they had duly challenged his right to the throne. After winning the ensuing dynastic conflict, Vasilii appointed his own son, Ivan, as his co-ruler some 15 years before his own death to ensure that Ivan would follow him in vertical succession. When Vasilii died in 1462, he adjured each of his four younger sons and his widow to obey Ivan as ruler of Muscovy. Yet, Vasilii left each of them a significant appanage, or *udel*, in the traditional manner. An appanage was a substantial group of provinces within the borders of Muscovy, given to male members of the royal family to support them in appropriate political, military and economic fashion. Appanage holders were forbidden to alienate the property, which reverted to the throne if the appanage holder's family died out. Until then, however, the royal sons and widow ruled as nearly independent sovereigns in their own appanages. As with the *boiars*, the turmoil of the civil war – as well as their father's will – urged the brothers to cooperate loyally with the throne in military and foreign policy matters. Ivan and his court, on the one hand, and his brothers, on the other, also trusted that subsequent events would define the brothers' role in decision making, their status in Moscow, and the limits of their independence to their own particular benefit.[9]

The growing number of notables at the Muscovite court after the civil war had an important secondary result. It was not only service princes and *boiars* who attended court in Moscow; those local elites and their own retinues – those who had formerly comprised local courts – perforce followed their leaders to Moscow. Some shifted their allegiance directly to the Muscovite court as a condition of their own prince's defeat; the possibility of greater rewards tempted others to serve the Grand Prince directly; some remained attached primarily to outlying courts. As a result, however, Ivan's court swelled not only with notables, but with *boiars*, courtiers (*dvoriane*) and lesser men (*deti boiarskie*) from other principalities. These men of uncertain loyalties joined Muscovites of the same standing to swell the sovereign's court.

From 1462 Ivan III was undisputed ruler of Muscovy, but he ruled over a court that was an unwieldy and unpredictable admixture of elites: *boiars*, vassals, allies, service princes and royal brothers. Ivan's and his court's expectations of one another were individually distinct, often idiosyncratic, based on historical loyalties and experience, conditions of the moment, tradition, locale and some degree of reciprocity, as well as a healthy respect for Muscovite power. In the aftermath of a destructive civil war, these men were generally disposed to be cooperative and cohesive. This inclination was often reinforced by poverty, defeat and intimidation. Nevertheless, in the 1460s, as men were added to the court, the new relationships needed reinforcement. Neither Crown nor courtiers could depend upon traditional habits, principles of service, or established loyalties to govern their interaction. And Muscovy's ability to pursue expansive military and international projects would depend on the reinforcement and stability of political patterns at court.

Moscow's military forces

In the early fifteenth century the Muscovite army was a rather unwieldy grouping of independent units. The Grand Prince's personal forces were an important and growing share of the total number of available fighting men; they included his *boiars*, courtiers and provincial servitors. The *boiars*, however, mustered for military duty attended by their own retinues of fighting men, whose primary loyalty was to their *boiar* commander. Men of the Muscovite royal family and service princes, responding to a call to arms from the Muscovite court, also appeared for service with their personal troops – the *boiars*, courtiers and provincials of their own courts. There was always the possibility that such calls to arms might not be honoured. The leaders of these separate units were then awarded army commands and duties for the duration of a campaign. The relative importance of their responsibilities and the placement of their personal troops directly reflected the commanders' relative standing at the Grand Prince's court. Inversely, military prowess might also advance the standing of a particular field commander upon his return to court. The close connections between the military prowess and the political standing of the elite were thus constantly reinforced.

At mid-century, the army had not recently undergone significant change. The military enjoyed no new technological or organizational advantages over its immediate competitors; technological change was relatively rare in this era. As far as we know, Muscovy's army in 1460 was not significantly different than its Muscovite predecessors, except that the number of men potentially available to Moscow, its *boiars*, allies, vassals, and appanages, grew as the court grew. However, mustering that variegated army under the command of *boiars* and other competitors for political power at court required considerable finesse until habits and principles of military service were developed and reinforced.

Military force in this era and region was overwhelmingly made up of cavalry-archers armed in the Mongol style, with hemp coats, or perhaps light chain mail, swords or sabres, and certainly powerful composite bows with arrows. These accoutrements and cavalry mounts, all of which each warrior brought with him, were relatively inexpensive, but they helped to create a highly mobile army, effective against both steppe and sedentary populations. Military training for cavalrymen was a matter of personal endeavour and daily experience. As a rule, the cavalry consisted of men of relatively high status accompanied by relatives, clients and perhaps combat slaves. Cavalry forces were used for small raids, border forays and larger military campaigns.

The Muscovite army on campaign took a relatively consistent form. The mass of cavalrymen was usually separated into divisions (sometimes called regiments), and then subdivided into hundreds, fifties and tens, each with its own commander. Much of the Grand Prince's court (*dvor*), which included *boiars*, service princes, allies and more lowly courtiers, served in the Great or Centre Division. This Centre was the most prestigious part of the army, unless the Grand Prince himself took the field as commander of his own, Sovereign's, Division. When a relatively small force took the field, the army was organized in three divisions: the Centre supported by the Right and the Left Wings; this was called a 'Small Array'.[10] Based on early sixteenth-century descriptions, it seems likely that, on the battlefield, the Centre Division typically met an enemy attack head on, while the wing divisions tried rapidly to envelope the opposing force. A larger Muscovite force was organized into a Large Array; here a Vanguard and a Rear Guard Division supported the Centre, Left and Right for a total of five divisions.

In the arrays, Muscovite courtiers joined provincial cavalrymen, those loyal to Moscow but not resident at court, and, separately, the troops and retinues who followed the Grand Prince's relatives, vassals and allies. A Tatar prince like the Khan of Kasimov, who served Muscovy, was a valuable and reliable auxiliary to the Grand Prince's army; the Khan commanded his own excellent cavalry. Peasant militias also might accompany an army on the move, although it is not clear if they had a specific military function. In addition, since cavalrymen were responsible for their own supplies, the baggage train was a disaggregate affair, in which peasants and personal servants guarded supplies belonging to particular individuals – an unwieldy and worrisome element in an otherwise very mobile force.

Gunpowder, its weaponry and tactics had not had much impact on these forces – or on Muscovite warfare more broadly – by the mid-fifteenth century. This was not due entirely to ignorance; Moscow was aware of gunpowder and its uses. More than a century earlier, the Muscovites had fired a small cannon at Mongol armies, and the Mongols themselves had had gunpowder weapons. In the early fifteenth century, cannon – probably European imports – were reported elsewhere in Russia, too. The recent civil war and hostility between Moscow and neighbouring Lithuania may have then slowed the transfer of information about recent technical developments in gunpowder warfare. By the mid-fifteenth century, the cannon in Muscovite Eurasia were largely station-ary, and principally used by defenders from behind fortress walls. Since artillery was unreliable as well as difficult to transport, it was rarely used even in battles over fortresses. Furthermore, the Eurasian landscape, sparse population and local military practices meant that the conquest of fortresses was not of central importance in the mid-fifteenth century. Other forms of gunpowder technology, such as hand-held firearms, became numerous only later. Under Ivan III, Muscovy would infrequently use handguns (muzzle-loaded matchlock weapons). Like its Tatar opponents, it found the then-current gunpowder technology to be largely inappropriate to battlefields and strategies geared to mobile cavalry troops.[11]

In the 1450s Moscow's armies were not particularly large, despite the growing number of men upon whom they might have drawn. The huge forces described in some sources probably never existed. It seems likely that command difficulties, logistics and other organizational limitations kept the armies to about 35,000 men, with additional men in auxiliary forces and the baggage train.[12] In Muscovy, more available men probably translated into the ability to call for more frequent campaigns, not to muster larger armies on any particular occasion.

The Grand Prince cautiously developed ways of calling directly upon his new provincial warrior-elite. For example, cross-border raids in the north-northeast were ordered by Moscow in 1462. The troops were led by a *boiar* who had long served Moscow, but most of the cavalry came from territories near the Kazan border whose allegiance to Moscow was less well established: Ustiug, Vologda and Galich. Men from these same ter-ritories were then mustered to defend Muscovite lands (and theirs) when the Tatars counter-attacked. Some of these men also joined later, larger campaigns against Kazan. Men like these might be summoned to fight by a viceregent from Moscow or by their own prince under Muscovite command. In the northeast there were good reasons for them to obey

Moscow's call. The enemy they fought was their own, and if they were successful, the booty was theirs. On one occasion, Moscow even offered food, apparel and arrows for men to guard their own borderlands over the winter.[13] Nevertheless, some provincials withheld their cooperation. Viatka and Perm were semi-independent territories, uncomfortably located between Moscow and Kazan, and they refused to cooperate with Moscow for fear of Tatar reprisals after Muscovite troops had left. As these examples suggest, Moscow's ability to muster provincial forces to fight in its name was growing at mid-century, but not routine.

Moscow used every opportunity to reinforce cooperation and define service to the royal court among newer and more exalted servitors. Military obligations between the Grand Prince and his newer vassals and allies were only sometimes defined by treaty. It was quite possible that individual commanders would fail to appear when called, dispute their roles with other leaders, or even withdraw from a campaign. Thus, mobilizing the full panoply of Muscovite allies and vassals alongside the court still required considerable political finesse. Ivan's brother, Iurii, was assigned to command defensive troops near his own lands in Moscow's name, before he led allied and Muscovite cavalry further afield. Members of the Iaroslav princely family commanded court troops in 1467 and again in 1469. In such situations, when not commanding the defence of their own lands, the royal brothers (and others whose loyalty and responsiveness was suspect) were often accompanied in their military endeavours by trusted *boiars* of the Grand Prince's court.[14] Muscovy's monarch was quite successful in manipulating the successful use of new military elites, but his interactions with them were neither stable (regulated) nor predictable. The importance of elite cooperation in military matters is underscored by the nearly exclusive focus of existing military records on such matters.

Beyond issues of command and logistics, Moscow's ability to muster men and resources for a military campaign also depended on its central administrative apparatus. Historians have frequently argued that the royal administration must have been developing specialized functions by the mid-fifteenth century, because recording military service, tax collection and so forth required it. However, surviving records from this era offer only rudimentary information on this topic and numerous others. In itself, this means little, since fires and wars subsequently destroyed a great many older Muscovite records. Nonetheless, some military appointment books have survived. These record the names and positions of commanders in particular campaigns; they specify that a commander or *voevoda* (who is named) led 'men of Viatka' or 'men of Vladimir', but they do not list the actual number or responsibilities of provincial troops.[15] Historians now speculate that appointment books were primarily records of courtiers' appointments and status, and were not intended to be records of military activities. Even viceregents (*namestniki*) received no written orders that can be discovered. General taxes were less important than might be imagined, when the army supported itself from its lands. Other taxes were presumably local, and their collection decentralized. This all suggests that administrative specialization and record keeping did not support military activity as directly as previously speculated.[16]

Muscovy in 1450 had considerable potential to move beyond its regional prominence on the edge of the Eurasian steppe. Indeed, over the next 150 years, even as it began to consolidate its many-faceted domestic political and military elements, new and competing interests would emerge. In the north the linking of the Scandinavian crowns, though precariously maintained in the fifteenth century, meant the beginnings of a formidable empire northwest of Novgorod. The Baltic Livonian Order would also pose a challenge to the three expansionist powers that surrounded it. Distant and powerful, Habsburgs and Safavids would shortly concern Muscovy, as would the Ottoman Empire, whose relations with Muscovy were often mediated by the Tatars on Crimea.

Under the leadership of Ivan III (r. 1462–1505), Vasilii III (r. 1505–33), and finally Ivan IV (r. 1533–84), Muscovite territory would expand by a factor of three and more. Most impressively, Muscovy absorbed eastern Russian principalities and conquered the Khanates of Kazan, Astrakhan and finally Sibir toward the end of the sixteenth century. Muscovite traders and soldiers then headed eastward towards the Pacific. As Muscovy expanded further southeast, it began its long contest with the Ottomans over the Caucasus. The Crimean Khanate to the south began the period as a Muscovite ally, but by the 1520s became a hostile Ottoman vassal. Moscow absorbed Novgorod and Pskov to its west, and its claims to western border territories spawned prolonged border wars, which eroded both the extent and the power of the Lithuanian Grand Duchy. The decline and collapse of Livonia also drew the surrounding powers into recurring conflict. As the sixteenth century drew to a close, however, Muscovite expansion in this direction stalled. Meanwhile, commercial, diplomatic and military relations developed with Ming China, the Safavids, the Ottomans and the kingdoms of central and parts of western Europe. Increasingly, sixteenth-century Muscovy was becoming a large, albeit somewhat unusual, bureaucratic empire, and increasingly operated in the context of other large empires.

Military change accompanied expansion. In important ways that change was camouflaged. That is, Muscovy in the 1580s still fielded an over-whelmingly cavalry force organized in three or five divisions. As before, the cavalry was largely made up of self-supporting elite archers on horse-back, who drew little from state coffers and who could be mustered either to defend themselves against raids or to launch more aggressive campaigns. The activities of this force continued to be of paramount socio-political importance, since elite status was still closely tied to military affairs.

These military continuities concealed some profound alterations. Rather than the 'assumptions' and 'practices' of the late fifteenth century, the army of the sixteenth century drew as a matter of routine on a much larger pool of better-integrated fighting men with a central, unified command. Behind the army stood a powerful court and a panoply of institutional supports and regulations. Service princes and royal brothers did little to disrupt musters or command by the 1590s. The Muscovite elite largely saw itself as the ruling element in a powerful autocracy where loyal milit-ary service by all landholders was a lifelong expectation. Although the cavalry was still largely self-supporting, many other things were carefully recorded and regulated by the bureaucracy: the numbers of horsemen, and the expectations and frequency of their service. Warfare was closely entwined with the development of the machinery of state to support it.

A growing state apparatus had also made it possible for the army to respond to Muscovy's changing international status and bring about gradual military change. Artillery rapidly developed into a Muscovite strength. The army included men skilled in siege warfare, and by the six-teenth century Moscow boasted a number of trained, salaried infantry regiments (arquebusiers and musketeers or *streltsy*), paralleling Ottoman and European developments.[17] These men, some of whom served year-round, were not of elite status. Muscovite tactics and strategy increasingly accommodated their new skills, altering siege and battlefield behaviour. The fiscal machinery to support such military necessities sputtered to life. Although Muscovy retained fundamentals of its former court politics and cavalry army, by the 1580s its army was also connected to new bureau-cratic power, which had made it possible for Muscovy to add elements to its army and attain new status as a regional power.

New combinations allowed Muscovy to come to terms militarily with a precarious geopolitical position. From about 1513 a hostile Crimea often made massive and deadly raids on Moscow's southern agricultural borderlands. To protect itself and to ransom the captives represented a major military and fiscal drain on Muscovy. An organized and effective defence against this threat, which could coexist and be coordinated with an army in battle array, was a durable achievement of the sixteenth century. As Muscovy's empire grew, it used a growing bureaucracy to mobilize the men and resources needed to claim and defend it.

By the late sixteenth century, however, even these notable successes did not relieve the growing pressures on the Muscovite military. The viability of self-supporting and semi-professional military forces was already in question elsewhere in Europe. The Muscovite army's failures in a recent war in Livonia brought that same question to the fore in Muscovy, since that war had undermined peasant economies and halted the distribution of new lands to support cavalry. Disciplined firepower had evolved among some Muscovite enemies, while Ivan IV's bizarre conduct sapped the court's political will for further change. In retrospect, it is all too clear that Muscovy's fifteenth and sixteenth-century successes had burst the bounds of its still tradition forms. How this all transpired is the story of the following chapters.

Notes

1 Carsten Gohrke, 'Zur Problem von Bevölkerungsziffer und Bevölkerungsdichte des Moskauer Rieches im 16. Jahrhundert', *FzOG*, vol. 24 (1978), 74.

2 See Janet Martin, 'Muscovite relations with the Khanates of Kazan and the Crimea, 1460s to 1521', *Canadian–American Slavic Studies*, vol. 17 no. 4 (1983), 435–53, for more detail.

3 The evidence for this assertion is based on titles used by Ivan and others to describe themselves. See Donald Ostrowski, *Muscovy and the Mongols. Cross Cultural Influences on the Steppe Frontier, 1304–1589* (Cambridge, 2002), 180–2.

4 Nancy Shields Kollmann, *Kinship and Politics* (Stanford, 1987) provides a detailed analysis in English of elite family politics in the fourteenth and fifteenth centuries. Here: 36–41.

5 Nancy Shields Kollmann, *By Honor Bound: State and Society in Early Modern Russia* (Ithaca, 1999), 176–7.

6 Ann Kleimola, 'Patterns of Duma Recruitment', in *Essays in honor of A. A. Zimin* (Columbus, OH, 1985), 232–58; S. Z. Chernov, *Volok Lamskii* (Moscow, 1998), 310.

7 Richard Hellie, *Enserfment and Military Change in Muscovy* (Chicago, 1972), 26; N. P. Pavlov-Sil'vanskii, *Gosudarevye sluzhilye liudi* (St Petersburg, 1898), 97.

8 A. V. Chernov, *Vooruzhennye sily Russkogo gosudarstva v XV–XVII vv. s obrazovaniia tsentralizovannogo gosudarstva do reform pri Petre I* (Moscow, 1954), 23.

9 R. C. Howes, ed. and trans., *The Testaments of the Grand Princes of Moscow* (Ithaca, 1967), no. 61, 137–42. See esp. 258, 260–1 for translation of relevant points.

10 This organization echoes pre-Mongol steppe cavalry organization. R. A. Rorex and Wen Fong, eds, *Eighteen Songs of a Nomad Flute. The Story of Lady Wen-Chi* (New York, 1974).

11 Chernov, *Vooruzhennye*, 28, 33–5, 38, 40; Hellie, *Enserfment*, 152–3 citing A. N. Kirpichnikov, 'Voennoe delo srednvkovoi Rusi', *Sovietskaia arkheologiia* 1/3 (1957), 62–5.

12 Brian L. Davies, 'The Development of Russian Military Power', in Jeremy Black, ed., *European Warfare, 1453–1815* (New York, 1999), 148.

13 Gustave Alef, 'Muscovite military reforms in the second half of the 15th century', *FzOG*, vol. 18 (1973), 77, cites K. N. Serbina, ed., *Ustiuzhnyi lietopis'nyi svod* (Moscow, 1950), 88.

14 Alef, 'Muscovite Military Reforms', 88; Chernov, *Volok Lamskii*, 307; Robert M. Crosky, ed., 'Trakhaniot's description of Russia in 1486', trans. E. C. Ronquist, *Russian History/Histoire Russe*, vol. 17 no. 1 (1990), 59; Iu. G. Alekseev, *Gosudar' vseia Rusi* (Novosibirsk, 1991), 67–8: but cf. A. A. Zimin, *Rossiia na poroge novogo vremeni* (Moscow, 1972), 98.

15 See V. I. Buganov, ed., *Razriadnaia kniga, 1475–1598* (Moscow, 1966), 18, for 1478.

16 Cf. Chernov, *Vooruzhennye*, 40, and his 'TsGADA kak istochnik po voennoi istorii Russogo gosudarstva do XVIII v', *Trudy MGIAI* (1948), 3 or 117, with Marshall Poe, 'Muscovite personnel records, 1475–1550: new light on the early evolution of Russian bureaucracy', *JfGO* n.f. 45 (1997), 364–5.

17 Cf. Colin Imber, *The Ottoman Empire* (New York, 2002), 264–81; I. A. A. Thompson, *War and Government in Habsburg Spain, 1560–1620* (London, 1976), 2–3.

CHAPTER 2

Creating a Muscovite army, 1462–1533

Overview

Construction began in 1485 on the great redbrick walls of the Moscow Kremlin. Eleven years later, Italian engineers, architects, their Russian counterparts and local artisans had nearly completed a dramatic, new, triangular fortress at the confluence of the Moskva and Neglinnaia Rivers. Eighteen imposing lookout towers (the spires were added in the seventeenth century) interrupt the exterior brick walls, which are more than 2 kilometres (1¼ miles) long and 3.5–6.5 metres (11–21 feet) thick. On the vulnerable landside, facing Red Square, they rise as high as 19 metres (62 feet). The new fortress, which replaced dangerously dilapidated, century-old, limestone fortifications, bore the architectural stamp of the Italian quattrocento. The interior boasted a complex of new, Italianate ecclesiastical and royal buildings, including the Granitovaia Palata and the Dormition Cathedral. Until about 1513, further Kremlin fortifications and interior buildings were added by Ivan III (r. 1462–1505) and then his son (Vasilii III, r. 1505–33). Imposing to Moscow's subjects as to its enemies, the Kremlin's qualities as a military stronghold were initially overshadowed by its significance as a symbol of Moscow's consolidation and expansion in the early sixteenth century.[1]

Muscovy added dramatically to its territories and to its international political influence during the 75 years following Ivan III's accession. First, Ivan and his heir, Vasilii III, 'gathered the Russian lands'. This phrase, 'gathering the Russian lands', speaks to Muscovy's further ambitions as well as describing actual achievement. Still, most Russian-speaking principalities near Moscow that retained any claim to independence in 1462 were annexed to Muscovy before the end of Ivan's reign in 1505. The city of Novgorod and its vast northern territories were the largest and most valuable of those additions. Although Novgorod had signed the Treaty of Iazhelbitsy with Ivan's father, bringing it closer to Moscow, leading Novgorodians did not hesitate early in Ivan's reign to negotiate with the Grand Duchy of Lithuania in the hopes of regaining independence. In 1470 Ivan responded by sending a large military force westward. Disagreements among the Novgorodians and Moscow's careful planning made it easily victorious.[2] As Novgorod's loyalty proved repeatedly suspect, Ivan sent more troops, made arrests, confiscated lands and imprisoned leading figures. By the 1490s Novgorod's integration into Muscovy was visibly underway. Novgorod's famous *veche* bell, symbol of its style of self-government, was gone, and the earthen walls of the town fortress had been replaced with brick ones in Moscow's Italianate style.[3] By 1523, if not before, cavalrymen based in Novgorod were fighting in Moscow's interests far from home.

The other northeastern principalities absorbed by Moscow were smaller, and their acquisition is reported in a less dramatic way. In 1485 the military surrounded Moscow's one-time arch-enemy, Tver, to prevent its prince from forging an alliance with Lithuania. As in Novgorod, the army mustered a large and intimidating force, with service princes, auxiliaries, royal brothers, provincials and the sovereign's court all taking to the field. Such ambitious pre-emptive military displays helped Moscow achieve its goals. Tver and other principalities were rapidly absorbed by Moscow under Ivan; Vasilii (r. 1505–33) later absorbed Pskov, Riazan' and Volok. Over the two reigns, then, Muscovy laid claim to all the lands north and northwest of the Pontic steppe from Lithuania to Kazan.

At the same time, Muscovy played an increasingly prominent role in the continuing competition for leadership on the steppe. This was achieved by military force, as well as by diplomatic initiative. In this case, however, Moscow's goals, and its successes, are best measured neither in territorial conquest nor annexation, but in political influence.

Especially at the beginning of the period, Moscow was able to extend its sway south and eastward largely as a result of its relationship with the Khanate of Crimea. The Khanate at this juncture occupied the peninsula of Crimea and a significant swath of the Kipchak steppe to the north. Although more sedentary than their predecessors of the Golden Horde, Crimeans retained a raiding and trading economy. Trading interests kept significant non-Muslim minorities in the principal cities; Muscovy too maintained a lively trade over the steppe. Crimea's political stability and military strength depended upon the ability of the Khan (of the Giray dynasty and Chingissid descent) to elicit loyal support and cooperation from his *beys*, leaders of the noble clans.

At Crimea's urging, a highly successful military alliance was negotiated between Moscow and the Khanate that lasted nearly 40 years from 1480 to 1519. The Grand Duchy of Lithuania, as a strategic response, allied itself with the Great Horde, which still aspired to regain the Golden Horde's former reach and glory. The two sets of allies tangled frequently, often to Muscovite–Crimean advantage. In one particularly notable example, in October 1480, the forces of the Great Horde positioned themselves south of the Ugra River, awaiting their Lithuanian allies and the first freeze that made cavalry movements easier, before attacking Muscovy. Muscovite forces drew up on the opposite bank. The Lithuanians, distracted by puni- tive Crimean raids on their southeastern borderlands and by a rebellion of Orthodox princes at home, never arrived. As time wore on, the Nogai threatened to attack the Great Horde's home pastures, and the Great Horde withdrew without a battle. This non-event became an important symbolic victory for Muscovy, even if it did not represent the end of Mongol control over Russia, as is sometimes implied. At the same time, it was a decisive setback for the Horde, one that was very much to Crimea's advantage. Crimea, whose rulers became (unruly) Ottoman vassals begin- ning in 1475, also brokered Moscow's relationship with its overlord. In return, Muscovy used its military forces repeatedly to help bring the third khanate, Kazan, under the dynastic sway of Crimea.[4] By supporting Crimean clients on the throne of Kazan throughout the late fifteenth cen- tury and in the early years of the sixteenth century, Moscow successfully promoted a triangular alliance that threatened completely to dominate the western end of the steppe.

By the 1510s, however, success undermined common interests, replac- ing the alliance with hostility. For one thing, Moscow's growing size and might changed the balance of power. Moscow's frequent military excur- sions and intensified commerce helped to decrease Crimea's role as steppe broker, increasing Moscow's direct influence over Kazan, and leading towards an unmediated relationship with the Ottomans. Crimea's destruc- tion of the Great Horde in the early years of the sixteenth century further eliminated one of its principal motivations for cooperating with Moscow.[5] By 1519 Crimea renounced the alliance; instead it became an intermittent ally of the Grand Duchy of Lithuania. Thereafter, Moscow had a power- ful enemy across the steppe in the Crimean Khanate. Moscow's southern frontiers were vulnerable. Its steppe foe was allied to the great military strength of Ottoman Turkey. Further, Crimea and Moscow now competed for influence in Kazan.

To the west, by contrast, Moscow's gains were reflected in territorial expansion. Military encounters with Lithuania ending in 1522 confirmed Moscow's control over a number of principalities to its southwest. The Grand Duchy of Lithuania, joined from 1386 in personal union with the Catholic Kingdom of Poland, shared a Jagellonian monarch, but resisted institutional, fiscal and military incorporation. Lithuania was one of Moscow's most persistent rivals; they competed over access to trade routes leading to the Balkans, conflicting rights to tax revenues, the activities of their steppe allies, and control over lands along the border between them. A number of the Lithuanian vassal princes and courtiers who lived along the Muscovite border were confessionally Orthodox, while the Grand Duke's court was tied to Catholic Poland. Moscow's efforts to woo the allegiance of these princes and absorb their lands into Muscovy led to wars, skirmishes, defeats and ephemeral truces in 1492–4, 1500–3 and 1512–22. In the end, Muscovy gained a new crop of service princes and their lands, whose location helped to justify Moscow's claim that it was heir to Orthodox Kievan Rus'. These impressive territorial gains between 1462 and 1533 were accompanied by growing Muscovite diplomatic and commercial interests in eastern and central Europe.

Consolidation

Domestic political consolidation, with corresponding implications for the army's reliability and loyalty, was key to this successful expansion. Over time, Muscovy proved successful in gradually attracting political loyalty while diffusing political rivalries and attaining some degree of administrative unity, but this was not simply achieved. Even the Principality of Moscow proper had never been governed as a single entity. When Ivan III became grand prince, his personal domains were primarily 15 major Muscovite towns. His rulership was far more extensive, including his family's Muscovite lands and the territory of Viatka. Although Ivan's brothers obeyed him as ruler of all Muscovy, each received lands within that realm over which they were supreme rulers. Ivan's eldest brother held the most substantial appanage of five Muscovite towns. The next brother had three major towns, and the two youngest another five between them. Under his father's will, Ivan received only one-third of the principality's total income, while his brothers and mother shared the rest.[6] Ivan held other lands, like Riazan', indirectly. Some were allied to Moscow by treaty and were governed separately. Still others were under Muscovite over-lordship but administered by Moscow as the separate principalities they had once been, sometimes by their own princes. In times of war, each of these territories dispatched its own troops to join the Muscovite army as a group. That these lands and their rulers were loyal to the Grand Prince was, for the most part, not in doubt. As matters stood, however, ruling this collection of disparate territories was far from simple.

As most historians understand this process, consolidation was achieved in large part on an elite and personal level. With one notable exception, the historical record does not emphasize military occupation after the con-quest of Russian-speaking principalities. Instead, gradual changes in the basic social and political tenets underlying life at the Muscovite court incorporated, even co-opted, formerly independent-minded elites into the Muscovite project. Negotiated agreements, incremental changes and finally more predictable rules came to govern their relationship with one another and with the Grand Prince, until, by the 1530s, the court was the arena within which powerful elites acted in concert and in collaboration with their monarch.[7]

Important members of the court did not cooperate as a matter of course with Ivan III (despite the consensus emerging from the civil war). The lifelong negotiations between Ivan and his younger brothers provide a particularly vivid example. Ivan III, not a generous sibling, did not parti-tion newly conquered and escheated lands, which by custom might have been divided among family members. Ivan nevertheless demanded that his brothers' military units participate frequently and fully in his many military adventures. When two brothers objected to this treatment in the 1470s, Ivan negotiated quite traditional agreements, offering each brother the new lands he demanded. In return, however, Ivan claimed more control over their status at his court, their funds, and the nature of their appanage courts. While the brothers did not dispute Ivan's position as grand prince, they continued to object to his avaricious and demeaning treatment of them.[8] When Ivan demanded the return of a senior Moscow courtier who had transferred his allegiance to a brother's court, they objected to his high-handed interference. Matters came to a head in late 1479, in the midst of particularly severe military pressures. Earlier in the year Ivan had dispatched a military expedition to Novgorod to forestall rebellion. After its return, Moscow awaited an attack by the Horde ('the stand on the Ugra'), and then Livonia attacked Pskov. At this precarious moment, Ivan's two brothers made their displeasure evident by withdrawing their troops. They took their own military forces (quite numerous by implication) out of the pool of Muscovite fighting men and marched westward toward Novgorod, where they entered negotiations with King Casimir of Poland as mediator. Fortunately for Ivan, this rebellious effort fizzled out, and he was able to negotiate a return of his brothers and their forces to the fold.

In subsequent treaties Ivan continued trying to erode the brothers' independence, but with limited success. By 1491 his eldest brother again refused to add his troops to the Muscovite army, which was then defending its Crimean ally. Ivan had him arrested, and he died in prison two years later. Ivan's two nephews also spent their lives in prison and exile, as their uncle fought against any resurgence of traditional appanage power. In these circumstances most remaining appanage rulers willed their lands to Ivan when they died. The appanage courts and their military forces thus came under Moscow's direct control, and the independence of appanage courts, generally, was curtailed. During Vasilii's reign, for example, appanage military contingents were successfully dispersed throughout the army, rather than serving together as a group. Nonetheless, after Vasilii himself died in 1533, his two remaining brothers were arrested to prevent them from claiming their rights in lateral succession.[9] In addition to confirming vertical dynastic inheritance, these events at last induced most members of the royal family to become an integral and subordinate part of Muscovite military and political affairs. Only a few pockets of appanage power persisted into the second half of the sixteenth century.[10]

While control over the royal family was being successfully asserted, Moscow also began to routinize cooperation among the competitive and powerful members of its court, and between the Grand Prince and the court as a whole. Powerful princes continued to join the Muscovite sphere in the late fifteenth and early sixteenth centuries. Well into the sixteenth century, however, there seem to have been no commonly accepted rules for admitting such individuals to the Muscovite court. Rather, they negotiated their entry based upon a number of factors, including the location, military and political importance of their principality to Moscow, the number of courtiers and fighting men they commanded and so on. This was particularly the case for members of the Tatar royal house. As descendants of Genghis Khan and heirs of the Golden Horde, they added cachet to the Muscovite court by their presence, as well as bringing excellent cavalry troops to Moscow's auxiliary forces. Their allegiance was therefore courted; it was rewarded with land and the continued personal command of their troops. At the Muscovite court, they carried higher ceremonial rank even than the royal brothers. The military skills and political might implicit in the presence of Tatar princes largely trumped any sense of cultural or religious difference.[11] Russian service princes carried less weight. In return for the loyalty of semi-independent Iaroslavl during the civil war, the son of its last ruler, his relatives and even his *boiars* were allowed to retain their lands after Iaroslavl's absorption in 1463. They soon appeared as important members of the Moscow court and as valued commanders in the Grand Prince's own army. By contrast, when Muscovy conquered a hostile but much weakened Tver in 1485, its princes and elites remained on their lands for some time after the conquest without access to the status or privileges of the Muscovite court elite.[12]

Even as princes came to Moscow to serve at Ivan's court, Muscovy often appointed its own viceregents, or *namestniki*, to govern newly incorporated areas. The responsiveness of these officials was ensured by their desire to win higher status and greater rewards at Ivan's court. At the same time, a man appointed to serve as a *namestnik* in a new territory had little time or opportunity to cultivate local ties near his own hereditary lands. The rule of viceregents thus helped encourage the great Muscovite clans to identify their interests with those of Muscovy at large, rather than with their own inherited lands. Meanwhile, the viceregents helped impose a degree of commonality and uniformity among newly incorporated areas.

Some adjustments to the structure of the court eased the acceptance of these new elites by the great clans who had long been in Moscow. Important offices and positions of stature undoubtedly grew in number during Ivan and Vasilii's reigns; frequent military action, the need for *namestniki* to govern new territories, and the growth of the court itself helped to create them. Still, the number of competitors at court outstripped available positions. Towards 1500, furthermore, service princes began to predominate among military appointments; during Vasilii's reign, the princely clans gained greater prominence, becoming *boiars* in their own right.[13] As a consequence, the total number of *boiars* was allowed to increase. Despite such adjustments, Moscow took forceful measures to prevent both princely and untitled clans from shifting their allegiance to other leaders such as the royal brothers.[14]

Further, precedence-ranking or *mestnichestvo*, a system of institutionalized competition amongst clans, developed over the span of Ivan and Vasilii's reigns. By providing rules for the resolution of disputes and rivalries between great families, it prevented fragmentation of the court through internecine strife. *Mestnichestvo* fundamentally identified seniority or place (*mesto*) within and among clans. *Mesto* represented relative importance, establishing and responding to a clan member's position at court ceremonials, in senior military appointments, and, as the system developed, for even lesser posts. Place and seniority in this system depended upon two factors. Service to the Muscovite court, not only of an individual, but also of his kin, was one element. Family genealogy, which could be real and mythologized, was the other. While an emphasis on service benefited established but untitled Muscovites, genealogy advantaged princely families. Advances in each category could be made by means of outstanding service or through an advantageous marriage alliance. The senior man in an important clan was eligible for selection as a *boiar* or *okol'nich'e* (a lesser rank added in the late 1400s). Ranking within and among clans allowed lesser members of a clan to compare their own status in their clan hierarchy to that of counterparts in other clans. Since status was always calculated relative to other clans, it followed that one should not serve as the subordinate to a man of lower place, nor command one of higher status. If a particular individual considered that these injunctions were violated in his own or another's appointment, he could request an interpretation from the Grand Prince. Complex rules and balances, scrupulously observed and enforced, directed and checked competition among Muscovy's most powerful families. The *mestnichestvo* system effectively integrated new and princely families into the court in a fashion acceptable to most parties. It limited disputes, distributed political power, and focused elite competition in Moscow rather than among regional power bases.

The exchange of views, consultation and advice between ruler and elite became a basic element of political and ceremonial life at court. Cooperation among the great families at court allowed them to exert very considerable influence on the ruler and, many have argued, to limit his options substantially. Neither Ivan III nor Vasilii III would consent even to see foreign ambassadors without his *boiars*. A particular case was the succession crisis of 1498-9. The death of his son, Ivan Molodoi, forced Ivan to select another heir, choosing between his grandson – Ivan Molodoi's son, Dmitrii – and his own second son, Vasilii. The choice of the grandson (1498) seemed to ensure the continued dominance at court of the powerful Patrikeev clan. The Patrikeevs not only had close ties to the new heir, but Dmitrii's youth delayed any opportunity for other clans to marry into the royal family. Ivan, however, disgraced the Patrikeev clan. Within a year, even though they were descendants of Lithuanian royalty and directly related to Ivan's own family, the senior Patrikeev men were tonsured as monks, imprisoned or executed. Many historians see this as the result of pressure exerted on Ivan by clans with consultative or Duma rank, who wished to equalize power at court and limit Patrikeev influence. By 1505 Vasilii had become the heir. It is a telling sign of Moscow's effective if recent consolidation that there was no hint of an appeal to an external or regional power.[15]

On the other hand, it is not difficult to adduce examples when the sovereign's will prevailed. Since he was responsible for elite clans' entry into court and service, the character of their appointments and the adjudication of *mestnichestvo* disputes, the sovereign's power in his relationship with them was correspondingly likely to increase. Thus, after Vasilii III remarried, he 'stacked the court', creating new *boiars* among his new wife's relatives to offset a group of *boiars* who favoured his brother's succession.[16]

Mestnichestvo and attendant political changes had several crucial implications from the perspective of this volume. The relatively orderly absorption of formerly independent princes into the Muscovite court provided the basis for their participation at the heart of Moscow's increasingly unified political and military decision making. Consolidation reinforced and regularized elite connections and interdependence with the Muscovite Crown. By the middle of the 1520s the behaviour of the Muscovite elite suggests that they no longer saw themselves as a group of disparate princelings. Instead they exhibited collective loyalty to the Muscovite court, within which context elite power and influence were debated and exercised. Their loyalty had ideological reinforcement in the Orthodox Church. Further, this consolidation of power increasingly confined high-level political (and military) decision making to the court itself.[17]

Political consolidation had other, direct effects on the army. Successful military service remained the road to advancement among and within elite families. Appointment to high army command reflected exalted status at court and offered the opportunity for further wealth and political power. By the late sixteenth century military commanders strove for further advancement in Moscow's service, not outside it. Even at the beginning of his reign, Ivan III had no need to reinforce loyalty to Moscow's goals by leading each military campaign in person. However, the appointment of untitled *boiars* serving as commanders alongside his royal brothers and service princes on the battlefield ensured the commitment and cooperation of the latter. By 1533 such careful reinforcement was less needed. Despite their great political power and even some remaining private retinues, titled and untitled families usually served loyally in the army, competing for the emoluments attendant on successful military service.[18] And as former princes and other elites were integrated into a single command structure, formerly separate troops melted into Moscow's own forces.

Despite its advantages, *mestnichestvo* also had potentially negative effects on the army. As elements in *mestnichestvo* calculations, military appointments were jealously watched and sometimes challenged because of their potential impact on an individual's or a clan's status.[19] Under such circumstances, a less gifted commander might be preferred, or army action might be delayed. However, disputes were still relatively infrequent in Ivan's time, and the existence of similar, if less formalized, arrangements in central Europe suggests that such difficulties were generally limited.[20] In Muscovy, in fact, commanders for a particular campaign were chosen from a relatively large pool of individuals who were both loyal and socially appropriate.

Growing unity and integration of Muscovite rule (and in turn of army command) was reinforced by redefining the allegiances of men below the rank of prince and *boiar*. At issue were the loyalties of men from former principalities and princely retinues, as their former commanders entered into new arrangements at the Muscovite court. During the latter part of the fifteenth century the most distinguished servitors of Iaroslavl, for example, or Vladimir, joined the Grand Prince's court when their princes did; there they competed with Muscovites of similar status. But Moscow also had still lesser servitors who lived in the provinces: *deti boiarskie* and *dvoriane*; so too did Vladimir and Iaroslavl. Frequently, such lesser men continued living in Vladimir or Iaroslavl, for example, although now they technically owed allegiance to Moscow.[21] These provincial servicemen typically enjoyed considerably less status and wealth than those men actually serving at court. For many provincials, military enterprise offered a significant source of booty and supplementary income, as well as an opportunity for advancement.

Ivan III and his successors in the end directly attracted the military support and loyalty of most such individuals. Incremental devices were used effectively. At first, as in 1462, such men were asked to serve locally to defend their own lands under their own commanders against their traditional enemies; only later were they asked to join Moscow's campaigns further afield. More broadly, provincial life gradually came into contact with institutions of Muscovite rule, sometimes through the *namestniki*; Ivan's *Sudebnik*, or Law Code of 1497, claimed authority for the Grand Prince over law courts in nearly all parts of Muscovy. Ivan III used that authority *inter alia* to limit peasant mobility to a two-week period in late autumn, after all fees and charges were paid.[22] The ruling presumably helped to ensure a steadier labour supply on provincial landholdings, so there was every incentive to acknowledge the Prince's writ.

The influence of *pomest'e*, or service landholding, after 1500 was particularly potent. One result of Novgorod's repeated attempts to break away from Moscow after 1470 was the confiscation of land from native Novgorodians, first from those elites hostile to Moscow, then on a larger scale from hostile and supportive landholders alike, and finally from the Church. Ivan claimed huge tracts of land in Novgorod for the Crown, while a few dispossessed Novgorodians may have received land in other parts of Muscovy. Novgorod thus proved an important anomaly in the structuring of a consolidated Muscovy; its experience was akin to seizure and occupation, and Novgorod's elites moved towards the court only after many were displaced. Ivan then exerted his authority by distributing confiscated land in Novgorod to loyal Muscovites, while reserving his patrimonial right to reclaim it. By 1500 numerous lesser men were awarded these lands. The right to remain on them became conditional upon loyal service as a cavalryman in the Grand Prince's army, although initially the peasants living on these lands were not 'his', nor did he control the amount of rent they paid. Over time, the utility to the Crown of *pomest'e* landholding, as a supplement to hereditary landholding, or *votchina*, only increased. *Pomest'e* ensured loyalty, and it reduced reliance on booty won in wartime, even as other sources of income for warrior-landholders disappeared. As long as Muscovy continued rapidly to expand, the resulting steady supply of available land guaranteed its usefulness over successive generations.

Once the connection between service and landholding had been established, the institution spread throughout Muscovy, offering an inexpensive way of supporting a large and loyal army of significant size. The granting of *pomest'e* obligated lesser, local men directly to the court in Moscow and ensured their loyal military service (even if that was not its original intent).[23] Vasilii, in particular, was increasingly able to call upon provincial and regional forces to fight Moscow's battles far from their homelands at minimal expense to the court. The result was to tie a middling layer of landholders tightly to the sovereign's service – a petty service elite accurately described as a 'middle service class'.[24]

The domestic consolidation of Muscovy and its new territories was a slow process, but political and social integration did develop in the first half of the sixteenth century. This had a broad impact on the army. What had been separate units united by common command became one army led by the Grand Prince or his appointee. Appanage and service princes, who had once commanded their own retinues or troops, gradually lost their autonomy; regional, even ethnic and religious differences were minimized by service to Moscow. By the time of Vasilii III, elite landholders from many different regions both commanded and filled the rank-and-file of the Muscovite army. Second, the relationship between the court and the army was reinforced by the process of integration. The primacy of military concerns, characteristic of Moscow's older warrior elite, was retained by the principality's newly consolidated court.

A final key element in the process of integration was the development of an identifiable administrative structure. Muscovite politics took place at court, where the *boiars* and *okol'nich'e* consulted with the Grand Prince; the inner grouping is often – if not strictly accurately – referred to as the Boiar Duma, or Boiar Council. In the provinces, political authority was exercised through viceregents (*namestnik*) who supervised judicial, fiscal, military and other duties with the aid of local deputies. The viceregents had their own ties to the court; indeed they were members of the court on assignment, and their personal status directly reflected the military importance, age and size of the towns and regions they governed. Viceregents were supported by local payments or 'feeding' (*kormlenie*). As previously indicated, the appointment of Muscovite viceregents in newly absorbed territories helped speed their integration.[25] These key activities, court politics and much of the work of the *namestniki* remained dependent upon personal ties of patronage, clan politics and individual interaction – not least with the Grand Prince.

Expansion in territory, the new size of the royal court, the number of viceregents and the growing military forces available to the Crown eventually did require a limited number of more formal new structures – to compile and maintain written records for the Grand Prince's household and court. These activities were not of direct political significance to the court and *boiars*, and they were largely independent of the personal politics of the court. State secretaries (*diaki*), clerks and scribes were quite isolated from the court proper, and those courtiers who supervised them were rarely *boiars*. After the mid-fifteenth century this record-keeping structure was still limited to four areas. Military service lists (*razriady*) exist from as early as the 1470s. Because they were primarily a record of elite status at court, entries indicate who held what army command; occasionally they identify the fighting men ('the men of Galich'; 'the men of Vladimir', and so on). Later, such documents acquired a more specifically military function, recording how many men served and how they were armed. Finally, the regularization of military service required a different kind of record keeping that allowed for greater continuity and predictability. Eventually, small administrative units developed to monitor such things, although historians are unable to agree on the date at which such specialization first took place.[26]

As Muscovy grew in size and developed a limited but unifying record-keeping capacity, a second task, tax collection, took on a new shape. Taxes once levied by numerous independent princes were taken over by a Muscovite treasury. Vasilii III's new military activities, in particular, needed financial support. New taxes were levied in cash and in kind to rebuild fortifications, to pay officials to supervise such work, and, under Vasilii III, even to pay for horses; some of these were quite local. A more general tax, *iamskie dengi*, helped pay in cash for the efficient relay messenger system inherited from the Mongols; the labour of peasants living near the post stations also supported the system. Other taxes paid for Vasilii's experimental infantry troops while they were on campaign, and for their gunpowder.

The granting of *pomest'e* was a third area that demanded increased record keeping. Which lands made up an estate, how many peasants lived on them, what rents they owed, and who served from them were all written down, first in Novgorod and then in other parts of Muscovy. Land cadastres recorded which servicemen died, how their families were supported, and which estates had been reassigned. Finally, Muscovy's broadening horizons increased its diplomatic activity; this required records of embassies, consultations, translations of diplomatic exchanges, and ceremonies at the Muscovite and foreign courts.[27]

Although of growing importance, the new record-keeping functions remained small and politically insignificant to the court. The record keepers were socially undistinguished and recognizable chiefly by their literacy. There were few specialized personnel or offices, except perhaps in military (*razriady*) and diplomatic matters.[28]

Over the reigns of Ivan III and Vasilii III, the Crown developed the ability to support, muster and command a larger and more integrated army. That force was increasingly able to function effectively both to defend its lands and to acquire new territory.

Military developments

A great deal of Muscovite military activity throughout the 1520s involved raiding. Like hunting, raiding was an intrinsic, almost daily part of life in the extensive steppe borderlands along the southern and eastern edges of the principality. The Tatar Khanates, the Nogai and the Viatchane, among others, included nomadic and semi-nomadic societies whose values, economic systems and military organization supported nearly constant readiness for these activities. The frequency of raids, especially in frontier areas, is often seen as an outcome of ecology and lifestyle – a kind of unfortunate, if high-impact, side effect of nomadism.

Raiding is a rather complex phenomenon. Unquestionably, Muscovy commonly dealt with small-scale raiding, a constant and debilitating 'little war' which broke regularly over the fringes of the forested steppe. Local, relatively undisciplined war parties attacked nearby communities, burned buildings and took domestic items, livestock and human captives for ransom or sale into slavery. This captured booty amply repaid the warriors, who were bow-and-arrow horsemen, sometimes armed with sabres or spears, providing them a profitable, even necessary, supplement to pastoralism. The Muscovite borders typically experienced multiple small attacks during a single campaigning season, as did northern China and the Habsburg–Ottoman borders.[29] Small raids frequently originated in decentralized and fragmented societies; even where there were governments or tribal federations putatively in charge, they could exert little political control over an activity so necessary to the economic survival of the attackers.[30] This 'little war' was a nearly constant element of Muscovite border life. When individual Tatar princes joined Muscovite service as loyal vassals, it diminished the number of those who roamed the steppe, free to attack lands to the north. Moscow's alliance with Crimea further limited, but did not eliminate, this cumulatively debilitating pattern.

'Raiding', however, equally applies to a range of more organized activity, including large, disciplined, military campaigns led by major political figures with clear political motives. In 1501, as on other occasions, Khan Mengli-Giray called upon every adult male in the Crimean population to present himself, bringing three horses, food and arms for a campaign against Kiev. Tribal officers arrived with units of 10, 100 and 1,000 men. These large armies approached frontiers along established tracks or *shliakhy*, depending on rapid mobilization and unexpected approach to surprise defenders. In the absence of opposing forces, the army split into smaller units to capture booty and people; that accomplished, they withdrew equally rapidly. In 1500 Tatar forces bottled up defenders in their fortresses, while others accompanied prisoners and booty safely beyond reach. Large-scale raids such as these had a political as well as economic impact. Crimean attacks on Lithuania in 1500 and 1501 carried off rich booty, but they also played a strategic role in Muscovite and Crimean foreign policy, distracting Poland and Lithuania from other military activity.[31] These large forays were later turned against Muscovy, which experienced major incursions in 1507, 1512, 1521 and 1531. Large-scale raiding of this sort was not peculiar to Crimea. Among others, the early Ottomans conducted similar kinds of military expeditions.

This brief discussion should be adequate to demonstrate that raiding was neither 'natural' nor a nomadic 'lifestyle'. It was a military strategy. Raiders made rapid and often well-coordinated incursions into vulnerable territory. Their purpose was not conquest: neither military occupation nor territorial takeover. Rather, their goal was to capture resources, to extract political or economic concessions, or to gain acknowledgment and prestige.[32] This accomplished, raiders withdrew as rapidly as possible, avoiding confrontation with an opposing military.

Steppe raiders in fifteenth and sixteenth-century Muscovy fit this description neatly. Booty, tribute goods, alliances and prestige interested them, not the occupation of sedentary communities. The Tatars used their own unshod steppe horses – small but fast and hardy animals that subsisted on forage and required little other support.[33] Tatar armies, as well as smaller raiding parties, deployed skilled bow-and-arrow horsemen, who fought standing in their stirrups. Highly-valued military skills were particularly easily cultivated by nomads and those often on horseback, and these were used to great effect. But, as military forces, the Tatar raiders relied on coordinated, speedy attack and equally well-coordinated, rapid withdrawal with minimal baggage and armour to protect themselves. They were not constituted to stand under attack, but to strike and withdraw.

To the modern reader, such 'raids' may not imply much military sophistication.[34] But it took logistics, advance reconnaissance, careful coordination and considerable political acumen to put the full Tatar army in the field. They were heirs to the discipline of the Mongol cavalry and the vast collection of Mongol military technologies.[35] Tatars had some professional military men and an awareness and knowledge of gunpowder weapons; indeed, a small infantry contingent was armed with arquebuses (muskets) as early as 1493.[36] But infantry and gunpowder weapons were ill-adapted to raiding strategies and did not receive major attention. Instead, raiding became a cornerstone of Tatar and other steppe societies, which became economically dependent upon the continual supply of tribute; slaves for farming, sale or ransom, and goods from raiding, reinforcing the pattern.[37]

For all that, Tatars and steppe nomads were by no means the only practitioners of the strategy on the Muscovite frontier. Raiding was not a one-way scourge, brandished by the Khanate's steppe warriors against peaceful, sedentary communities. In reality, there was no hard-and-fast line between agricultural and steppe life. The Muscovite frontier was a settlement zone, rather than a political borderline. Some Muscovite peasants were slash-and-burn agriculturalists, so they shifted location with some frequency. The cavalrymen who were their landlords were not exclusively agricultural managers, but trained themselves and any other servicemen who accompanied them in the use of bow and arrow on horseback through daily experience. Realistically, some of them were also part-time pastoralists. There seems little reason to doubt that Muscovites who themselves lived in the borderlands indulged in small-scale raiding on their own neighbours, as occasional bandits or more regular warrior-raiders.[38] Cossacks, people who resisted permanent settlement and moved more completely into the fluid border zone, appeared in the Muscovite south in the mid-fifteenth century.[39] Cossacks, wanderers, refugees and other steppe-border peoples were hired for pay directly into the Muscovite military in the sixteenth century precisely for their steppe skills.[40] Cossacks settled near Smolensk on the western border frequently harassed the Lithuanians in the early 1500s, for example.[41] Many of the Tatars who had moved to Muscovy retained a more pastoralist life than their Slavic neighbours. Others took to the steppes, living as raiders for the campaigning season.[42] Belgorod and Azov Cossacks preyed on the Crimeans.[43] Muscovy's 'little war' had raider-participants on both sides.

More formal Muscovite military exchanges also used the strategy of raid and counter-raid. In 1462 Muscovy sent a raiding force into Komi territory, and then into Perm Velikaia – its intent apparently to collect booty and to intimidate, but certainly not to conquer. Tatars unsuccessfully responded in kind, resulting in a Muscovite counter-raid against tribes on the Iugra in 1465, as a result of which the latter paid tribute to Ivan III.[44] It is not difficult to discover other Muscovite conflicts (not only against Tatars) where the intent was punitive, to inflict damage, to garner the upper hand politically, but not to occupy territory or capture fortresses.

Raiding warfare, beyond its economic and psychological significance on the frontier, gave fundamental shape to the Muscovite army and its usages. Its organization and accoutrements reflected the central importance of this particular kind of warfare and its key place in military practice. Muscovy's predominantly light cavalry army was organized for speed and mobility. Its auxiliaries and irregulars included a religiously and ethnically diverse group, whose participation was valued for precisely those characteristics: Cossack troops, Tatars under their own noble leadership, the

Cheremis and the Mordvinians.[45] Cavalry accoutrements were geared for light weight and speed. Muscovy eschewed the raising of large cavalry horses, unlike its counterparts further west, purchasing small steppe ponies from Crimea annually.[46] The Muscovite government supported its troops by allowing them to collect booty, even selling Christian prisoners to the Nogai and Crimea for the slave trade.[47] Furthermore, raiding with its relatively rapid attack and withdrawal, tended to limit the time actually spent campaigning; since elite warriors were also active in agriculture, they could not in any case spend all their time campaigning but had to be at home on their land with some regularity.

The army's battlefield conduct conformed to its overall strategic orientation.[48] Muscovite forces engaged in major field battles, although they were not commonplace. When it did so, troops often bunched tightly in the centre of the battlefield, to withstand attack as long as possible. Meanwhile, cavalry massed on the wings enveloped the enemy, attacking from the flanks and the rear. The cavalry would fire a volley of arrows, then join hand-to-hand combat with sabres. These tactics allowed for little manoeuvrability on the battlefield, although quite detailed plans might be made in advance.[49]

The Imperial ambassador, Sigmund von Herberstein, whose accounts of his 1517 and 1526 visits to Muscovy provide many of our earliest descriptions of Moscow's army, was evidently not attuned to raiding strategies, their advantages or requirements. He accurately but unenthusi-astically reports that Muscovite battle order in the early sixteenth century relied upon speed and ruses, rather than prizing the ability to stand under fire. The Muscovite vanguard lured opponents into ambush or created an ambush for an unsuspecting enemy, as at the battle of Mit'kove field (on the Vedrosh River) against Lithuania in 1500.[50] A reconnaissance division was first noted as part of Moscow's army in 1524, departing in advance of the main force, for exactly that purpose. Herberstein further notes, less than admiringly: 'In their campaigns . . . their single tactic [is] to attack or flee in haste' and '. . . they attack their enemies defiantly but do not persist long'.[51]

The emphasis inherent in all these arrangements should come as no surprise, however, since Muscovy had been part of the Mongol–Tatar military world for generations.[52] These military arrangements are also generally congruent with Muscovy's political practices. That is, as it con-quered new territory, as far as one can tell, Muscovy was inclined to attack and harass a neighbouring principality, subjecting it to raids until its prince capitulated. Massive demonstration of force was another tactic.

With Novgorod as an outstanding exception, written accounts do not emphasize military occupation as a sequel; rather, it was the inclusion of the elite into Muscovy's courtly *cursus honorum* that completed the process. Even after 1462, this remained an effective *modus operandi*, and much about raiding and its fundamental military principles continued to dominate the Muscovite army for several more generations.

Moscow's military effectiveness can also be explained by the army's comparatively simple administrative and fiscal apparatus, as revealed in a growing written record. A significant percentage of the population was involved in military endeavours, but only on an occasional or part-time basis. Drafted peasants preceded the army to prepare roads and other military necessities for the arrival of the troops. Elite cavalrymen-landholders supported, mounted and armed themselves and any retainers and slaves from agricultural land. When they went to war, they carried as little as possible. Ivan III, for example, preferred to release half of each regiment to forage near Novgorod in 1477, rather than encumbering the army with a baggage train. Foraging also served the psychological purpose of terrorizing local inhabitants.[53] Warriors received, in addition to booty, medals and supplemental payments for successful campaigns.[54] Cavalrymen were called upon as needed and in rotation, typically half in the spring and half in the late summer. This arrangement permitted Moscow to make maximum use of its growing military numbers. For cavalry, training was a matter of personal responsibility during the off-season. During the reign of Vasilii III, written records indicate that there were periodic cavalry musters, where weaponry and mounts were reviewed. What they do not show is how many men served from a particular landholding and what arms they carried. With military command changing from one campaign to another, it was possible for an individual to lead a small troop in one rotation and serve in the ranks in another. A contemporary Polish painting suggests that senior commanders were identified simply by headgear. At the very top, Ivan III and Vasilii III did not typically command their own troops, although Vasilii clearly believed in the usefulness of appearing personally to his troops.[55] This simple but comprehensive organization made it possible for the throne to muster at low cost considerable numbers of fighting men, if only for short periods.

Despite a continuing orientation toward raiding cavalry, at least two transformative developments were launched within the Muscovite military order in the early sixteenth century. First, Muscovy began to develop more effective defences against incessant raids from the steppe. This was a matter of resource mobilization through record keeping and administrative change, rather than technical innovation. Local defence of borderlands by resident landholders probably developed spontaneously; log palisades and small earthworks appeared along the usual Tatar approaches, or *shliakhy*, where horsemen crossed the Oka and Ugra Rivers for trade, military and political purposes. By the middle of the fifteenth century there were small wooden forts next to some *shliakhy*. Fortifications served as protection for local inhabitants, but some individual fortresses also began to dispatch patrols to watch for the approach of large raiding parties. It was an activity for which Cossacks, hired for cash, were particularly prized.[56] From the time of Ivan III, there is evidence of Moscow's involvement in this kind of defence. The garrisoning of fortresses, if it meant year-round absence from estates, was potentially a vexed question. In 1469 Ivan paid and supplied his brother Iurii's men as they guarded the borders for much of the winter. Focusing relatively small units on vulnerable points could be effective. In 1472, because there was advance news of a large Tatar force approaching, the main army was even ordered to gather at Serpukhov as the fortress garrison at Aleksin fought a holding action; hearing of the force gathering at Serpukhov, the Tatars did not advance beyond Aleksin.[57]

Such defensive efforts received increasing support after 1500. Moscow used funds from new taxes to build more fortresses under the supervision of an appointed fortress steward. An effort to coordinate defences was launched. A few fortresses were linked to form defensible segments. Military men garrisoned these fortresses in season, and the army met regularly at pre-arranged points in anticipation of Tatar attack. It was in this context that mobile fortresses, or *guliai gorod*, appeared, as will be seen below. The importance of a more organized defence grew with the collapse of the alliance between Moscow and Crimea in the 1510s, after which large Crimean raids became more frequent and threatening. Army activity was to some degree coordinated with local defence by 1518. By 1527, fortresses and troops in Pereiaslavl-Riazansk, Kashira, Kolomna, Tula and Odoev were in place to protect the borderlands, easing the southward advance of agricultural settlement thereafter.[58] This was explicitly a defence against raiding, as Muscovy placed fortifications across a wide front in the way of highly mobile and rapid offensives. Moscow's steppe defences became a more centrally organized effort than defence in Poland and Lithuania, which continued to rely on field confrontations and privately maintained fortresses that were unable to hire many defenders. The difference grew more important as the Muscovite system became increasingly efficient.[59] Furthermore, the ability to build and garrison fortresses proved to have important implications, not only on the south-eastern frontier, but also in the west.

In addition to investing in territorial defence along the steppe, Ivan III and Vasilii III increased the use of firepower in the Muscovite army by importing artisans and engineers and investing new resources. Ivan III was particularly interested in the contemporary development of new weaponry and military architecture in southern Europe. His concern may have been encouraged by developments in Poland and Lithuania, where brick and stone fortresses loomed. This did not represent a rejection of raiding cavalry, which remained both effective and powerful in the field.[60] But new artillery and other innovations did offer new possibilities, in particular for siege warfare. Muscovy in this era tended to capture fortresses and towns by persistence (such as surrounding a fortress or starving out the inhabitants), rather than by frontal assault.[61] In the relatively vast and under-inhabited spaces of eastern Europe, cavalry remained key for blockading fortresses, skirmishing with sortie parties, and supplying the besiegers.[62] But artillery and siege expertise offered a way that a cavalry army might bring sieges to a more rapid finish.

Innovations were quickly adopted. In the 1460s Muscovy produced forged iron cannon in several cities. Ivan's invitation to Aristotel Fioravante, an architect and military engineer from Bologna in the 1470s, was followed by the foundation of the *Pushechnaia izba*, where gunpowder was produced and brass cannon were forged from imported brass. Most fifteenth-century artillery was still used on fortress walls, but gun carriages and 'trunnions', or balancing pins, made cannon more mobile towards the turn of the sixteenth century. Where possible, heavy artillery was moved not overland but by water. Fioravante accompanied the Muscovite army as it used its artillery in 1478 against Novgorod, against Kazan in 1482, and in 1485 against Tver. Early in the sixteenth century Muscovite forces at Pskov, Kazan, Fellin, Serpensk, Orsha, Vyborg and Smolensk also used cannon. Muscovites were not at first very expert cannoneers, but artillery fire played its part, at least diverting defenders' attention while an assault took place elsewhere. By 1513, Muscovy, its heavy cannon protected by earthworks and supported by peasant labour, successfully bombarded the major fortress of Smolensk.[63]

Fioravante introduced further technical and engineering information with military significance. He built a pontoon bridge over the Volkhov in 1477 and taught the Russians to fire denser brick. Applying his countrymen's expertise, Fioravante introduced new[64] Italianate fortress design for artillery forces, with straight, thicker curtain walls, niches for guns and turrets, and slightly projecting corner towers as the focus of defences. Major construction projects used new techniques and materials, while Moscow's new officials helped organize and support the work from taxation. The Moscow Kremlin was built first, followed by Novgorod, and then Pskov, Ladoga, Kopor'e, Iam and Ivangorod, with its modern, rectangular citadel. Fortresses at Nizhni Novgorod, Zaraisk and Tula were major projects under Vasilii III. These fortress bastions were also symbols of Muscovite unity – outlining the borders, not of the old principality of Moscow, but of a greater Muscovy whose frontier defences protected all its component principalities.[65]

Moscow's innovations in the use of firepower initially relied on foreign artisans and mercenaries. Moscow's enemies anticipated as much; Sweden, German and Baltic cities tried, some harder than others, to embargo military goods and experts moving eastward.[66] It is unlikely that the effort was overwhelmingly successful. The movement of military and other personnel both to and from Europe was limited, but it was not only the embargo that militated against it. Fioravante and his Italian colleagues were among the most skilled of the foreigners who nonetheless served the Muscovite army directly and indirectly during the late fifteenth and early sixteenth centuries. A foreign quarter appeared in Moscow, where Italian and German bombardiers lived. These Europeans served nearly everywhere the army fought, fighting alongside Muscovites despite linguistic, ethnic and religious differences.[67] In the first half of the sixteenth century, however, Muscovy began replacing some Europeans with Muscovites. The new service was considered socially inferior to the cavalry exclusively manned by the hereditary elite, and Muscovite artillerymen and other specialists were drawn from the taxpaying population. Nor did military service of this sort did earn elite status. Instead, like the Cossacks, Muscovite artillerymen and siege experts were contract servicemen (*sluzhilye liudi po priboru*) who were trained, supplied, and settled in their own suburbs.[68] By the 1520s the army had a separate artillery force, often with elite Muscovite commanders and officers. At first, command of low-status artillery troops did not convey high status, the way that cavalry command did. As it turned out, artillery command gradually became a means for gaining access to such higher levels of command by families of slightly lesser standing.[69] Artillery production and use, especially in siege conditions, fitted without great difficulty into the existing framework of politics and cavalry army. Over time, the artillery developed into an area of particular Muscovite skill and expertise.

Muscovite firepower was not restricted to cannon, however. Muscovy shortly introduced small numbers of infantry with firearms. Arquebuses were used at the 'stand on the Ugra' in 1480, and troops of arquebusiers (*pishchal'niki*) existed by 1504–8. Vasilii III even used a group of 1,000 *pishchal'niki* in the annexation of Pskov and on the southern frontier.[70] These men were evidently recruited from particular towns; they certainly were not hereditary landholding warriors like those that made up the cavalry. Their training was brief, their weapons not their own. Like the rest of the army, they were evidently called out at need and dispatched home after military action was over for the year.[71]

The appearance of even a few troops with gunpowder weaponry required some accommodation from a highly mobile cavalry army. The Muscovite reactions seemed largely tactical, on the battlefield. The *pishchal'niki* required protection as they took their weapons off their firing stands, reloaded and prepared to fire again. Artillery likewise took some time to prepare for firing. Since Muscovite cavalry forces did not use pikes nor did the army have infantry pikemen to protect those using artillery and firearms, the *guliai gorod* or 'mobile fortress' served the purpose. These long interlocking parallel wooden walls first appeared in 1522, providing protective covering for infantry and artillery alike during battle; they were particularly secure against Tatar bows and arrows. Although it could be laboriously moved, the *guliai gorod* hardly encouraged freewheeling infantry manoeuvres. Rather, these walls or circled baggage wagons (*Wagenburg* or *tabor*) provided shelter that allowed both infantry and artillery to function on a cavalry battlefield without changing the army's fundamental structure. Indeed, the *guliai gorod* also served as a haven for cavalry to regroup, further justifying a change that benefited the limited number of guns on the Muscovite battlefield. By contrast, given the private nature of most cavalry provisioning in this era, the Muscovite army was slower to develop a logistical arm to manage the baggage train, even when the need for gunpowder supplies required it.

These two new developments – defensive capability on the steppe and gunpowder weapons – appear to have been direct responses to the particular requirements of the Muscovite situation at the turn of the sixteenth century. First, Muscovy began to develop a layered territorial defence for the agricultural population on the steppe's edge. Although the cavalry was organized for steppe encounters, stationary fortress-style defence proved much more effective in protecting sedentary agriculturalists, focusing and localizing the use of cavalry and other troops effectively. At the same time,

Muscovy responded to innovations in fortress building, the development of infantry and field artillery appearing near its western borders.

One should not fall into the trap, however, of envisioning Muscovy as fighting two separate kinds of warfare – one against the Tatars and another in the west. The effectiveness and applicability of both innovations on both fronts were clearly appreciated by Muscovite commanders. If arquebuses were used in the annexation of Pskov, Muscovites also brought them to the stand on the Ugra. New fortresses were built at Vasil'sursk near Kazan, and at Ivangorod in the west. Cavalry raids and the *guliai gorod* were a staple of war against Lithuania as well as in the east. Muscovite diplomacy responded to its Muslim Tatar neighbours to the east and south, and to its European Christian neighbours to the west in a coordinated, unified fashion. So too did the Muscovite military use military and technological innovation to develop a coordinated, unified response along all its frontiers.

Notwithstanding their significance, the appearance of military innovations did not generate a profound review of military priorities or organization. Mobile cavalry warfare, its tactics and strategies, remained militarily and economically effective for the Muscovite rulers through the mid-sixteenth century. New unified ways of marshalling Moscow's men and resources gave the principality regional advantages. Moscow used these to organize new defences and launch gunpowder weaponry. Notably, however, military men even in the newer parts of the army lived at least partly on the old fiscal system. Although they might be paid in cash, many were also settled in a 'suburb' with access to land. A mixture of old and new that maintained the overall shape and thinking of its cavalry forces served Muscovy well through the middle of the sixteenth century. The organization, command and support of the cavalry forces were closely tied to Muscovy's social and political structures. In fact, as Muscovy reinforced those structures while integrating its new holdings, the basic structure and organization of its steppe army were themselves reaffirmed and strengthened.

Wars of expansion

Muscovite expansion during the reigns of Ivan III and Vasilii III illustrates the impact of political consolidation and a growing range of Muscovite military strategies and capabilities. Some of Moscow's success in adding vast territories and accruing corresponding regional power followed from its consolidation: careful diplomatic negotiation, marriage politics and the threat of military force, rather than outright warfare. But Muscovy also engaged in numerous military actions against a variety of foes – Kazan, Lithuania, Livonia, Sweden and other Russian principalities. Cavalry raids remained a staple of this military activity, but Muscovy's new capabilities allowed larger and more frequent incursions, which proved particularly useful in gaining political influence, rather than conquering territory. In addition, Muscovy increasingly developed and used military strategies that depended upon the building, capture and maintenance of fortresses. Such strategies were often related to Moscow's newly available firepower.

Under Ivan III, in particular, Muscovy's military strength for the most part was launched in short campaigns and raids that were not themselves intended to conquer or occupy territory. As Moscow's organizational abilities grew, it could dispatch two or more sizeable armies towards the same destination within a single calendar year, sometimes accompanied by gunpowder weapons. For the most part however, each particular campaign remained brief. This is consistent with Moscow's goals, its preferred strategies, and the nature of its cavalry forces. For an army made up largely of men who trained, armed and supplied themselves, time to supervise estates was also a necessity.

Moscow's early campaigns against the Khanate of Kazan offer a clear example. For the latter part of the fifteenth century, Muscovy's principal military goal there was not conquest, but the exertion of political influence on behalf of its Crimean ally. The importance of Moscow's new organizational abilities in preparing for frequent and sizable campaigns should not be underestimated. Muscovite armies moved toward Kazan in the late 1460s, in 1486–7, and again in the late 1490s to intervene in succession disputes, placing and supporting clients of Crimea on the Khanate's throne. These campaigns did not always succeed in their immediate aims, but Moscow's frequent presence threatened Kazan's independence.

In the early sixteenth century Moscow's new intentions, to exert more influence in Kazan on its own behalf, did little to change its military strategy. At the beginning of his reign, in particular, Vasilii relied on large and frequent punitive raids. When Kazan detained merchants and its ambassador in 1506, Muscovy called out its troops for not one, but two, expeditions in rapid succession. As in Ivan's reign, Muscovite raids and campaigns under Vasilii III did not destroy Kazan's sovereignty or conquer its territory; that was not their goal.

The cumulative impact of frequent Muscovite incursions took its toll, helping to undermine Kazan's political stability. Moscow's influence was inconsistent, however, and Kazan remained a formidable enough opponent, protected in part by the difficulties Muscovite armies had in reaching

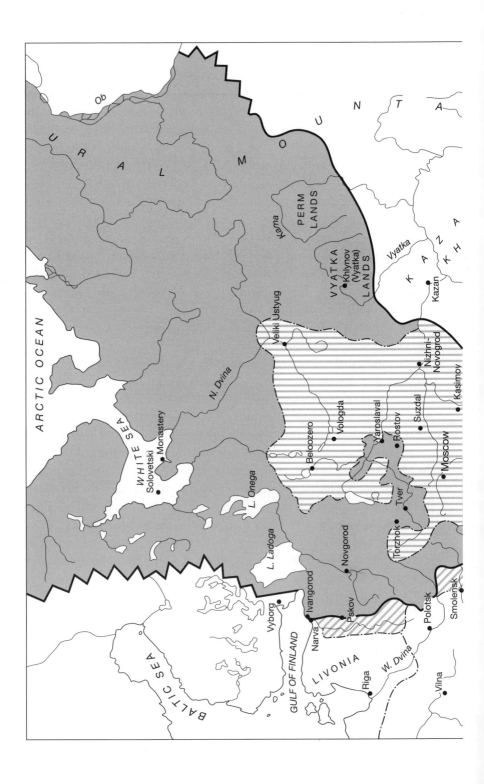

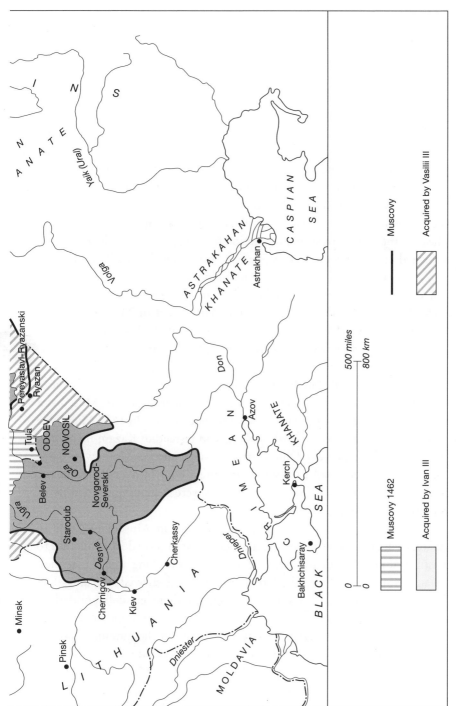

MAP 2 *Muscovy, 1462–1533* (adapted from Chew, Allen Frank, *An Atlas of Russian History: Eleven Centuries of Changing Borders* (Yale University Press, 1971))

its capital. The two Muscovite campaigns in 1506 were thrown back, and Kazan finally released Moscow's ambassador only as the 1507 campaign season approached. From 1520 to 1523, Kazan reacted with increasing hostility to Moscow, culminating in the 1523 murder of a Muscovite envoy to the Khanate.

As Moscow prepared to deliver a military rebuke for this event, its forces tried a new strategy, which involved territorial encroachment on the approaches to the Khanate. This time, the army built a forward base on the upper Volga, the fortress of Vasil'sursk. The new fortress reduced the impact of the time and distance that had to be traversed by an army moving toward Kazan; until then, both had been an element in Kazan's defence. Vasil'sursk also reflected Muscovy's new military capabilities. Slow-moving infantry,[72] heavy artillery, and siege machinery were sent ahead to the new fortress, in preparation for their use against the Khanate's principal citadel. Like other steppe-edge fortresses, however, Vasil'sursk had to be maintained by a year-round military contingent, a requirement not easily met by cavalry-landholders.[73] In this case, the new strategy yielded no immediate advantage. Tatar harassment of Muscovite forces *en route* from Vasil'sursk to Kazan in 1523 limited Moscow's ability to besiege Kazan, by depriving the attackers of food and supplies. As a result, perhaps, the political goal of the expedition was only partly successful. A new khan took the throne following the campaign, but he was a Crimean who was interested in promoting peace and cooperation with Moscow; a compromise candidate rather than a Muscovite puppet. In 1524 Muscovite merchants traded through Nizhni Novgorod instead of Kazan; thereafter, an uneasy truce prevailed until after Vasilii's death. Moscow became increasingly determined to assert more direct control over the Khanate, which some elements of Muscovite society were beginning to identify as an ideological enemy.[74]

Fortress strategies also figured increasingly in Muscovite–Crimean military encounters, as the two states' relationship turned from alliance to hostility under Vasilii III. Both sides evinced declining interest in their alliance after 1500. Once the Great Horde was destroyed, the allies had less reason to cooperate, and they competed, rather than collaborated, to establish preponderant influence over Kazan. Vasilii's reluctance to pay tribute, in the form of large gifts to the Khan and his nobility, did not make matters easier. Unofficially, Crimeans began raiding the Muscovite borderlands; there were 17 large-scale attacks before 1520, and numerous smaller ones. Muscovite defences proved of some value, though each side scored its victories.

The particular vulnerabilities of fortress defence were emphasized as Moscow's relationship with Crimea worsened and a Crimean–Lithuanian alliance was signed in 1519. Two years later, while much of the Muscovite army was fighting in the west, Khan Muhammed Girey launched a full-scale attack against the Muscovite frontier. On this occasion the raiders swept past undermanned and unsupported border defences; fast-moving raiders were in little danger of attack from the rear. One contingent swung eastward, while another reached and encircled the capital city itself. Ironically, Moscow's only enemy to surround the Kremlin in nearly a century did not rely upon the artillery that its new fortress had been designed to withstand. Muhammed Girey retreated when promised tribute and gifts by the city's Tatar commander, a converted Chingissid and Vasilii's brother-in-law. The Crimean forces withdrew with numerous prisoners and booty. Moscow's frontier fortresses alone had offered little protection against a major attack. The Khan's success encouraged Vasilii himself to head the annual army musters in 1522; infantry and artillery reinforced frontier defence. A new fortress at Kolomna became the centre of coordinated defence, a significant organizational accomplishment.[75] The annual requirement that the army muster against raiders, however, emphasized the army's focus on mobile cavalry and raiding strategies. The construction and maintenance of stationary fortress defence was its silent partner.

The goals of Moscow's intermittent border wars with its western neighbour and rival, the Grand Duchy of Lithuania, were quite different. Here, the annexation of territory was explicitly at issue. In particular, Muscovy challenged Lithuania's overlordship over principalities that had once been a part of Kievan Rus'.

The Grand Duchy shared many military characteristics with Muscovy, including the use of raiding strategies with the goal of devastating border territories before campaigners returned to their own agricultural concerns. As rivals for steppe influence, each allied itself with Tatar forces as the opportunity arose. The Grand Duchy did not demonstrate significant technical advantages over Moscow. Like its eastern neighbour, Lithuania had no standing infantry until the second half of the sixteenth century, in this case for administrative and political reasons. Like Poland, with which it shared a dynasty, Lithuania had not invested central resources in border defences. It is hardly surprising, then, that Muscovite–Lithuanian border wars were at least in part wars of attrition and negotiation, where raids and campaigns functioned as a form of political and military inducement to local princes to transfer their allegiance.

However, Lithuania, Poland – its partner in the Dual Monarchy – and nearby Livonia had relatively high density of urban enclaves, with stone rather than wooden fortresses and defensive walls. Livonia in particular was dotted with fortresses, some of them of recent German design. Their forces evinced some familiarity and skill with artillery in the early sixteenth century, and some Lithuanians were hired by Muscovy as siege specialists.[76] Although Muscovy undoubtedly applied its artillery, siege machinery and gunpowder troops wherever it fought, it was from warfare on its western front that these had been adapted, and wars for territorial gain here in the early sixteenth century demanded their frequent use. By the early 1500s, fighting on this front had become part of a complex diplomatic and military equation. Large Muscovite armies moved repeatedly westward (as they did toward Kazan). Sieges and battlefield confrontations, practised against stone fortresses in the west, appeared with greater frequency in the east.

From 1480 to 1491, however, Muscovy conducted frequent small raids and some larger operations across the Lithuanian border, and Lithuania responded in kind. For this decade and the following one, under pressure from this kind of activity, a number of Orthodox large landholders and princes transferred their allegiance to Moscow. One study argues that the new Muscovites were those who had been marginalized both politically and geographically at the Lithuanian court. Out of a desire to protect their lands from Muscovite depredations, and to improve their status as they became eligible for positions and rewards at the Muscovite court, they shifted allegiance; religious concerns were of lesser import.[77] The absorption of these border principalities was thus initiated by military raids, but completed by the negotiated inclusion of their rulers into the Muscovite court. The princes of Novosil, by becoming active Muscovite allies, tried to retain a degree of independence for themselves. Others brought their lands and servitors with them directly into the Muscovite court. The Bel'skii family left their lands behind to become direct dependents of Moscow. When the Muscovite court divided western frontier territories into separate military commands, Bel'skii commanded a border district that lay between his old Lithuanian and his newly awarded Muscovite lands. Such positive incentives coupled with persistent military pressure from Moscow resulted in the addition of a significant stripe of territory to its western reaches.

On news of Grand Duke Casimir's death in 1492, Muscovite pressure intensified with the dispatch of a large campaign force toward Lithuania. Some Lithuanian territory, such as Viaz'ma, capitulated with little fighting.

Other towns, including Liubutsk, Mtsensk, Serpeisk and Meshchovsk, had to be captured by siege from princes who had less interest in defecting to Muscovy. At Serpeisk in particular, Lithuanian forces from Smolensk reinforced the defence; when captured the town was burnt. Muscovy was broadly successful in capturing and holding fortresses. By 1494 a treaty consolidated its gains. Ivan's daughter, Elena, married the new Lithuanian Grand Prince, Alexander, while Lithuania conceded the claims inherent in Ivan's title, 'Sovereign of all Russia'. Princes who were compliant and had already defected to Moscow retained their lands. While Moscow returned some of the territories its forces had conquered, the treaty acknowledged its acquisition of lands that encircled on three sides the Lithuanian principalities near the Ugra River. The newly won areas were often integrated into Muscovy through princely collaboration, not by conquest and occupation.[78]

Muscovy's active military presence near the eastern end of the Baltic intensified its contact with this rather different world. The knights of the Livonian Order attacked Pskov in 1480, and Ivan counter-attacked. Peace treaties were signed only in 1493, in conjunction with the Lithuanian agreement.[79] In pursuit of an aggressive commercial policy against Livonia and the Hanseatic League of trading cities, Ivan closed down the Hansa's headquarters in Novgorod, and built a rival trading port and fortress at Ivangorod (adjacent to Livonian Narva), its rectangular design again tailored to withstand artillery warfare.[80]

Further north, Denmark, recognizing Muscovy's growing importance in the eastern Baltic, solicited Muscovite cooperation against Sten Sture of Sweden. Denmark wanted to reconstitute the Scandinavian Union; Muscovy hoped to redefine its Finnish border. Ivan's successful raids on the Finnish frontier provoked the Swedish bombardment and sack of Ivangorod. Moscow captured it once again and rebuilt it after a six-year truce ended the fighting in 1497.[81]

Muscovy's enhanced stature was also promoted by diplomatic contacts. Ivan opened communication with the Hungarian Crown and the Habsburg Emperor, Maximillian II. Moscow had established a fruitful understanding with Steven of Moldavia in the 1480s, which was cemented by a marriage between Ivan's then-heir and Steven's daughter. A Moldavian–Crimean alliance in the early 1490s completed a triangle threatening Poland and Lithuania. Poland's subsequent attack on Moldavia, an Ottoman vassal, generated a punitive Ottoman counter-attack against Poland and Lithuania in 1498. During this same era, the first Muscovite ambassador presented himself at the Ottoman court.[82]

When Muscovite–Lithuanian conflict resumed between 1500 and 1503, Ivan attacked with two armies, one from the south-east and a second towards Briansk and Dorogobuzh. At first there was limited resistance to Muscovite encroachments. The army took a number of cities, and powerful principalities quickly transferred their allegiance to Moscow. Lithuania lost a major battle at the Vedrosha River in 1500. Shortly, however, Lithuania marshalled its defence, and the fighting become more complex and less mobile, although Muscovite armies fought for relatively brief campaign seasons. Furthermore, Muscovy's actions provoked regional reactions: Hungary threatened to help Lithuania; Lithuania's ally and neighbour, Livonia, opened another front, raiding lands around Pskov and Ivangorod, while Muscovite forces responded with a victorious march to Dorpat and northward to Narva. Both the Great Horde and Crimea joined the fray.

In 1502 Ivan launched a grand campaign toward the key fortress of Smolensk. The attacking army was politically and militarily important, led by Ivan's third son and commanded by a panoply of experienced military leaders. Further support for the attack was held off by determined Livonians, and the campaign proved a disappointing failure for Muscovy. Its army may not have been at full strength; inadequate artillery supplies and poor strategy are also mentioned. The elaborate alliance system nurtured by Muscovy at most prevented Lithuanian troops from reinforcing Smolensk. Despite Muscovy's uneven performance, a six-year truce, signed in 1503, acknowledged *de facto* the spectacular territorial gains made by Moscow over Ivan's reign – the conquest or absorption of nearly one-third of Lithuania. The agreement, however, was an unstable one, and raiding and minor fighting continued along the border for years.[83]

War resumed (1508–22) after both Alexander and Ivan were dead. Lithuanian Prince Glinskii fomented rebellion against the Lithuanian throne, now occupied by Alexander's brother, Sigismund. Defeated, Glinskii fled to Moscow where he became a prominent member of the Muscovite court. Matters were complicated by the breakdown of Moscow's Crimean alliance. Muscovy's activities were twice interrupted by significant Crimean attacks on its southern borders. On the other hand, Moscow this time benefited from Livonian support.

A principal Muscovite objective remained the capture of Smolensk and its formidable fortress. The final inclusion of Pskov into Muscovy in 1510 helped prepare for another advance on Smolensk.[84] Repeated short campaigns against the city were next. Raids were followed by an unsuccessful six-week siege of Smolensk in early 1513. Later the same year, Muscovy laid siege to the town for four more weeks. Mercenaries and military experts were sent for from the Habsburg Empire. A third attempt in summer 1514 captured the city and fortress quickly; the city was bombarded from the surrounding hills.[85]

The war dragged on; Moscow was unable to regain its initial momentum. A Muscovite army was severely defeated as it crossed the Dniepr near Orsza (Orsha) in 1514 (see the cover illustration); artillery and mercenary infantry units were cleverly coordinated with Polish and Lithuanian cavalry. Although Lithuania then recaptured a number of cities, it was unable to retake Smolensk; in 1517 Lithuania also launched an unsuccessful siege of Opochka. Thereafter, Muscovy focused on cross-border raiding as an incentive to concluding an agreement. Livonia attacked Poland in 1519; this effort, in the long run unsuccessful, was paid for with Muscovite money.[86] The arrival of Crimean troops outside Moscow in 1521 only added to the desirability of the five-year truce reached in 1522 and extended until 1534.

By 1530 Muscovy had proven itself capable of repeatedly fielding large campaign armies of light, mobile cavalry supported by artillery and small, temporary infantry contingents. Raiding by cavalry troops continued to hold an important place in Muscovite strategy; and raiding-style tactics also persisted on the battlefield. Growing numbers of wooden, stone and brick fortresses on Moscow's periphery made the effective defence and capture of fortresses a concern. Individual campaigns were rarely of great duration, but prolonged warfare with such units over an extensive terrain was also perfectly possible, as indicated by Vasilii's war against Lithuania. In these respects, Muscovy was more successful in attaining its goals in the west than against Kazan and Crimea. Against these latter enemies, despite the innovative building of Vasil'sursk and the beginning of layered steppe defences, Moscow was less successful; it was Crimea, not Lithuania, which surrounded Moscow in 1521. For military reasons, as well as sociopolitical ones, then, the dominance of light, mobile cavalry in the Muscovite army seemed likely to persist for some time.

Conclusions

When Vasilii III died in 1533 the outline of a unified Muscovite service army was in place, although some appanage and service princes retained a degree of independence. At the heart of the military were hereditary servicemen-landholders (*sluzhilye liudi po otechestvu*), who commanded and filled the ranks of a light cavalry army. Predominantly mobile cavalry in orientation, Muscovite military forces benefited from integrated, loyal service from the elite of a newly expanded principality. The most exalted elements of the army were members of *boiar*, princely, and other ranking clans, who commanded armies, governed and defended key territories, but also acted as political advisers; their personal and patronage links throughout the court constituted their political power. Around these key figures in Moscow were others of lesser stature who fought in the army as members of the Muscovite court. Outlying territories also had hereditary servicemen who served in the army, at first to defend their own lands, and then in broader Muscovite endeavours.

Military service was an important element in the basic political, social and economic structures of the Muscovite principality. It was an integral component in competition among elites for social and political promin- ence; as a result, their personal interests were tied closely to their service to the Crown. Further, effective service from this entire group depended upon the support of individual servicemen and their military activities from landholdings worked by peasants. For many hereditary servicemen, land (and thus their economic well-being) was also conditional on their prompt appearance for military service when called. The availability of service land (*pomest'e*) for a growing population required a continuing stock of unclaimed land in newly conquered territories; indirectly, in other words, it was sustained on the remarkable military triumphs of Muscovite arms to 1533. The army staffed and supported by these interlocking social, political and economic systems reflected, in its organization and usages, the central importance of mobile cavalry warfare to Muscovite life.

At the same time, the army also included some small and relatively new elements. Some of the men involved in these newer areas were foreign spe- cialists in artillery, military architecture and gunpowder troops. There were also Muscovites who were recruited into service (*sluzhilye liudi po pribory*); unlike the hereditary landholding cavalry, these Cossack patrols, artillerymen, siege specialists and the arquebusiers were not of the social and political elite. Some were unusual in that they specialized in the use of gunpowder technology; others were connected to Muscovy's steppe defence and small administration. In small numbers, they co-existed effec- tively with Muscovy's dominant cavalry and were regularly used on all military fronts. The Lithuanian War ending in 1522 proved a showcase for some of their developing skills. There was some limited adjustment to their presence in the army's structure and practices.

By the first third of the sixteenth century Muscovy had established itself as a successful regional power. It did not quail before the challenge from its steppe competitors; on its western borders, it claimed and won from Lithuania many of the principalities that had once belonged in Kievan Rus'. If its most recent experiences in Lithuania suggested that organizing and mobilizing resources to sustain fortress sieges and numerous battlefield encounters were taxing, its army was certainly capable of sustaining the territorial expansion needed to maintain its principal troops. This was the situation in 1533 when Vasilii III died, leaving a regent and his three-year old son to steer Muscovy further.

Notes

1 E. V. Anisimov, *Illiustrirovannaia istoriia Rossii* (St Petersburg, 2003), 62; William C. Brumfield, *A History of Russian Architecture* (Cambridge, 1993), 99; A. S. Ramelli, 'Il cremlino di Mosca, esempio di architettura militare', *Arte Lombarda*, vols 44/45 (1976), 130–8.

2 See Evgenii Andreevich Razin, *Istoriia voennogo iskusstva*, vol. 2 (Moscow, 1955), 312–18 for greater detail.

3 Brumfield, *History*, 72.

4 V. E. Syroechkovskii, 'Puti i usloviia snoshenii Moskvy s Krymom na rubezhe XVI veka', *Izvestiia akademiia nauk SSSR* (1932) 200–4, 217, 224; Michael Khodarkovsky, *Russia's Steppe Frontier* (Bloomington, 2002), 77–91; Janet Martin, 'Muscovite relations with the Khanates of Kazan and the Crimea, 1460s to 1521', *Canadian–American Slavic Studies*, vol. 17 no. 4 (1983), 443–5.

5 Martin, 'Muscovite relations', 447; Khodarkovsky, *Russia's Steppe Frontier*, 91–100.

6 R. C. Howes, ed. and trans., *The Testaments of the Grand Princes of Moscow* (Ithaca, 1967), no. 61, 137–43; English translation, 241–67.

7 V. D. Nazarov's work, particularly as summarized in 'Gosudarev dvor v Rossii konsa XV-srediny XVI vv', (unpublished paper, Culture and Identity in Muscovy Conference, Los Angeles, 1993).

8 Iu. G. Alekseev, *Gosudar' vseia Rusi* (Novosibirsk, 1991), 141.

9 Janet Martin, *Medieval Russia, 980–1584* (Cambridge, 1995), 248; Nancy Shields Kollmann, *Kinship and Politics* (Stanford, 1987), 157; Gustave Alef, 'The Age of Ivan III' *FzOG* (1986), 164–76.

10 Nancy Shields Kollmann, *By Honor Bound: State and Society in Early Modern Russia* (Ithaca, 1999), 8; S. M. Kashtanov, 'Udely i udel'nye kniazia', (unpublished paper, Culture and Identity in Muscovy Conference, Los Angeles, 1993).

11 Donald Ostrowski, *Muscovy and the Mongols. Cross Cultural Influences on the Steppe Frontier, 1304–1589* (Cambridge, 2002), 54–9; John H. L. Keep, *Soldiers of the Tsar. Army and Society in Russia, 1462–1874* (Oxford, 1985), 77–8.

12 S. B. Veselovskii, *Feodal'noe zemlevladenie v severo-vostochnoi Rusi* (Moscow, 1947) I, 301; Gustave Alef, 'Muscovite Military Reforms in the second half of the 15th century', *FzOG*, vol. 18 (1973), 87–8, 90, 95; A. A. Zimin, *Formirovanie boiarskoi aristokratii v Rossii* (Mocow, 1988), 293, points out that the appanage courtiers lost their titles, however.

13 Ann Kleimola, 'Patterns of Duma Recruitment', in *Essays in honor of A. A. Zimin* (Columbus, OH, 1985), 233; A. V. Chernov, *Vooruzhennye sily Russkogo gosudarstva v XV–XVII vv. s obrazovaniia tsentralizovannogo gosudarstva do reform pri Petre I* (Moscow, 1954), 20.

14 In 1479 Ivan Vladimirovich Obolenskii-Lyko tried to defect to Ivan's brother, Boris, when he (Obolenskii-Lyko) was in disgrace with Ivan III. Ivan went to great lengths to arrest and imprison him.

15 Nancy Shields Kollmann, 'Consensus Politics: the dynastic crisis of the 1490s reconsidered', *Russian Review*, vol. 45 (1986), 235–67; John V. A. Fine Jr., 'The Muscovite Dynastic Crisis', *Canadian Slavonic Papers*, vol. 8 (1966), 198–205.

16 Kleimola, 'Patterns', 235; cf. Kollmann, *Kinship*, 144–5 for opposing view.

17 M. E. Bychkova, *Sostav klassa feodalov Rossii v XVI v* (Moscow, 1986), 43, 96 passim. Exceptions: A. A. Zimin, *Rossiia na poroge novogo vremeni* (Moscow, 1972), 149.

18 Alef, 'Muscovite military reforms', 86–7.

19 Razin, *Istoriia*, vol. 2, 307.

20 Michael Hochedlinger, *Austria's Wars of Emergence: War, State and Society in the Habsburg Monarchy, 1683–1797* (Harlow, 2003), 92–4; Dianne L. Smith, 'The Muscovite officer corps, 1475–1598', (Ph.D. dissertation, University of California, Davis, 1989) reminds us of the contemporary Austrian precendence system, and of the nineteenth-century British naval seniority system. Further, the US army still prevents an officer from serving beneath another of the same rank who was promoted after him: 332.

21 S. Z. Chernov, *Volok Lamskii* (Moscow, 1998), 65, 84, 193.

22 '*Sudebnik* of 1497', in H. W. Dewey, ed., *Muscovite Judicial Texts, 1488–1556* (Ann Arbor, 1966), 7–21, esp. Article 57.

23 Janet Martin's recent work suggests that the first land grants by Ivan III to men of lesser social stature in Novgorod were not initially connected to a service obligation, but that that obligation existed by 1523. Janet Martin,

'Some observations on the creation and development of the *pomest'e* system in Novgorod during the reign of Ivan III', unpublished paper presented at the 35th AAASS, 2003. V. B. Kobrin, 'Stanovlenie pomestnoi sistemy', *IZ*, vol. 105 (1980), 150–95, argues that the purpose of the *pomest'e* system was, among other things, to keep land in secular hands and prevent its absorption by the Church.

24 The term is Richard Hellie's. His, *Enserfment and Military Change in Muscovy* (Chicago, 1972), 21ff.

25 H. W. Dewey, 'The Decline of the Muscovite *namestnik*', *Oxford Slavonic Papers* 12 (1965), 21–39.

26 AN SSSR II, *Ocherki istorii SSSR Period feodalizma konets XV v.-nachalo XVII v.* (Moscow, 1955), 120; Marshall Poe, 'Muscovite Personnel Records, 1475–1550: new light on the early evolution of Russian bureaucracy', *JfGO* n.f. 45 (1997); G. B. Gal'perin, *Forma pravleniia Russkogo tsentralizovannogo gosudarstva XV–XVI vv* (Leningrad, 1964), 74–85; *Razriadnaia kniga, 1475–1598* (Moscow, 1966), 18, 21.

27 N. O. Zeziulinskii, *O konnozavodskom diele* (St Petersburg, 1889), 16; A. A. Zimin, *Rossiia na poroge novogo vremeni* (Moscow, 1972), 144; P. N. Miliukov, *Spornye voprosy finansovoi istorii Moskovskogo gosudarstva* (St Petersburg, 1892), 15; P. O. Bobrovskii, *Perekhod Rossii k reguliarnoi armii* (St Petersburg, 1885), 95f.; B. N. Floria, 'Sbor torgovykh poshlin i posadskoe naselenie', *IZ*, vol. 118 (1990), 333.

28 A. A. Zimin, 'D'iacheskii apparat v Rossii vtoroi polovine XV-pervoi treti XVI vekakh', *IZ*, vol. 87 (1971), 219–56.

29 V. V. Karagalov, 'Oborona iuzhnoi granitsy Russkogo gosudarstva v pervoi polovine XVIv.', *Istoriia SSSR* vol. 17, no. 6 (1973), 140–8.

30 Khodarkovsky, *Russia's Steppe Frontier*, 16–17, 20.

31 V. P. Zagorovskii, *Istoriia vkhozhdenie tsentral'nogo chernozem'ia v sostav Rossiiskogo gosudarstva v XVI vek* (Voronezh, 1991), ch. 2, part 1.

32 Archer Jones, *The Art of War in the Western World* (Chicago/Urbana, 1987), 55–6; Gunter Erich Rothenberg, *The Austrian Military Border in Croatia, 1522–1747* (Urbana, 1960), 27.

33 L. J. D. Collins, 'Military organization and tactics of the Crimean Tatars in the sixteenth and seventeenth centuries', in V. J. Perry and M. Yapp, eds, *War, Technology, and Society in the Middle East* (Oxford, 1975), 259.

34 Naomi Standen, 'What do nomads want?' in Reuven Amitai and Michael Biran eds, *Mongols, Turks and Others* (Leiden, 2005), 129–74, recently argues that raiding is not a 'primitive' strategy; but cf. R. Grousset, *The Empire of the Steppes* (New Brunswick, NJ, 1970).

35 Thomas Allsen, 'The circulation of military technology in the Mongolian Empire', in Nicola Di Cosmo, ed., *Warfare in Inner Asian History (500–1800)* (Leiden, 2002), 265–93, esp. 286.

36 Collins, 'Military organization', 259–60.

37 After the fall of Constantinople in 1453, the Turks depended upon the Black Sea coast to feed them, which required more slaves to farm. Martin, *Medieval Russia*, 314. Muscovy's tribute, ransoms and other payments to the Tatars were called *pominki* or presents.

38 Zagorovskii, *Istoriia*, 86–7; Syroechkovskii, 'Puti i usloviia', 208; cf. Naomi Standen, 'Raiding and frontier society in the five dynasties', in Nicola Di Cosmo and Don Wyatt, eds, *Political Frontiers, Ethnic Boundaries and Human Geographies in Chinese History* (London, 2003), 160–91, who argues the same for the Chinese steppe edge.

39 N. I. Nikitin, 'O proiskhozhdenii, strukture, i sotsial'noi prirode soobshchestv Russkikh kazakov XVI-serediny XVII v.', *Istoriia SSSR*, no. 4 (1986), 168–9ff.

40 Bobrovskii, *Perekhod*, 70–1; Zagorovskii, *Istoriia*, 90–1.

41 *DAI*, vol. 1, doc. 26, 23–6, for example.

42 Syroechkovskii, 'Puti i usloviia', part III, 205–6.

43 Bobrovskii, *Perekhod*, 99.

44 Martin, 'Muscovite relations', 438–9, 447–8.

45 Sigmund von Herberstein, *Description of Moscow and Muscovy* (New York, 1969), 23 on the Mordvin; 25–6, 37 on border life; 35–6 on border 'thieves.'

46 Zeziulinskii, *O konnozavodskom diele*, part I, 16.

47 Bobrovskii, *Perekhod*, 99.

48 'Zamechaniia inostrantsev XVI veka', *Otechestvenniia zapiski*, vol. 25 (1826), 97.

49 Hellie, *Enserfment*, 29.

50 Brian Davies, 'The rise of the Muscovite army', typescript, 10; S. M. Solov'ev, *Istoriia Rossii* (Moscow, 1960), vol. 3, 114.

51 Herberstein, *Description*, 78; A. Baiov, *Kurs istorii Russkogo voennogo isskustva*, vol. 1 *Ot nachala Rusi do Petra* (St Petersburg, 1909), 44.

52 Don Ostrowski, 'Troop mobilization by the Muscovite Grand Princes, 1313–1533', in Eric Lohr and Marshall Poe, eds, *The Military and Society in Russia, 1450–1917* (Leiden, 2002); S. K. Bogoiavlenskii, 'Vooruzhenie russkikh voisk v XV–XVII vv', *IZ*, vol. 4 (1938), 258–9.

53 Razin, *Istoriia*, vol. 2, 307; Smith, 'Muscovite officer corps', 3, 13, 40–3; Herberstein, *Description*, 79–80; Chernov, *Vooruzhennye*, 35; Hellie, *Enserfment*, 29.

54 Baiov, *Kurs istorii*, 67; Smith, 'Muscovite officer corps', 86.

55 Smith, 'Muscovite officer corps', 3, 13, 40–3.

56 Baiov, *Kurs istorii*, 68; Chernov, *Vooruzhennye*, 29; Razin, *Istoriia*, vol. 2, 305.

57 Alef, 'Muscovite military reforms', 78; Chernov, *Vooruzhennye*, 28, describes a similar event in 1517.

58 M. N. Tikhomirov, *Rossiia v XVI stoletii* (Moscow, 1962), 415.

59 V. V. Kargalov, 'Zasechnye cherty. Ikh rol' v oborone Russkogo gosudarstva v XVI–XVII vekakh', *Voenno-istoricheskii zhurnal*, no. 12 (1986), 64–5; Dmitri Bagalei, 'K istorii zaseleniia stepnoi okrainy Moskovskago gosudarstva', *ZhMNP* vol. 245 (May, 1886), 90–1.

60 V. E. Syroechkovskii, 'Puti i usloviia snoshenii Moskvy s Krymom na rubezhe XVI veka', *Izvestiia akademiia nauk SSSR* (1932) 198.

61 Hellie, *Enserfment*, 159; Herberstein, *Description*, 79.

62 Robert Frost, *The Northern Wars. War, State and Society in Northeastern Europe, 1558–1721* (Harlow, 1993), 60–2.

63 N. F. Gulianitskii, *Gradostroitel'stvo Moskovkogo gosudarstva XVI–XVII vekov* (Moscow, 1994), 59–60; Davies, 'Army', 8; Chernov, *Vooruzhennye*, 37–8; A. A. Zimin, *Rossiia na rubezhe XV–XVI stoletii* (Moscow, 1982), 106; Razin, *Istoriia*, vol. 2, 346.

64 The Kremlin's design was 'new' for Muscovy. However, it reflected the soon-to-be outdated artillery-resistant design of the Milanese fortress, rather than angled bastions advocated by Alberti's *De Re Aedificatoria* in 1485, and built by the French and others after the mid-1490s.

65 Geoffrey Parker, *The Military Revolution. Military Innovation and the Rise of the West, 1500–1800*, 2nd ed. (Cambridge, 1996), 9; Zimin, *Rossiia na poroge*, 97; Razin, *Istoriia*, vol. 2, 308; S. M. Zemtsov and V. L. Glazychev, *Aristotel' F'oravanti* (Moscow, 1985), 132, 134, 142; Ramelli, 'Il cremlino de Mosca', 130–8; Mikhail Isaevich Mil'chik, *Krepost' Ivangorod: novye otkrytiia* (St Petersburg, 1997), 14–18.

66 Thomas Esper, 'A 16th-century anti-Russian arms embargo', *Jahrbücher für Geschichte Osteuropas* 15 (1967), 187; Erik Tiberg, *Moscow, Livonia and the Hanseatic League, 1487–1550* (Stockholm, 1995), 232–8.

67 By contrast, the Tatar cavalry did not always participate in Russian campaigns.

68 *Ocherki istorii SSSR*, 126–7; Zimin, *Rossiia na poroge*, 143; Smith, 'Muscovite officer corps', 126–7; Razin, *Istoriia*, vol. 2, 336.

69 Smith, 'Muscovite officer corps', 137–8; Zimin, *Rossiia na poroge*, 144.

70 Hellie, *Enserfment*, 157–8; Zemtsov and Glazychev, *F'oravanti*, 135.

71 Chernov, *Vooruzhennye*, 30; S. A. Gulevich, *Istoriia 8ogo pekhotnogo Estlandskago polka* (St Petersburg, 1911), ch. 1.

72 The early infantry was called *sudovaia rat'* since these military units also arrived by boat. Razin, *Istoriia*, vol. 2, 306.

73 Jaroslaw Pelenski, *Russia and Kazan. Conquest and Imperial Ideology (1438–1560s)* (The Hague, 1974), 50; Razin, *Istoriia*, vol. 2, 355.

74 Pelenski, *Russia and Kazan*, 52.

75 Khodarkovsky, *Steppe Frontier*, 97–100; Martin, *Medieval Russia*, 325; Kargalov, 'Oborona', 141, 145.

76 Zimin, *Rossiia na poroge*, 153; Razin, *Istoriia*, vol. 2, 325–6 notes Muscovy's growing capacities for fortress building and artillery.

77 M. M. Krom, *Mezh Rus'iu i Litvoi* (Moscow, 1995), 130–1; Zimin, *Rossiia na rubezhe*, 95–7, cites orthodoxy as the reason for the defections.

78 Razin, *Istoriia*, vol. 2, 318; Alef, 'Muscovite military reforms', 104–5; Zimin, *Rossiia na rubezhe*, 97–104.

79 See William Urban, *The Teutonic Knights. A Military History* (London, 2003), chs 11 and 12, for further details.

80 Hellie, *Enserfment*, 158; Mil'chik, *Krepost' Ivangorod*, 119–32.

81 Mil'chik, *Krepost' Ivangorod*, 32–45; the Swedes set wooden buildings in Ivangorod alight with burning arrows; they did not capture it with artillery. Tiberg, 137.

82 N. A. Smirnov, *Rossiia i Turtsiia v XVI–XVII vv* (Moscow, 1946), vol. 2, 70–2.

83 Krom, *Mezh Rus'iu i Litvoi*, 131, 229; Razin, *Istoriia*, vol. 2, 320–5; Zimin, *Rossiia na rubezhe*, 178–96. J. L. I. Fennell, *Ivan the Great of Moscow* (New York, London, 1961), ch. 8, has a narrative in English.

84 Its independent trade was undercut; Muscovite administrators and garrisons installed; it was then specially refortified by Moscow in 1517, 1524–7. Zimin, *Rossiia na poroge*, 121, 123.

85 A. V. Dulov, *Geograficheskaia sreda* (Moscow, 1983), 219; Herberstein, *Description*, 79, was unimpressed.

86 Razin, *Istoriia*, vol. 2, 351–4.

CHAPTER 3

The army that won an empire

Overview

After a troubled 14-year regency, Vasilii III's son and heir, Ivan IV, became the first Muscovite tsar (*cesar*) in 1547. The imperial implications of his title proved increasingly apt during the following extraordinary half-century, as Moscow was ruled by Ivan and his son, Fedor (Theodore). Muscovy acquired still more territory, more ethnically and religiously diverse populations, and confronted the new military challenges associated with imperial and territorial aggrandizement.

Ivan IV, known to English-speakers as Ivan the Terrible, reigned child and adult for 37 years from 1547 to 1584. It was a tumultuous period that witnessed extraordinary governmental reform and military success, such as the conquest of the mid-Volga region. It also included devastating defeat and destruction, particularly during the *oprichnina*, 1565–72, when Ivan terrorized his subjects from a separate and arbitrarily defined kingdom within Muscovy. Interpretation of Ivan's reign, the causes and long-term impacts of its events, has long provoked serious disagreement among historians.[1]

During this period the Muscovite military inevitably suffered from some of the dramatic reversals of policy and erratic behaviour that characterized life and politics under Ivan IV. In retrospect, however, the consistency of Muscovy's ambitions and the nature of its foes helped to focus military activities throughout Ivan's reign and into Fedor's around a few broad themes. The Muscovite military during this period was very active, attacking and conquering the Khanates of Kazan and Astrakhan in the 1550s. Expansion on to the lower Volga and toward the Caucasus stimulated brief encounters with the Ottoman Empire and several attacks on the

Khanate of Crimea. Finally, the disintegration of political power in Livonia tempted Ivan to attack this strategically and commercially valuable territory on the eastern end of the Baltic. This generated prolonged regional conflict among Muscovy, Poland-Lithuania and Sweden from 1558 to 1582, and again from 1590 to 1595. A permanent undercurrent to all other military activity was the need to defend Moscow's southern frontiers against Crimean raids, which intensified as Moscow expanded.

This near-feverish pace of engagement played out in a variable and volatile political and social environment. Disputes at Ivan's court during his regency threatened its political equilibrium. On reaching his majority, Ivan attempted to stabilize *boiar* relations; in 1565, he abandoned that for the bizarre arrangements of the *oprichnina*, and then replaced the *oprichnina* with other increasingly erratic arrangements. Finally, with defeat in the Livonia War inevitable, Ivan subjected the court's political arrangements to a further devastating blow in 1581, when he murdered his son and heir in a fit of fury. In the ageing ruler's last years, the childlessness of the remaining legitimate heir, Fedor, created the prospect of a major succession crisis.

Perhaps the chief catalyst for military change during the reign of Ivan IV lay in the scale of Muscovy's quite persistent, if unevenly pursued, expansion. Prior to 1550, Muscovy had absorbed numerous Russian principalities, partially by administrative encroachment and partially by enfolding newly subordinate elites into the Muscovite court. Even Novgorod, whose resistance was more than once suppressed by military force, was envisioned and eventually administered in ways parallel to the central institutions of Muscovite rule. The same could not be said of Ivan's mid-sixteenth century conquests. Expansion in the second half of the sixteenth century brought territories more difficult to incorporate and control. This situation was aggravated by a political ideology that, with increasing insistence, identified Moscow with Eastern Orthodox Christianity and its enemies (including some of its conquests) with other faiths. Moscow's army found itself defending Moscow's right to rule in its new lands, as well as defending the new borders. The Khanates of Kazan and Astrakhan remained hostile and prone to frequent rebellion after conquest. During the Livonian War, Moscow retained conquered territory when it could persistently defend its claim to both land and fortresses. The situation along Moscow's southern frontier was not so very different, as Crimean raids launched themselves with increasing fury at border fortresses that marked the advance of Muscovite agriculture southward. Alongside campaigns and punitive raids, Moscow's military needs came to include the garrisoning of many more fortresses.

Cumulatively, then, expansion created an empire that in turn strained the existing military and unequivocally demanded adjustment. First, Muscovy needed to be able to raise troops reliably, predictably and in significant numbers to raid, reconnoitre and do battle along increasingly wide-flung borders. Muscovy responded by trying to regulate, improve and then demand further service from its *pomest'e* cavalry, a force whose members were the country's landholding elite.

Second, and perhaps more significantly, the growing demand for troops to staff garrisons and defend fortresses at the edges of Moscow's empire required more permanent and year-round forces.[2] Elite *pomest'e* cavalrymen, who were part-time warriors and part-time managers of their estates, could fulfil this requirement only exceptionally. Moscow met the demand with 'contract servicemen' (*sluzhilye liudi po pribory*). The Russian phrase indicates that the men were recruited, rather than born into military service. By the standards of the time, they were therefore of lesser social standing than the elite landholding cavalry. In the time of Ivan IV, the need to deliver massed firepower on the battlefield ensured that the most numerous contract servicemen were musketeers (*streltsy*) – not only Moscow's first standing troops, but infantry and cavalry trained in the use of gunpowder weaponry; these were battlefield and fortress units. There were more gunners and artillerymen, sappers, stockade defenders and even gatekeepers than under Vasilii III. Moscow also added significantly to its resident troops: Cossacks and others who staffed garrisons in return for small nearby plots of land. Many of these men served collectively; groups of Cossacks held land communally rather than individually. Although of differing quality and training, these units all helped to develop Muscovy's fortress siege and defence capability. In addition, although Tatar princes continued to command very high status, the rank-and-file of non-Russian troops – that is, from vassal principalities or non-Christians – were also nominally contract servicemen. Collectively, the contract servicemen represented a considerable change in the social make-up of the Muscovite armed forces after the middle of the sixteenth century. Excluding the non-Russians, up to one-third of the forces available to Ivan and his son, Fedor, were contract servicemen. There is little indication that these particular servitors were chosen specifically to counterbalance hereditary servicemen, despite a low-grade political and social antipathy between elite warriors and the tsar's lower-status soldiers.[3]

As these changes took place, the number and role of foreigners in the Muscovite military as advisers and combatants only grew. There were some 4,000 foreigners employed by the army under Ivan IV. Specialists from Lithuania, Italy and elsewhere came to Moscow, despite Livonia's ongoing embargo. Muscovites serving in the Polish armed forces were both observers and conduits of change. The impact of the newcomers was formidable.[4] During the second half of the sixteenth century Muscovy invested heavily in new gunpowder technology and design, improving its siege capabilities with heavy artillery for use against fortress walls, engineering, sapping and mining. Construction on 150 town fortresses was completed; some were simple wooden structures, but others were brick or stone and artillery-resistant in design. Muscovy also launched a programme of artillery and firearms production with some Russian masters, and began training its infantry, partly under the tutelage of central and west European mercenaries. Field artillery came into its own. In these technical respects, Muscovy under Ivan IV seems to have been very much *au fait* with contemporary developments.[5]

While these changes were very important and their scale significant, they still did not represent a broad reorientation of Muscovite military practice. The raiding strategies and high mobility of *pomest'e* warriors were much esteemed for both military and political reasons.[6] The importance of the steppe and Muscovy's growing empire on the steppe edge also remained – in the campaigns against Kazan and the annual muster against Crimean raids, and in the new investments in contract servicemen and fortresses to defend the frontier. The political importance and military significance of the cavalry warrior and landholder was not challenged until quite late in Ivan's reign.

Adjustments to meet the particular military strengths of Livonia, Lithuania, Poland, Sweden and the Ottoman Empire in the latter part of the sixteenth century took place within the context of a steppe army. Developments in gunpowder weaponry and their deployment, however, remained largely compatible with Moscow's military orientation. Moscow's efforts to deal with the most visible and technical of these (innovations in fortress design, the organization of troop supply, new artillery and other weaponry, fortress construction and garrisoning) were quite successful. Further west, in the 1590s, Europe began using new manoeuvres and tactics for armed infantrymen, such as those spearheaded by Counts Maurice (1567–1625) and William Lewis of Nassau (1560–1620). But Moscow's immediate neighbours, Poland and Lithuania, did not have numerous standing troops. Mercenary forces and Sweden's rapidly evolving peasant militia were the most innovative nearby military experiments; Muscovy's new standing infantry and cavalry were used somewhat differently, but did not fare badly. Over the long run, it would be the less visible, structural problems revealed by prolonged warfare that would pose the most intractable problems for a growing Muscovite Empire, as for its immediate neighbours to the west.

Kazan

Military developments were not an important element of the Regency, 1533–47. A government riven with internal dissent had difficulties in discouraging some 20 large Crimean raids along its frontiers. Muscovite influence in the Khanate of Kazan declined so far at the same time that a Muscovite client prince was dethroned even during a Kazanian civil war.[7] The Regency's various confrontations with the Tatars may have helped shape Ivan's military goals and attitudes, but the government of the era did little to alter military organization or policy.

The pace of military events began to pick up after Ivan's coronation. With strong ecclesiastical support, Ivan's government moved to conquer Kazan. While the defeat of an Islamic state now offered a powerful ideological incentive, both the Orthodox Church and the Muscovite elite also hoped to add to their lands and estates. However, the army sent against the Khanate in 1547 failed. Russian chroniclers attributed this to an unseasonable thaw on the Volga: 'cannons and many muskets were lost in the water . . . many [people] went out onto the river ice . . . and were drowned'.[8] Muscovy renewed the attack in the winter of 1549–50, after the death of Khan Sefa Girey, a powerful leader allied to the Crimean royal family. After 11 days outside Kazan in the driving rain, the Muscovites again withdrew, their siege over. Both incidents suggest (neither for the first nor the last time) that Kazan was far enough from Moscow that getting an army there and back in a single campaign season strained Moscow's logistical capacities unless conditions were nearly ideal.[9] As they withdrew, Muscovite troops moved to remedy this by building and garrisoning a new fortress at Sviazhsk on the right bank of the Volga. Unlike its predecessor, it was within the Khanate, not far from the capital of Kazan itself. Thereafter, with a restored Vasil'sursk, it served as a second forward base for military operations.[10]

The fortress at Sviazhsk had an effect. From 1551 nearby peoples, such as the Mordvin, Chuvash, Mari, Tatar and Udmurt, declared allegiance to Moscow. Threatened by the fortress and its garrison, Kazan once again accepted a khan who was a Muscovite client. The abrupt assertion of Muscovite power also stimulated resistance. When Moscow's client, Khan Ali, departed before presiding over the final absorption of Kazan, negotiations over the Khanate's political future sparked open revolt among the

Tatars; peoples such as the Chuvash on the right bank supported it. Moscow prepared to launch another major campaign against Kazan in 1552.

Military reform

Nearly simultaneously with the Kazan campaigns, Ivan's government initiated a series of reforms that would have important impacts on the army. The government improved its own ability to manage its military resources, in part through more oversight and regularization of the cavalry service. At the same time, permanent troops were created, and Muscovy invested further in artillery and engineering forces. Some of these reforms, such as artillery and engineering improvements, were motivated by the failed Tatar campaigns. Others, particularly those relating to the *pomest'e* cavalry, were connected to political events at Ivan's court.

As part of reforms in the 1550s, significant new military expenditure took place on Moscow's southern frontiers. Recent Crimean attacks on that frontier had been timed to divert Muscovite activities against Kazan. A line of fortresses, stretching through Kolomna, Serkin, Serpukhov, Kaluga and Ugra, already blocked such raids. Ivan's government strengthened this line, making Tula the centre of defensive military activity. Construction on a second line of fortresses began in the late 1550s. New fortifications appeared further south, at Rylsk, Novgorod Seversk, Orel, Novosil, Riazhsk and Shatsk; local people were enrolled to man garrisons where possible. Old and new log fortresses were then linked by cavalry barricades, earthen walls and stretches of forest to constitute a new more southerly boundary against the Crimeans. Such defences relied heavily on local ecology, particularly heavy forestation, where cavalry found it more difficult to manoeuvre than on the open, grassy steppe.[11]

Muscovy also formed its select musketeer regiments, or *streltsy*, beginning in 1550.[12] These troops were notably more efficient than the seasonally mustered, poorly trained *pishchal'niki* who had appeared in Vasilii III's army and again in the mid-1540s. By contrast, the *streltsy* were paid, permanent troops, who trained regularly and who did not disband. The first 3,000 musketeers were organized in troops of 500 called *pribory*. The rank-and-file enrolled voluntarily – free men, but not taxpayers – but their sons were expected to follow. On joining, each musketeer received a grain allowance, a garden plot near his assigned location, and 4 to 7 rubles in annual salary. The troops were identifiable by their red caftan-length uniform coats. They carried axes and arquebuses (muskets), and were drilled in precision firing, as far as that was possible with contemporary firearms. Unlike the rank-and-file, *strelets* officers were hereditary servicemen; their titles and functions echoed exactly the spare command structure of the cavalry forces: a hundredsman commanded two fiftiesmen, and each of these, five tensmen.

Moscow's first musketeer units served as a palace guard. In action with other troops, however, their role became the delivery of massed firepower. Typically, musketeers fired in unison from behind some kind of fortification – fortress walls, a moat or the *guliai gorod*; additional protection was provided by cavalry forces. Muscovite infantrymen did not numerically dominate the army, nor did they operate as independent units on the battlefield. In battle, musketeers standing behind a long expanse of *guliai gorod* could easily deliver fire across a broad field, in cooperation with the *pomest'e* cavalry troops who supplemented their protection. The tactical possibilities for the musketeers in such circumstances were limited, however. They could not easily shift positions and move about a battlefield, in part because they were commanded by a limited number of officers. Thus, they did not typically indulge in hand-to-hand fighting, remaining instead behind their protective walls. Interestingly, confidence in these troops became such that their failures were usually attributed to mismanagement of the *guliai gorod*.

This use of musketeers was relatively distinctive. West European infantry of this era often manoeuvred more easily, but on a confined battlefield in compact infantry squares bristling with pikes for self-protection[13] – a different response to somewhat different military situations. It was only very late in the sixteenth century that there is a record of Muscovite musketeers firing volleys from long, more exposed lines.[14] This experiment (under the aegis of European officers) was roughly contemporary with the use of volleys in the Dutch army, but it remained a rarity in Moscow where the traditional positioning of the *streltsy* already delivered a broad field of fire.

Permanent, standing regiments of musketeers rapidly proved valuable in another respect. Musketeers appeared with increasing frequency as the residents of provincial cities. As paid forces, they could sustain year-round garrison duty, unhampered by the need to return seasonally to estates and farmlands to sustain themselves. By the end of the century, there were 20,000–25,000 *streltsy* scattered geographically throughout the realm.[15]

It has been argued that the musketeers were created to counter Polish and Swedish infantry of the era,[16] and indeed they served precisely that function during Ivan's reign. The organization of the Muscovite army,

however, was more integrated and unified than this implies, and musketeers' responsibilities both broader and more integral to the army's activities. As the date of their creation suggests, musketeer units first saw battle
duty in the wars against Kazan, where their role was to supply firepower
at sieges rather than to do battle with other infantry.[17] Ivan Peresvetov,
a court publicist of the era, had earlier recommended the creation of
standing troops to garrison fortresses against the Tatars along the steppe
frontier, and musketeers were also heavily used as garrison troops – and
not just against the Tatars.[18] Much of our information about the motiva-
tion for the creation of infantry or other Muscovite military innovations
must be deduced from results. The growth and development of musketeer
troops in Ivan IV's reign suggests that they were, in the end, a response to
military demands that were integral to the expansion of the Muscovite
Empire in its entirety.

As expensive but valuable musketeer troops were added to the army,
so were other contract servicemen. Other, less numerous, paid and trained
forces, such as artillery gunners (who learned on the job) and experts in
mining and sapping, complemented musketeers' roles at a siege or in a
garrison. These troops made use of the technical and manufacturing developments mentioned earlier. A significant number of contract servicemen
were Cossacks, many of them runaways who lived on the steppe edge; a
few Cossacks had acted as Muscovite auxiliaries for some time. Under
Ivan IV some became resident troops – 'fortress Cossacks'. In return for
limited 'pay' – shares in collective land grants, perhaps some cash and tax
exemptions – they lived near the frontier fortresses and were ready at a
moment's notice to defend them. Despite their obvious resemblances to
pomest'e cavalry, the Muscovite government usually categorized Cossacks
with musketeers and others of lower social status and less wealth. This
lower social status did not entitle Cossacks to *pomest'e* land or to the
stature of the cavalry. These fortress Cossacks should not be confused
with more independent Cossacks, who lived in colonies beyond Muscovy's
reach on the lower Don and Dniepr, for example.[19]

The usefulness of these troops notwithstanding, Muscovy found it very
expensive to pay for professional fighting men. Especially by comparison
with the landholding cavalry, year-round cash salaries, training and maintenance for growing numbers of troops required considerable government
resources. Greater administrative specialization within the Muscovite
government provided part of the answer. In 1577 a special administrative
unit, the Musketeers Chancellery, appeared to regulate many of the contract servicemen, particularly the musketeers and the 'fortress Cossacks'.

The new musketeers' tax, which it levied on productive agricultural land, was not based on new sources of income, but focused instead on extracting more of existing resources for government use. Furthermore, the new tax took the amount needed to support the troops and divided it among available tax-paying units in order to arrive at assessments.[20] Inevitably, the tax-paying population did not grow as fast as the rapidly expanding numbers of musketeers, and the tax became increasingly burdensome. Fiscal pressure was exacerbated by the impact of the Little Ice Age on agriculture, and the competing economic pressure of supplying *pomest'e* cavalrymen through successive years of war. As the number and cost of musketeers continued to grow towards the end of the century, interim reimbursement devices were used; awarding provincial musketeers tax-free trading status or land made them more independent of state salaries. This had contradictory effects. It did resolve fiscal pressure, but it also undermined the musketeers' value as permanent troops by directing their attention to non-military pursuits. The greater their detachment from year-round military pursuits, by the end of the century, the greater their similarity to the town Cossacks.[21]

An increasingly active and diverse Muscovite military, in this and other cases, contributed fundamentally to the development of greater fiscal and administrative regularity. Intensified record keeping and a more specialized administrative office helped to regularize and mobilize Moscow's army, as well as pay for it. The preponderance of this effort seems to have been directed at the *pomest'e* cavalry.

There was a concerted effort to improve the collection of taxes and raise revenues for spending on the army's expanded ventures. Land surveys early in Ivan's reign identified who was in possession of arable lands, so unclaimed territory could be assigned to new *pomest'e* holders. Similarly, Ivan's government also tried to recover lands that had been deeded to churches and monasteries. A new kind of land assessment used in this process revised how taxes were levied, and distributed the tax burden more widely. Viceregents (*namestniki*) and the 'feeding' system that supported them (*kormlenie*) were gradually phased out and tax farming diminished. The new local officials, such as town elders, had less individual power and were more easily supervised. The fees and taxes they collected were regularized and recorded, so that larger sums made their way to the centre.[22] To increase its resources, Muscovy encouraged commerce down the Volga, to the Baltic and through the White Sea, which was then taxed. Various important trading partners were involved, including the Ottomans, the English (who discovered a northern route to Muscovy in the 1550s) and

Baltic merchants. The Muscovite economy was quite prosperous at least into the 1560s. It supported a growing tax burden, and state revenues expanded.[23]

A more formal and precise accounting of army service replaced what had apparently been recorded only in the memory of local magnates and elders. Beginning in 1552, the year of the Kazan campaign, the administration prepared lists of local cavalrymen *prior* to cavalry musters. From the age of 15 until his retirement, injury or death, a cavalryman's appearance at regular army musters was now confirmed in writing. At such an event, a scribe recorded the mounts, accoutrements and general preparedness of each cavalryman and those accompanying him. The purpose was to enforce a minimum standard, not an upgrade of arms. Chain mail or a reinforced jacket, an iron helmet, bow and arrows and a sabre remained standard for a mounted warrior. Cavalrymen who appeared without the requisite items were fined. After a muster, the cavalryman (and his attendants) were dismissed, sent on siege duty, distant campaigns, or south to join units preparing to aid any frontier fortresses under Tatar attack.[24] Regularization extended further. Cavalrymen from some territories began to receive predictable assignments, to fight in the same parts of a particular division year after year. In other words, servicemen from Murom might be regularly assigned to the Centre Division of an army departing on campaign. Further, the same group of men was appointed as their officers from year to year. Command and placement thus became relatively consistent from season to season.[25]

In 1556 Ivan's government introduced service norms, which for the first time formally spelled out the service responsibilities that attached to landholding. According to the Ordinance on Service, a landholder had to supply for his sovereign's service one mounted cavalryman, fully armed and provided, from every 400 acres of good arable land. If the cavalryman was sent on a distant campaign, the landholder was required to send a second horse, a reserve mount, with him. The decree implicitly registered a new claim, because these service norms applied equally to *votchina*, or inherited lands, as they did to *pomest'e* land. A cash supplement was offered for exceeding the service norm. Landholders met or exceeded the norms by bringing outfitted combat slaves to the musters, in addition to baggage slaves. Richard Hellie calculates that about one-third of the combat forces under Ivan IV were slaves.[26] Compliance with the Ordinance became the minimum requirement for retaining service land, earning the cash allowance offered to cavalrymen, even for obtaining promotion with attendant larger land grants and higher status. Efforts like these to regularize compliance, including penalties for failure to meet service norms, centralized ordinary army service, helped create cavalry units of predictable size and structure, and simplified ready response.[27] Over the length of Ivan's long and militarily active reign, the standardization of military service (as well as taxation and payment) also proved an ideal vehicle for raising service requirements.

This level of standardization required considerable expertise with records, and more clearly differentiated administrative units within the Muscovite government followed. Specialized departments (called *izby*, lit. huts) were clearly evident by the 1540s and 1550s. From 1566 a separate *Razriadnaia Izba* dealt with the cavalry troops, their musters, appointments and military regulation. The growing importance of a bureaucracy was reflected in a name change late in the century, as government departments became chancelleries. The Military Chancellery (*Razriadnyi Prikaz*) became the central agency for much of army regulation and oversight. To some degree, it coordinated the activities of other military chancelleries, such as the Musketeers Chancellery, which appeared in 1577.[28] The growing importance of administration was also reflected in two new elite ranks. *Dumnyi dvoriane* and *dumnyi d'iaki* were new participants in the inner circles of political power, the Boiar Council. The latter in particular was reserved for the holders of important administrative positions.

Reforms introduced for political reasons also had an impact on the military. In an effort to restore greater stability at court, it has been argued, Ivan and his ruling circle attempted during these early years of his reign to counteract the collective political importance of the great *boiar* families or perhaps to reinvigorate the capital's service population. For example, in 1550 Ivan ordered that 1,000 cavalrymen who were not high-ranking courtiers be awarded lands near Moscow and with it the right to participate in court life. In the same vein, *boiars* and other members of the court also found their aspirations channelled, perhaps even limited. The move away from viceregal government in the provinces, for example, increasingly confined *boiar* service and advancement to the arenas of court and army.[29] Finally, the power of precedence (*mestnichestvo*) to affect the military was somewhat limited. Certainly, rulers used remonstrance to mitigate its impact on army activities from the outset. But precedence disputes had become increasingly common at the Muscovite court under Ivan IV. When status disputes among commanders disrupted the Kazan campaign of 1549, Ivan initiated the practice of declaring a campaign null with regard to precedence-ranking, or *bez mest*. That is, the military posts held in such a campaign did not count in subsequent precedence (*mestnichestvo*)

calculations, and questions about the precedence implications of such post-
ings were disallowed. The practice of nullifying precedence for a campaign, with its implication of some meritocracy in the high command,
became increasingly common in subsequent years. Ivan's rulings appear to
have regulated rather than eliminated precedence ranking, however.[30]

Other government actions supported the economic viability of a large
cavalry force. A general Law Code in 1550 repeated a 1497 injunction,
which allowed peasants to leave the estates where they lived only after the
harvest was in and their debts paid. This insurance against wilful departure helped some landholders retain labour more easily. As it became
customary to award land to (each of) the sons of *pomest'e* holders as they
came of age, Muscovy prepared to meet that obligation through land
retrieval and registration, as mentioned above.[31]

Finally, the first Assembly of the Land, or *zemskii sobor*, brought
representatives of the clergy, elite and provincial cavalrymen-landholders,
administrators and merchants to Moscow in 1549 to consult with the Tsar.
The Assembly provided a new channel for information from the provinces
to reach the centre, a substitute for the *boiar* viceregents, who were being
phased out. Its second meeting in 1556 registered consensus over Moscow's
entry into the Livonian War.

The lineaments of empire

With these reforms providing critical support to its activities, an army
against Kazan departed in early June 1552, with Ivan himself at the head
of his troops. The logistics of the approach were well calculated on this
occasion. Slower-moving army contingents – the musketeers, artillery and
supplies – travelled down the Volga by boat to the prefabricated wooden
fortress at Sviazhsk. Although a Crimean attack on the frontier attempted
to divert troops moving overland, that effort was unsuccessful; cavalry
forces led by Gorbatyi arrived at Sviazhsk in mid-August. Despite careful
planning, it had taken nearly six weeks for the army to reach Kazan.
Given the short campaigning season, the inherent problem in military
logistics is quite clear. How could Muscovy move its cavalry, never mind
the infantry, artillery and supplies it now needed, across sparsely inhab-
ited distances of steppe land (and back), without exhausting the campaign
season and depleting the supplies accompanying the army?

Muscovy was lucky in 1552, because Kazan did not hold out for long.
From Sviazhsk, a reunited army moved nearly unimpeded toward Kazan,
where it besieged the capital city. The Centre and Advance Divisions

approached the city from the southeast and camped on Arsk plain as in 1550.[32] Attacks by Tatar forces from the east impeded the Russians as they constructed a three-tier siege tower and surrounded Kazan with trenches and stockades, in preparation for bombardment; the musketeers providing fire until the Russians were dug in. With the annihilation of the Tatar troops, the siege was joined in earnest. The city of Kazan, once the barriers imposed by distance were removed, was at a considerable disadvantage. Its forces were not as numerous as the Muscovites, although they included both infantry and cavalry. The defenders were provided with both muskets and cannon, although the Kazan fortress was not designed to withstand steady artillery fire. Mining of the town's access to water doomed the fortress, although Moscovite *pomest'e* troops engaged in fierce hand-to-hand combat before they finally took the city on 2 October 1552.[33]

The fall of the city of Kazan, however, was not a prelude to a peaceful absorption of the Khanate. Further military operations to establish control lasted several more years. During the 1552 siege, much of the capital was sacked, and its population died in the fighting or abandoned its walls. Kazan was rebuilt as a Russian city and a centre of Russian Orthodox Christianity. The walls of the Zilantov Uspenskii monastery were included in the new fortifications. Defences at Alatyr (1552) and Cheboksary (1552) in northern and central Kazan also required garrisons to reinforce Moscow's grasp of the Khanate outside the capital. Although some Tatars declared their allegiance to Moscow, guerrilla warfare against the occupiers began almost as soon as the capital fell. Two years of open rebellion in 1553–4 were followed by punitive Russian campaigns that slaughtered thousands and devastated large tracts of territory. In their wake, three or four more monasteries were built, whose fortifications supported existing fortress towns. Meanwhile, a Tatar suburb reappeared outside the walls of Kazan.

Even then, establishing Muscovite rule was neither easy nor rapid. No less than three punitive campaigns were sent from Moscow in 1556 to deal with rebellions. Three garrison towns by 1558, and another three in the mid-1570s, helped to complete a fortified line facing the open steppe from within the former khanate. Despite continued resistance, *pomest'e* lands were gradually distributed to military personnel, including some Tatars. In some respects, Kazan was taken into the Muscovite state using devices individually tried elsewhere on previous occasions – the dispossession of elites, reassignment of lands, the construction of fortified defensive lines. It was also accompanied by devastating punitive war, the construction

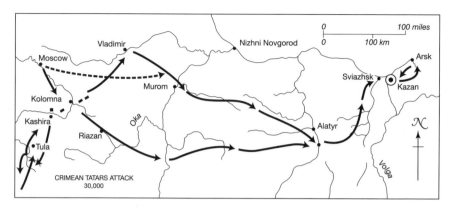

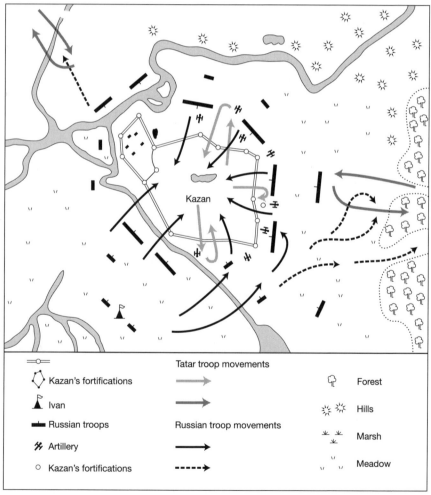

MAP 3   *The Kazan campaign, 1552*

of fortresses and their military occupation. Even so, Kazan was not as fully integrated into the central government as Novgorod or Tver. Its Muslim princes were not inaugurated into the *cursus honorum* of the Muscovite court. In Kazan itself, local land and military affairs were administered through a single territorial chancellery, the *Kazanskii dvorets*. Kazan remained a quite separate element within Muscovy. So did its troops and those of other non-Russians, who were clearly identified as distinctive elements in the Muscovite army.[34]

Still, Moscow's influence and power spread rapidly south and eastward from Kazan. Factions within the Nogai Horde, whose lands stretched across the southern Volga, had intermittently allied themselves with Muscovy for some time already. After the fall of Kazan, Muscovite troops installed a Nogai prince in Astrakhan in 1554. When the prince and his Nogai confederates turned against his Muscovite garrison, Muscovy responded by sending more troops to reinforce the installation of a Russian governor (*voevoda*) in 1556. Once established, the Russian presence in Astrakhan severely undermined Nogai self-sufficiency, although Muscovy continued to rely on the Nogai to distract, if not defeat, Crimea. In 1555 Muscovite influence expanded eastward to the Khanate of Sibir, which began paying tribute to Moscow.[35]

Moscow's conquests in the east meant that its empire now exercised some control over vast new territories, including the northern end of important trade routes that ran the length of the Volga, southward across the Caspian and westward to Constantinople. Quite abruptly, Moscow loomed much larger in central Eurasia and on the steppe. These conquests carried ideological power. Although it is doubtful that the conquests were primarily motivated by such concerns, Muscovy did not fail to portray itself at home and to its western neighbours, especially to Poland, as a champion of Christianity over Islam.[36] The great cathedral of St Basil the Blessed in Moscow, begun in 1551 and completed in 1558, celebrated the victory over Kazan and reflected the importance of the conquest as seen from Moscow. Significant as this ideological perspective was, Ivan was quite willing, as he addressed his new subjects, to accept the homage due a descendant of the Golden Horde, and to assert on some occasions that Islam and Christianity could co-exist in his domains.[37]

Conquest opened new territories for settlement and occupation. The fall of Kazan and Astrakhan of course implied the annexation of new lands, which were eventually used to support *pomest'e* cavalrymen and their families. Furthermore, they opened the way to further eastward colonization. Privileges assigned to major trading families allowed a few families like the Strogonovs to exploit opportunities for exploration. They hired armed bands and sent them eastward, establishing small islands[38] of Russian fortification and settlement in their search for fur and fur hunters. Most famously, towards the end of Ivan's reign, the Cossack Ermak defeated the Khan of Sibir and occupied his principal city in 1582. Although Ermak and most of his followers were killed shortly thereafter, Moscow sent military reinforcements to follow private initiative, when it could, claiming and garrisoning outposts in Sibir and, rapidly, further east.

These achievements certainly demonstrated the value of the army's preparations during the immediately preceding period. Although there would later be accusations of military incompetence and mistakes,[39] the campaigns against Kazan in 1552 and Astrakhan in 1556 were both obviously successful, fully justifying Muscovy's investments in gunpowder technology and troops, its logistics preparations, and its effective use of Cossacks, musketeers and regular *pomest'e* cavalry under the command of court appointees. Even the punitive expeditions that followed the conquest were effectively staged, if undoubtedly brutal.

The political and diplomatic stresses generated by the fall of Kazan changed steppe politics and placed significant pressure on Muscovy's military institutions, particularly on its ability to mobilize men and resources and organize their use. This was particularly evident in Muscovy's dealings with Crimea and its Ottoman overlords. The Khanate of Crimea under Khan Devlet Girey persistently refused to acknowledge Muscovy's conquest of Kazan and Astrakhan. The Crimean royal family continued to claim them for itself. After 1556, therefore, Crimea was at loggerheads with Muscovy, unwilling to compromise even occasionally. Instead, it intensified formidable and debilitating attacks along Muscovy's frontier, often in collaboration with Muscovy's Lithuanian foe. Moscow responded with a series of direct but unsuccessful attacks on Crimea in 1557, 1559 and 1560. These campaigns, which were the subject of intense policy debate at Ivan's court, neither diminished Crimean depredations along the frontier, nor undermined the military power of Khan Devlet Girey on his home territories. Crimea was out of reach. Moscow's Nogai allies were similarly unable to provide consistent relief from the Khanate's raids on Muscovite territory. The conquest of Kazan exacerbated the problem of defending the Muscovite southern frontier, which remained a persistent and increasingly intransigent military problem, notwithstanding greater state supervision over newly fortified defensive lines.[40]

Expansion brought Muscovy face to face with the Ottoman Empire, then at the height of its power.[41] Sultan Suleyman tried, even before Kazan fell, to counteract Muscovite expansion with steppe alliances, but the Ottoman Empire's struggles with both Persia and the Habsburgs delayed a focused response. By then, Muscovy was extending its sphere of authority around Astrakhan; it entered into an alliance with Kabarda in the central Caucasus, which was soon cemented by Ivan's marriage to the Kabardian princess. Muscovy' presence there threatened Ottoman interests.[42] Cossack raiders from nearby encampments disrupted Ottoman communications eastward. Furthermore, from Astrakhan, Muscovy could and sometimes did disrupt pilgrimage routes, as well as Ottoman military and commercial connections with central Asia. An Ottoman military response against Muscovy, supported by Crimea's claims to Kazan, was contemplated from at least 1563.

Ottoman Turkey's first military attack on Muscovy was launched in spring 1569 after nearly two years of preparation. The landing of an Ottoman army had only reluctant support from the Crimean Khan, who feared the presence of his Ottoman overlord almost as much as the Muscovite threat. First, the Empire planned to build a canal between the Don and Volga Rivers. Such a canal offered important military advantages, allowing Turkish ships to move between the Black and Caspian Seas, giving the Empire easy access not only to Astrakhan, but also to the northern Caucasus and Persia. Next, the Ottomans planned to supply their armies for a campaign against Astrakhan via the canal. Muscovite officials, deeply concerned about the presence of the Ottoman colossus to their south and heavily engaged on their western border, were relieved when the Ottoman expedition largely self-destructed. The canal proved impossible to dig, particularly in the single summer season allowed.[43] Without the canal, the nearly legendary Ottoman supply system was unable to sustain the army as it approached Astrakhan. Initially, the Ottoman forces chose to winter over outside Astrakhan before attacking. Their Crimean allies, fearful of the Ottoman presence, urged them to return to the Black Sea without delay. Contemporary sources suggest that the Crimeans even sowed dissent among the Turkish troops.[44] Given the possibility of both Persian and Russian attack, the Ottoman commander finally decided to withdraw across the open steppe to Azov, despite the immense logistical problems that presented. Less than a third of the original force made it back.[45]

To all appearances, the campaign represented a devastating Ottoman failure. The grandiose nature of the canal project and the failure to establish riverine access between the Black and Caspian Seas doomed the military effort dependent upon it. Without water access, Constantinople was no more able to supply its army in the barren and under-populated steppe than Moscow. Well into the eighteenth century, this fundamental problem plagued Ottoman–Muscovite warfare from both sides. Even the Tatars, when accompanied by Ottoman janissaries and guns, succumbed to this problem.[46] But in political terms, the expedition was less of a failure than it appeared. Muscovy's awareness of Ottoman sensibilities and of the profound threat represented by Ottoman–Crimean military cooperation was reinforced. Over the next few years Moscow reopened trade and pilgrimage through Astrakhan and destroyed the fortress it had built on the Terek River. After a particularly devastating Crimean raid, which reached Moscow in 1571 and prompted Ottoman praise for its vassal, Ivan IV was apparently willing to discuss the 'return' of Astrakhan and perhaps even Kazan.[47]

Several important military issues emerged from the conquest and occupation of the former Khanates of Kazan and Astrakhan. First, these events significantly reinforced Muscovy's need for a numerous army – to fight on the lower Volga and to combat resistance in Kazan. Even after 'pacification' efforts in 1553–6, the retention and defence of the Khanate required the nearly constant presence of Muscovite troops.[48] The more efficiently and predictably men could be gathered for these purposes, the less pressure it represented both on the men and on the military apparatus.

The conquest of Kazan and Astrakhan also reinforced newer military requirements. The situation in Kazan made particularly clear the need for permanent, garrison troops. Standing units, trained in the use of firearms, were stationed in the fortresses, supplementing the cavalry presence on the frontier. Contract servicemen were prominent in Kazan garrisons generally by the 1560s, and over half the Kazan town garrison. This situation intensified similar demands from the southern frontier, reinforcing the usefulness of musketeers and Cossacks. Tsar Fedor's government tried to reinforce the garrisons with *pomest'e* servicemen, by issuing more land grants in Kazan to loyal Muscovites and cash supplements to loyal Tatars in Muscovite service. Such actions helped to domesticate Kazan as they had Novgorod.[49]

On the other hand, Kazan and Astrakhan delivered valuable cavalry troops led by Tatar commanders to the Muscovite army; they supplemented other Tatar troops from the Nogai Horde and the Khanate of Kasimov.[50] Putting loyal garrison troops in Kazan while Tatar cavalry fought in Livonia demanded an administrative system capable of efficiently mustering Muscovy's fiscal, manpower and technological resources. As fighting persisted, the reform and regularization of the military begun in

the 1550s particularly helped to bolster Muscovy's military power throughout the 1560s.

The Livonian challenge

Long before its position on the Volga was assured, Muscovy engaged itself
in another demanding conflict, the Livonian War. Livonia lay between
Muscovy and the Grand Duchy of Lithuania to Muscovy's north-east. By
the second half of the sixteenth century it represented a loose association
of elements: some rich trading cities belonging to the Hanseatic League,
alongside the remnants of a once-powerful Roman Catholic crusading
order, and a selection of other ecclesiastical holdings, some of which were
openly contemplating a conversion to Protestantism. Not only was a
central authority lacking, but internal conflict was rife in the 1550s. Ivan
was quick to make the most of it. On the pretext of demanding ancient
rights and dues, Ivan moved troops rapidly toward the common border in
1557. To maximize the consternation of unprepared Livonians, the two-
pronged Muscovite attack was led by the Tatar Khan of Kazimov and
two other Tatar princes, with Russian *boiars*. Their forces included Tatar
and *pomest'e* cavalry, Cossacks, musketeers and a significant artillery
train.[51]

Under this assault, the Livonians were slow to muster their own forces.
Although Livonian towns and orders were well protected by numerous
castles, many recently fortified, and individual cities like Dorpat (also
known as Derpt, Iur'ev or Tartu) were well armed, the Muscovites were
stunningly successful in this less familiar military landscape for most of
the period 1558–62. In 1558, for example, Muscovite armies took Narva
and Dorpat, and besieged Reval; the Livonians retook only Wesenberg.
The following year, another Muscovite campaign army occupied much of
central Livonia before signing a six-month truce, during which interval
Muscovy sent an army against Crimea. The city of Fellin succumbed
to Muscovite forces in 1560. At Ermes in August 1561 the Livonian
Order's remaining cavalry forces were drawn into an attack on the main
Muscovite army, and their disastrous defeat eliminated the Order's own
forces. Livonians sought foreign protection for their cities and bishoprics.

The early successes had recognizable characteristics. Muscovite forces
carried out numerous short campaigns and victorious sieges. Musketeers
were an important part of siege activity, firing from behind entrenchments
and wooden walls, well protected by Muscovite and Tatar cavalrymen.
Moscow's artillery was successfully deployed in support of these sieges. The

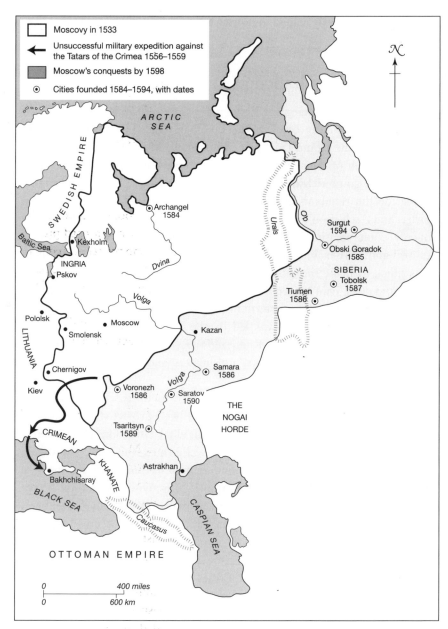

MAP 4 *The expansion of Muscovy, 1533–98* (adapted from Gilbert, Martin, *Atlas of Russian History* (Marboro Books, 1989))

fighting was not continuous, however. There were seasonal interruptions, and campaigns were halted by brief periods of truce. The lands around Livonian fortresses and cities suffered near devastation as a result of Muscovite military actions. By 1560, those Livonians who could had retreated to the remaining castles to avoid expert cavalry raids in which the Muscovites carried off booty, supplies and prisoners. The havoc wreaked by Moscow's troops was compounded by local outlaws and by mercenary troops who went on the rampage after Livonia hired but could not pay them.[52]

Thereafter, however, the nature of the war altered, expanding its scope and changing its character. Rapid, even devastating, Muscovite victories brought Livonia's other neighbours into the war, staking claims to lands within that disintegrating polity. Danish forces arrived in 1560; the Swedes in 1561; Lithuania proclaimed its interest in southern Livonia the same year and took Riga under its wing in 1562. Effectively, Livonia was divided among four nearby powers. As a result, the conflict quickly became a consuming regional war, which brought new and greater military pressures to bear on a Muscovite army fighting on many fronts.

In the northern part of Livonia, long-standing hostility between Denmark and Sweden directed the pattern of activity. Denmark purchased the Isle of Osel off the Livonian coast for its king's brother. In order to claim its purchase, Danish forces had to suppress a serious Estonian peasant rebellion. By 1561, however, Sweden was claiming the right to protect the towns of Reval and Pernau and most of present-day Estonia. Long-standing hostilities between the two Scandinavian powers ignited seven years of warfare, lasting from 1563 to 1570. Muscovy allied itself with Sweden, while its long-standing enemy and neighbour, Poland-Lithuania, joined Lübeck in supporting the Danes. Both Poland-Lithuania and Muscovy, however, were primarily engaged against one another in Livonia and further south, and neither took much action in the Scandinavian conflict. In the long run, the Seven Years' War was remarkable for the Scandinavian states' developing ability to fight a sustained land and naval war, rather than for concrete gains by either side.[53]

Further south, the Lithuanians superintended the dissolution of the Livonian Order of Crusading Knights in 1561–2, taking Riga and the Order's southern lands under Lithuanian protection. Moscow and Lithuania prepared for confrontation, each hoping to fight with a coalition behind it. There were border skirmishes and raids. Campaigns in 1561 and 1562 were inconclusive. Then, Muscovy launched a major campaign against the city of Polotsk in Lithuania in December of 1562. The town was strategically located to help decide the fate of Muscovy's armies in Livonia. It also ruled a wealthy and populous territory. Dynastic claims figured largely in justifying the attack. Polotsk was a part of Ivan's claim to the lands of Kievan Rus, and the Lithuanians and Poles had declined to accept Ivan's title as 'tsar' since his coronation. The religious significance of the attack was trumpeted in terms not unlike the conquest of Kazan.[54]

Details of this successful Muscovite campaign are unusually rich, thanks to extant chronicle accounts and the earliest official count of the Muscovite army on the move. These forces numbered more than 31,500 men. About one-fifth of the troops were non-Russian; Tatars from Kazan, Astrakhan and the Nogai Horde, among others, fought as an integral part of the Muscovite army. The campaign's leadership included prominent Tatars. Although the Tatars were accompanied by *boiar* 'minders' from the court, they appear to have exercised full powers of command. Tatar troops were used both as advance guards and as offensive troops, who inspired terror in those whom they fought; meanwhile, their engagement in Livonia kept them from potentially subversive involvement at home.[55] The rest of the army included landholding cavalrymen from Moscow and 17 other districts. Some 38 per cent of the army – 12,000 musketeers and artillerymen – was contract servicemen. Led by Ivan himself, the entire force left from Velikie Luki with seven divisions containing three artillery units. Engineering and logistics were well organized; even provisioning for the siege troops was considered. Bridges were built ahead of the army, with towers and artillery brought up to the front in a timely fashion, despite other heavy military traffic.[56]

The Muscovite cavalry quickly established control of the Lithuanian countryside around Polotsk. On the battlefield around the city, the gunpowder troops played a vital role. Musketeers and artillerymen,[57] positioned on an island and on the shores of the Dvina, responded to bombardment from the city and provided cover for assaults by the Centre Division of the besieging army. They set fire to a fortified tower near the river and later were instrumental in the capture of the town of Polotsk. After the town fell, the main fortress fought on, although Lithuania was unable to provide relief or reinforcement. The Muscovite artillery resumed bombardment, and within another week the siege was over. Although Muscovy treated the garrison troops with leniency, there are records of the looting and burning of the town by the army, the destruction of non-Orthodox places of worship, and large numbers of men, women and children taken captive.[58] A garrison was left behind as Ivan and the army returned to Moscow after two months of winter duty. Under Muscovite military leadership, the fortress walls were restored and new outlying forts added to the existing ones. The capture of Polotsk nicely illustrates the Muscovite army's ability to execute a well-planned, expert and brief siege in favourable conditions.

The taking of Polotsk, however, marked the end of Muscovite successes as war on multiple fronts took its toll. Losses and setbacks began to mount as Ivan fought to retain his Livonian conquests. Meanwhile, Lithuania bolstered its capacity to respond, pouring money into the war. In 1564 Muscovite troops lost a battle to the Lithuanians on the Ulla River near Orsha/Orsza (south-east of Polotsk) due to blunders by the leadership.[59] This was followed by the desertion to Lithuania of Prince Kurbsky, a politically prominent and successful general of the Kazan campaign. Another major loss to Lithuania followed at Chashniki in 1565, while large Crimean raids continued to strike Moscow's southern frontiers.

Even as military events took a turn for the worse, Muscovite attention was forced towards domestic events. In a fit of fury, perhaps sparked by the losses in Lithuania, Ivan rejected his court and left the capital for the town of Aleksandrova Sloboda, about 96 kilometres (60 miles) away. To the consternation of his subjects, he shortly thereafter divided his realm into two parts. The lands he chose to rule personally, called the *oprichnina*, were withdrawn from the kingdom, and many landholders were dispossessed. Under Ivan's tutelage, the *oprichnina* developed its own administration and army, which eventually included 15,000 musketeers and Cossacks. Meanwhile, the rest of Muscovy, called the *zemshchina*, was separately administered. In the terror that followed, the *oprichnina*'s forces were turned against Muscovites whom Ivan suspected of treason. In 1570 they were used for a particularly vicious sack of Novgorod.

It is hardly surprising that Moscow's position in the war against Lithuania worsened during this period of intense internal discord. Internal problems were compounded by external ones. The Grand Duchy of Lithuania was united with the Kingdom of Poland to become the Commonwealth of Poland–Lithuania in 1569. Whatever its drawbacks, the union gave Lithuanians more direct access to the military resources of richer and more populous Poland. The possibility of Swedish–Commonwealth cooperation against Muscovy loomed, and Muscovy's military position was further threatened when the Ottomans launched the 1569 attack on Astrakhan, discussed above.

Remarkably, Muscovy mounted a military response, despite internal upheaval. The *zemshchina* shared responsibility for defending the southern frontier with *oprichnina* forces. Similarly, while the *zemshchina* organized, paid for and dispatched armies westward to Lithuania and Livonia, *oprichnina* forces also served there. These cooperative military efforts were not successful, in all likelihood because of internal upheaval rather than military incompetence or corruption.[60] As an expedient, Ivan proposed to the King of Denmark's younger brother in Osel that he rule Livonia as a Muscovite vassal. Muscovite troops proved ineffective under the younger brother's leadership, however. Ivan then hired a Danish corsair to help the Muscovite effort by creating a mercenary navy in the Baltic; after capturing a few ships, the episode was rapidly terminated by the King of Denmark's arrest of the would-be admiral.[61]

In 1571 the military situation reached its nadir, when the Crimean Khanate launched a raid in force at Muscovy's southern border. It is unclear exactly why the joint *oprichnina–zemshchina* forces on guard failed in their efforts to halt the attack. It is likely to have been the result of many factors: the troops may have been demoralized; their joint command may have induced confusion; the political disorders certainly hindered military responsiveness. To the considerable admiration of his Ottoman overlord, the Crimean Khan broke through the defences, raced northward to Moscow and sacked the city's environs before returning homeward. This is the moment when Ivan briefly considered relinquishing Astrakhan and perhaps Kazan, to stave off further devastation.[62]

Crimean raiders at the gates of Moscow brought the *oprichnina* to an official and rapid end in 1571-2, although Ivan's erratic behaviour did not cease. The first military efforts of the reunited government were a reform of the southern frontier defences and the renewal of serious military activity against Lithuania in Livonia proper. Muscovy held 22 fortress-cities with permanent garrisons, many of which were on the southern fortified lines. Their troops included many contract servicemen: musketeers, gunners, gatekeepers and Cossacks.[63] They were supported by *pomest'e* cavalrymen on 'siege duty'. Assigned only to those with small land grants or unable to serve far away, 'siege duty' troops were the poorest of *pomest'e* holders, whose status and economic condition was perilously close to service contract Cossacks.[64] The unusual nature of service in southern fortresses was reinforced in 1571 by the creation of a specialized frontier service. Rotas of guards for six-week tours of duty were established at all major fortresses from 1 April to the onset of winter. Guards were supported by patrol units that travelled long, predetermined routes south of the defensive lines on the outlook for telltale signs of Tatar approach. The patrol units were numerous enough to pass nearly every segment of the frontier on an almost daily basis. As needed, the patrols and guards alerted local garrisons, warned local populations to take cover, and called upon the cavalry units, who were seasonally posted to strategic points along the defensive line to do battle with the enemy.[65] The establishment of specialized local guards and patrols could not defend the southern frontier alone, but they substantially improved security along this border. In 1572 the Crimean Khan, expecting a still under-defended frontier, attacked again. A carefully deployed Muscovite battle array at Molodi successfully repelled the attack, and undermined the Khan's credit in Constantinople.[66]

Muscovy's renewed interest in the Livonian War after 1577 met with limited success. Muscovy's ability to muster men and resources was not infinite; when it returned to war, it did so in Livonia rather than in a reinvigorated Lithuania. A Muscovite campaign in 1572 retook Wittenstein (in present-day Estonia), while Russian vassal, King Magnus, ineffectually besieged the city of Reval. By 1575 Muscovy had captured Pernau and devastated much of central Livonia. Subsequently, Muscovy conquered Dünaburg, Kokenhausen and other towns in Polish Livonia. Little besides Reval, Riga and Osel remained free of Muscovite occupation.

In 1576, however, other forces entered the fray again. The Swedes, from their foothold in Reval, redoubled their efforts. Swedish troops defeated the Muscovites near Pernau, then made a rapid and unexpected strike at the Muscovite border, taking Narva and Ivangorod in 1581. King Magnus enjoyed a brief resurgence, as Livonian towns chose his rule over their neighbours'. After a long interregnum, Stefan Batory was elected king of the newly united Polish–Lithuanian Commonwealth, and the Polish Diet voted money to support war again Ivan. The Commonwealth soon forced Muscovite garrisons to relinquish some of the conquered fortresses, to the satisfaction of local residents.[67] In 1579 Batory recaptured Polotsk and then swiftly turned his forces against Muscovite towns. A Lithuanian-led army took Velikie Luki from a small Muscovite garrison.[68] Kholm fell in 1580, and Stefan Batory besieged Pskov for five months in 1581–2, at the same time as the Swedes attacked Muscovy further north.

Although its military administration remarkably continued to function from 1577 to 1582, Muscovy was exhausted. It had been at war nearly without interval since the mid-1550s. Although its involvement in Livonia had been at first intermittent, Moscow's absences from the field had not represented periods of recuperation and renewal. Rather, during lulls in the Livonian fighting, Moscow put garrisons along its new borders, battled rebellions in Kazan, and confronted more than 20 significant attacks from Crimea. Intensified demands for military service of all kinds were the nearly inevitable result of continued warfare on so many fronts.[69] The accelerating pressures of war were compounded by the political discord and economic confusion of the *oprichnina*. The Terror and the impact of its attendant political uproar deepened less visible dislocations. The prosperous commerce of the mid-sixteenth century went into steep decline. Some landholders whose lands were grabbed for the *oprichnina* were resettled in Kazan, only to be repatriated later.[70] The speed with which newly conquered lands in Livonia were disbursed to Muscovites suggests that productive lands to support *pomest'e* cavalry forces were in short supply at home.[71] The economies of central Russian landholders were, by the mid and late 1570s, feeling the economic impact of estate-holders who went off to successive years of war rather than managing their estates. Their peasants, overtaxed and overburdened by the late 1570s, had begun to sell themselves into slavery or simply to flee to the frontiers. After 1580, in an effort to stem the tide, limitations on peasant movement were introduced. Flight continued; some of the landholders, themselves impoverished, would follow the peasants in the next decades.

The military consequences were predictable and costly. The backbone of the cavalry forces, the *pomest'e* landholders, failed systematically to appear at musters. If they did present themselves at musters, many deserted, forcing the government to send troops to look for them.[72] The total number of available cavalrymen dwindled. In Livonia and Lithuania, Moscow made up the numbers as far as it could with Tatar and other non-Russian troops, who represented an increasing proportion of the men under arms in the latter part of the war.[73] The proportions of Cossacks, musketeers and other contract servicemen also inched upward, although Muscovy lacked the resources to pay for substantial numbers of them. Still, more than half the men initially gathered to defend Pskov in 1580 were contract servicemen. Despite these efforts, the overall size of the army on campaigns gradually declined.[74] Sustaining such pro-longed military effort, for Muscovy as for its neighbours, was nearly impossible.

By the early 1580s Moscow was forced to call a truce in its war against Sweden and the Polish–Lithuanian Commonwealth. In the truce of Iam Zapolskii between Muscovy and the Commonwealth, Ivan abandoned all his conquests and claims in Livonia, in order to prevent King Stefan Batory from renewing his attack on Pskov; the former border between Lithuania and Muscovy was substantially restored. A three-year truce with Sweden in 1583 left Moscow with only a toehold on the Ingrian coast; Narva and Ivangorod remained in Swedish hands.

Tsar Fedor

The situation in which Muscovy was left at Ivan's death in 1584 was little short of catastrophic. Politically, socially and economically, the country and its inhabitants were under profound stress. Somewhat surprisingly, Ivan's feeble son, Fedor (Theodore, r. 1584–96), reigned for a decade and a half in relative peace, partially as a result of policies introduced by his ambitious chief adviser, Boris Godunov.

Some of the notable accomplishments of this reign were military. A renewal of fighting between Sweden and Muscovy after 1590 culminated in a peace at Teusino in 1595, which was more acceptable to Moscow. The Livonian War had ended on a nearly intolerable note for Muscovy, with the Polish–Lithuanian Commonwealth emerging ascendant, and the once-weak Swedes making significant gains. After Stefan Batory's death, however, leadership crises preoccupied both the Commonwealth and Sweden; these political events and limited economic recovery in parts of Muscovy were the background to the Swedish–Muscovite War of 1590–5. Fighting on both sides was undertaken only with great caution, and campaigns were followed by truces and recuperative periods. Muscovy's initial attack convinced Sweden to relinquish Iama, Korpor'e and Ivangorod on the Baltic coast, but Muscovy was unable to capture Narva. In a subsequent campaign, Muscovy devastated Vyborg and Åbo, but Sweden was unable to take back Ivangorod. With this brief demonstration of its military abilities, Moscow proved content, particularly given the possibility the Commonwealth might enter the war.[75] In addition to Ivangorod and Korpor'e, Muscovy gained Ingria and Kexholm.

In the decades following Ivan's death, the long-term value of Muscovy's frontier defence became clear. As the heartland of Muscovy depopulated under persistent economic and military pressures, people of many stations in life moved outward towards the frontiers – sometimes relinquishing their social position to do so. Boris Godunov, first as regent and later as tsar in his own right, exploited this migration when he ordered the building of new fortresses. Livny and Voronezh (1586), Elets (1592), and Belgorod, Oskol, Valuiki and Kromy (1593) formed new segments of a fortified line closer to the steppe. Finally, Tsarev Borisov (1599) was built astonishingly far to the south. Well fortified, it was surrounded by earthworks and garrisoned by nearly 3,000 men, about two-thirds of them were infantry with firearms in 1600.[76] Army units, assembling to defend the frontier, began to meet far south of the Oka River. As garrisons, settlers and fugitives moved in around these towns, the zone of Muscovite settlement advanced southward – by some 480 kilometres (300 miles) between Ivan's death and the century's end. A similar, if less rapid and more interrupted process was underway in Kazan, where more fortress building enforced Muscovite control and bolstered the advancing frontier. New fortified towns staked out more islands of Russian space in the vast-nesses of Siberia.[77]

The successes of Muscovy's military and agricultural colonization generated a debilitating response. The Dniepr Cossacks attacked and burnt Voronezh shortly after its construction, for example.[78] Rebellion and insubordination persisted in Kazan in the 1580s and 1590s, and restoring control was expensive. Fedor's government sent troops, when efforts to encourage loyalty through Christianization and other devices had very limited success.[79] Both Crimea and its Nogai neighbours were hostile to Moscow in this era, although inconsistently. Crimea was tolerant of Moscow and the Don Cossacks as required by its enmity to Lithuania and the Dniepr Cossacks or by its obligations to its Ottoman overlords, for example.[80] But Crimea also recognized the implication of Moscow's advancing frontier defences. In 1587–8 and again in the early 1590s as the new fortifications were being completed, there were successive, large Crimean attacks on the southern frontier. In the 1590s, yet again, an attack broke through the fortifications. Crimean forces reached Moscow and burnt down its suburbs, but withdrew rather than attack the city's fortifications. It would be the last time the Crimeans would get so close to the capital. In the 1590s, however, Moscow agreed to resume its payments to the Khanate.[81]

A military crisis?

With historical hindsight, it seems clear that the military events of the late sixteenth century impelled Muscovy to face two complex problems. One of these was the recent erratic functioning of the Muscovite service state, that interlocking political and military organization which had served Muscovy so well as it expanded to imperial dimensions. Although its basic structures persisted, the political equilibrium at court, where Tsar consulted with *boiars* and service princes, was seriously disturbed under Ivan IV: by a contentious regency, by Ivan's wildly erratic political behaviour, by a new emphasis on administration, by the presence of Assemblies of the Land, and by the resulting change in *boiar* power. Any efforts made in Fedor's time to restore a balanced leadership were undermined by the absence of an heir.

Equally important were the changes to those basic political and economic relationships that had sustained the court's hierarchy from the grassroots up. These hinged upon a symbiotic exchange of productive land and elite status in return for service to the Tsar. *Pomest'e* was its basic building block; the *pomest'e* cavalry its result. The character and duration of the Livonian War, in combination with effects of Ivan's erratic politics, challenged the basis of this exchange. First, there simply was not enough productive land to meet demand. Only one son of a *pomest'e* cavalryman could take over his father's land. Other sons usually claimed their own *pomest'e* from the state. The scions of great families inherited family lands (*votchina*) free and clear, but many of them also needed the supplemental support of *pomest'e* land, after generations of subdividing their personal lands into parcels for each and every offspring. The intense competition for unclaimed *pomest'e* land was for a while offset by military conquests, which added new land stock. The events of the *oprichnina* and the failure of the Livonian War, however, critically exacerbated the problem, in part by cutting off the supplies of new land. As early as the 1560s, a landless *pomest'e* cavalryman who lived off a brother's or a father's lands while awaiting his own land grant was by no means unheard of.

The land itself, actual acreage, was not the sole issue. If the system was to work, viable agricultural acreage needed peasant labour to work it. Maintaining the labour supply required steady population growth and peasants willing to till the *pomest'e* fields. The Livonian War created serious economic pressures on the peasantry, because it generated both higher taxes to support the musketeers, artillery, fortress building, and high private demands for support for their *pomest'e* landholders on frequent and distant campaigns. This pressure, on top of the wanton destructiveness of the *oprichnina*, destroyed most peasants' ability to work the landholders' land. Peasants simply fled, depopulating the central districts, moving to richer estates or into newly opened southern territories, or perhaps beyond Muscovy's boundaries. The impact on landholders of peasant flight was not uniform. Peasants were quickest to leave small estates where pressure was greater. They might even be lured to larger estates (nearby) where conditions were substantially better.

Unfortunately, the results were militarily very consistent. Many ordinary *pomest'e* cavalrymen, even those who began the wars with viable estates, were unable by the late 1570s to sustain military service. In the 1570s and 1580s some stayed home to farm for themselves, or to prevent their remaining labourers from departing. Punishing either the *pomeshchiki* or the peasants was of little avail. When peasant movement was formally restricted, it was too late, and it did not resolve the plight of the smaller estates. Finally, even the brief respite of the 1590s was undermined by crop failures and famines in 1600.

Together, there were socio-political, as well as military, implications. Without *pomest'e* land and peasants, the *deti boiarskie* and *dvoriane* lacked the standard markers of hereditary elite status. They also lacked the means to serve, to recoup their standing, or even to support themselves. As 1600 approached, many of them headed for the southern fortresses to recoup their fortunes or to the Cossack settlements beyond the borders, where they swelled a volatile, armed and discontented group of fellow refugees and long-time residents.

It is not clear that this combination of circumstances forced a reconsideration of Muscovy's basic military values towards the end of the sixteenth century. That is, elite Muscovites certainly perceived that *pomest'e* troops were unreliable or inappropriate in some circumstances; fewer would have questioned the value of *pomest'e* cavalry in general.[82] Not only the threatening political situation, but also the continuing military usefulness of any cavalry in eastern Europe militated against the questioning of established principles. Cavalry charges were a key element in offensive warfare. Cavalry defended against border raiders, but they also undertook reconnaissance, foraged beyond a devastated battlefield, or destroyed economic assets as they passed. Mobility was invaluable for a state whose defensible points and military targets might be 1,500 kilometres (950 miles) apart, with or without riverine approaches. The Muscovite instinct about the importance of cavalry was shared by other governments fighting in east Europe. Cavalry continued to represent nearly half of the Swedish, Ottoman and Polish–Lithuanian armies, as well as Moscow's, for another hundred years.[83] Thus, issues of cost, military effectiveness and no doubt inertia encouraged a continuing attachment to *pomest'e*-style cavalry, in particular. Contingents of Muscovite cavalry nearly annually met to confront Tatar raiders. In such circumstances, speed, mobility and seasonality were appropriate characteristics. They had recently proven their worth, particularly in the early years of the Livonian War. A skilled self-supporting cavalry archer, whose training encompassed a lifetime of hunting on his own estate, could still fire several shots for every one fired by a slow-loading musket in the hands of a trained soldier, whose salary and equipment were costly to the state. In many circumstances, even in 1600, Muscovy would not necessarily have wished for another kind of cavalry discipline or for the cavalry to carry gunpowder weaponry (although cavalrymen carrying firearms were encouraged by being listed separately and receiving gunpowder).[84]

However, other kinds of innovations and additions to the *pomest'e* army were by the late sixteenth century not only acknowledged as important; they absorbed increasing funds and attention. Fortress building, defensive arrangements and artillery production had significantly reinforced the army's successes. Standing troops, particularly those trained in the use of muskets, had richly rewarded Muscovite investment by delivering massed firepower (if not tactical manoeuvrability). They had proven themselves generally reliable and resilient under military stress, during the Livonian War as in border garrisons. However, political and economic crisis discouraged any reconsideration of their place in the Muscovite military by the end of the sixteenth century. The organization of *streltsy* and their battlefield capacities remained quite compatible with the dominant *pomest'e* forms. Nor did the Muscovite government of the late sixteenth century make any politically costly attempt to convert *pomest'e* servicemen to these kinds of duties. Instead, an entirely new set of lower status troops were established – contract servicemen including musketeers, artillerymen and some Cossacks. Little significance was attributed to their intermediate social status, but Muscovy's consciousness of their military importance was visible in their growing numbers throughout the second half of the century. As the state's resources dwindled towards the end of the century, however, Muscovy was forced to pay these valuable soldiers, not the direct salaries in cash and in kind they had originally received, but by older means, such as tax exemptions and access to land. At key moments, such expedient, if potentially harmful, measures maintained and even expanded contract service troops, particularly for garrison service.

The Muscovite court in the waning years of the sixteenth century had no difficulty in seeing the gravity of the political (and military) crises that it faced, but its fiscal and economic resources were under severe strain. Under the circumstances, Muscovy lacked the immediate capacity to improve its military situation or further integrate its military. Temporary expedients, such as awarding the musketeers trading privileges or trying to halt peasant movement, had only short-term benefit and some did long-term harm. Until the overwhelming issue of succession to the now-nearly-defunct Muscovite royal line was resolved, however, Muscovy would also lack the political will to initiate any transformative changes.

Notes

1 *Russian History*, vol. 46 no. 2 (1987) is largely devoted to such a debate, for example. More recently, see the useful comments in Isabel de Madariaga, *Ivan IV. First Tsar of Russia* (New Haven, 2005), x–xv.

2 See A. Baiov, *Kurs istorii Russkogo voennogo isskustva*, vol. 1 *Ot nachala Rusi do Petra* (St Petersburg, 1909), 69–70, on the changing kinds of servicemen under Ivan IV.

3 Richard Hellie, *Enserfment and Military Change in Muscovy* (Chicago, 1972), 267. Hellie, 161, and John H. L. Keep, *Soldiers of the Tsar. Army and Society in Russia, 1462–1874* (Oxford, 1985), 60, argue that military needs motivated the introduction of the *strel'tsy*. M. R. Brix, *Geschichte der alten russischen Heeres-Einrichtungen* (Berlin, 1867), 93, over-emphasizes their role as a political counterweight to the *pomeshchiki*.

4 Hellie, *Enserfment*, 267; Thomas Esper, 'A 16th-Century anti-Russian Arms Embargo', *Jahrbücher für Geschichte Osteuropas*, 15 (1967), 182–3.

5 Hellie, *Enserfment*, 156–7; A. V. Chernov, *Vooruzhennye sily Russkogo gosudarstva v XV–XVII vv. s obrazovaniia tsentralizovannogo gosudarstva do reform pri Petre I* (Moscow, 1954), 100; Evgenii Andreevich Razin, *Istoriia voennogo iskusstva*, vol. 2 (Moscow, 1955), 400–1.

6 The baggage train that followed Moscow's army to Polotsk-Orsha in 1564 included only 5,000 vehicles for 17–18,000 men. This average of one cart per three or four men is surprisingly close to the Tatar standard of one cart for every five men. L. J. D. Collins, 'Military organization and tactics of the Crimean Tatars in the sixteenth and seventeenth centuries', in V. J. Perry and M. Yapp, eds, *War, Technology, and Society in the Middle East* (Oxford, 1975), 259.

7 V. V. Kargalov, 'Oborona iuzhnoi granitsy Russkogo gosudarstva v pervoi polovine XVIv.', *Istoriia SSSR* vol. 17, no. 6 (1973), 141; Jaroslaw Pelenski, *Russia and Kazan. Conquest and Imperial Ideology (1483–1560s)* (The Hague, 1974), 52.

8 *PSRL*, vol. 20 part 2, 473–5, 477; also cited in AN SSSR II *Istoriia Tatarii v materialakh i dokumentakh* (Moscow, 1937), 113–15.

9 Chapter 3, section 'Lineaments of empire', 78–85, offers a more detailed example.

10 Razin, *Istoriia*, vol. 2, 355; *Istoriia Tatariia*, 123. Forward garrisons still were not commonplace, but the Lvov chronicle explicitly states that this was the purpose of Sviazshk. *PSRL*, 20/2, 497; *Istoriia Tatariia*, 114.

11 D. I. Bagalei, *Ocherki po istorii kolonizatsii stepnoi okraine* (Moscow, 1887), 36; V. P. Zagorovskii, *Belgorodskaia cherta* (Voronezh, 1969), 23.

12 A. V. Chernov, 'Obrazovanie streletskogo voiska', *IZ*, vol. 38 (1951), 283–4, points to the probability that there were some musketeers at Kazan earlier (1646–7).

13 Geoffrey Parker, *The Military Revolution. Military Innovation and the Rise of the West, 1500–1800*, 2nd ed. (Cambridge, 1996), 18.

14 Dobrynichi; see Chapter 4.

15 Chernov, *Vooruzhennye*, 46–50, 82–5; Hellie, *Enserfment*, 162–3.

16 M. I. Markov, *Istoriia konnitsy*, 5 vols (Tver, 1886–96), vol. 3, 110, cited in Hellie, *Enserfment*, 161.

17 *PSRL*, vol. 20 no. 2, 519; *Istoriia Tatariia*, 120–1.

18 A. A. Zimin, 'I. S. Peresvetov i ego sochineniia', in A. A. Zimin and D. S. Likhachov, eds, *Socheneniia I. Peresvetova* (Moscow, 1956), 175.

19 Chernov, *Vooruzhennye*, 86–91; Baiov, *Kurs istorii*, 68, 70; Zagorovskii, *Belgorodskaia*, 29–30.

20 P. N. Miliukov, *Gosudarstvennoe khoziaistvo v pervoi chetverti XVIII stolietiia i reforma Petra Velikago* (St Petersburg, 1905), 42–67.

21 Chernov, *Vooruzhennye*, 84–5.

22 H. W. Dewey, 'The Decline of the Muscovite *namestnik*', *Oxford Slavonic Papers* 12 (1965), 37–8; 'Sudebnik 1550', in B. D. Grekov, ed., *Sudebniki XV–XVI vv.* (Moscow, Leningrad, 1952).

23 Marc Zlotnik, 'Muscovite Fiscal Policy', *Russian History*, vol. 6 (1965), 253.

24 *Akty Moskovskago gosudarstva*, vol. 2 no. 85; Razin, *Istoriia*, vol. 2, 306–7, 327–30, 338–41; Chernov, *Vooruzhennye*, 75–82.

25 K. V. Petrov, ed., *Kniga Polotskogo pokhoda, 1563* (St Petersburg, 2004), 39.

26 Richard Hellie, *Slavery in Russia, 1450–1725* (Chicago, 1982), 468.

27 R. G. Skrynnikov, *Ivan Groznyi* (Moscow, 1975), 60; Baiov, *Kurs istorii* 68; Brian L. Davies, 'The development of Russian military power', in Jeremy Black, ed., *European Warfare, 1453–1815* (London, 1999), 153. Regularization also solidified a socio-military ranking system, with men of three provincial grades theoretically eligible for promotion to the four grades of service from Moscow (above which were only Duma ranks). See the excellent summary in Keep, *Soldiers of the Tsar*, 29–34. This focus created the 'service city'.

28 P. O. Bobrovskii, *Perekhod Rosii k regul'iarnoi armii* (St Petersburg, 1885), 64, 66; Marshall Poe, 'Muscovite Personnel Records, 1475–1550: new light on the early evolution of Russian bureaucracy', *JfGO* n.f. 45 (1997), 372–5.

29 Von Staden says Ivan needed his *boiars* for warfare. H. Von Staden, *The Land and Government of Muscovy*, trans. T. Esper (Stanford, 1967), 63.

30 R. B. Miuller and N. E. Nosov (eds), *Zakonodatel'nye akty Russkogo gosudarstva vtoroi polovine XVI-pervoi polovine XVII veka kommentarii* (Leningrad, 1986), 10–11, summarizes the literature; A. A. Zimin, 'K istorii, voennykh reform 50kh godov XVI v.', *IZ*, vol. 55 (1956), 347–8; Chernov, *Vooruzhennye*, 53.

31 Accurate land cadastres also expedited tax collection. Bobrovskii, *Perekhod*, 69.

32 M. G. Khudiakov, *Ocherki po istorii Kazanskogo khanstva*, reprint (Moscow, 2004), 22–3; map, *Istoriia Tatarii*, 120. Estimates of army size vary wildly. Janet Martin, *Medieval Russia, 980–1584* (Cambridge, 1995), 352; Hellie, *Enserfment*, 270.

33 Michael Khodarkovsky, *Russia's Steppe Frontier* (Bloomington, 2002), 105; I. P. Ermolaev, *Srednee Povolozh'e vo vtoroi polovine XVI–XVII vv.* (Kazan, 1982), 26; Hellie, *Enserfment*, 162; S. L. Margolin, 'Vooruzhenie streletskogo voiska,' in N. L. Rubenshtein, ed., *Voenno-istoricheskii sbornik* (Moscow, 1948), 93.

34 Matt Romaniello, 'Absolutism and empire. Governance on Russia's early modern frontier', (Ph.D. dissertation, Ohio State University, 2003), 22–3; his handout on 'Muscovite frontiers' at AAASS roundtable, Boston, 6 Dec. 2004; Pelenski, *Russia and Kazan*, 268; Khudiakov, *Ocherki*, 130–8; *Istoriia Tatariia*, 157, 168–9; Ermolaev, *Srednee*, 26, 28, 36.

35 Khodarkovsky, *Russia's Steppe Frontier*, 112–13; Ermolaev, *Srednee*, 23.

36 Pelenski, *Russia and Kazan*, 265.

37 Nomadic peoples addressed Ivan as 'the white tsar'. He did not use the term himself, although 'Tsar of Kazan' and 'Tsar of Astrakhan' presumably implied it. Khodarkovsky, *Russia's Steppe Frontier*, 44, 114.

38 Valerie Kivelson, AAASS, Boston, 6 Dec. 2004.

39 J. L. I. Fennell, ed., *The Correspondence between Prince A. M. Kurbsky and Tsar Ivan IV of Russia, 1564–1579* (Cambridge, 1955), 114–15, 138–9. There has been a prolonged debate over the authenticity of this correspondence.

40 Johannes Renner, *Livonian History 1556–1561*, trans. Jerry S. Smith and William Urban with J. Ward Jones, Baltic Studies, vol. 1 (Lewiston, NY, 1997), 103, 114; V. D. Koroliuk, *Livonskaia voina* (Moscow, 1954), 27–8, 44. Muscovite expeditions against Crimea were also supported by the Cossacks of the Zaporozhian Sech, who continued attacks on the Ottoman Black Sea coast even after Muscovy desisted. Chantal Lemercier-Quelquejay, 'Un Condottiere Lithuanien du XVIe siècle: Le Prince Dimitirj Vishnevckij et l'origine de la Sech Zaporogue d'après les archives Ottomanes', *Cahiers du monde russe et soviétique* vol. 10 no. 2 (1969), 267–70.

41 Carter Vaughn Findley, *The Turks in World History* (Oxford, 2005), 115.

42 P. A. Sadikov, 'Pokhod Tatar i Turok na Astrakhan v 1569 g', *IZ*, vol. 22 (1947), 143.

43 The current canal is 100 kilometres (63 miles) long; the Soviet building effort took from 1948 to 1952.

44 Simon Mal'tsev, 'Russian envoy in Ottoman captivity', in Sadikov, 'Pokhod', 147.

45 Halil Inalçik, 'The origin of Ottoman-Russian rivalry and the Don-Volga canal', *Ankara Üniversitesi Yilligi* I (1946–7), 61–91; Sadikov, 'Pokhod', 152.

46 D. L. Smith, 'Muscovite Logistics', *SEER*, vol. 71 (1993), 42 n. 20. For an eighteenth-century Russian example see Bruce W. Menning, 'G. A. Potemkin and A. I. Chernyshev', in David Schimmelpenninck van der Oye and Bruce W. Menning, *Reforming the Tsar's Army. Military Innovation in Imperial Russia from Peter the Great to the Revolution* (Cambridge, 2004), 277.

47 Khodarkovsky, *Russia's Steppe Frontier*, 117; G. D. Burdei, 'Molodinskaia bitva', *Uchenye zapiski instituta slavianovedeniia*, vol. 26 (1963), 63; Halil Inalçik, 'Osmanli-Rus rekabatinin inensei ve Don Volga kanal tesebbüsü', *Ankara Üniversiteesi Yilligi* I (194–7), 61–82, 107–111 (English); Alexandre Benningsen, 'L'expedition turque contre Astrakhan', *Cahiers du monde russe et sovietique* (1967), 427–46.

48 *PSRL*, vol. 13 (M, 1965), 523, 528. *Istoriia Tatariia*, 127, mentions further rebellions in 1572 and 1582.

49 *Istoriia Tatariia*, 125, 128, 189–90.

50 Janet Martin, 'Tatars in the Muscovite Army during the Livonian War', in Eric Lohr and Marshall Poe, eds, *The Military and Society in Russia, 1450–1917* (Leiden, 2002), 365–88.

51 Martin, 'Tatars in the Muscovite Army', 366, 381; Janet Martin, 'Multiethnicity in Muscovy', *Journal of Early Modern History*, vol. 5 no. 1, 5; Knud Rasmussen, *Die Livlandische Krise, 1554–1561* (Copenhagen, 1973), 226.

52 Renner, *Livonian History*, 37–9, 113–15, 121, 175.

53 Robert Frost, *The Northern Wars. War, State and Society in Northeastern Europe, 1558–1721* (Harlow, 1993), 36.

54 Sergei N. Bogotyrev, 'Battle for the divine Sophia? Ivan IV's Campaign against Polotsk and Novgorod', in Eric Lohr and Marshall Poe, eds, *The Military and Society in Russia, 1450–1917* (Leiden, 2002), 326; D. M. Aleksandrov and D. N. Volodikhin, *Bor'ba za Polotsk mezhdu Litvoi i Rus'iu v XII–XVII vekakh* (Moscow, 1994), 88–90.

55 Martin, 'Tatars in the Muscovite Army', 374–5, 382–3; Sapunov, A., ed., 'Razriadnaia kniga Polotskogo pokhoda tsaria Ioanna Vasi'evicha 1563g', *Vitebskaia starina*, 34–7; *Kniga Polotskogo pokhoda, 1563*, 45–63; Renner, *Livonian History*, 40. This estimate of army size seems to follow contemporary military lists. R. G. Skrynnikov, *Rossiia posle oprichniny* (Leningrad, 1975), 45–6. But, cf. Bogatyrev, 'Battle for the divine Sophia?' 381; Aleksandrov and Volodikhin, *Bor'ba za Polotsk*, 111.

56 Martin, 'Tatars in the Muscovite Army', 374; *Kniga Polotskogo pokhoda, 1563*, esp. 58–63.

57 Chernov, 'Obrazovanie', 290 reports the presence of *pishchal'niki* also.

58 Chernov, *Vooruzhennye*, 50–1; Skrynnikov, *Rossiia*, 120; *Kniga Polotskogo pokhoda, 1563*, 64, says 11,000 captives were taken. In a similar incident, Ivan ordered the 'elimination' of a town: 'so that henceforth a town will not be here'. 'Razriady' Nikolai Novikov, ed., *Russkaia istoricheskaia biblioteka*, vol. 14 (1790), 279–90.

59 Chernov, *Vooruzhennye*, 51.

60 Chernov, *Vooruzhennye*, 62, and D. L. Smith, 'The Oprichnina Army of Ivan the Terrible', (typescript), both argue that the *oprichnina* forces were 'field worthy', if not successful.

61 Razin, *Istoriia*, vol. 2, 374; Koroliuk, *Livonskaia* 73ff.

62 Chantal Lermericer-Quelquejay, 'Les Expéditions de Devlet Giråy contre Moscou en 1571 et 1572', *CMRS*, vol. 13 (1972), 557–8. Giles Fletcher, 'Of the Russe Commonwealth', in L. Berry and R. Crummey, eds, *Rude and Barbarous Kingdom* (Madison, Wisc., 1968), 193, offers a contemporary description.

63 Razin, *Istoriia*, vol. 2, 334 n. 1.

64 E. N. Shchepkina, *Starinnye pomeshchiki* (St Petersburg, 1890), 6–7.

65 *AMG*, vol. 1, docs 1, 2, 1–5; I. D. Beliaev, 'O storozhevoi, stanichnoi i polevoi sluzhbe', *ChOIDR* 4 (1846); S. L. Margolin, 'Oborona russkogo gosudarstva ot Tatar', in N. L. Rubenshtein, ed., *Voenno-istoricheskii sbornik* (Moscow, 1948), 18–23, lists precise patrol routes.

66 V. I. Buganov, 'Dokumenty o srazhenii pri Molodiakh v 1572', *Istoricheskii arkhiv*, no. 4 (1959), 174–7; Lemercier-Q, 'Les Expéditions', 558–9. Muscovite troops were about 10 per cent musketeers; 25+ per cent contract servicemen – 3,800 Cossacks. Skrynnikov, *Ivan Groznyi*, 185–6.

67 Aleksandrov and Volodikhin, *Bor'ba za Polotsk*, 120; W. Nowodworskii, *Bor'ba za Livoniiu, 1570–1582* (St Petersburg, 1904), 158.

68 Koroliuk, *Livonskaia voina*, 101; K. Olejnik, *Stefan Batory, 1533–1586* (Warsaw, 1998), 142–3.

69 'Rozriady 1576', *RIB*, vol. 14 (1790), 308–13; Buganov, 'pri Molodiakh', 167–74, shows the organization detail of moving armies to the southern front.

70 R. G. Skrynnikov, 'Oprichnaia zemel'naia reforma', *IZ*, vol. 70 (1961), 226–30.

71 N. F. Demidova, ed., 'Stolbtsy del moskovskikh prikazov', in Hieronim Grala et al., eds, *Pamiatniki istorii vostochnoi Evropy*, vol. 3 (Moscow, Warsaw, 1998), 122–96. These documents reassign conquered land as *pomest'e*.

72 V. I. Buganov, 'Dokumenty o Livonskoi voine', *Arkheograficheskii ezhegodnik* (1960) docs 1, 2; B. N. Floria, 'Dokumenty pokhodnogo arkhiva kn. V. D. Khil'kova, 1580', in Hieronim Grala et al., eds, *Pamiatniki*, doc. 28; Skrynnikov, *Rossia posle oprichniny*, 45–6, 49.

73 Martin, 'Tatars in the Muscovite Army', 384–7.

74 Although the conclusion seems accurate, there is debate about exact sizes of Muscovite armies. See discussion in Martin, *Medieval Russia*, 367 n. 19 on Skrynnikov and others. P. P. Epifanov, 'Oruzhie i snariazheni', *Ocherki Russkoi kul'tury XVI veka* (Moscow, 1977), 298, points out the declining worth of Russian arms and armour.

75 S. M. Soloviev, *History of Russia*, vol. 13, *The Reign of Tsar Fedor*, trans. W. D. Santoni (Gulf Breeze, Florida, 2002), 47–8, 52.

76 Bagalei, *Ocherki po istorii*, 38, 49.

77 See, for example, Basil Dmytryshyn et al., *Russia's Conquest of Siberia* (Oregon Historical Society, 1985), vol. 1, 8, 9.

78 Khodarkovsky, *Russia's Steppe Frontier*, 123; Hellie, *Enserfment*, 175; Bagalei, *Ocherki po istorii*, 38, 42–50.

79 *Istoriia Tatarii*, 128; Khodarkovsky, *Russia's Steppe Frontier*, 123; Pelenski, *Russia and Kazan*, 274–5.

80 Colin Imber, *The Ottoman Empire, 1300–1650. The Structure of Power* (Palgrave, 2002), 65–71; N. A. Smirnov, *Rossiia i Turtsiia* (Moscow, 1946), vol. 1, 134, 149–50.

81 Hellie, *Enserfment*, 98, 177; Khodarkovsky, *Russia's Steppe Frontier*, 124; E. V. Anisimov, *Illiustrirovannaia istoriia Rossiia* (St Petersburg, 2003), 81.

82 Fletcher, 'Of the Russe Commonwealth', 179–80.

83 C. B. Stevens, 'Evaluating Peter's Army', in Eric Lohr and Marshall Poe, eds, *The Military and Society in Russia, 1450–1917* (Leiden, 2002), 153–4.

84 Buganov, 'pri Molodiakh', 169, 174.

MAP 5   *The Livonian War and the time of troubles, 1558–1619* (adapted from Frost, Robert I., *The Northern Wars* (Pearson Education, 2000))

The sixteenth century – successes and limitations

Muscovy during the late fifteenth and sixteenth centuries was in many respects a stunningly successful expansionist state. By conquest, as well as by diplomatic manoeuvre and clan politics, the Muscovite Grand Principality had absorbed a variety of nearby principalities, city-states and central Russian khanates by the mid-1550s. Some of its successes were due more to the changing balance of international politics than specifically to Muscovite actions. Nonetheless, as it added new territories, the Muscovite royal house also shifted from the contentious lateral succession system common to the Riurikide clans generally to an apparently more stable primogeniture under Moscow's own Daniilovichi. Muscovy's gradual merging of independent political entities into a dynastic union developed some administrative apparatus that helped integrate disparate territories into a more uniform state. Finally, and perhaps most surprisingly, military forces identified with separate political units were gradually united into a single army under the command of the Muscovite Grand Prince, surprisingly unaffected by feudal-style regional and personal loyalties.[1]

To the south and east, Muscovite expansion had reached a broad frontier zone (neither the concept of state sovereignty nor the notion of precise borderlines applied here). This was an area of political and military confrontation involving Muscovy, indigenous groupings across the Siberian north, khanates in Crimea and across central Asia, the formidable organized military might of the Ottoman Empire, and, furthest to the east, China. It was also a zone of cultural adaptation and confrontation. Sedentary peasant agriculturalists coexisted (unhappily) with feuding semi-nomadic, livestock-herding communities, where the forests met the steppe; it was where Islam met mutually hostile Roman Catholic and Eastern

Orthodox Christianity, and where centralizing military-fiscal bureaucracies negotiated with powerful but loosely organized tribute-based confederations. These cultural frontiers did not necessarily coincide with one another or with existing political entities; significant overlap was more common. The Orthodox principality of Moscow, for example, had Tatar-Mongol landholders and Tatar cavalry units in its armed forces; at its convenience, Muscovy also encouraged Cossack steppe encampments and freebooting cossack behaviour that it otherwise labelled nomadic 'banditry' and 'piracy'.

For more than three centuries the steppe zone had been the primary focus of Muscovy's military and political activities. The Muscovite army was a rapidly moving light cavalry force that could be mustered on short notice; elite culture and political symbolism were deeply connected to steppe life and warfare. In the 1520s and 1530s, as in the preceding century, the Russian army had the structure, social composition and support appropriate to a rapidly moving light cavalry;[2] in many fundamental ways, this would hold true for the next hundred years.

By the middle of the sixteenth century, however, Muscovite expansion westward met an equally expansionist Polish–Lithuanian Commonwealth and Kingdom of Sweden. Given the geopolitical positions and political ambitions of the latter two governments, each was influenced (albeit in its own particular way) by the very rapid military change taking place further west and south. Sixteenth-century military establishments in west-central Europe and the Ottoman Empire shared an emphasis on artillery and siege warfare, the building of fortresses, the creation of trained infantry regiments to fight around and in defence of the fortresses, and government structures that could pay and supply them; new tactics and drill for infantry followed. Implemented on any significant scale, these military changes required adaptation of central state structure, the availability of cash reserves, and significant social adjustment.

Muscovy was conscious of the need to remain competitive through military innovation, particularly as its dynastic and territorial rivalries with Sweden and the Commonwealth became more important. Russian siege and field artillery was quite highly developed; Russia fortresses that faced west were built increasingly to the latest specifications, and its small paid standing infantry (*streltsy*) was capable of delivering massed fire-power. These changes were not introduced to conform to a monolithic European military model. On the contrary, what historians have called 'the gunpowder revolution' took many forms, within and outside Europe. Muscovy developed and used such innovations alongside its mobile, light cavalry, an unusual combination that suited its geopolitical situation and its imperial ambitions. Military reforms and the careful manipulation of steppe politics were richly rewarded with its conquests of Khanates of Kazan and Astrakhan in the 1540s and 1550s.

Russian participation in the Livonian War (1558–83), however, almost spelled an end to this highly successful system. Although at first victorious in Livonia, the intensity and length of the conflict overextended the Muscovite military. As a result, a severe crisis of the Muscovite political system followed. Beginning in the 1560s, Moscow's light cavalry forces in Livonia evinced growing difficulty in supporting themselves from gentry estates or even through battlefield plunder. Moscow's efforts to compete in battle with the combined economic weight of Lithuania and Poland led it to impose increasing taxes. Money was needed to help sustain the cavalry, and to pay for artillery, the infantry and military construction. Serious depopulation of central and western European Russia resulted, as both peasants and their masters moved towards the steppe zone to escape the demands of war and political terror at the centre. Further disintegration of the agrarian economy meant a decline in taxes and other state moneys to sustain the war effort. On the field of battle, first exhaustion and then losses to both Swedish and Commonwealth forces followed. These economic problems and the failure of further territorial expansion called into question the ability of the state to provide service estates (*pomest'e*) for the next generation of the elite – a provision that was at the heart of the political relationship between the Muscovite ruler and the elite.

Reconstruction of these central political relationships, seriously damaged by the Livonian War and the events that followed, dominated Muscovite developments well into the seventeenth century. The new configurations emerged only after civil war and restoration; their final forms had a far-reaching impact on the character of military change on the Eurasian frontier.

Notes

1   Janet Martin, *Medieval Russia* (Cambridge, 1995), 300–1, offers a felicitous summary.

2   Sigmund von Herberstein, *Description of Moscow and Muscovy* (New York, 1969), 78, describes the Russian cavalry as 'in haste'.

1598–1697

CHAPTER 4

The political prelude to military reform

Overview

Muscovy's entry into the seventeenth century was far from auspicious. After 1598, when Muscovy's ancient Riurikide dynasty came to an end with the death of Tsar Fedor, the country descended into nearly two decades of civil war, violent strife and foreign occupation.[1] For 20 years, choosing a new monarch and establishing the legitimacy of a new dynasty (whether in battle, by 'election', through propaganda or the manipulation of popular culture) were the pre-eminent political issues. It was military survival, more than systematic change, that preoccupied successive governments in Moscow. First, Tsar Boris Godunov (r. 1598–1605) and his son Tsar Fedor, r. 1605, and then Tsar Dmitrii, r. 1605–6, and Tsar Vasilii Shuiskii, r. 1606–10, faced rejection of their leadership; from 1604 onwards potent military opposition concentrated in the southern part of the country. The collapse of the political centre after 1610 brought Swedish and Polish forces into Muscovy, initially at the invitation of Russian political elites. The foreign presence generated a patriotic response encouraged by the Russian Orthodox Church. Russian military forces based in the provinces eventually reconquered Moscow in 1612. This period, evocatively known as the Time of Troubles, came to a formal end in 1613 with the selection by general acclamation of Tsar Michael Romanov, a relative by marriage of Ivan IV. However, military action, especially against Sweden and Poland, did not end until agreements were signed at Stolbovo and Deulino in 1617 and 1619.

After the turbulent decades of the Troubles, there can have been little doubt in any observer's mind about the superior efficacy of disciplined, trained troops, carrying firearms and led by numerous officers. Both musketeers (*streltsy*) and mercenaries leading European-style troops frequently played decisive roles in battles, out of proportion to their numbers. The ease with which Muscovy's immediate neighbours, Sweden and the Polish–Lithuanian Commonwealth, intervened in strife-torn Muscovy towards the end of the Troubles confirmed this observation. Both countries commanded, among others, trained, tactically manoeuvrable troops led by numerous officers. When Michael's government determined to regain territory lost to these neighbours after 1618, trained, professionally led troops, with an emphasis on infantry, seemed the only way to reach that goal.

While Muscovy's military needs were apparently clear, their attainment was threatened by complex socio-political and fiscal barriers. Michael Romanov's court, especially in the early years of reconstruction, had little choice but to emphasize its links and similarities to the norms of the Riurikide dynasty of Ivan IV and his predecessors. Rhetorically, such claims bolstered the legitimacy of the new royal family and promoted the return of a politically safe and ordered style of life. In practical terms, a return to the service state with its *pomest'e*-based service 'nobility' garnered support from important elements of the former political elite. It also offered to restore, at minimal cost, some sort of military force to a war-torn and financially destitute country.

Renewed emphasis on elite service to the Crown highlighted complex and durable problems. Clearly, *pomest'e* servicemen would or could no longer fight effectively. As Tsar Michael initially strove to drive out foreign troops and quell persistent rebellion, he was frequently forced to rely on the superior fighting ability of Cossack troops, although he manifestly disliked them. By 1630, despite policy initiatives and a general economic recovery, at least 40 per cent of hereditary *pomest'e* servicemen[2] could still not sustain the most basic and old-fashioned campaign service. Worse still, for reasons of social prestige, they would not willingly enrol and train in troops that had the desirable new characteristics. Instead, the Restoration government had perforce to hope that these poorest servicemen could still do useful duty in frontier fortresses, where the disadvantages of their poverty and military style might be more easily overcome.

These circumstances supported and even fostered the ordinary hereditary servicemen's fears about the erosion of their social and military standing. For hereditary servicemen, the availability of land and the retention or retrieval of peasants to work it thus acquired particular importance under the Restoration; land and peasants reinforced their political importance and offered the hope of restored economic viability. Other fears were directed against 'upstart' Cossacks and the contract servicemen who had formed such an important and growing arm of Ivan IV's army. Whatever the distaste they inspired in the Crown and the Russian military elite, they had confirmed their military worth during the Troubles, and their lesser political and economic status made them less able to resist moulding into new military forms. Clearly, an important prelude to creating desirable, disciplined, trained troops lay in identifying a group of men that could be enrolled without creating a storm of political and social protest against the fledgling monarchy.

A second barrier was economic and administrative. Paying for large numbers of permanent, year-round professional troops was a serious burden on an under-productive agricultural economy and a hard-pressed network of towns and markets, even as the economy recovered. But Muscovy gradually developed an effective bureaucracy that could identify and extract available resources from both. Growing numbers of experienced chancelleries remained centralized in Moscow, obedient to the monarchy, and uninterested in supporting regional or political disloyalty. Innovations in regional administration permitted the extension of stronger central authority to the provinces, untrammelled and increasingly effective, as the country began to recover.

Michael's government chose to spend money rather than forcing the highly charged issue of the *pomest'e* servicemen. It accelerated recruiting highly paid mercenaries to command new-style regiments (filled with foreigners and Russians of mixed social origin) for a Muscovite war on the Commonwealth in 1631.[3] After enormous short-term outlay, an army of 34,500 men, nearly half new-style troops, besieged the fortress of Smolensk from 1632 to 1634. In the midst of the protracted siege, the government's sense of purpose was deflected by the death of Filaret, the Tsar's father and the chief proponent of the war, and by devastating Tatar attacks on the neglected southern frontiers. The army was withdrawn in defeat, and most of the foreigners sent home.

The Romanov government next focused its military attention on the southern frontier, building and manning extensive fortifications there. While this effort restored and greatly enhanced the country's defensive capabilities, it also developed into a tacit means of circumventing some of Moscow's most pressing politico-military questions. As a result, Muscovy renewed its claims to the Pontic steppe. Given its new administrative and military capabilities there, it was able to transform the south into the new jumping-off point for territorial expansion.

Meanwhile, threatened by failing support, the Romanovs and their *boiar* allies reluctantly imposed limitations on the peasantry. Landholder retrieval rights were extended in the 1620s and 1630s. Then, in 1649, a new Law Code tied peasants to the land in perpetuity as serfs. An indirect product of rebellion in the capital, serfdom constrained and shaped military (and many other) decisions for the next 200 years.

The Troubles begin

The Time of Troubles is sometimes dated from the accession to the Muscovite throne of Tsar Boris Godunov, r. 1598–1605. A member of a landholding family of middle rank, Boris first became a favourite at the court of Ivan IV, then brother-in-law to the heir, Fedor, and eventually his regent, since Fedor was incapable of ruling alone. Godunov's rise to the throne after Fedor's death was preceded by prolonged infighting among *boiar* clans at court and followed by a purge of Godunov's enemies. An experienced head of state and legitimately connected to the Ruirikide dynasty by marriage, Godunov ascended to the throne with the approval of a hastily convened Assembly of the Land to reinforce his legitimacy.[4]

As ruler, Godunov continued to pursue some of the military and diplomatic initiatives of Fedor's reign. Troops promoted further expansion into Siberia and embarked on a failed expedition to Dagestan. New wooden border fortresses – Tsarev Borisev (1599) and Tomsk (1604) – protected settlement beyond the established defensive lines. In the west, Smolensk was rebuilt with massive thick, high rectangular walls and the multi-storey defensive towers characteristic of the region.[5]

By contrast, the importance of contract servicemen, a growing element of Ivan IV's army, was downplayed by Boris's government. A great many of them were implicitly demoted to part-time fortress defenders, rather than salaried battlefield troops. In the years since the Livonian War, musketeers and artillerymen had come to rely on trade to supplement unpaid government salaries; Boris officially enrolled them as members of Muscovy's tax-paying urban communities, instead of preserving their military identities. Additional responsibilities and controls were imposed on Cossacks and other servicemen near the southern border fortresses. These policies created considerable hostility towards the government.[6]

Instead, European mercenaries, who were cogniscent of the latest techniques but had few local political loyalties, became Godunov's preferred troops. Initially, there were about 2,500 of these men in Muscovy, including the French memoirist, Captain Jacques Margeret. Within a few years, Godunov employed at least 4,000 foreigners, as many as Ivan albeit in different positions.[7]

At the same time, Godunov's government invested heavily in the principle of elite military service to the state. The political and military predominance of the *pomest'e* cavalry could hardly be challenged by a fledgling dynasty. Rather, Godunov tried to reinvigorate it by precisely the kinds of actions that *pomeshchiki* themselves demanded. All assumed that adequate peasant labour on their estates assured returning prosperity to these hereditary landholders and cavalrymen, and that prosperity in turn assured the return of their military prowess.

There was reason enough for concern, even a decade after the end of the Livonian War. Peasant farming, and the taxes peasants paid, were in precipitous decline. Around Novgorod, only 5–10 per cent of peasant homesteads were still actively farmed; vacant lands abounded. The situation was somewhat better around Moscow, where some 30–40 per cent of lands were still under cultivation.[8] Many peasants, who had not yet decamped for the frontier and a freer if more precarious life, sold themselves into slavery, became monks, or moved to larger estates, whose relative wealth provided some cushion against hard times. For small landholders, such depopulation was catastrophic.

Godunov's government responded by extending the Forbidden Years of the 1580s, when the traditional right of peasants to change locations and landlords during two weeks in the autumn was temporarily rescinded. By 1602, virtually all peasant movement was categorically forbidden.

Neither the political nor the military gamble worked. Peasant flight continued, so did peasant disturbances. *Pomest'e* cavalrymen remained ill-prepared and reluctant to appear for military service. This was not entirely Boris's fault. Muscovy plunged into economic catastrophe, as bad weather, the cumulative effects of the Little Ice Age, and resulting famine took hold. Government charity and the Tsar's personal famine relief were incapable of stemming the tide. Troops were used to control hungry and displaced marauders.

The failed gamble had dramatic effects. Popular hardship, dislocation and growing fiscal crisis helped create widespread dissatisfaction. Most uncharacteristically, the reaction extended far beyond the *boiars*, who dominated Russia's political decision making, to smaller landholders and to other, traditionally non-political parts of the population. Although it may have been broadly motivated by contemporary conditions, it was articulated as a religio-political questioning of Boris's legitimacy.[9]

A rival claimant to the throne focused the discontent. This was Dmitrii Ivanovich, Ivan IV's youngest son born of his seventh wife, Maria Nagaia. Dmitrii's story bears a strong resemblance to the English 'Princes in the Tower', supposedly murdered by Richard III. Dmitrii Ivanovich would not normally have been considered a legitimate heir to the Muscovite throne, because his mother's marriage was non-canonical. Nonetheless, as his half-brother Fedor had no heirs, the infant Dmitrii began attracting political plots as soon as his father died in 1584. With supporters and relatives, he was therefore exiled to protective custody in Uglich, where he died in 1591. An apparently neutral government-appointed commission of the time investigated Dmitrii's death and cleared both Tsar Fedor and his regent, Godunov, of any complicity in the death. The incident was then apparently forgotten.

In 1603, however, a young man claiming to be Tsarevich Dmitrii Ivanovich, miraculous survivor of an assassination attempt, announced himself from the relative safety of the Polish–Lithuanian Common-wealth.[10] The true origins of this Dmitrii are unknown, although it seems unlikely that he was anything other than a pretender, knowingly or not. Whatever his origins, Dmitrii's claim to be the 'true tsar' rapidly gained support, especially in the southern borderlands. In 1604 he crossed the border into Muscovy from the south-west to claim his throne, triggering a prolonged period of turmoil.

Cossacks at the margins

The southern borderlands of Muscovy played an important and complex part in military events of the Troubles beginning in 1604. Unlike the centre, this region had recently seen significant popular immigration, even opening new territories. Much of the influx was spontaneous, not initiated by the government. Former *pomest'e* landholders, their former peasants, former military slaves, even *streltsy*, gunners and other trained military men found their way south beginning in the 1580s. Many had been abandoned by a fiscally insolvent state; others certainly felt themselves ill-used.[11]

Some fugitives settled in the forested steppe, where the Muscovite state was not slow to make use of their presence. After a Tatar raid reached Moscow in 1591, Godunov repaired and extended Ivan's fortified line with six new fortress towns in the deep south to protect new residents.[12] The fortresses were garrisoned by contract servicemen, such as *streltsy*, transferred from the central provinces. Some migrants were willing to serve in return for a modicum of state support and protection, after the fashion of 'fortress Cossacks'. When it could, Moscow paid salaries, awarded landholdings, organized further construction, occasionally provided food and ammunition, and in extreme situations defended the colonists with its army. By sponsoring military colonization and supporting agricultural expansion, the authorities drew in and tried to incorporate volatile migrant and fugitive populations. In some cases, the effort was success-ful, but it also attracted a good deal of resentment. Nonetheless, no other effort to colonize the Pontic steppe by governments along its edges was as systematic or state-sponsored.[13] The presence of these fortresses aggres-sively advanced Muscovite claims southward.

Other migrants from central Russia did their best to move beyond the expanding reach of the Muscovite government. Raiders, herders and traders lived at the steppe's edge; these included a variety of non-Russians such as the Kalmyk, Chuvash, Cheremis and Nogai, as well as transna-tional Cossack encampments that accepted some of the migrants. The life of Cossack encampments is easily and frequently romanticized as free, democratic and 'knightly';[14] it was also precarious and unstable. The Don Cossacks in the Muscovite south-east, and the Zaporozhian Cossacks on the Dniepr rapids in southern Ukraine, were the largest and most politic-ally significant of the encampments. Both of these 'Cossack hosts' were at least a century old by the Time of Troubles. Other small groups scattered along the steppe edge from the Ottoman border to east of the Don also supported themselves by raiding. According to their stated intentions and beliefs, raids from these Cossack encampments on the western steppe were explicitly directed against infidel Tatar and Ottoman settlements; in prac-tice banditry and piracy were not always so discriminating.

The military significance of Cossacks on the steppe had grown during the sixteenth century. Their combat readiness and their relatively easy access to firearms (unusual elsewhere on the steppe) made large groups of Cossacks from the Hosts welcome allies or auxiliaries to the Muscovite army – or to the Polish–Lithuanian Commonwealth. Individuals and smaller groups of Cossacks who were willing to settle remained valued front-line defenders for the southern fortresses as 'fortress Cossacks'. Cossack allegiance was perhaps even more precarious than that of migrants further north. Loyalty from the Hosts and fortress Cossacks depended heavily on Muscovy's continued support and sponsorship in cash and goods.[15] Furthermore, Cossackdom broadly claimed considerable independ-ence, and encroachments by an organized state were often much resented. In particular, the Godunov government's pressure on Cossack populations generated considerable resentment.

Although the Cossacks were certainly a transnational phenomenon along the steppe borderlands, their ethos and reputation exerted considerable influence on the diverse Muscovite frontier population of which they were a part. In part, diversity on the Muscovite frontier concealed some quite surprising homogeneity. For example, many southerners' daily lives afforded them rough-and-ready military experience and survival skills, even if some were trained troops and others not. Many fit within a relatively narrow economic stratum; there were few prosperous landholders and most depended on their service to sustain them. Financial or political difficulties in Moscow threatened their lifestyles and such marginalization called into question their loyalties. As a result, many also shared a certain disregard for Muscovite social conventions and settled state-imposed order. Distinctions between hereditary and contract service were often observed in the breach, and flexible, fluid populations substituted for more stable, permanent communities of central Muscovy. Some, but not all, southerners espoused a rather simple Orthodox 'patriotism', which exalted Orthodox Muscovy as against heathen and infidel border peoples.

Many of these qualities, shared by Cossacks and Muscovite frontiersmen, epitomize the Cossack lifestyle; it made them suspect in the eyes of many of their compatriots. Southerners of varied social backgrounds were a key element in the military campaigns of the Time of Troubles. Their dependence upon and ambivalence towards the Muscovite state brought them northward towards Moscow, sometimes to fight against the Muscovite establishment. They were often broadly referred to as Cossacks; the term was not meant as a compliment, but clearly distinguished between the marginalized south and the Muscovite heartland.

Civil war

Muscovy endured nearly ceaseless fighting and civil war(s) from 1604, when the royal claimant Dmitrii Ivanovich appeared in south-west Muscovy with Cossack and Polish troops, until after 1613, when Michael Romanov was enthroned. Although royal authority in Moscow remained in the hands of Boris Godunov until his death in 1605, fighting between the claimant and government forces spread through the south-west and the south. Once Boris's son, Fedor (r. 1605), replaced him, however, the political and military advantage shifted rapidly to Dmitrii Ivanovich, who triumphantly entered Moscow in mid-1605 and ruled there as Tsar Dmitrii I until his assassination a year later. His successor, Tsar Vasilii Shuiskii, was one of the conspirators responsible for his predecessor's assassination. For the next five years (1606–10), Shuiskii reigned over much of northern and central Muscovy, but was unable to suppress or co-opt spreading rebellions led by Bolotnikov, a putative 'Tsarevich Peter', and various troops enthusiastically supporting the claims of another Dmitrii Ivanovich. In an effort to recover from his increasingly untenable situation, Shuiskii gave Sweden a piece of north-western Muscovy in return for the loan of Swedish troops. Not only did this action bring the Polish–Lithuanian Common-wealth into the war, but it rapidly resulted in Shuiskii's being forced to quit the throne. Shortly thereafter, Polish troops arrived in Moscow to install, by invitation, Wladyslaw of Poland as his successor. For rather obvious reasons, these years of the Troubles are often referred to as the period of foreign intervention.

The study of these successive conflicts has produced little consensus about their causes. A dominant interpretation of the period, drawing on Soviet historiography, focuses on its characteristics as a social revolution – a reaction against enserfment or, more plausibly by Cossacks and others the reaction against the increasing constraints of an expanding state. While reactions against the growth of the state and against new levels of exploitation no doubt set the stage, simplistic social explanations are difficult to sustain. The armies of nearly all participants included a range of different social and economic groups. Also important is the regional nature of the conflict; most of the civil war pitted the south and south-west of the country against the capital and the north. One study argues that a general concern over royal legitimacy interacted with broad concerns over changing state and military power during a period of serious economic collapse.[16]

From a military perspective, indeed, an important explanatory variable must be the inability of the Muscovite state to meet fundamental expectations on the part of its military personnel, particularly in the parts of the country where much of the population lacked other resources. The state's failures eroded loyalty and undermined already diminished military capacity. At important points during conflict, there was astonishingly little difference between the army of a major bureaucratic state and those of the dedicated but impecunious anti-government forces.

Not at the beginning, however. Tsar Boris (r. 1598–1605) was well informed about the claimant Dmitrii's activities in 1604, but he evidently did not take them seriously. The Crown made surprisingly few advance preparations. Late that year, when the claimant crossed the border into the south-west corner of Muscovy, some 4,000 troops accompanied him; they included some Polish mercenaries and Cossacks. Dmitrii's claim to be the true tsar, his eloquence and charisma in front of his troops was bolstered by local distaste for Boris's recent activities. An army of local military men quickly gathered around Dmitrii, and a number of nearby fortresses transferred their loyalties to him without a shot. Even with such unpredicted and enthusiastic support for Dmitrii, however, the few loyal government forces in the south-west enjoyed some advantages. At Novgorod-Seversk, for example, a few loyal, well-supplied and officered musketeers of the regular garrison held off Dmitrii's forces; the attackers had no field artillery.[17]

As Dmitrii's forces grew, Tsar Boris called government units to arms. The number of men responding was limited by other military responsibilities – an army in the Caucasus and men in other border garrisons. Further limitations were imposed by continuing poverty among the *pomest'e* cavalry and some hostility to Boris's frontier policies. Still, the resulting force of musketeers (*streltsy*), some 13,000 *pomest'e* cavalry, their military slaves, peasant conscripts and about 2,500 European mercenaries, was larger than Dmitrii's.[18] Limited logistical support was provided by the Military Chancellery. Government troops still had to forage. But, as they moved into hostile territory, they were fortunately not as dependent upon local goodwill and supplies as Dmitrii's army.

Contemporary accounts of the first encounters between the two armies, deep in the Muscovite south-west, emphasize above all the key role of the trained troops on each side. A first confrontation, in front of the besieged fortress of Novgorod-Seversk, was carried for Dmitrii by the determined assault of three trained and cohesive Polish cavalry units against Boris's Right Wing. Apparently stunned government forces offered little response, while Dmitrii's Cossack forces evinced what became legendary loyalty, skill, and determination on his behalf.[19] A second encounter at Dobrynichi shortly thereafter began with another attack led by Polish cavalry units on the government's Right Wing. At first, the well-coordinated Polish attack appeared to carry the field. Then, all the massed firepower of government forces was loosed on the main regiments of Dmitrii's army, who were advancing to claim the battlefield. Trained musketeer (*strelets*) regiments fired from behind a *guliai gorod* or mobile fortress. Long lines of other infantry also delivered a broad field of fire in a very west European style, perhaps at the urging of Captain Margeret of the mercenaries. Dmitrii's army fled precipitously. Significantly, Margeret's mercenary cavalry immediately gave chase, inspiring some *pomest'e* units to do the same. Government victory was secured, while the rest of the army paused to claim whatever booty it could from the field.[20] Dmitrii's army was devastated, losing not only its victorious enthusiasm and momentum, but most of its infantry and accrued artillery.

Boris's army, however, was unable to build upon its victory. The commitment of Cossacks and local garrison forces to Dmitrii gradually outweighed government troops, reinforced from the north but operating in hostile territory. Boris's death in April 1605, leaving the throne to his son, Fedor, generated nearly wholesale desertion of the Godunov cause. The value of trained troops with firearms, already demonstrated at Dobrynichi, was further underscored as a few thousand loyal government *streltsy* successfully delayed the approach of Dmitrii's exhausted and impoverished 30,000-man army to Moscow.[21] Nonetheless, the new tsar entered Moscow in triumph in June 1605.

Tsar Dmitrii (r. 1605–6) pursued policies whose military and political inspiration differed little from Boris Godunov's. He reinforced and elaborated restrictions on peasant movement and issued new land grants, presumably in a continuing effort to relieve desperate poverty among hereditary military servicemen and retain their support.[22] Aware of military developments elsewhere, Dmitrii invested in Muscovite artillery production and requested information about the latest military developments; the translation of a book of European military tactics may have begun in Moscow under his aegis. Finally, Dmitrii bolstered the capital's troops by hiring Captain Margeret and fellow mercenaries who had remained faithful to the Godunovs to the end.[23] Other plans, including a crusade against Islam (and more specifically against the Turko-Tatar fortresses near Azov), never came to fruition. Dmitrii's reign ended abruptly within a year of his crowning. As Moscow prepared for his wedding to a Polish Catholic princess, a group of conspirators involving both the Shuiskii and Golitsyn *boiar* clans organized the assassination of Tsar Dmitrii and the accession of Vasilii Shuiskii. Rumours that Tsar Dmitrii had once again escaped assassination by his political enemies began to circulate almost immediately among his supporters.[24]

Although Vasilii Shuiskii (r. 1606–10) was the scion of a major *boiar* family and had been a political player at court since before the reign of Boris Godunov, his appearance on the throne in no way marked a return to politics as usual. Economic and social dislocation intensified. The central issues confronting Muscovite society – the inability of the state to sustain the servicemen on whose military and political support it relied or to incorporate the marginalized men this created – remained. Shuiskii's understandable failure to solve them deepened the political crisis and plunged Muscovy into further years of internecine fighting. Almost immediately, anti-government forces assembled again, but rejection of Tsar Vasilii, which was particularly strong in the south, did not unify behind a single leader. Rebellious forces led by Ivan Bolotnikov claimed southern fortress towns in Dmitrii's name. Another pretender, Tsarevich Peter, soon led Cossack forces out of the south-east. These and other forces mustered in the name of Dmitrii Ivanovich. When a figure claiming to be Dmitrii himself finally put in a belated appearance, the Polish–Lithuanian borderlands immediately rallied to his support.[25]

In many respects, this more diffuse second wave of rebellion recalled the support for Dmitrii I. The southern borderlands remained an important source of anti-government support; after 1606, the very different region between Tula and the capital was also key to rebel successes. Despite its regional character, a fairly broad cross-section of Muscovite society found itself in the rebel camp: *pomest'e* cavalry, musketeers, Cossacks, townspeople, non-Slavs and others.[26] The visible participation of ex-military slaves in this and other anti-government forces led to a reduction in the use of combat slaves in the army after the Troubles.[27] Once again, those suffering diverse social and economic ills were united by an openly avowed, broad political and religious concern with legitimacy.

Although the government generally drew its forces from a more stable part of the country, its access to effective Russian troops gradually declined, despite the best efforts of talented military men such as the Tsar's nephew, Prince M. V. Skopin-Shuiskii.[28]

Given the widening devastation of warfare, the impoverishment of the central state and of Muscovy's fighting men, military similarities among the contending parties grew. Each side offered land grants, peasants and, when they could, cash payments to *pomest'e* cavalrymen. Cossacks received food supplies, payments and sometimes the right to collect food or contributions from a designated area. Reliance on such troops perforce increased as the Troubles continued. The services of foreign mercenaries were courted by both sides as an effective, if impermanent, answer to the situation; the conclusion of numerous European wars offered a rich selection of such troops available for hire. But paying them posed its own challenges.[29]

Renewed fighting from 1606 brought only stalemate. Vasilii Shuiskii's government bolstered its cavalry forces with artillery and used non-Slavic troops to frighten its opponents,[30] but its attack on rebel forces in the south broke up within the year. A rebel push northward then besieged but could not capture the capital city. Supply shortages threatened the besiegers as well as the besieged. In this inconclusive situation, Shuiskii still retained the loyalty of most of the north and much of the capital's elite. Meanwhile, a rebel counter-capital appeared at Tushino, just outside Moscow. Some *boiars* from the capital (including the Romanovs) defected to Tushino, where a shadow bureaucracy fell into place; the rebel forces there were largely led by Polish officers and their numbers bolstered by Polish mercenaries.[31]

A year later, the stalemate was broken, if not by military action. The rapacious activities of an army trying to support itself without the benefit of regular central taxation and organization alienated many from the rebel cause. At Tushino mercenaries went unpaid; rival claimants and resistance groups appeared. The encampment declined into late 1609, when the claimant, Dmitrii, abandoned it to political and military disarray.

Foreign armies

The Polish–Lithuanian Commonwealth, Sweden and even, to some extent, Crimea had by this time all been drawn into the political vacuum in neighbouring Muscovy. Once Dmitrii I's death removed his threat against Tatar–Ottoman forces at Azov, even the Crimean Tatars launched raid after raid at Muscovy's relatively undefended southern frontier.

In 1608, hoping to defeat the rebel forces at Tushino once and for all, Tsar Vasilii Shuiskii agreed to transfer Korela and its vicinity to Sweden, if Sweden provided him with 5,000 troops.[32] The 3,000 mercenaries actually raised by Sweden briefly supported Shuiskii's troops, but largely abandoned their erstwhile allies when it became clear that Tsar Vasilii was unable to pay them as agreed. By 1612 Swedish troops were in Novgorod and Ivangorod, and occupied a considerable swath of territory southward towards Pskov, as well as around Lake Ladoga.

Men of the Polish–Lithuanian Commonwealth, by contrast, were involved in the Troubles from their inception. Initially, Polish troops provided unofficial aid to the rebels. By 1609 the Polish army advanced into Muscovy to attack the recently renovated Muscovite fortress at Smolensk. At the same time, the leadership of Dmitrii II's rebel forces, abandoned by their putative leader, began negotiating with the Commonwealth to replace Shuiskii with Wladyslaw, son of the Commonwealth's King Sigismund. Polish troops also hoped to forestall Swedish forces, whose arrival in Korela threatened Livonian territories that the Commonwealth had gained during the Livonian War. Events initially favoured the Commonwealth. Shuiskii was deposed in 1610, and Commonwealth forces moved quickly across western Muscovy despite the presence of yet more Swedish mercenaries. At first, the Polish forces supported Prince Wladyslaw's claim to the Muscovite throne, but their efforts soon took on the appearance of direct conquest.[33] A Polish garrison, bolstered by German mercenaries, occupied Moscow in 1610–11.

However, the Polish presence in Moscow and elsewhere attracted strong resentment. The city of Novgorod, for example, surrendered to the Swedes, insisting that the Swedes, whose developing military techniques made them formidable opponents, support Muscovite efforts against the Commonwealth. While some *boiars* responded by negotiating with the Polish occupiers of Moscow, many Muscovites acquired a lasting distaste for foreigners, for foreign regiments such as those that went over to the Poles in 1610, and for Muscovites in power who dealt with them.[34] To political issues of the first importance – such as royal legitimacy and the fate of the service state – were added the desire to dispense with the foreign forces and restore order.

While resistance developed simultaneously in several places, Muscovy's provincial cities provided the organizational basis for reunification. The Muscovite practice of mustering the cavalry by province had created something very like a provincial militia with a corporate sense.[35] Ongoing trade in the north and east sustained a relatively prosperous and well-connected merchantry. Direction from Patriarch Hermogen in Moscow and local church and military notables allowed towns like Nizhni Novgorod and Iaroslavl to muster and support significant forces.[36]

The first efforts to unite against Poland (1610–11) foundered on such shoals as copycat pretenders and *boiar* rivalries; status competition, regional loyalties and jealousy among the commanders of anti-Polish forces also played a role. Further, the presence of so many Cossacks in central Muscovy aroused unease and hostility from some *pomest'e* cavalry, whose military and social roles the Cossacks appeared poised to appropriate.

A subsequent campaign led by Minin, a butcher from Nizhni Novgorod, and Prince Pozharskii, a member of a minor aristocratic house, proved more successful, in part because of carefully negotiated political alliances. Cossack leaders were incorporated into the Muscovite system with grants of lands and peasants; hereditary servicemen were generously offered further *pomest'e* and support. The townsmen and musketeers (*streltsy*) who formed infantry regiments were paid from merchants' cash reserves. As far as possible, the inevitable and indeed necessary *boiar* political negotiations were distanced from the army. As Muscovite troops closed in around Moscow, the Commonwealth attempted to relieve its garrison in the Kremlin. In October 1612, however, the garrison surrendered to the besieging Muscovite forces; King Sigismund's efforts to reinstate it that December were unsuccessful.[37] Military forces based in the provinces, organized in large part by a coalition of towns, had achieved reunification.

The surrender of the isolated Commonwealth garrison did little to correct the disarray and lack of preparedness among Muscovy's military forces. The professional troops who had so clearly demonstrated their efficiency during the Troubles had become a rarity in Muscovy. Although the victorious army was better supplied than its predecessors, the majority of Muscovite troops were part-time units, individually prepared to use steppe-style armaments and accoutrements. Experienced Cossack fighters fought alongside inexperienced urban militias and peasant draftees. Ominously, given their organizational importance, the *pomest'e* cavalry demonstrated little military advantage in weaponry or training over the townsmen and peasantry.[38] Despite individual skills and commitment, Muscovite military forces at the end of the Troubles were ill-prepared to confront those who fielded tactically disciplined or professional troops.

The Restoration

The immediate business of Moscow was the restoration of a monarch. In 1613, on a wave of general support (and his family's propaganda), young Michael Romanov became tsar. As it turned out, his legitimacy was readily accepted both by an Assembly of the Land and the great *boiar* clans.

The choice of a dynasty was only a prelude to the complexities of restoration. One early objective was principally military in nature. Swedish and Commonwealth troops still occupied significant portions of western Muscovy. A Cossack force, supported by provincial cavalry, moved westward to confront Swedish contingents exhausted by prolonged fighting. The Peace of Stolbovo (1617) returned Novgorod and other inland cities, while Sweden retained the eastern littoral of the Baltic as a buffer zone. By contrast, Muscovy had little success against the Commonwealth, beyond preventing a reoccupation of the capital in 1617. The Truce of Deulino, signed in 1619, awarded the Commonwealth a swath of territory from Smolensk to Chernigov. Its reconquest became a particular goal of Tsar Michael's father, Filaret, who returned from Poland to Moscow as a result of the treaty; he became the Russian Orthodox Patriarch and the principal force behind the throne.

The long-term intentions of the new monarchy as it attempted to restore social order, military discipline and solvency to a war-torn country appear mixed. In some ways its efforts proclaimed a sixteenth-century conservative restoration – implicitly a politically charged recreation of the socio-military structures of the sixteenth-century service state. The great *boiar* families willingly offered their support to the new dynasty in 1613, particularly since Michael's powerful father, Filaret, remained in Polish captivity.[39] They were richly rewarded for their continued loyalty and participation with lands, peasants, and positions at court and in the army. Their return to accustomed (if not even more privileged) positions at the apex of Muscovite political power was only briefly tempered by the knowledge that many had cooperated with foreign occupiers.

There were some early indications that provincial *pomest'e* landholders and cavalrymen would also return to their traditional places within the elite. The early Romanov government followed in the political footsteps of the Minin-Pozharskii army of 1612–13, offering some *pomeshchiki* unusually large land claims and cash supports for their participation. Men of the Smolensk region, whose lands had been lost to the Common-wealth, received land claims in a south-western province instead.[40] New surveys and land cadastres recorded and regulated the state of *pomest'e* landholding. Subsequent legislation protected the social status of these hereditary servicemen, by limiting such landholding to already established families. After an initial brief rise in taxes, *pomest'e* lands were relieved of some taxes, and the cost of restoration was shifted to townspeople. The Forbidden Years were extended, and the peasantry's relationship with landholders worsened. Gradually, a slow agricultural recovery began. By the 1620s peasants were even moving into Muscovy from the west. The economic condition of some small landholder cavalrymen improved.[41] Once again, however, the provincial *pomest'e* cavalrymen-landholders generally failed to recover their economic and military viability. There were continuing concerns over their ability and willingness to serve.[42] Significant numbers of them were assigned to less demanding fortress defence.

Meanwhile, the resurgent bureaucracy that supported the political and military reconstruction was not at all 'traditional'. The pre-war system of mustering servicemen by town, which had functioned so well at the end of the Troubles, was strengthened. Impressed by the recent effectiveness of military town governors (*voevody*), Moscow installed them in greater numbers and more systematically than before. Government thus became more immediately local and more focused on the military.[43] The central government also expanded rapidly, nearly doubling the number of chancelleries during the two decades following the Troubles. A new census of the population preceded a revision of *pomest'e* and hereditary land grants records; these became the basis for tax collection, military service records, and the issuing of cash grants and bonuses to poorer servicemen. As the instruments of systematic local oversight, the town governors became a lynchpin of the restored military record keeping, representing the *Razriad*, or Military Chancellery, the *Pomestnyi* or Landholding Chancellery, and numerous others. Gradually, over the following decades, the more detailed reporting[44] of provincial affairs to the centre that followed also limited the capital's need to convene the Assembly of the Land.

Contract servicemen, on the other hand, did not as a group profit from their prominence during the Troubles and reunification. Rather, they were often 'restored' to positions and locations of less significance. For example, new *streltsy* (still Moscow's only trained troops) were enrolled, but many were stationed in provincial fortresses, where financial shortfalls limited the number who received cash salaries. The number stationed in Moscow declined.[45] Similarly, the Restoration government firmly rejected any permanent acknowledgment of the Cossacks, despite their unquestionable military importance in 1610–13. Thus, Cossack troops were prominent in the fighting against the Swedish and Commonwealth presence until 1617. Meanwhile, Cossack troops still in the Muscovite heartland were purged. Some fugitives were denied the right to continue as Cossacks, and some were forced (back) into the peasantry. Cossack commanders were disciplined, while a few were promoted into the regular military as service landholders.[46] While a small number of individual Cossacks succeeded in integrating into northern Muscovite society in varying guises, Cossack units there and their presumed rebelliousness continued to generate suspicion.[47]

Under pressure, Cossack relationships with the Muscovite state appeared by the 1620s to return to something very like their sixteenth-century state. Many returned to the frontier or to the Hosts, where they resumed their roles as garrison fighters or more independent men-at-arms. In other words, Cossacks seemed to rejoin the Muscovite service hierarchy as contract servicemen, and as the advance guard of colonization and expansion.

But once the Cossacks had largely returned to frontier and border territories, their continuing advantages as fighters led to a gradual change in their position. Once more a few received the right to claim small individual plots of land, which blurred, but did not necessarily raise, their formal status. Some Cossack officers received cash supports and the right to claim land in the south on a par with entry-level hereditary servicemen. By mid-century, their military importance was acknowledged with the creation of a separate Cossack Chancellery, and thousands of Cossacks were transferred to the regular field troops.[48] Such a combination of accommodation and restriction temporarily stabilized their relationship with the Muscovite state, offering Cossacks greater rewards but within greater constraints.

At the same time, the large Cossack encampments beyond the frontiers re-emerged as volatile and politically charged steppe entities. In the 1620s, while the Commonwealth was intensely involved elsewhere, the Zaporozhian Cossacks contemplated opportunistically attaching themselves to Moscow, bringing reconquered lands with them.[49] Similarly, Don Cossack forces and boats successfully captured the fortress of Azov from the distant but formidable Ottoman Empire in 1637. Unable to hold it themselves, they repeatedly proffered it to Muscovy, illustrating at once their political liabilities and their military prowess. Muscovy on this occasion refused the offer.

The results of the Romanov Restoration in the early seventeenth century were thus far from 'traditional'. The larger group of *boiar* clans around Tsar Michael and his father, Patriarch Filaret, did not just resume their accustomed positions; they gained ascendancy. Less exalted hereditary servicemen retained political significance. But even where their prosperity was restored, the political status of such men was threatened by their lack of military promise. Thus important questions about the future significance of service to the Crown remained unanswered. Meanwhile, many contract servicemen were increasingly concentrated in service on the frontiers and in the provinces; there, Cossacks and others like them, seemed among the most promising military forces, a fact which aroused considerable anxiety among *pomeshchiki*. The central government, with the greater access to local conditions promised by more intense regional administration, was increasingly able to manoeuvre outside its traditionally defined sphere.

The Smolensk War

Russia's effort to recapture the fortress and hinterland of Smolensk from the Commonwealth, known as the Smolensk War of 1632–4, was only one element in continuing instability along Muscovy's western border. Zaporozhian Cossack actions helped both to instigate and to defeat Ottoman–Crimean attacks on the Commonwealth in 1620 and 1621; Cossack–Commonwealth relations in the aftermath led to rebellion by 1630. Swedish troops returned to stake their claim to the eastern Baltic, where they fought against the Commonwealth. Swedish successes led to Sweden's direct intervention in the ongoing Thirty Years' War (1618–48), and Sweden's transformation into a major military power. Still hostile to the Commonwealth, Sweden also encouraged Muscovy's desire to recapture Smolensk. When King Sigismund of Poland died just as the Truce of Deulino was expiring, Muscovy moved rapidly toward war.

By 1630 the Muscovite army had not been called up to face an international conflict in nearly four decades. The records enumerated about 100,000 men available to fight on Muscovy's behalf, listed in traditional categories. Some 27,400 hereditary servicemen, once the heart of the army, were registered for military service. Despite the efforts of the preceding decades, only 15,850 of them were judged capable of serving in the field army. The other 11,550 were relegated to fortress service and local defence only; some 2,000 of these had no lands; some cavalrymen were so poor that they had no mounts. The same military registers revealed a slightly higher proportion of contract servicemen than was common even in the late sixteenth century.[50] These included more than 33,000 musketeers (*streltsy*), whose experiences of the past decade had prepared them more for fortress rather for battlefield service. While communal lands and tax-free trade had helped to sustain their troop numbers, those arrangements undermined their original status as trained, standing troops. There were also 11,500 Cossacks and more than 4,000 artillerymen, gunners and the like. Artillery contingents were well represented and well supplied. Beginning in the late 1620s, guns, gunpowder and shot had been stockpiled; armaments manufacture began in earnest in 1632 under foreign supervision.[51] Tatars and non-Russian irregulars made up the remaining numbers, about one-fifth of the available force.

The traditional categories, used by Muscovy to identify its military servitors, were symptomatic of some of the military problems faced by the Romanov government as it prepared for war against the Commonwealth. The balance and use of cavalry with infantry, the creation of tactically responsive officer structures, and regular if not full-time training had gained enormously in importance since the Livonian War in Sweden and, in a different fashion, in Poland.[52] Moscow's records (and its political thinking) emphasized the social origins of its troops and the methods by which they were recruited and sustained. The military qualities of a unit and any new military priorities were more difficult to ascertain from these listings: the musketeers (*streltsy*) were not all professional troops; some hereditary servicemen could no longer support battlefield or even cavalry duty, and so on.

Muscovy's leadership was well aware of the challenges implicit in fighting its western neighbours. At least in part, the point had been clearly made during the Troubles; furthermore, Moscow had since received military advice, equipment and technical assistance from Sweden – in return for grain subsidies after 1628.[53] Beginning in 1630, at Filaret's insistence, Muscovy therefore began to add a new kind of infantry regiment to its army – with an officer corps that was numerous, tactically responsive and by implication professional – as well as reinforcing its siege and artillery capabilities. Foreign officers were hired from among the mercenary forces fighting in central Europe. Large salaries ensured that Muscovy's recruiters would not return empty-handed. In 1630 Alexander Leslie, a Scot who man who had fought for both the Commonwealth and the Swedes, arrived to serve as a military adviser. Men like Leslie hired the officer corps of entire regiments overseas to train Muscovites in the latest infantry techniques, which they had acquired through personal experiences in both Sweden and the Netherlands.[54]

But the social implications of the older military categories remained important to Muscovite servicemen, and the new regiments did not always conform to their concerns. Thus when 2,000 landless hereditary servicemen were asked to become infantrymen (*soldaty* in the new, salaried infantry regiments), few answered the call, since service as foot soldiers and under foreign officers impugned their status. The new regiments were eventually filled. However, they were largely composed of contract servicemen such as Tatars and Cossacks, disgraced hereditary servicemen, and finally conscripted taxpayers (townsmen and peasants) – all of which only reinforced the social stigma of infantry service in the new regiments. In 1632 a new cavalry regiment (*reitary*) was created. Landless hereditary servicemen responded more willingly, so more cavalry and some dragoons were added. Higher rates of pay for *reitar* cavalrymen, though sensible, reinforced existing social convictions.

All told, ten of these regiments, called 'new formation regiments' (*polki novogo stroia*), were formed before and during the Smolensk War. More than 10,000 *soldaty* or infantrymen fought alongside a large cavalry troop (*reitary*) and one dragoon regiment, whose members were trained to fight both on horseback and on foot.[55] Each new regiment had a hierarchical command structure in the new style: colonel, lieutenant colonel, major, captain and so on – proportionately more than a Muscovite hundred (*sotnia*). Almost all the officers and some of the rank and file were foreigners, usually Europeans. The social discipline and military preparation of such troops was not altogether new to Muscovy, since the *streltsy* had somewhat similar training; but it was new to these men. In preparation for the launch of war and the siege of Smolensk, the bureaucracy began gathering food and military supplies, and fortifications specialists turned out in force.

In the end, the army led westward by General Shein to besiege
Smolensk in 1632 was the largest mustered by Muscovy since early in
the Livonian War, about one-third of Muscovy's available fighting men.
More than half the army was new-formation regiments, mostly infantry,
with foreign officers, paid and armed at government expense. Alongside
them, slightly more than one-third of the force was hereditary servicemen
– *pomest'e* cavalry still organized in its traditional hundreds (*sotni*).
Contract servicemen, including more Cossacks and non-Russians than
streltsy, made up the remaining 16 per cent.[56] Although the new regiments
were expected to be the strong arm of the military (as had earlier been
the case with the *streltsy* and artillery), the army retained its traditional
overall structure and command. The undertaking, in its entirety, was
enormously expensive for Muscovy. At the start of the war, it was paid
for from carefully accumulated government cash reserves and, as these
dwindled, from rapidly escalating taxation.[57]

The Smolensk War (1632–4) pitted this army against a very large,
modern fortress, recently refortified by the Muscovites themselves but now
quickly reinforced and defended by comparatively few Commonwealth
troops. Commander Shein, who was familiar with the fortress from his
command there in 1609–11, surrounded it with a complicated system of
earthen siege works and trenches. Observers were impressed by the quality
of the Muscovite infantry, the abundance of supplies and matériel available to the besieging forces,[58] and the ability of Shein's artillery to deliver
withering bombardments. By 1633 it seemed that the Commonwealth
garrison might soon be starved out. Newly elected King Wladyslaw, however, quickly organized a relief force, which surrounded the besieging
army. Unable to extricate his men, Shein surrendered to the Polish commander early in 1634.

A variety of reasons have been offered for Muscovy's ignominious and
perplexing defeat at Smolensk. The Muscovite army had abundant supplies
and a clear numerical advantage. The *streltsy* and new formation infantry
performed creditably. Eyewitnesses also testify to effective Muscovite
firepower and field fortifications. There seemed to be little doubt about
the performance of these parts of the army. Some historians attribute the
defeat, in the teeth of such advantages, to inept command, interference
from Moscow, or a distrust of foreign mercenary commanders. The spring
thaw (*raspustitsa*) perhaps stalled the arrival of Muscovite artillery at key
moments.[59] A significant problem also lay with the Muscovite cavalry
(rather than the new infantry). Wladyslaw's relief army included a significant contingent of hussars. These small semi-professional cavalry units,

whose structure made them mobile and tactically responsive without a hierarchical officer structure, pinned the besieging infantry in its trenches. Meanwhile, the Muscovite cavalry was not as well outfitted, cohesive, or responsive as the Polish hussars who had recently proven their mettle even against the Swedes.[60] Nearly all of Moscow's mounted units, even the new formations, consisted of *pomest'e* cavalrymen, some of whom were reluctant to serve and unable to provide for themselves well in the field. As an economizing gesture, the newer *reitar* units were not given the statutory number of officers.

Events far from the battlefield also undermined the military effort. When the Tsar's father died in 1633, his successor as head of Tsar Michael's government did not have his strong commitment to the reconquest of Smolensk. No relief force was dispatched to help Shein, surrounded in the siege trenches around Smolensk. With the death of Gustavus Adolphus of Sweden, Muscovy withdrew its grain subsidy and Swedish involvement in Muscovite affairs ceased in 1633. Meanwhile, the Commonwealth drew support from the Crimean Tatars, who raided the relatively unprotected Muscovite south, the field army having relinquished its usual role in southern defence. The Peace of Polianovka confirmed Polish conquests at Deulino, in return for which Wladyslaw withdrew his claim to the Muscovite throne; in addition to the expenses of the war, Muscovy paid an indemnity. General Shein and others were executed for suspected pro-Polish activities; the new formation regiments were disbanded and foreign officers dismissed according to the terms of the Treaty.[61]

Despite the brevity of their existence, these new formation regiments of the 1630s in many ways defined the shape of military reform for most of the century. The focus of change was and long remained the creation of a numerous, tactically manoeuvrable infantry. Men of mixed, largely non-elite social background and officers from central and eastern Europe made up these new units.[62] The musketeers or *streltsy*, regardless of their military contributions up to and including Smolensk, were not retrained but served in homogenous units of their own.[63] The political and social convictions of the hereditary servicemen remained largely unchallenged. Traditional cavalry hundreds were filled by the more prosperous, while poorer hereditary servicemen enrolled in new formation cavalry (*reitary*) units under the understanding that they would return to the hundreds once they were materially able. Training these *reitar* units was a low priority, so that in some ways they remained close to *pomest'e* cavalry. These military choices were partly impelled by complex socio-political realities (who was available, capable of, willing to serve, and under what

THE POLITICAL PRELUDE TO MILITARY REFORM   133

conditions) and by financial expediency. But in the 1630s there was also a persistent military demand for light, mobile cavalry, only part of which was met by Cossacks.

Muscovy's great wall

The defence of Moscow's southern borderlands against Crimean raids had long attracted the attention of its military men. In the 1570s Ivan IV's government organized a reasonably effective defence against such raiders. A frontier service patrolled the steppe edge; as necessary, they alerted garrisons along a fortified line of connected fortresses strategically placed across Tatar approaches. These fortresses sheltered local inhabitants and fought a holding action as the field cavalry moved southward from muster points on the Oka River to confront and halt the enemy.

This system was reinforced under Michael Romanov. The southward movement of population since the 1580s meant that there were already two tiers of fortress towns. The newest fortresses, furthest south, relied heavily on cavalry – to patrol, to report Tatar approaches, and to chase off smaller contingents. Towns along the defensive line further north relied more heavily on infantry to defend their fortresses,[64] since cavalry units from the main campaign army mustered annually along the nearby Oka River, to answer the call of the patrols and to repulse larger attacks. For this cavalry, seasonal availability and high mobility were entirely appropriate military qualities. Their important role in southern defence reinforced the existing mobile, light cavalry orientation and organization of the Muscovite army.

These arrangements continued to function quite effectively, despite uneven attention to artillery and fortification in the 1620s,[65] until the demands of the Smolensk War prompted the withdrawal of the Oka River troops. As a result, in 1632 and 1633, Crimean detachments passed the southern tier of towns and raided as far north as Sepukhov and Kolomna.[66]

In the aftermath of the Smolensk defeat, Tsar Michael's government determined to defend its southern settlements with another fortified line, much further south. This protected a new swath of rich agricultural land, promised to support *pomest'e* cavalry, and personally enrich the governmental elite. In the long run, however, the new border defences impelled Muscovy to intensify military pressures on its population, experiment further with new formation and peasant troops, and develop new regional military institutions. They also gradually undermined the *pomest'e* cavalry's last significant military role, and circumvented its military demands.

Between 1635 and 1653 military forces worked intensively to construct new border defences.[67] Once renovations were complete on the existing fortresses along the frontier, new towns and connecting wooden and earthen fortifications were built. The Crimean Tatars, directly attacking the builders and their new fortresses, endeavoured to reverse or arrest such massive expansion. By 1653, however, the fortifications (called the Belgorod abattis line or *Belgorodskaia cherta* after the city at its centre) were complete, stretching about 800 kilometres (500 miles) from Tambov, through Voronezh on the middle reaches of the Don River, southwestward through Old Oskol and Belgorod, before heading almost directly west to Akhtyrka.

Once complete, the Belgorod abattis line had a dramatic impact. Tatar raiders were rarely able to break through. When they did, the impact of their attacks was severely limited. The land north of the line, no longer vulnerable to devastating raids, was rapidly claimed by new settlers over the next decades. The well-garrisoned Belgorod line also served as a constraint, holding back peasant flight and military colonization into the open steppe. New defence lines, built eastward to Simbirsk in the 1640s and 1650s and southward to Izium in 1680, extended Muscovy's controlled colonization of the steppe. By contrast, the neighbouring Commonwealth, whose defence against the Tatars still relied principally on the army's response to raids, expanded southward far more tentatively, if more freely.

There was relatively little about the construction of the Belgorod defences that suggests major innovation. The fortifications themselves were of a well-established type: wooden palisade fortresses with watchtowers connected by stretches of dense (protected) forest; earthen moats and walls; and barriers of spiked, crossed logs helped prevent the passage of cavalry at particularly vulnerable spots. Dutch and French fortifications specialists did introduce some novel elements, thus continuing the earlier practice of introducing military change across the Empire. In addition, artillery assumed a growing role in the defence of larger fortresses, particularly by the 1670s.[68] But these were useful supplements, rather than vital components in the design.

The building of the defensive line was innovative, however, because of the new levels of resource mobilization that it represented, on the heels of an expensive and unsuccessful war. To build the new line while under Crimean attack required investments of cash, men and resources on a nearly unprecedented scale over an 18-year period; as an achievement, it was certainly on a par with the occupation of Kazan in the preceding century. The new Chancellery of Fortress Construction between 1638 and 1644 supervised many of the relevant functions. Construction alone cost in excess of 100,000 rubles and involved the labour of many thousands of men. To support this effort, the government required major infusions of cash. Taxation did not drop after the Smolensk War as one might have expected, but in many quarters actually rose. Still more importantly, men were mustered to build the new line and defend the builders in the sparsely populated south. The construction of the Belgorod line illustrated some of the ways in which the Restoration had created, not sixteenth-century Muscovy, but a powerful military-fiscal state.

Mustering the manpower required was perhaps the most dramatic example of the state's new abilities. Up to 1,100 hereditary and contract servicemen, with artisans, some peasants, food and military supplies for all, were gathered to build and defend *each* of the 25 segments of the defences each season – without undermining Muscovy's other military projects. The finished fortresses also required a near tripling of permanent garrison troops in a still sparsely populated region. Various devices were tried, including the enrolment of fugitives, provincial musketeers and Cossacks into the garrisons. As before, such garrison servicemen often included contract servicemen who received collective landholdings to support their military activities, which were largely nearby and seasonal.[69] But this alone was not enough.

In the late 1630s and 1640s, as the abattis line was under construction, the real threat of Crimean attack led to new experiments with military recruitment. These began with a revival of the new formation regiments for use on the southern frontier. As early as 1636–7, the government ordered veterans of the new formations southward to defend the construction effort as a particular Tatar onslaught was expected. Infantry in particular being in short supply, payment and weapons were also offered to freemen and hereditary servicemen who volunteered for duty. But for financial and other reasons, these so-called new formation troops were not standing or professional troops; one year's muster returned home after a season's service to be replaced by a new muster the next season.[70]

These calls-to-duty produced inadequate numbers. Seasonal conscription of the peasantry followed, patterned on conscription for military labour in the sixteenth century and on peasant military recruitment during the Troubles.[71] The first peasant conscripts were paid, fed and supplied while they trained and stood guard, before returning to their villages for the winter. Variants were quickly introduced to lower the cost and improve military effectiveness. In the mid-1640s prosperous peasants living near the frontier were conscripted for garrison service as a group; they made up one or more new formation dragoon regiments in return for tax exemptions.[72] Their own farms supplied food, mounts and even money for their weapons, as they trained and served during the military season in nearby garrison towns. In the winter their families and fellow villagers supported them. From among less prosperous peasants, the infantry took one adult man in four for similar self-sustaining service. Some peasants were even given lands in return for permanent if seasonal service.[73] Filling southern garrisons in this way proved both inexpensive and quite effective. The southern peasantry was relatively prosperous, and the resulting troops had an interest in defending their own fields and villages. In emergencies, such as the war over Ukraine in the 1650s, these troops were also drawn into the field army. In such cases, when such garrison servicemen served away from home, their military efforts required state support to avoid impoverishing them.[74]

This combination of peasant conscription and new formation service proved a first step in moving the Muscovite army away from its emphasis on seasonal elite service toward mass conscription into trainable regiments. That is, the new regiments had a numerous officer corps, brief training, and were not dependent upon elite service to the state. At this early stage, however, they also appeared to be a low-status variant on elite service and they had the effect of reinforcing the homogeneity of southern settlement. Economically, at least, there was little variance between the peasants drawn into southern regiments and local residents who were contract servicemen. As a result, however, local *pomest'e* cavalrymen found it difficult to retain peasant labour near the frontier. Many hereditary servicemen had only two or three peasant households, and not a few worked the land themselves.

The new troops, their recruitment and organizational character were quickly reproduced elsewhere. On the local level, they promised a less politically charged, viable military alternative to elite service. Variations on the southern arrangements appeared in the north-western frontier region[75] and formed the basis of broader conscription efforts in the 1650s.

The demands of the southern military project led to the creation of a new kind of regional military administration, which provided a framework for more rapid military change in the 1650s.[76] Larger numbers of resident southern troops required careful coordination. Southern military men were selected for service either in local units of the campaign forces or in southern garrisons. Garrisons had to coordinate their activities with the main forces of the *pomest'e* cavalry, which met annually along the

Oka defence line until 1646 and thereafter in Belgorod, to be called if a Tatar attack was spotted by patrols further south.[77] Gradually, however, the garrisons became competent to deal with most Tatar attacks themselves, effectively superceding the field cavalry. As this happened, coordination among garrisons became a more significant issue. Stocks of arms, artillery, matériel, and grain were needed in each frontier fortress, and provisioning was gradually undertaken through increased local collections and central chancellery activities.[78] But communication between garrisons, the availability of men and distribution of supplies still had to be coordinated. These requirements were particularly difficult to meet. The main forces of the Muscovite army had long been run largely through the powerful Military Chancellery or *Razriad*. Since there were only a few year-round standing troops, which were administered by separate chancelleries, the Military Chancellery initially lacked the institutional structures and coordination for large numbers of standing military units.[79] The problems involved in coordinating resident garrison troops along the frontier intensified as the total number of men involved grew; even a town like Userd had a garrison of more than 800 men by 1651.[80]

To meet these requirements, Moscow experimentally consolidated military administration on the regional level. A military-administrative district was created around the town of Belgorod in the 1640s under the umbrella of the Military Chancellery; the Belgorod District (*Belgorodskii razriad*) was an adaptation of an older system, by which the landed servicemen from a particular set of towns were usually mustered to defend a particular area.[81] Throughout most of Muscovy, military and civilian decision making took place in the capital. Typically, a military governor (*voevoda*) would report directly to Moscow, where his reports were coordinated with those of other governors, and corresponding orders returned to each. Beginning in the 1640s, however, the Belgorod District gradually unified year-round command over all the troops who lived and served in the growing number of towns (35 and up) along and behind the Belgorod defence line. About half the troops were field regiments raised from the region, whose commander bore overall responsibility for the Belgorod District. The remainder was garrison troops, whose units were immediately commanded by their town *voevoda* and ultimately by the Belgorod District commander.[82] Individual assignment and reassignment to garrison and to field forces were shifted to meet institutional needs and reflect military capacity. By the 1650s a new administrative arrangement, akin to a coordinated regional government, was developing under the leadership of the Military Chancellery. In combination with the unusual

social and economic homogeneity of its inhabitants, this regional administration allowed for unprecedented and localized experimentation with
military techniques and organization. As a consequence, the south soon
became a launching pad for new territorial expansion.

The political price

The events of the Restoration cumulatively thus undermined rather
than re-established the military superiority and social status of ordinary
hereditary servicemen. The many problems inherent in the exchange of
land and status for military service had only deepened with new military
demands after the Troubles. For many hereditary servicemen, the markers
of their elite standing simply continued to erode. Their political links
to the court changed as a bureaucratic state moved into the provinces
and as military promotions from the provinces to the capital declined.
New military values, continuing poverty and longer campaigns resulted
in less willingness and less ability to serve effectively. Although the ownership of *pomest'e* land was restricted to those whose fathers had held
hereditary status, this had done little to restore or shore up their position.
A continuing point of contention was the retrieval of peasant labour.
That is, the holders of smaller estates, to whom the loss of even one
peasant was significant, petitioned the government repeatedly in the early
seventeenth century to extend or remove any limitations on their right
to retrieve fugitive peasants. The response was contradictory. Limitations
were reluctantly extended from five years to nine and ten. At the same
time, because southern defences were under construction and Tatar attack
threatened in 1635, the government refused to return any refugees at all
from the south. In short, decisive action about the rights of landholders to
retrieve fugitive peasants was avoided during the first half of the seventeenth century.

Matters came to a head in 1648. Riots began in Moscow, when a
petition addressed to the Tsar from townspeople was turned away unread.
Historians studying the riots point to the tensions induced by bureaucratization and the loss of traditional political culture; the domination
of that bureaucracy by corrupt and self-serving *boiars* was a particular
focus of discontent. After Tsar Michael's adviser, I. B. Cherkasskii, died in
1642, Michael's final years were dominated by F. I. Sheremetev, whose
rule appears to have focused on gaining personal wealth and status. After
Michael's death in 1645, B. I. Morozov led the young Aleksei Mikhailovich's
government; although Morozov's administrative talents were many, he

too systematically used the government apparatus for personal enrichment. Under his leadership, a census was taken in 1646–7, which clearly documented the location of peasant (and urban) households, but his promises to facilitate the pursuit of runaway peasants came to naught. The new Tsar quickly found himself under pressure.

The rioters were initially disciplined by Moscow troops, but shortly disgruntled musketeers joined the townspeople. The mob plundered the establishments of leading members of government; several were killed, and a fire burnt much of the capital. Even the hereditary servicemen in the capital refused actively to support the young Tsar and his government. As a new government tried to bolster its support among hereditary servicemen with land grants and cash supplements, an Assembly of the Land was hastily convened by popular request.[83]

Over two years' time that meeting generated a new law code, called the *Ulozhenie*.[84] The *Ulozhenie* was above all the quintessential document of a growing bureaucracy. It attempted to codify the legal rulings of the Muscovite monarchy and a social order for its subjects. On a rather elementary level, such codification simplified the tasks of taxation and conscription – and these shortly became the administrative basis of new infantry regiments. It offered more extensive and careful definitions of the various duties and responsibilities of the Muscovite population to the central state than had been previously seen. *Inter alia*, it reinforced service norms and obligations for the landed. This codification had the effect of enacting more rigid divisions in Muscovite society.

As the *Ulozhenie* reinforced the outlines of a fiscal-military bureaucracy, caste lines hardened. For example, greater restrictions were imposed on the movement of townsmen. But the chief casualty was what remained of peasant freedom. The time limitation on the retrieval of fugitive peasants was entirely removed, and the government itself became more directly involved in the process of retrieval. The new conditions greatly increased the control exerted by small landholders over their peasant labour, and the conditions of peasant life, already 'nasty, brutish and short', took a further nosedive. These restrictions on the peasantry were not always in the best interests of the state. Controlled expansion into the steppe by fugitives, including peasants, and their enrolment in local garrisons had arguably achieved some important goals from Moscow's perspective; in practice, the government did not scruple to disregard the *Ulozhenie* on occasion. In this respect, the *Ulozhenie* looked like a major political victory for the hereditary servicemen.[85] It guaranteed them peasants to work the land – land that was already exclusively theirs.

It was nonetheless a pyrrhic victory. The Muscovite political system had long assumed a degree of consensus among its landed elite, a consensus mediated by the great *boiar* families and the principles of service to the Crown. There had been numerous indicators since the Troubles that this consensual model and its underlying principles were fraying. Lesser hereditary servicemen complained about the great magnates and about the administrative character of the new government, especially over the control of labour and the distribution of wealth. The collapse of consensus implicit in those complaints and in the 1648 riots were not healed by the *Ulozhenie*. Ordinary servicemen, who might be called the gentry in English, were increasingly frozen out of the court, as the likelihood of promotions from the provinces to Moscow, and from the Moscow ranks to the court itself continued to diminish as the century wore on. However, the guarantees of land and peasants apparently lulled even the poorest of *pomest'e* holders into a kind of quiescence. From 1650 the government could generally assume a tacit acceptance from *pomest'e* holders in the heartland. Nonetheless, it acted with great caution as it moved towards the new army that was its goal.

In other words, although the Law Code of 1649 reinforced gentry support of the Crown, it did not reconfigure elite service to the Crown. The military advantages of professional standing troops, who trained and served year round and were paid for doing so, were increasingly clear. The siege of Smolensk demonstrated that hiring mercenary troops to fill that role was extremely expensive, more expensive than Muscovy could comfortably afford. Given its size and its southern neighbours, furthermore, Muscovy required a numerous army. Although Muscovy was at a disadvantage given the relative absence of prosperous agriculture and developed commerce, many other governments were experiencing similar difficulties. The social rigidification and enserfment of the *Ulozhenie* at once set the political stage and limited Muscovy's practical options for organizing a native army, by pinning the taxpaying population in place for both recruitment and taxpaying purposes. How Muscovy's existing military classes could be persuaded to serve in an army defined by professionalism and military capability, not social rank and status, however, was a question urged only by the beginning of the Thirteen Years' War.

Notes

1 Detailed discussions of the Time of Troubles in English are to be found in Ruslan Skrynnikov, *The Time of Troubles. Russia in Crisis*, ed. and trans.

Hugh Graham (Gulf Breeze, Florida, 1988); Sergei Platonov, *The Time of Troubles*, ed. and trans. J. T. Alexander (Lawrence, Kansas, 1970); and more recently Maureen Perrie, *Pretenders and Popular Monarchism in Early Modern Russia* (Cambridge, 1995) and Chester Dunning, *Russia's First Civil War* (University Park, Penn., 2001). Important contemporary accounts in English include Captain Jacques Margeret, *The Russian Empire and the Grand Duchy of Moscow*, ed. and trans C. S. L. Dunning (Pittsburgh, 1983) and Conrad Bussow, *The Disturbed State of the Russian Realm*, ed. and trans. G. Edward Orchard (Montreal, 1994).

2 Hereditary servicemen at several 'ranks' constituted a kind of Russian gentry; they are referred to here by the landholding privilege which distinguished them collectively and which was a key military and political issue in the seventeenth century.

3 Richard Hellie, *Enserfment and Military Change in Muscovy* (Chicago, 1972), 170; E. D. Stashevskii, *Smolenskaia voina, 1632–1634* (Kiev, 1919), 12, 56.

4 See Ruslan Skrynnikov, *Boris Godunov*, ed. and trans. Hugh Graham (Gulf Breeze, Florida, 1982), ch. 9, for further details.

5 See Evgenii Andreevich Razin, *Istoriia voennogo iskusstva*, vol. 2 (Moscow, 1955), 159; V. V. Kostochkin, *Gosudarev master Fedor Kon'* (Moscow, 1964), 71–119.

6 D. I. Bagalei, *Materialy dila istorii kolonizatsii i byta stepnoi okrainy Moskovskogo gosudarstva* (Khar'kov, 1886), vol. 1 no. 2, 10; R. V. Skrynnikov, *Rossia v nachale XVII v.* (Moscow, 1988), 106–7, 111, 114–15; Dunning, *Russia's First Civil War*, 69, 88–9; N. G. Anpilogov, *Novye dokumenty o Rossii konsa XVI–nachala XVII v.* (Moscow, 1967), 381–3; I. N. Miklashevskii, *K istorii khoziaistvennago byta Moskovskago gosudarstva. Pt. I Zaselenie i sel'skoe khozaistvo iuzhnoi okrainy XVII veka* (Moscow, 1874), 62–3.

7 Hellie, *Enserfment*, 169; Stashevskii, *Smolenskaia*, 9; A. Baiov, *Kurs istorii Russkogo voennogo isskustva vyp. 1 Ot nachala Rusi do Petra*; (St Petersburg, 1909), vol. 1, 119, says 9,000 'by some accounts'.

8 D. F. Maslovskii, *Zapiski po istorii voennago iskustva v Rossii* (St Petersburg, 1891), vol. 1 no. 64, 192–3; Hellie, *Enserfment*, 94–7, 106, to which I am broadly indebted for its discussion as well as this specific material.

9 Maureen Perrie, *Pretenders*, 245–6. Daniel Rowland, 'Did Muscovite Literary Ideology Place Limits on the Power of the Tsar (1540s–1560s)?' *Russian History/Histoire Russe* vol. 49 no. 2 (1990), 125–55, on religious views on the tsardom.

10 Konrad Bussow, *The Disturbed State of the Russian Realm*, trans. G. E. Orchard (Kingston, Ontario, 1994), 8, offers a contemporary version of the tale.

11 Skrynnikov, *Boris*, 78; V. P. Zagorovskii, *Belgorodskaia cherta* (Voronezh, 1969), 7, 21–4.

12 Elets, Kromy, Belgorod, Oskol, Valuiki and Tsarev-Borisov all appeared between 1592 and 1600.

13 Zagorovskii, *Belgorodskaia,* 23–5 and more detailed discussion in D. I. Bagalei, 'K istorii zaselenie', *ZhMNP* vol. 245 (May 1886) and seq. A quite similar state-sponsored military colonization of the steppe took place under the Han dynasty in China, however. Peter Perdue, 'China, Inner Asia, and imperial expansion, 1500–1800', lecture at Colgate University, 27 Sept. 2002.

14 See, for example, the contemporary comment of Chevalier comparing the Zaporozhians to the Knights of Malta (with appropriate religious overtones) mentioned in Serhii Plokhy, *The Cossacks and Religion in the Early Modern Ukraine* (Oxford, 2001), 21.

15 Bagalei, 'K istorii', 94, 104–5; A. V. Chernov, *Vooruzhennye sily Russkogo gosudarstva v XV–XVII vv. s obrazovaniia tsentralizovannogo gosudarstva do reform pri Petre I* (Moscow, 1954), 88–9; Zagorovskii, *Belgorodskaia,* 54–64; Philip Longworth, *The Cossacks* (New York, 1970), 14ff. Cossacks also appeared in other provinces as part of local forces.

16 See summary in Dunning, *Russia's First Civil War*, 4–5.

17 Isaac Massa, *Short History of the Beginning and Origins of These Present Wars in Moscow*, trans. and intro. G. Edward Orchard (Toronto, 1982), 76–7; R. G. Skrynnikov, *Rossiia v nachale XVII v.* (Moscow, 1988), 143, 147–8.

18 Skrynnikov, *Rossia v nachale XVII v.*, 55–7; Dunning, *Russia's First Civil War*, 146, 150–6; in Margeret, *Russian Empire*, 141 n. 149, Dunning estimates the mercenary contingent at 2,500 and adds a key proviso – which is that they were usually particularly well supplied and provisioned.

19 Bussow, *Disturbed State*, 423.

20 Margeret, *Russian Empire*, 62–4; Chernov, *Vooruzhennye*, 84; Bussow, *Disturbed State*, 40.

21 Massa, *Short History*, 101–2; Chernov, *Vooruzhennye*, 108, notes the general loyalty and utility of the musketeers.

22 Hellie, *Enserfment*, 101.

23 Margeret, *Russian Empire*, xviii–xix, 69, 98–9, n. 36.

24 Margeret, *Russian Empire*, 75; see Dunning, *Russia's First Civil War*, chs 12 and 13, for a detailed narrative.

25 Chernov, *Vooruzhennye*, 112.

26 Perrie, *Pretenders*, 172.

27 Richard Hellie, *Slavery in Russia, 1450–1725* (Chicago, 1982), 471.

28 V. A. Zolotarev, ed., *Voennaia istoriia otechestva* (Moscow, 1995) vol. 1, 159. (hereafter *VIO*). G. N. Bibikov, 'Opyt voennoi reformy, 1609–10', *Istoriia SSSR* vol. 19 (1975), 3–16, further argues Skopin-Shuiskii's interest in Europeanizing military reform.

29 *Idem* comments on the better training and provisions available to government forces.

30 Chernov, *Vooruzhennye*, 111.

31 Jan Piotr Sapieha and Roman Ruzinski. Dunning, *Russia's First Civil War*, 395.

32 Vyborg (1609); Chernov, *Vooruzhennye*, 114. Some of the Swedish troops would defect to the Polish side at the Battle of Klushino later that year; Bussow, *Disturbed State*, 132.

33 Sonia Howe, ed., *The False Dmitrii. Described by British Eyewitnesses* (New York, n.d.), 129; see Hetman Stanislas Zolkievskii, *Expedition to Moscow. A Memoir* (London, 1959), 75–80, 87, 91 on the importance of *strelets* and mercenary units.

34 Dunning, *Russia's First Civil War*, 420; Platonov, *The Time of Troubles*, 124, 126.

35 A. A. Novosel'skii, 'Raspad zemlevladeniia sluzhilogo goroda v XVII g', *Russkoe gosudarstva v XVII veke* (Moscow, 1961), 231.

36 Brian L. Davies "The foundations of Muscovite military power', in Fredrick Kagan and Robin Higham, eds, *The Military History of Tsarist Russia* (New York, 2002), 29; Platonov, *The Time of Troubles*, 146–7.

37 *VIO* I, 167.

38 Hellie, *Enserfment*, 168.

39 Bussow, *Disturbed State*, 167; Perrie, *Pretenders*, 219–20; Robert O. Crummey, 'The fate of Boyar clans, 1589–1613', *FzGO*, vol. 38 (1986), 254–5.

40 The *pomeshchiki* in question proved unable to register their claims, however, and many of them were still leading a town-based, landless existence later in the seventeenth century. Hellie, *Enserfment*, 53.

41 V. M. Vorob'ev, 'Konnost', liudnost', oruzhnost; i sbruinnost' sluzhilykh gorodov pri pervykh Romanovykh', in Iu. G. Alekseev et al., eds, *Dom*

Romanovykh v istorii Rossii (St Petersburg, 1995), 93–108; *AMG*, vol. 1, doc. 259. My thanks to Brian L. Davies for bringing the first citation to my attention. Also E. D. Stashevskii, *Ocherki po istorii tsarstvovaniia Mikhaila Fedorovicha* (Kiev, 1913; The Hague reprint, 1969), vol. 1, 375.

42 Novosel'skii, 'Raspad'; Chernov, *Vooruzhennye*, 124; *AMG*, vol. 1, docs 90, 116, 124. There was also plenty of service avoidance. *Ibid*, docs 89, 114.

43 B. N. Chicherin, *Oblastnaia uchrezhdeniia Rossii* (Moscow, 1856), 338–9.

44 *Voevody* even reported on behaviour likely to cause urban fires. *AMG*, vol. 1, docs 219–20, 244.

45 Financial need remained a driving element in the restoration government throughout the 1920s. See Stashevskii, *Tsarstvovaniia*, vol. 1, 109; Chernov, *Vooruzhennye*, 126–7.

46 Stashevskii, *Tsarstvovaniia*, vol. 1, 111; Platonov, *Time of Troubles*, 168–69.

47 Stashevskii, *Tsarstvovaniia*, vol. 1, 124.

48 Keep cites *AMG*, vol. 1, doc. 285. Cossacks in Siberia were less constrained in both their military activity and their status, but this subject will not be discussed here.

49 Plokhy, *The Cossacks and Religion*, 277.

50 Chernov, *Vooruzhennye*, 125, 130; Stashevskii, *Smolenskaia voina*, 3–4.

51 Stashevskii, *Smolenskaia*, 4–5.

52 Robert Frost, *The Northern Wars. War, State and Society in Northeastern Europe, 1558–1721* (Harlow, 1993), 107–9, 128.

53 B. F. Porshnev, *Muscovy and Sweden in the Thirty Years' War, 1630–1635*, ed. Paul Dukes, trans. Brian Pearce (Cambridge, 1995), 58–9.

54 Stashevskii, *Smolenskaia*, 103, 109; Porshnev, 72, emphasizes not only the Dutch model after which the troops were trained, but also the Swedish innovations to it.

55 Stashevskii, *Smolenskaia*, 320; Brian L. Davies, 'The Development of Russian Military Power', in Jeremy Black, ed., *European Warfare, 1453–1815* (London, 1999)', 164; William M. Reger, 'In the Service of the Tsar: European mercenary officers and the reception of military reform in Russia, 1654–67', (Ph.D. dissertation, University of Illinois at Urbana Champaign, 1997), 24.

56 Hellie, *Enserfment*, 271.

57 P. O. Bobrovskii, *Perekhod Rossii k reguliarnoi armii* (St Petersburg, 1885), 90, also mentions a 40 reichsthaller loan.

58 *AMG*, vol. 1, docs 347, 362, 366.

59 Hellie, *Enserfment*, 172–3; William C. Fuller Jr., *Strategy and Power in Russia, 1600–1914* (New York, 1992), 21–34.

60 Stashevskii, *Smolenskaia*, 134, 171, 195; Bobrovskii, *Perekhod*, 120; Frost, 57–8, 146–7.

61 Reger, 'In the service', 24.

62 Stashevskii, *Smolenskaia*, 127–30; Givi Zhodraniia, *Ocherki iz istorii frankorusskikh otnosheniii kontsa XVI i pervoi poloviny XVII vv.* (Tbilisi, 1959) 409, 465, points out French mercenary participation.

63 S. L. Margolin, 'K voprosu ob organizatsii i sotsial'nom sostav streletskogo voiska v XVII v.', *Uchenye Zapiski MOPI* (1953), 83–9.

64 Stashevskii, *Smolenskaia*, 237, 241.

65 Zagorovskii, *Belgorodskaia*, 54–5; A. A. Novosel'skii, *Bor'ba Moskovskogo gosudarstva s Tatarami v pervoi polovine XVII veka* (Moscow, 1948), 435–6; Stashevskii, *Smolenskaia*, 245ff.

66 Zagorovskii, *Belgorodskaia*, 68.

67 Zagorovskii, *Belgorodskaia*, ch. 2, 3.

68 C. B. Stevens, *Soldiers on the Steppe* (DeKalb, Illinois, 1995), 172–3.

69 Zagorovskii, *Belgorodskaia*, 26–8, 240–3.

70 Chernov, *Vooruzhennye*, 137–8.

71 Bobrovskii, *Perekhod*, 94; Chernov, *Voruzhennye*, 136.

72 Aleksandr-Dol'nik and Vtorovoi, eds, *Drevnyia gramoty* kn. 3 (Voronezh, 1853) docs 111, 35.

73 G. M. Belotserkovskii, *Tula i Tul'skii uezd v XVI i XVII vv.* (Kiev, 1914), 23 n.; S. A. Belokurov, 'O pribore liudei iz raznykh gorodov v soldatskii stroi', *CHIODR* vol. 1 no. 4 (1902) 10–11.

74 E. V. Chistiakova, 'Volnenie sluzhiklykh liudei', in AN SSSR II, *Russkoe gosudarstvo v XVII veke* (Moscow, 1962), 257ff. describes the Elets town garrison's available land and labour, for example.

75 Chernov, *Vooruzhennye*, 143.

76 Peter B. Brown, 'Early Modern Russian Bureaucracy: the evolution of the chancellery system from Ivan III to Peter the Great, 1478–1718' (Ph.D. dissertation, University of Chicago, 1978), 473.

77 Hellie, *Enserfment*, 178–9.

78 Aleskandr-Dol'nik, doc. 108; S. K. Bogoiavlenskii, 'O pushkarskom prikaze', in D. I. Bagalei (ed.), *Sbornik statei chest' M. K. Liubovskogo* (1917; reprint Dusseldorf, 1970), 363, 380 shows a variety of personnel and coordination before 1650; Zagorovskii, *Belgorodskaia*, 245ff.

79 Zagovoskii, *Belgorodskaia*, 169.

80 Ibid., 103, 141; Stevens, *Soldiers*, 34.

81 Chernov, *Vooruzhennye*, 170; Peter Brown, 'The pre-1700 origins of Peter the Great's provincial administrative (*guberniia*) reform', (unpubl. 1992), 4.

82 Prince N. I. Odoevskii took command of Belgorod's field and garrison regiments for the first time in 1646, as Moscow prepared once more for Tatar attack. After 1653 the Belgorod commander also had a permanent military administration in the fortress-town of Belgorod (or sometimes Kursk). When representatives of other chancelleries came to the region, they too operated through the regional command centre. (Any local or chancellery representatives already present in the 1640s, however, continued as before.)

83 Valerie A. Kivelson, 'The Devil Stole his Mind. The Tsar and the 1648 Uprising', *American Historical Review* (1993), 735, 738, 740–1.

84 Richard Hellie, ed. and trans., *Sobornoe Ulozhenie: The Muscovite Law Code of 1649* (Irvine California, 1988), also *PSZ*, vol. 1.

85 See Hellie, *Ulozhenie* ch. 11, 16, 17, 19.

CHAPTER 5

The Thirteen Years' War, 1654–67

Overview

The occasion for testing Muscovy's new political arrangements and fledgling new formation troops was not long in appearing. In 1648 Cossack Hetman Bohdan Khmelnytsky raised the banner of rebellion against the Polish–Lithuanian Commonwealth. The cause had deep roots in the religious, social and military disputes of Ukrainians with Royal Poland, the dominant partner in the Commonwealth of which Ukraine was a part. Initially, Khmelnytsky's rebellion was successful against poorly led and politically divided Polish forces, but Cossack unity and Cossack victories were difficult to sustain. Khmelnytsky appealed for Muscovite help. After several years' hesitation, Muscovy signed the Pereiaslav Agreement with Khmelnytsky in 1654, putting Ukraine under its protection. That event set off a prolonged war over the fate of Ukraine between Moscow and the Commonwealth; this confrontation soon involved the other military powers of eastern Europe. Muscovite victories against the Commonwealth and its invasion of Lithuania at the beginning of the Thirteen Years' War helped prompt Sweden's entry into the fray. A second northern war (1655–60) renewed fighting by Muscovy, the Commonwealth and Sweden over possession of the south-eastern Baltic littoral. Later, as fighting in Ukraine began to wane in the 1660s, a resurgent Ottoman Empire allied itself with disgruntled elements of Cossackdom, sending Turkish troops to fight in Ukraine and Poland.

The Thirteen Years' War itself (1654–67), between Muscovy and the Commonwealth, ended with the Treaty of Andrusovo. A triumphant Muscovy gained an enormous swath of territory from Smolensk to Chernigov, part of Witebsk, Left Bank Ukraine, and temporary control over Kiev. A devastated Royal Poland retained only Right Bank Ukraine. The division of Ukraine into two pieces, and the complexities of Ukrainian politics, ensured that Andrusovo was not a lasting peace. Directly or indirectly, Muscovy continued to battle over a divided Ukraine with Ottoman, Polish and other supporters of Ukrainian hetmans for much of the rest of the seventeenth century. The renewal of Muscovy's imperial aspirations was thus played out against a background of constant warfare.

The Thirteen Years' War transformed Muscovy militarily. Building on its earlier experiments and using its new political capital, it developed mechanisms that allowed it quite rapidly to turn its back on some elements of its steppe warfare inheritance. The resulting army had numerous new formation regiments. Many of these were officered by European mercenaries – professionals who provided much of the expertise needed to absorb steppe and other troops into the new regiments; a few of the new officers were even Russian. The Muscovite army also boasted an important infantry presence (*soldaty*), whose ranks were quite reliably filled by national peasant conscription. As older cavalry hundreds (*sotni*) were cautiously downplayed, more armed hereditary servicemen were drawn into the new formation cavalry regiments (*reitary*). These troops were partially sustained by new institutional, financial and technical support. Although the army's central command retained its previous structure until the end of the war, by the late 1660s Muscovy was on the road to a complete recasting of its military forces.

At the same time as these changes took place, the size of Muscovite armies in the field climbed steeply. Muscovy had a growing number of military commitments: garrisoning fortresses on the steppe frontier, in Siberia, forward posts along the western frontier, and a multi-front war. Furthermore, fighting the Thirteen Years' War proved to have a high human cost. Nonetheless, Muscovite decision makers successfully mobilized to put more and more conscripted soldiers into the field at a time.

Muscovy's insistence upon these two characteristics for its army was costly. Muscovite troops during the Thirteen Years' War were almost all seasonal or semi-permanent. There were fiscal and political reasons for this. The cost of maintaining new-style regiments in particular was quite high, even if the regiments were not permanent – they required food, officers, supplies and pay while on the march. Sensible military and fiscal priorities led Muscovy to choose more regiments, rather than a smaller army of permanent units. Furthermore, semi-permanent forces probably generated fewer complaints and less broad economic impact than permanent ones. The absence of both gentry and peasants from their agricultural roles for a campaign season or two was quite different from their permanent departure.

The devices adopted to achieve this extraordinary military transformation, though eventually rewarded with substantial territorial gain, brought hardship and rebellion in their wake. Taxes rose and inflation skyrocketed. In the long run, continued and extreme pressures on the south, whose structure, location and organization made it particularly vulnerable to military demands, reawakened the Cossack question in a new guise. From 1668 to 1672, even as fighting continued over Ukraine, rebellion led by the Don Cossack, Sten'ka Razin, swept the south and the Volga.

Ukrainian prelude

Ukraine occupied an uneasy place in the Polish–Lithuanian Commonwealth. Some problems had mixed social and religious roots. The much-debated position of the Orthodox Church hierarchy in Ukraine, where Catholic Poland supported the Uniate Church, was an ambiguous and highly politicized cause of tension. The growing influence of the largest landholders from Poland at the expense of minor local nobility was also a significant source of contention.

Against this background, Ukrainian Cossacks were a principal cause of regional volatility and instability within Royal Poland. Registered Cossacks were military men-for-hire, whose presence on the Polish payroll had made them the socio-economic elite of Ukrainian Cossackdom. Most registered Cossacks lived in newly settled, even urban, areas along the Dniepr River, where they had with difficulty acquired a significant degree of political and juridical autonomy. Royal Poland's strict limits on the number of Cossacks on the 'Register', and its chronic inability (and disinclination) to pay their stipends were sources of discontent. Registered Cossacks shared fiscal-military concerns with the petty Ukrainian nobility, who also depended upon being hired to fight along the frontier or in Commonwealth armies for their livelihood and their social status. For such military men, serving the Polish Crown was neither reliable nor enriching. Ukraine also had a population of poorer, unregistered Cossacks. Unregistered Cossacks who lived on agricultural lands were increasingly pressured to become serfs on large estates. The most restive unregistered Cossacks, however, congregated south of the settled regions, at the Zaporozhian Sech, an encampment in the Dniepr rapids area where they were led by their own elected hetman. In 1648, this was Bohdan Khmelnytsky.

During wars against the Ottomans in the 1620s, some Ukrainian tensions briefly resolved themselves, as Poland enlisted more Cossacks and petty noblemen to defend Poland from external attack. The respite was brief. As peace returned, Poland dismissed its armies and reduced the Cossack Register to a bare minimum. Protest and rebellion among the unregistered Cossacks over their position became nearly endemic, while registered Cossacks and the local Orthodox population took unpredictable and often inconsistent parts in the discontent. A rebellion of unregistered Cossacks in 1637–8 was harshly suppressed. A Polish commissioner replaced the elected hetman, the Cossack Register was limited again, and the enserfment of unregistered Cossacks was mandated.

Briefly, it appeared that the expansionist aims of the Commonwealth's king, Wladyslaw IV (r. 1632–48), offered release from intensifying tensions in Ukraine. The Polish Diet, however, curbed his plans, fearful of their cost and their potential for conferring greater royal autonomy. Wladyslaw's secret attempts to raise a Cossack force to aid him fell through. By the mid-1640s, the situation in Ukraine had not improved; indeed, internal instability and external insecurity were on the rise.[1]

In 1648 rebellion against the Commonwealth developed under the leadership of the Cossack Hetman Bohdan Khmelnytsky. Khmelnytsky began by allying himself with Poland's long-time enemy, the Crimean Tatars. The Cossack cause, with its religio-nationalist overtones, quickly garnered support in Ukraine proper. Cossack victories against divided Polish leadership during the interregnum following Wladislaw's death followed in stunningly rapid succession. After 1648–9, however, it was difficult to maintain political or military unity among the Cossacks, and Khmelnytsky's second and third campaigns proved less successful. As Poland prepared to renew its efforts under newly elected King Jan Casimir (r. 1648–68), Khmelnytsky appealed for international support, first to the Ottomans, and then to the Muscovite Tsar, Aleksei Mikhailovich (r. 1645–76). Muscovy hesitated for several years: it was the era of the 1648 rebellions, the writing of the *Ulozhenie*, the beginning of liturgical reform, and final construction on the Belgorod defence line. The Muscovite leadership was under no illusions about the consequences of supporting Khmelnytsky. Both military and diplomatic preparations for war were underway even as an Assembly of the Land was called. When the Assembly consented, Khmelnytsky signed the Pereiaslav Agreement with Muscovy in 1654. The intentions of each party have been the subject of acrimonious dispute ever since.[2] Muscovy sent 4,000 men to aid Khmelnytsky in

Ukraine, but mustered its major forces to recapture Smolensk and surrounding Belarus. The Thirteen Years' War had begun.[3]

Preparation for war

As understood by Aleksei Mikhailovich's chief advisers (the *boiar* B. I.
Morozov, displaced by the Moscow mob in 1648, was replaced by I. D.
Miloslavskii), military preparedness in the mid-1650s entailed continuing
change. The hiring of foreign officers had resumed in the 1640s; so had
the production and purchase of firearms.[4] The revival of new formation
regiments, begun as an element of southern defence, had by the 1650s
spread to the field forces. A complex of chancellery and sub-chancellery
level organizations appeared to direct and to supply the new troops; there
was even a basic medical service. These military preparations did not disregard Muscovy's older forces. *Pomest'e* cavalry hundreds, Cossacks and
musketeers were still the vast majority of the armies moving westward
in the 1650s. But the dimensions of the changes were such that a major
redirection of Muscovy's military order could (and would) take place
during the war.

Change was only gradually introduced. Muscovy's dependence on its
pomest'e cavalry, Cossack and musketeer troops was undeniable at the
beginning of the Thirteen Years' War. As the fighting started, the total
number of musketeers in the army rose; they were particularly heavily
used in fortresses along the southern frontier and elsewhere. Cossacks
were also well represented; they too were inexpensive resident troops
along the frontiers. However, their low service status made them less
touchy about the social implications of their service. Some 20,000 were
moved towards the front in new formation cavalry units (*reitary*) during
the war, while others – especially recent migrants from Ukraine to the
Muscovite frontier, called *cherkassy* – served as separate Cossack troops.
Meanwhile, the number of *pomest'e* cavalrymen available to serve remained
large, although poverty and status concerns discouraged some from service
on distant campaigns, carrying firearms, or willingly submitting to retrain-
ing as *reitary* or new formation cavalry. Nonetheless, until after 1660,
such cavalrymen were a numerically important presence in the army.[5]

At the same time, Moscow had resumed its hiring of foreign officers in
the 1640s. As earlier, the principal role for these military immigrants was
the evaluation, organization, training and leadership of new formation
regiments (*polki novogo stroia*). Generous pay scales and the end of the

MAP 6   *The Thirteen Years' War, 1654–67* (adapted from Gilbert, Martin, *Atlas of Russian History* (Marboro Books, 1989))

Thirty Years' War in central Europe ensured that recruiters were successful. Since the Muscovite bureaucracy actually tested expertise before hiring, and positions were not subject to inheritance or purchase, the new formation officer corps was, by Muscovite standards, an unusually professional body of men, whose expertise was sustained by regular foreign correspondence and by the influx of new men.[6]

Foreign officers were introduced cautiously. Muscovites generally exhibited considerable hostility to non-Orthodox foreigners living and working in their midst, and Aleksei temporized on their status, isolating most of them at first in the Foreign Quarter in the outskirts of Moscow.[7] Similarly, the Tsar encouraged foreign officers to suggest military improvements, but asked that they relay such ideas directly to him instead of telling a possibly antagonistic superior.[8] By 1652, further, foreigners were denied landholding rights unless they converted to Orthodoxy, making them more dependent on government pay and food supports; and foreign officers frequently had to establish their authority without much support from Muscovite officialdom.

For all that, foreign officers in the Muscovite army made important contributions from the beginning of the Thirteen Years' War. Through training, personal behaviour and ongoing technical assistance, they illustrated a new style of organization and fighting to the troops. Originating from a variety of locations and cultures, from Scotland to the Ottoman Empire, these officers soon ranged far beyond the metropolitan centre, to the battlefront and to the provinces. Their presence was persistent and prolonged in the southern frontier garrisons, in particular. Furthermore, although foreigners continued to dominate the higher ranks in most new formation regiments for the duration of the war, some hereditary servicemen serving in the new formation regiments were gradually promoted into the lower ranks of new formation officers.

Officers' and other specialists' long-term residence in Moscow and the provinces launched a new cultural shift, as Muscovites (and elite Muscovites in particular) became familiar with and overtly adopted 'foreign' (especially European) ideas and customs. Immediately, however, officers in the new forces had little or no relationship with political authority or power at court, where the new style military expertise, per se, carried little weight. Service in the new formation officer corps, in point of fact, was considered socially degrading by the highest-born Muscovites and their families. Although individual officers personally liked by the Tsar did achieve the high status of advising him directly on military affairs, the direction and generalship of war rested primarily in the hands of the older-style army and its politico-military elite. The immediate impact of foreign advisers and serving officers was largely limited to military, even battlefield, matters.[9]

The manning of the new formation infantry forces (*soldaty*), although among the most complex of the subsequent innovations to execute, was politically among the easiest. The presence of settled dragoons and infantrymen, the state peasants resident on the southern and north-western frontiers described in the preceding chapter, represented the initial step. The enlistment of serfs and state peasants elsewhere in the country was the next step. A very limited conscription began based upon the 1646 census, which counted households rather than cultivated acreage. In a few areas, set conscription rates, such as one man per 10–20 households, were introduced. Over the next decades, similar household conscriptions developed into a relatively reliable basis for national recruitment, and proved key to the army's ability to grow rapidly in the 1660s. In the case of serfs the eventual return of surviving conscripts to their fields after a season or a campaign minimized the reaction of landholders. The new rigidities of Muscovite society generally eased the identification of recruits and the staffing of the army, although *pomeshchik* privilege limited its application.

But the infantry was never intended to be an exclusively peasant force. Attempts were made from the beginning to draw upon existing military expertise. In 1652–3, 8,000 non-taxpayers (that is, neither townspeople nor peasants) were recruited to serve in infantry regiments at Iablonov on the southern frontier; others followed at Smolensk. Young men coming of age in musketeer families were directed to the new infantry regiments. For men who had lost hereditary service status during the Troubles, enrolment in these new infantry regiments represented a partial reinstatement. However, when impoverished but registered hereditary servicemen were ordered to enrol as infantrymen or dragoons, they resisted such assignments as before; as before, such orders were rather feebly enforced. Once recruitment was underway, calculations of pay, supplies and encampment needs began the process of outfitting the new troops.[10]

Manning the new formation cavalry (*reitary*) regiments followed the staffing of infantry units. From March 1654 the order went out to enrol new regiments. Those called upon were the descendants of hereditary servicemen, who themselves had not yet been registered for the *pomest'e* cavalry. After enrolment, the new *reitary* nonetheless claimed land and cash supports like their brethren in the *pomest'e* cavalry hundreds. On the battlefield, however, men in these new units were different from the cavalry hundreds: they had some regular training with firearms (for a month in the autumn and just before a campaign), and their officer structure made them more tactically manoeuvrable.

These cavalrymen were not enthusiastic about their new assignments. Service in the *reitar* regiments was made palatable by the regiments' social homogeneity and by the promise that *reitar* cavalry could return to the hundreds once their personal circumstances permitted it.[11] But as the war dragged on, more cavalry was needed. As the army grew in size, cavalry was (and remained) an important element of east European military action. By 1660 some cavalry hundreds were transmogrified into *reitar* cavalry, on the simple principle that new formation troops were superior to the older variety. As the proportions of new formation troops in the army grew, however, Cossacks, peasants and others were also pressed into *reitar* cavalry service, despite the violation of social status that implied. Such men were removed from their regiments once the war was over.[12] A cautious military transition was underway, as the elite of the cavalry hundreds moved into less prestigious new formation cavalry units.

The production and purchase of firearms were also an important element in military preparations. The Kremlin Armory and the Tula armaments factory produced flintlock muskets to arm dragoons and infantry along both the western and the southern fronts. The new guns were both faster firing and lighter than older muskets. Thus Muscovy produced some weaponry of its own, but it also imported foreign musket locks to affix to guns produced in Muscovy. Other firearms were purchased abroad in large quantities; diplomatic representations to Sweden, Denmark, the Netherlands and others prepared the way for Muscovite attempts to purchase these goods. For the most part, guns were issued to the troops for training or on entry into battle; they were reclaimed at the end of the exercise. Fortress and field artillery were also produced in greater volume at the Cannon Yard (*Pushechnyi Dvor*) in Moscow.[13]

Within a brief period, new chancelleries appeared to administer to new military needs: the Dragoons, the Cavalry, and Artillery Manufacture Chancelleries. Muscovy was less successful in dealing with the long-term financial issue of how to pay for the new troops. In 1646 Morozov tried to replace the country's two principal direct taxes with an indirect surcharge on salt. Instead of filling the state's coffers, the salt tax generated outrage and declining revenues, and the salt monopoly was abolished the following year. Not long thereafter, alcohol sales were limited, and grain was sold abroad to pay for arms.[14] As for other early modern states, the revenues to pay for professional forces threatened to be an ominously intractable problem.

The purpose of both the growing size and the reorganization of Muscovy's military forces was clear as Muscovy's armies moved westward in 1654. New administrative abilities moved troops and supplies to several key points along the long frontier simultaneously. About 6,000 men moved towards Ukraine to support Khmelnytsky; about one-third of them garrisoned the fortress at Kiev. A significantly larger number of men, including nearly 7,000 new formation infantry in three separate but closely coordinated commands, stood on the Belgorod defensive line in anticipation of Crimean attack; the Crimeans were deeply opposed to any Muscovite presence in Ukraine. These were the lesser of Moscow's men under arms, in part because of Khmelnytsky's relatively strong position. Muscovy's principal interests in war against the Commonwealth were signalled by the main field army of 41,000 men moving towards Smolensk and led by the Tsar himself; the new formations in particular were well supplied from forward bases at Velikie Luki. The main army was flanked on the north by the Left Wing and south by the Right Wing, armies of about 15,000 men each. Another 20,000 Cossacks moved northward from Ukraine to support the main forces. These armies made significant use of the south's new organizational structure. The new formations were an important presence, but not yet a large proportion of the field army in the field.[15]

Success turns bitter

Muscovy's efforts on the Belarussian–Lithuanian front were at first stunningly successful.[16] Smolensk fell in November, and Muscovite troops advanced along the frontier. After many Muscovite units were dismissed for the season late in 1654, the Commonwealth focused its efforts unsuccessfully on the retaking of Mogilev in the north and on the region of Bratslav in the south. Muscovite units reunited under Tsar Aleksei's leadership in the spring headed almost directly west into Lithuania, while other troops occupied Polotsk and Witebsk. Twenty thousand Cossacks started north from Ukraine, capturing towns as they went. Moscow occupied Borisov, Minsk, Grodno and Kovno. By August 1655 Muscovy had taken the Lithuanian capital at Vilno. The triumphs came to an end only when Muscovite troops in the north attempted to conquer Swedish-held Riga late in 1656. The siege began late in the season with an army that was tired, far from its borders and its supplies. Riga itself was well defended and readily supplied from the sea. Moscow sustained the action only for a few months before it withdrew.[17] A truce with Poland came late in 1656; Tsar Aleksei put himself forward as a candidate for the Polish throne.[18]

In this era, the Muscovite army confronted a Commonwealth in disarray. The defenders were outnumbered, and military indecision among Commonwealth commanders was complicated by profound political disagreement. Towns fell easily to Muscovite forces, whose infantry and artillery forces showed to particular advantage in siege situations. The Tsar's personal intervention in command probably helped morale; it seemingly unified the many distinct corps involved.[19]

But the Lithuanian victories were also costly. Both the Ukrainians and the Muscovites devastated the territories where they fought. Despite the care taken to provision troops, there were acute shortages and foraging was rife; Cossack forces from Ukraine brought particular supply and coordination problems. Muscovites did not fail to take prisoners (for slave sales), pillage, attack Jewish populations, or execute those who resisted. Finally, putting large armies in the field for three successive campaign seasons, as always, considerably strained available men and matériel; mustering Moscow's still seasonal armies and monitoring their turnover required real fiscal and organizational effort. What is more, the implosion of the Commonwealth and the presence of Muscovite troops near the Baltic brought Sweden into the war.

Furthermore, conditions in Ukraine were rapidly worsening. Khmelnytsky's successful 1654 campaign was quickly overshadowed. By early 1655 the Crimeans turned against him decisively and allied themselves with Poland. Muscovy responded by sending members of its new formation corps from the Belgorod district into Ukraine. Nevertheless, Tatar attacks devastated parts of Ukraine before the Crimeans negotiated an armistice and withdrew in November 1655. Although allied troops then rushed to lay siege to Lviv, one of the few cities still loyal to Poland, they subsequently withdrew in return for payment. The Ukrainian effort was unravelling over internal disagreements, the Tsar's actions and the international situation.

Meanwhile, in mid-1655, Sweden entered the war. Its first goal was to win Ducal Prussia from the Danes. A thoroughly professional Swedish army, recently so successful in the Thirty Years' War, then moved southward, so rapidly and efficiently that some Polish mercenaries even joined the Swedish army in the hopes of better, or at least some, pay. Devastated Lithuania first accepted Swedish protection and then signed a treaty uniting itself with Sweden. The Commonwealth, it appeared, was on the verge of dissolution. Muscovy declared war against its formidable Swedish neighbour, but was content to launch only a lackadaisical campaign into Livonia in 1657 before signing a truce in 1658. After a bravura campaign with insufficient forces, however, King Charles of Sweden was forced to pull back, northward. Sweden had to be content with a victory over Denmark and the long negotiation with the Commonwealth of the Peace of Oliva, 1660.[20]

During this interlude, Moscow's attention was being drawn southward to Ukraine where, after Khmelnytsky's death in 1657, his successors were unable to control the volatile mix of domestic and international interests focused there. Concerned about Muscovy's evident interest in Lithuania and the Polish Crown instead of Ukraine, Ivan Vyhovsky, Khmeltnytsky's able secretary and successor, chose to negotiate with both Crimea and Poland. Two Muscovite forces with Cossack supporters, sent to defend the Pereiaslav Agreement, were decisively defeated at Konotop in 1659 by Vyhovsky and his Crimean allies. This defeat allowed the Crimeans to circumvent Muscovite defences on the western end and ravage the Muscovite south.[21]

Ukraine promptly erupted into a period of intense civil war. As Ukraine interests splintered and a variety of leaders emerged, successive hetmans tried to reunite Ukraine, by variously enlisting support from and promoting competition among Muscovy, Poland and Crimea. In 1659 the Cossacks themselves rejected Vyhovsky's leadership, electing Khmelnytsky's son, Iuri, to replace him. When Moscow sent troops to reinforce its sovereignty and its relationship with Khmelnytsky, however, Polish forces, released in 1660 from battling the Swedes in the north, appeared in Ukraine supported by their Crimean ally. Khmelnytsky, defeated in battle, transferred his allegiance to Poland. Nearly an entire Muscovite force was then lost at the battle of Chudnov in 1660.[22] By this time, Ukrainian support for the Muscovite alliance tended to focus on Left Bank (or eastern) Ukraine, while support for alliance with Royal Poland was likely to be on the Right Bank (western Ukraine). Khmelnytsky and his successor tried to recapture the Left Bank with Polish and occasional Crimean support. Muscovite forces helped the newly elected (1663) hetman of the Left Bank, Ivan Briukhovetsky, resist them. Throughout this period, Tatar attacks on the southern borders persisted. Although exhaustion and stalemate now bedevilled both Muscovite and Polish forces, not everyone was prepared to settle. Briukhovetsky, on the Left Bank, conceded more power to Moscow in 1665. Petro Doroshenko, newly elected (1666) Right Bank hetman, began by swearing allegiance to the Commonwealth; very soon, however, he moved to drive the Poles out of the area south-west of Kiev by negotiating powerful outside support; he took the field at the head of joint Cossack–Crimean forces, supported by Ottoman janissaries.

The threat of Ottoman involvement finally helped bring Muscovy and the Commonwealth to an agreement. When fighting between Moscow and the Commonwealth had resumed in the north in 1658, the tide quickly turned against Moscow. The Muscovites, who were relying heavily on local foraging to feed their troops,[23] found themselves harassed by partisan bands. The Polish heavy cavalry worked to great advantage against Muscovite forces, especially where the Muscovite infantry was unprotected by fortifications. At Polonka in 1660, for example, events deprived the Muscovite infantry of both fortifications and cavalry protection, and the undefended foot soldiers were slaughtered by the Polish cavalry troops. Muscovite retreat across the Lithuanian front followed, only to be arrested at Mogilev in 1662. At this point, both Moscow and Poland lacked the resources and willingness to continue. The devastated Commonwealth could no longer pay its mercenaries; Muscovite forces, paid in debased coinage, barely held the field. In 1664 a Commonwealth campaign in the north briefly drove the Muscovites back onto their own territory near Pskov, but further hostilities were forestalled by civil war in the Commonwealth (1665–6) and then the threat of Ottoman involvement in the south.

The Thirteen Years' War ended as Muscovy and the Commonwealth, each exhausted by its efforts, signed a 13-year truce at Andrusovo in 1667. The agreement awarded much of Belarus to Muscovy with Smolensk, Chernigov and part of Witebsk. Right Bank Ukraine, west of the Dniepr, remained within the Polish part of the Commonwealth. Muscovy took Left Bank Ukraine, east of the Dniepr, and Kiev, the latter for a brief period. This demarcation proved durable, and it had a lasting cultural and political impact. Muscovy and the Commonwealth also shared responsibility for Zaporozhe and its Cossacks and cooperated in keeping the Ottomans and Tatars from occupying Ukraine.

Several elements of this agreement were at best provisional and would provoke continuing military encounters. Polish negotiators granted Kiev to Moscow for two years, hoping that they could clear Ukraine of Cossack rebels (and Doroshenko in particular) and reclaim the city. Although discussions about Kiev were regularly revived, Muscovy never relinquished it, defending its hold with arms and in negotiations. More immediately important, the division of Ukraine took place without consideration of the existing situation there. Polish Ukraine was in fact dominated by Doroshenko and his allies. They were not inclined to accept Andrusovo. Doroshenko's popularity, if not his troops, extended to the Left Bank, where Hetman Briukhovetsky's less-than-independent stance toward Muscovite centralization was far from universally appreciated. Finally, under the circumstances, the signatories' ability to exert influence over the Cossack encampment at Zaporozhe seemed highly unlikely.

The foundations of a new army

Muscovy's involvement in the Thirteen Years' War brought very high casualties on and off the battlefield.[24] Civilian losses were significant. This war's impact on civilians, a subject that merits greater attention from historians, was catastrophic, particularly in the Commonwealth and Right Bank Ukraine. Khmelnytsky's earliest victories in Ukraine were followed by massacres of non-combatant Jews, Catholic priests and Polish nobles. During the Crimean attack on the Muscovite south in 1659, more than 4,000 farms were lost and more than 25,000 prisoners carried off. Battlefield encounters were every bit as hard on civilians; some 18,000 local residents died in the aftermath of the Muscovite capture of Mscislaw and Vilno. The Muscovites burnt both Kopysi and Dubrovna, rather than turn them over to the Poles. Despite these events, Muscovy made some effort to minimize even civilian losses in 1654–5.[25]

Battlefield casualties were also very high. Jan Pasek, a minor Polish nobleman serving with Czarniecki's forces, noted in his memoirs that the siege of Friedrichs-Odde in 1657 resulted in the loss of 20,000 Swedish and Danish lives.[26] Muscovite casualties seem particularly high towards the end of the Thirteen Years' War. Nearly 5,000 men died at Konotop in June 1659. The campaigns of 1660 had much more serious consequences. As many as 30,000 Muscovites are said to have died in the siege of Lachowicze. At Polonka, also in 1660, Pasek observed that Polish troops 'were slaughtering them [the Muscovite infantry] like sheep'.[27] In Ukraine that same year, fighting among the various participants involved more than 100,000 combatants; the Poles and Tatars took 20,000 Muscovite prisoners after the battle of Chudno alone, including the commander V. B. Sheremetev; most of the rest of his 36,000-man force had already been killed in battle. Some 19,000 more died near Polotsk in 1661 and another 10,000 at Buzhin in 1663. Whether or not these casualty figures are precise, they clearly reflect the fact that contemporaries saw unprecedented carnage. And indeed Muscovite forces appear to have suffered particularly severe losses, even without reckoning the numbers and the cost of ransomed prisoners, another element in the high cost of war.[28]

Over the course of the war, high battlefield casualties appear to have speeded the decline of *pomest'e* cavalry units. From the beginning of the war, many *pomest'e* cavalrymen had been reluctant to serve. Threatened with the loss of their honour and their status, and entreated with offers of cash supports, the total number of enrolled hereditary servicemen still declined during the war; fewer still reported for duty, although some sent substitutes. Muscovy did not have the administrative skills, resources, or organizational structure to enforce their obligations.[29] More importantly, Muscovy's leaders cared little about restoring these cavalry forces. Their military usefulness was in steep decline. Their seasonal presence at the front could require the Muscovite army to spend the first part of its spring campaign clearing areas conquered the preceding year but infiltrated after some of the troops had left for the winter. Even during a single season, plundering, foraging and desertion resulted when their personal supplies ran short. Their lack of battlefield discipline compared poorly with the Polish hussars, and they had failed to distinguish themselves even in fighting against the Ukrainian Cossack forces. The carnage of the war accelerated the decline of *pomest'e* cavalry in the army. Sheremetev's army of more than 40,000 in Ukraine just after Konotop in 1659 included merely 7,000 hereditary cavalrymen, or 17–18 per cent; after 1661, they simply ceased to appear in the field army as independent units.[30]

The relentless demand for more men did not permit *pomest'e* holders simply to withdraw, of course. The emphasis on reassigning hereditary servicemen in non-traditional ways increased, particularly after 1659–60. Some of the least prosperous were detailed to garrison service. Many more were enrolled in the new formation regiments, especially the cavalry (*reitary*), whose numbers grew from 2,000 to 18,000 by 1663. As a palliative to hereditary servicemen whose status was threatened by the presence of Cossacks and others, hereditary servicemen served in units segregated by social status. By further purging the ranks of the *reitary* after the war, Muscovy encouraged the misleading impression that the *reitary* would become as socially exclusive as the cavalry hundreds had once been.[31]

From the 1660s the new formation cavalry became an important component of the Muscovite forces. Cavalry generally remained an important element of Moscow's army, as it did of all east European forces into the eighteenth century. But Moscow was unused to investing in cavalry forces, and in the midst of war it invested only in a limited way in its new formation, elite-dominated *reitary*. Like the new formation infantry, these troops had a denser, more hierarchical command structure, with both foreign and Muscovite officers. While this made the new units tactically more responsive,[32] the rank and file had only limited training, and lacked morale and cohesiveness. In part, this can be attributed to the ingenious fiscal tactics Muscovy perpetuated, as it struggled to maintain large numbers of men in the field. That is, the state acknowledged its obligation to pay cavalrymen of the new formation between 6 and 15 rubles a year and two measures (*chetverti*) each of rye and oats to support themselves and their horses. In practice, however, those salaries were paid only when the men were on active service. Furthermore, when men of the hereditary elite presented themselves for service and were enrolled in new cavalry units (*reitary*), they still received *pomest'e* grants very much like those their fathers and uncles had received. 'Salaries' owing to such *reitary* were then docked or withheld according to the size of their lands, as the grant of service land still carried the obligation for a serviceman to arm, equip and supply himself at least partly at his own expense. Smaller changes suggested a new relationship: for example, the military occasionally sold weapons to poorly equipped *reitary*.[33] These arrangements, although they undermined the military qualities of the new troops, allowed Muscovy to continue putting numerous cavalry forces in the field. Nevertheless, these new troops appeared more reliably for service and served with greater success than their predecessors.

But it was the new formation infantry, not the new cavalry, that largely met Muscovy's manpower and military needs after 1659. Wartime losses and experience hastily accelerated the move to new formation infantry. Obviously, the Muscovite military had been aware for some time of the tactical importance of infantry. New formation servicemen had already been raised on the frontier by combining calls for volunteers with peasant conscriptions. In the 1640s southern peasants were inducted into new-style infantry and settled dragoon regiments, trained by foreign officers and commanded by a foreign colonel.[34] In 1658, however, such limited peasant conscription was replaced by a more broadly based effort: one man was drafted from every 25 taxable households throughout much of Muscovy. There were exemptions for the hard-pressed frontiers and slightly different recruitment norms for other regions. Although the exact rate of the conscriptions would change, the drafts themselves continued – and frequently, as Muscovy rapidly increased the number of its new formation troops. This was very close to mass national conscription, and it recurred in 1659, 1660, 1661 and 1663, with other partial drafts filling the shortfalls. Overall, it drew about 100,000 men into the military during the last years of the war. A great many would be killed, die of disease, desert, or be taken prisoner. Nevertheless, in 1663, the army had some 50,000 infantrymen in its *soldat* regiments; even after the war was over, about half that number remained on the rolls.

The use, growth and replicability of infantry on this scale allowed Muscovy to remain in the field for the final years of the war despite the appalling casualties. It was a politically expedient response; peasant recruits were levied into infantry regiments without political protest, and they quickly supplied badly needed front-line field forces. It was also militarily expedient. Trained infantry was assumed to be necessary by the upper levels of Muscovite government, and front-line officers routinely reported when Muscovite forces – or the Polish enemy – suffered for lack of soldiers. The introduction of conscripted peasant troops on a national scale, even if they were not all standing forces, marked a major and permanent transition in Muscovite military organization.[35]

New troops entering the field on such a scale created numerous difficulties. The long-suffering peasantry bore yet another heavy burden. Even as the men who laboured in the fields were sent to fight, their households continued to pay taxes and even, in some cases, support their landlords at the front. Consequent peasant flight and economic distress led to some limited reductions in the numbers recruited after 1660.

Mass recruitment made demands on the state and its infrastructure. Foot soldiers did receive some, even substantial, support from their government while they were in service away from home. They were paid in cash-and-grain, supplied with arms (rapiers, pikes, hand grenades, armour and muskets) and matériel at the front. Firearms were particularly closely guarded, being the charge of a special officer called the *capitaine d'armes* (*kapiten darmus*), who issued them to the soldiers just before battle was joined. Infantry training and leadership, dominated by expensive foreign officers, were designed for field manoeuvrability and efficient firearm use. Muscovite troops were also accompanied by regimental artillery and artillerymen.[36] But like the *reitar* regiments, far from all the new formation infantry units of the Thirteen Years' War were regular troops. Salaries went unpaid except on active duty. Seasonal dismissals had the salutary effect of returning serfs to their work in the fields. Landlord support for recruits journeying to the front, or even at the front, was demanded where possible.[37] Cash stipends proved too small to pay the high cost of food near the front; as with many contemporary armies, foraging for food was an important source of sustenance for Muscovite troops.[38] Some soldiers received land in lieu of payment. There were shortfalls in both the numbers and the quality of the new troops.

Payment and provisioning quickly became key issues in Moscow's ability to keep its new troops in the field. Muscovy had faced the high cost of maintaining new formation troops once before, during the Smolensk

War, and it had responded by dismissing them after two years. The annual cost of maintaining the army in the 1650s, even before these changes took place, has been calculated at more than 3 million rubles. Later in the war, the officer corps and two standing select infantry regiments alone cost an impressive quarter million rubles a year. Despite the devices adopted to reduce their cost, the rapidly growing new formation forces after 1658 were, to say the least, prohibitively expensive. By 1663 the active army alone cost four times what it had in 1630. Muscovy's state income in the 1660s can only be estimated, since the Muscovite state did not produce a unified state budget until the 1680s. It is nonetheless very clear that such demands were large relative to the national economy and exceedingly difficult to meet.[39]

Even partial payment for less than year-round service proved very difficult for the Muscovite budget to sustain.[40] To the west, growing commercial economies produced new kinds of cash reserves, which might be taxed for military support. New institutions were used to marshal economic resources in new ways, and the development of credit made international borrowing yet another method available to sustain a military establishment at war. For Muscovy, as Aleksei Mikhailovich quickly discovered, such options were not realistic. The additional resources that could be levied from Muscovite commerce were very limited. While the government's right to tax was not institutionally constrained, new sources of taxable wealth were difficult to discover and most chancelleries resorted to replication and hypothecation, rather than innovation. Foreign institutions lent little to a country that lacked deep reserves and a national budget. Muscovy waged war largely on its own resources. For the Thirteen Years' War, the Muscovite government did try to arrange foreign and domestic loans. It raised taxes and added a couple of extraordinary cash levies. Finally, and most dramatically, it debased the currency, paying its army (and others) in copper coinage with the same face value as silver coins. Although these were initially accepted at nearly their nominal value, eventually serious price inflation set in. Merchants accepted the army's copper pay only at radically discounted rates, if at all. Indeed, the state itself began to specify that taxes should be paid in silver. For men on and near the front, pay and food allowances became grossly inadequate to the purchase of food and other necessaries. The army grumbled and threatened; some foreign officers applied to return home. This had little effect until copper riots in the capital forced the government into withdrawing the copper currency in 1662–3. Faced with such constraints, the government resumed the sale of liquor concessions, as the need for cash overcame scruples about the sale of alcohol.[41]

Such financial expedients in the short run did not, in the long run, lead to improvements or even regularization of Muscovy's cash revenues. Rather, the government relied on expansion and institutionalization of an older practice, that of removing whatever expenses possible from cash transactions and the market. *Voevoda* G. G. Romodanovskii, in charge of provisioning in 1655, collected oil and grain in kind to offer the troops. On other occasions, foreign officers received Siberian furs in lieu of the cash owed them.[42]

Food allowances paid to members of the army in kind were helpful instances of non-cash, off-market transactions. When the troops received grain, in lieu of a cash allowance for food, the government avoided the complication of inflated food prices near the front. Delivery of food in kind to the front could also help avoid the shortfalls occasionally to be expected from Russia's fledgling markets. Supply in kind was hardly a new idea. Muscovy had long collected grain as a tax-in-kind to support its standing musketeer troops. On the frontiers, local grain taxes-in-kind provisioned siege granaries, offered emergency aid, or provided grain for specific ends, such as tribute for the Don Cossacks. First the musketeers' grain tax and then special southern levies were redirected to provide grain in kind to the front in 1655, 1656, 1657 and 1662.[43] Although the resulting amounts still fell short, and new formation troops deserted because of hunger, the value of in-kind supply was quite clear.[44]

As infantry recruitment escalated in the early 1660s, so did food deliveries to front-line troops, particularly as allowances and salaries paid in copper coinage led to high inflation. Beginning in 1663, the Grain Chancellery (*Khlebnyi Prikaz*) fed some troops from escheated and confiscated estates and other sources; the musketeers' grain tax from the Musketeers' Chancellery fed others; and the Military Chancellery's grain department (1664) fed still others with grain from a now-annual southern tax in kind.[45] Priority in disbursement went to new formation infantry. Musketeers received grain only after the more valuable troops had been paid.[46] This off-market, organizationally disjointed effort by no means represented nationally organized provisioning. However, the systematic attempt to feed the most valuable troops on campaign again signalled a transition in Muscovite military organization.

In particular, it became clear that Muscovy would be well repaid by permanent, year-round military organization at the regional level. The Belgorod military-administrative district provided grain and men for the front, at the same time as its garrisons defended the Tatar frontier. The Novgorod and Smolensk administrative districts, created along the north-western front at the beginning of the war, also demonstrated a surprising capacity for supporting the new formation troops. About 1665, the western provinces of the growing Belgorod district were broken off to form a new Sevsk military district. With the development of more unified regional administration, Muscovy's ability to muster resources was greatly enhanced. Towards the end of the war significant numbers of Muscovite field troops were identified specifically by district, as permanent, regional military organization took on greater importance.[47]

The sum total of changes in the Muscovite military establishment by the end of the Thirteen Years' War was transformative. Early in the war Muscovy had about 100,000 military men on its registers; particular campaigns drew on about 40,000 of these men, while others remained in garrisons and off duty. At this early point in the war the army was one-third musketeers and more than half *pomest'e* cavalry. By 1663 nearly 80 per cent of men on the military registers had been transferred or enrolled into the new formations, generally acknowledged to be superior troops. Even more interestingly, the army of the 1660s was as much as 40 per cent infantry, with 25,000 new formation soldiers and the rest musketeers. The most valuable units in the army were regularly, if briefly, trained by foreign officers. Indeed, the widespread presence of foreign officers meant persistent new military influences.[48] The state acknowledged that it owed its new-style units salaries, provisions and (in the case of the infantry) firearms and matériel while they were in the field. Organizational changes and greater institutional permanence increased Muscovy's ability to mobilize its resources more fully.

In the process, the first steps toward a mass, national army categorized by training and capabilities were taken. Although still carefully segregated by regiment, the impoverished gentry served as soldiers and cavalrymen in new formation regiments – as did peasants and contract servicemen such as Cossacks and musketeers. Social sensibilities, particularly of the gentry, though cautiously treated, clearly took a back seat to the military capacities of the Muscovite state.

The commitment to these changes was consistent, if cautious. Undeniably, there was both political and cultural resistance to these transformations; institutional support for the new forces was frequently based on adaptations of older landholding, taxation and other arrangements. Ominously, the financial underpinnings of change were far from stable or well formed. Unmistakably, for all that, increasing experience with Polish troops, Habsburg mercenaries and the Swedish army urged Muscovy in the direction of the 'Euro-Ottoman standard of parity' – that is, an army whose organization, tactics and resources could deal not only with the steppe, but which was learning rapidly from the expertise of its near European neighbours.

There are nonetheless important qualifications to this description of the Muscovite military. In the post-war period Muscovy pulled back on its commitment to social mixing in the regiments. Cavalry regiments, in particular, were given a peacetime veneer of social exclusivity. Still, the old cavalry hundreds remained a rarity after the Thirteen Years' War. Further, in the 1660s, the training of most new formation regiments was a matter of practical and personal experience. That is, foreign officers had brief training sessions with cavalry troops, and they lacked a common cavalry training reference. Since the common written repertoire for infantry training was limited to a printed, translated Dutch manual and a Muscovite manuscript from the turn of the century, *soldat* training in practice also depended largely on the abilities, insistence and expertise of individual officers.[49] Although the foreign officers in question were often competent, professional, and knowledgeable, the diversity of their efforts complicated troop coordination and tactical responses. Furthermore, except for regionally based troops, the new formation regiments moved quickly from recruitment to battlefield, where their experience strongly if briefly shaped their own abilities. Some foreign officers, like the highly placed Scots mercenary Patrick Gordon, consequently did not rate their battlefield readiness very highly. This notwithstanding, new formation troops during the Thirteen Years' War showed signs that they could manoeuvre under fire and withdraw in an orderly manner – from the besieged town of Borisov, and, notably, the retreat at Liakhovichi in spite of heavy losses.[50] The new formation regiments by their persistent presence served an over-extended Muscovite army well.

Some of the capabilities of the new formation regiments derived as much from their military environment as from their training. Infantry, like their musketeer predecessors, functioned effectively in conjunction with fortifications and entrenchments, which allowed them to 'deliver heavy firepower from a secured position'. On the steppe, Muscovite troops made similar effective use of the *wagenburg*; the Hungarians and Turks, among others, also used this tactic. The crowding of troops within the shelter of baggage carts and the moving walls of the *guliai gorod*, allowed Muscovites to move slowly across exposed terrain even while under attack, as at Konotop and Chudnovo.[51]

Some important advantages of the new formations lay in their underlying organization as much as in their tactical abilities. The new ability to recruit large numbers of troops, train them and provide for them, had developed in the relatively unified southern frontier districts, which faced Crimea. When such troops later appeared on the national level, their stability and new comprehensive responsibilities were clearly advantageous.

For all these innovations, both financial crisis and the absence of an overall institutional coordination for military affairs (regarding provisioning, for example) impeded the war effort. In many respects, the result was ·a semi-standing, semi-permanent army. This was reflected in the situation of the Military Chancellery (*Razriad*), whose peacetime responsibilities were both lighter and different from its wartime ones.[52] Nevertheless, the ability to recruit men persistently, to outfit them for the field, maintain them there and to campaign season after season, was a important result of the victorious Muscovite effort in the Thirteen Years' War.

After Andrusovo

Andrusovo emphasized Muscovy's new role as a European diplomatic player. Aleksei Mikhailovich's chief negotiator at Andrusovo envisioned that the cooperation of the Commonwealth with Muscovy might be the beginning of a larger common effort against the Ottoman Empire. The government sought acknowledgement and interest from the Habsburgs, France, England, Spain, the Netherlands, Denmark, Sweden, Brandenburg, Venice and Persia.[53]

But, the Treaty of Andrusovo did not end the fighting in Ukraine, which continued sporadically for at least a decade.[54] Developments in Ukraine in the five years after Andrusovo were complex, involving not only Right and Left Bank Ukraine, but also the other major armies of the region: Crimea, the Ottoman Empire, the Poland–Commonwealth and Muscovy.

At the moment of the treaty, Ivan Briukhovetsky, supported by Moscow, was hetman of the Left Bank. Muscovy, hoping to solidify its authority over the Left Bank, had established the Little Russian Chancellery (*Malorossiiskii Prikaz*) in 1662,[55] as an administrative unit governing Muscovite garrisons in major Left Bank fortresses (including Kiev) and levying taxes and payments to support them. This activity, directed towards incorporating the Left Bank into a functioning Muscovite system, was deeply resented.

Although Hetman Doroshenko on the Right Bank aspired to reunite Ukraine, he was still unable to do so without outside support. At first he was primarily involved in battling the Polish forces that had recently taken

the field against him. Meanwhile, under the terms of an agreement negotiated with Doroshenko early in 1668, Hetman Briukhovetsky on the
Left Bank led an anti-Muscovite uprising. Once that uprising appeared
to succeed, both Doroshenko and some of Briukhovetsky's own supporters turned on the Left Bank Hetman, who was replaced by one of
Doroshenko's lieutenants. Reaction was almost instantaneous. Moscow
divided the 40,000 men (including nearly 20,000 musketeers) still on alert
in the south into two forces and dispatched them to Ukraine: to crush
the Left Bank in a pincer movement, to relieve remaining Muscovite garrisons, and to protect Muscovite control over Kiev.[56] At about the same
time (1668–9), Doroshenko and the Zaporozhian Cossacks began to
negotiate with the Ottoman Empire to grant Ukraine protectorate status.

   As a result, Ukrainian reunification was short-lived. Doroshenko
returned to his Right Bank capital, Chyhyryn (Chigirin). Muscovite forces
arrived at the town of Nezhin and attacked Doroshenko's lieutenant
on the Left Bank, Demian Mnogogreshnyi. Rather than withdrawing,
Mnogogreshnyi negotiated an agreement with Moscow and became hetman of the Left Bank early in 1669. As Muscovite rule returned to the Left
Bank, southern army units supported new garrisons in Left Bank towns
and protected Muscovy's extended western borders.

   Meanwhile, Doroshenko's attempts to negotiate more autonomy
increased international tensions, pitting the Ottomans and the Tatars, first
against Poland and then against Muscovy. Having reached an agreement
with the Porte, Doroshenko himself undertook to negotiate a settlement
with Poland. Supporting their new client and ally, Hetman Doroshenko,
the Ottomans complained to Moscow about Cossack attacks on their
Black Sea strongholds and about the presence of Muscovite armies
near Kiev. Muscovy filed reciprocal complaints with the Porte about
Crimean attacks on the Muscovite south. Negotiations began about the
terms of Andrusovo and then about control over their clients, Crimean
and Cossack.[57] As the two empires moved cautiously toward more open
conflict, garrisons across the Muscovite south remained on alert; the
Belgorod and Sevsk military districts collected grain and other necessaries
to sustain the Muscovite forces on the Left Bank, since Muscovite taxation of the Left Bank was counterproductive. But it was events in southern
Poland and western Ukraine that finally brought Ottoman troops into the
fray. The Polish–Lithuanian Commonwealth tried to isolate Doroshenko
by creating a rival Left Bank hetman. In response, Doroshenko and Sultan
Mehmed IV launched a large and successful campaign against Poland,
which captured Kamianets-Podol'skii. In the subsequent Treaty of Buchach

(1672), Podol'ia and Cossack Ukraine were ceded to Turkey as an independent protectorate.

The scene was set for open conflict between Muscovy and the Ottomans over Ukraine; intermittently this remained a central issue for Muscovite politics and its military for the rest of the century. It would have been difficult at the time to imagine that further Muscovite successes could emerge from the devastation and further fighting in Ukraine. Muscovite troops in the south had battled hard to retain Andrusovo's gains. Sustaining Left Bank garrisons, protecting their borders and, as far as possible, their hard-won prize of Kiev, stretched the Muscovite military administration very thin. On the other hand, Ottoman troops, supported by Doroshenko and Crimea, seemed capable of overwhelming any east European armies in the area.

Demographic changes in Ukraine inflamed Turkish–Crimean concerns about Muscovy. Conditions in Left Bank Ukraine and the protection of Moscow's defensive line furnished a dramatic and stable contrast to the lengthy and ruinous conflict on the Right Bank. There, the devastating impact of troop movement and fighting encouraged the population to emigrate. Some western Ukrainians went eastward into the Muscovite Ukraine – settling Cossack regimental territories on the Left Bank of the Dniepr. Others moved still further east. After initial enthusiasm, Muscovy became reluctant to accept so many settlers from such a turbulent and potentially disloyal population into the provinces behind the defensive line. Instead, it encouraged new Cossack settlement in the Slobodskaia Ukraina, the largely empty lands south-east of the Muscovite defence lines. As the population grew (and grow it did, especially in the 1670s),[58] the Cossack Slobodskaia Ukrainia became an integral part of Muscovy, albeit organized on its own terms. Hesitantly but irreversibly, the frontier of Muscovy's settlement advanced southward, to the continuing concern of Crimea, in particular.

Despite this unanticipated gain, pressures on the population of southern Muscovy persisted or even increased after 1667. Moscow certainly anticipated renewed conflict. Although some foreign officers were dismissed at the end of the war,[59] the southern military districts of Belgorod and Sevsk held their field regiments and its officer corps at full strength.[60] Demands on relatively poor southern servicemen with small plots of land increased after Andrusovo, rather than reverting to pre-war levels. Military inspectors were forced to draw deeply upon the region's reserves. In service families with three adult men, all three were forced to serve: the ablest to go on campaign with the army, the remaining two respectively to farm the

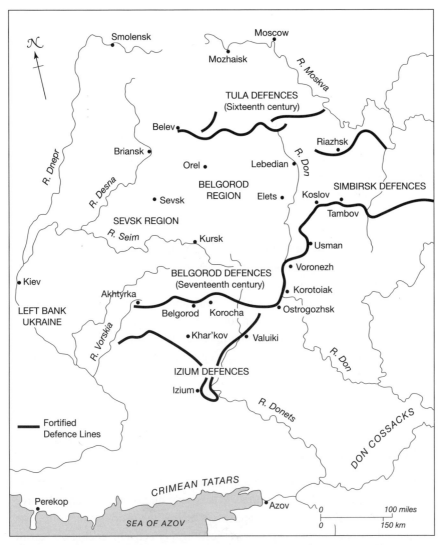

MAP 7 *Muscovy's southern frontier in the seventeenth century* (adapted from Stevens, Carol Belkin, *Soldiers on the Steppe: Army Reform and Social Change in Early Modern Russia* (Northern Illinois University Press, 1995))

family holding and to serve in the local garrison. In the interior provinces, where Tatar raids had not penetrated in nearly two decades, military inspectors chose to quickly and deliberately deplete the garrisons; only those fortresses directly on defensive Belgorod line were staffed at full strength. Odd economic and administrative devices appeared, such as the creation of 'service families' by artificially grouping single male smallholders for mutual support.[61] In addition to recruitments, escalating in-kind collections of grain further burdened farmer-servicemen. Given the threat of war with the Ottomans, the loyalty of the Don Cossacks was courted with grain shipments from Voronezh. Garrisons at Kiev and in Left Bank Ukraine could not be sustained by cash payments and market purchases in that increasingly hostile and war-torn region. Kiev, too, began to draw on the southern regions.[62] It became increasingly difficult for farmer-servicemen (and the districts) to meet the multitudes of demands imposed upon them.

Manpower and economic pressures quickly generated a response. Complaints poured in against new norms and requirements that short-changed local agriculture and garrison defences. Garrison troops in Left Bank Ukraine and Kiev, left in place for years without replacements, became increasingly indignant or simply deserted. Although the south was not alone in feeling the pinch of ongoing military preparedness, its burden was disproportionate. When Muscovy had little relief to offer its best-organized military provinces,[63] its residents were not reluctant to take matters into their own hands.

Other frontiers

The military sponsorship of expansion was not limited to Muscovy's western borders or the Pontic steppe. Muscovy's highly successful defensive system against the steppe was replicated, as the Belgorod fortified line was extended eastward from Tambov to the Volga, effectively fencing off Kazan from the lower Don basin. With this exception, however, the role of the military in expansion eastward took different forms.

The arrival of the Kalmyks on the lower Volga at mid-century threatened the stability of the region to the south-east of the Tambov–Samara fortifications. The Kalmyks fielded a fairly formidable and numerous force of disciplined cavalrymen, which they used for steppe-style raiding expeditions.[64] Muscovy was unable to apply its defensive line strategy against them, since fortifications of this kind would interrupt a valuable trade route between the middle Volga and Astrakhan, on the Volga delta. Instead, in the seventeenth century Muscovy signed a succession of treaties with the Kalmyks – in return for annual payments, personal presents, the promise of extensive pastures and duty-free trade. After the middle of the century, these treaties successfully neutralized the Kalmyk threat. A loosely structured political alliance between the Kalmyks and the Muscovite government in the Volga basin effectively if tentatively extended Muscovy's reach into the steppe. The Kalmyks turned their raids away from Russian settlements, attacking instead the Ottoman client state of Crimea. The Crimeans were forced to build their own defensive lines to protect themselves and their Nogai allies from these raids; the Khanate also maintained coastal defences to deflect Cossack naval raids in the late 1660s and early 1670s.[65]

Over the longer term, however, Muscovy's expectations, that the Kalmyks could be used as auxiliaries to their army and docile allies who would raid on command, were destined for frequent disappointment. The Kalmyks actively built and maintained their own relationships with peoples on and across the steppe.[66] Under pressure, Muscovy fortified some small and medium-sized towns, without linking them in a defensive line. The presence of the trade route and the lesser geopolitical importance of the region meant that the lower Volga basin did not attract the attention or the resources that had unified a militarized population, military administration and fortified defence line further to the west.[67]

During this same period, the long arm of Muscovite military bureaucracy extended through Siberia to reach the Pacific coast. The Muscovite presence in Siberia was represented by a series of isolated outposts; these offered quite different military challenges than contiguous regions with a significant agricultural population. In the Siberian north, the Siberian Chancellery supplied and staffed a string of small fortresses,[68] essentially repeating over an ever-growing distance the 'well-tried pattern of exploration and settlement, subjugation of local tribes, and the establishment of fortified posts (ostrogi)' developed during its sixteenth and early seventeenth-century expansion.[69] Private mercantile activity and the state's collection of fur tribute (iasak) elicited attacks and rebellion from indigenous peoples. In the northern taiga, such rebellion was rarely sustainable for long against the bureaucratic resources of the Muscovite Empire moving eastward towards the Pacific.

By comparison with northern Siberia, expansion south-eastward along the steppe edge remained difficult well into the eighteenth century. Here Muscovy confronted strong and sustained resistance by steppe peoples. Its strategy was to accumulate information about adjacent groups, with a view to soliciting Kazakh and others' cooperation in the protection of the old but still active steppe trade routes. Ongoing battles between the Kazakhs and their neighbours continuously disrupted this strategy, while Moscow's efforts to convert its Muslim neighbours and subjects to Orthodox Christianity heightened resistance. As a result, confrontations continued to take place frequently along the southward-facing Siberian border.[70] Only in the eighteenth and nineteenth centuries were resources dedicated to the building of defensive fortified lines east of the Urals. This, in turn, paved the way for the Russian Empire's claims to broader, more conventional control over the region.[71]

Frontier activities were a slow drain on Moscow's military and bureaucratic resources. Efforts to control the Volga basin, Siberia and inner Asia did not occupy centre stage in Moscow during the seventeenth century, militarily or in any other way. In the latter part of the century, however, frontier affairs brought Muscovy into direct confrontation with another large, expansionist and bureaucratic empire – China. To solidify control over Siberia east of Lake Baikal, Muscovy built the fortress of Nerchinsk in 1659. Thence Muscovite traders and small military groups moved southward into the Amur valley; by 1665 Muscovy was building the fort of Albazin to protect Russian traders on the middle reaches of the river. In 1685, however, China attacked and took Albazin. Although Muscovy recaptured it promptly, the Chinese were unwilling to withdraw from the Amur valley and particularly reluctant to allow Muscovy the opportunity of negotiating an alliance with the Dzhungar Mongols.[72] News of the ongoing conflict led to the dispatch of an ambassador, Golovin, to negotiate with China. As instructed, he relinquished territory, but not Muscovy's trading ambitions. The Treaty of Nerchinsk, signed in August of 1689, formalized a Muscovite withdrawal from the Amur River area for nearly 200 years.[73] In fact, this retreat was nearly simultaneous with the failure of a major Muscovite attack on Crimea. News from the east travelled slowly, however, so Nerchinsk surely played no part in the negative political reaction that greeted the Crimean failure.

The significance of Muscovy's remote and near eastern territories should not be ignored, however. China certainly occupied a secondary or even tertiary position in Moscow's constellation of adversaries. The ongoing competition, and intermittent conflict, with the Ottoman Empire during the last two-and-a half decades of the century over the long common border from Ukraine to the Urals ensured that it remained so. However, Moscow continued to invest funds and military effort in supporting its claims in Siberia. For one thing, Siberian furs comprised a significant proportion of Muscovite state revenues throughout the latter part of the

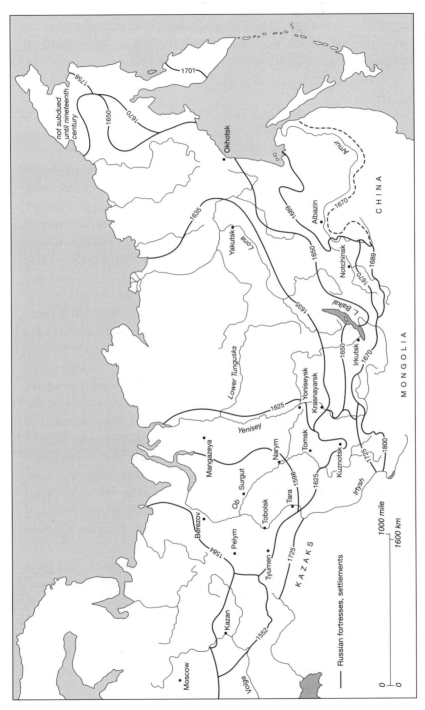

MAP 8   *The Russian presence in Siberia* (adapted from Forsyth, James, *A History of the Peoples of Siberia: Russia's North Asian Colony, 1581–1990* (Cambridge University Press, 1992))

seventeenth century, and disruption was highly undesirable. Furthermore, steppe politics in the east, and Kalmyk influence in particular, had an immediate impact on the western steppe – the Nogai, the Khanate of Crimea and the Cossack settlements on the lower Don.

Rebellion

By the 1660s the Cossack population on the lower Don had grown significantly. Recent migrants to the area included fugitives from central Muscovy, from the southern provinces, and even from Ukraine. As the size of Don Cossacks settlements grew, so did the difficulty of sustaining them from meagre agriculture resources, raiding and trading. Muscovy continued to send grain and other supplies southward to the Cossacks by boat from Voronezh, but these amounts had never been intended to support an entire community. By the late 1660s, as the Thirteen Years' War drew to a close, the relatively prosperous registered Cossacks and less prosperous newer arrivals were uncomfortably divided. After 1667 the leadership of Sten'ka Razin provided the opportunity for growing numbers of the poorer Cossacks to engage in traditional raiding and piratical expeditions. Crimea's new defences thwarted their efforts on the Don, so Razin and his followers turned their attention to the Persian shores of the Caspian.[74] Although successful enough to attract some servicemen from southern Muscovy,[75] these expeditions did not remain lucrative for long, and Razin turned homeward. Then Muscovy's regular shipment of grain and supplies to the Cossacks on the Don fell short of expectations. This placed even the wealthier Cossacks at risk, and the Don burst into rebellious resentment against Moscow. Razin's forces, gathering numbers, occupied Tsaritsyn and Astrakhan in 1670. Then they continued northward along the Volga towards the settled south-eastern corner of European Muscovy, some of them turning westward along the southern defensive lines.

The Cossack rebellion found fertile ground in the southernmost parts of the Belgorod district. Frontier garrisons were often riven by considerable tension and contradictions; indeed, some had rebelled before in 1648–9.[76] Contract servicemen of the older forces, garrison Cossacks and musketeers resented their declining military status and disliked any demands for year-round military service. Their neighbours and relatives were under constant pressure to supply food and recruits for front-line troops. These were, after all, not the musketeers of the capital whose political and military role included guarding the court, but provincial musketeers, whose salaries and food supports had long ago been sacrificed in favour of the new formation infantry. Some were easily moved to support rebellion.[77]

Powerful though fiscal and social concerns were, they were allied to other causes of discontent. Popular opposition to the authority of the Church took a variety of forms on the frontier, but the Cossacks in particular sometimes associated it with resistance to political and other changes. Among other things, this distaste was directed against foreign officers and military styles. Such concerns fuelled social disgruntlement in some frontier towns, and, at times, served as a catalyst for the religious and political utopianism.[78]

As Razin's forces approached from the south-east, Muscovite garrisons and even some ranking military officers went over to the rebels in towns such as Ostrogozhsk and Ol'shansk, declaring themselves for Sten'ka Razin and his brother, Frol'ka. Elsewhere large expanses of countryside declared their allegiance to the Cossacks; the Slobodskaia Ukraina in the south-west proved fertile ground for rebellion, and the possibility of alliance with Zaporozhian Cossacks of Ukraine was bruited. While Frol'ka Razin mustered support in the south-southwest, Sten'ka continued northward up the Volga towards Simbirsk and the end of the extended fortified line. Until he reached Simbirsk itself, Razin met with considerable success among frontier garrisons and outposts in this region too. The Razin rebellion was, in a real sense, the most successful raid on the defensive lines since their construction at mid-century.

In the end, however, the military organization of the frontier held. Bonus pay and extra ammunition were issued to garrisons along the fortified lines, while town governors assessed the loyalty of troops and requested reinforcements.[79] Unable to capture Simbirsk late in 1670, Razin retreated southward towards the Don. He was pursued by newly assembled battlefield troops – who came from Moscow rather than Belgorod and Sevsk. Commanders in Tambov and Voronezh held the eastern front, while Prince G. G. Romodanovskii, still in command (*voevoda*) of the Belgorod district's field army, moved quickly against Frol'ka Razin. As hetman of the Left Bank, Demian Mnogogreshnyi contributed Cossack troops to suppress rebellion in the Slobodskaia Ukraina just to his east.[80] The rebellion was over quickly. Registered Don Cossacks captured both Razins as they retreated to the Don and delivered them to Moscow. Astrakhan was the last Razin stronghold to fall in 1671. Shortly thereafter,

Muscovite soldiers were posted to a garrison on the Don, and the Don Cossacks thereafter were required to swear an oath of loyalty to the Tsar in Moscow.

Rebellions of such size and intensity were uncommon, but resistance to Moscow's seventeenth-century military, financial and administrative innovations was not, particularly when change was accompanied by the imposition of stronger state structures. Razin spawned many copycat and parallel disturbances. An uprising in the far north at Solovetskii Monastery was triggered by its rejection of religious reform. In Siberia native populations struggled against Muscovy's representatives. Other examples, though less dramatic and militarily less threatening, abounded in the 1670s. Powerful ecclesiastics and court elites maintained private armed bands, and banditry persisted, difficult if not impossible to suppress. The limits of state power and its control over military force were clearly visible in Muscovite life.

Conclusions

During the protracted military encounters of the mid-seventeenth century, several important and visible changes took place in the Muscovite army. The most noticeable of these was perhaps Moscow's new ability to put men in the field, campaign after campaign, replacing battlefield casualties while still maintaining minimum defences. Given the high casualty rates and the duration of the war, the relatively reliable, persistent replacement of front-line troops helped Muscovy gain substantial territory in the Right Bank and the important city of Kiev at the Treaty of Andrusovo in 1667. The new capability also sustained the involvement of Moscow's troops in the region after the peace was concluded and helped hold that territory even in the face of local rebellion and foreign power involvement.

Although it might have been spurred in part by the reluctance of hereditary servicemen to serve, this new capability was focused in large part on filling new formation regiments. All these troops were highly valued for their tactical potential and battlefield manoeuvrability, as the immense sums spent to officer these regiments with skilled foreigners attest. In particular, peasant conscription regularly filled the new formation infantry units, or *soldaty*, whose numbers and training began to offer Muscovy new military possibilities.

But in addition to changing battlefield configurations, the Thirteen Years' War helped to launch a new socio-military perspective in Muscovy.

For one thing, the number of lower status units in the Muscovite military appeared to grow dramatically. By 1663, for example, identifiable hereditary servicemen were a minority in a large army. At least 70,000 men, by contrast, joined to potential ranks of musketeer, Cossack, soldat and artillery units. Similar proportions can be identified in the armies of the Doroshenko campaigns from 1667 to 1669. At first glance, this might appear to be an extension of Ivan IV's increased use of contract servicemen in the late sixteenth century. This alone would be a misleading conclusion, however. It was more significant that these men, petty hereditary servicemen and peasants, all joined that growing proportion of all troops in new formation regiments. In these regiments, social status appeared to take second place to the military qualities of the troops. In practice, these new regiments pushed – even transgressed – the limits of unstated, commonly accepted rules and accommodations to hereditary and contract service. Thus, during the Thirteen Years' War, a significant number of troops were categorized on the basis of their military qualities, not primarily on social rank. The presence of the foreign officer corps, with a claim to hierarchical and meritocratic command structure, was another element in an apparent transformation of organizational perspective.

Less visible, but equally important to military change, were administrative changes that supported the new formation troops. The internal reach of government increased, at personal cost to Muscovy's peasants, other taxpayers and petty servitors. The move towards mass national conscription, state-supplied salaries, food, firearms and matériel on a grander scale made it possible to create more new formation regiments. Many of the administrative innovations derived, directly or indirectly, from the unified military districts of southern Muscovy, and pressed hard on those areas. Such permanent coordinating institutions and their growing ability to manage resources at the regional level were key developments at mid-century.

Muscovy's ability to sustain the innovations of the Thirteen Years' War, however, was unsteady. The army's size, regularly at least 40,000 men on campaign out of the 100,000 available, made it capable of fighting simultaneously on a long frontier over prolonged periods. It also made the army very expensive. Copper riots, attempted loans and irregular payments clearly show that Muscovy skated close to the financial edge. Muscovy was not capable of supporting its numerous troops year-round, nor did it conscript on that basis. Instead, with a very few exceptions, some men were supported with salaries, food, arms and matériel some of the time. With a few exceptions, they did not train and drill regularly. The army's performance in the field was sometimes satisfactory, but rarely stellar. The expertise that underlay it was uneven. A native strength in artillery and fortifications developed further, and the Tsar was advised and supported by a committed group of advisers and foreign officers. Cultural and political resistance was strong, however, and until the last years of his reign even Aleskei Mikhailovich's leadership of reform was muted by the need for some degree of consensus and accommodation. As a consequence, the army was 'semi-standing, and semi-regular', dependent in large part on the service devices of the previous century.

The military changes of the Thirteen Years' War, all told, represented a precarious compromise between far-reaching changes geared for military success and the need to maintain social and political support among a persistent and self-defined military elite. Muscovy started moving unreliable *pomest'e* troops into new regiments; at the same time it felt obliged to acknowledge the expectations of these elite cavalrymen, even if it sidestepped or did not entirely fulfil them.[81] The older understandings of elite military service to the state were silently eroded, but not gainsaid. The government at the same time began the process of supporting many of its troops, but only for part of the year and as far as traditional cash and in-kind reserves would carry it. Change was so hedged by the political and cultural reaction of Muscovy's political and social elite that much of it was accomplished by disproportionate pressure on the most accessible population in the south. Pressures there had in the end to be balanced against Cossack rebellion.

Military change and the political balancing act underpinning it brought significant consequences in their train. The gain of new territory in Ukraine was the immediate result of warfare. In the Slobodskaia Ukrainia and elsewhere there was a significant advance of settled, bureaucratic empire into the steppe. This generated reaction from the Cossacks of the Don, Ukraine and Zaporozhe, who as a result of Muscovy's southward movement attacked and raided the Ottoman Black Sea littoral. The continued presence of Muscovite troops during continued fighting in Ukraine against Doroshenko and in the aftermath of Razin itself reinforced Muscovy's continuing southward advance. The Cossacks found themselves under tightening Muscovite control across the south, from Zaporozhe through the Slobodskaia Ukraina to the Don. Into the next quarter century, Muscovy's military and diplomatic interests remained firmly focused on the south. As an extension of these concerns, it would confront the Ottoman Empire itself in battle during the last quarter of the seventeenth century.

Notes

1 Frank Sysyn, 'Ukrainian Social Tensions before the Khmelnytsky Uprising', in Samuel Baron and Nancy S. Kollmann, *Religion and Culture in Early Modern Russia and Ukraine* (DeKalb, Illinois, 1997), 69–70.

2 The agreement bore quite different interpretations for the signatory parties. In this sense as in others, it was characteristic of Muscovy's relationship with other steppe peoples. Michael Khodarkovsky, *Russia's Steppe Frontier* (Bloomington, 2002), 138; Andreas Kappeler, *The Russian Empire* (Harlow, 2001), 64.

3 Mobilization order, March: *PSZ*, vol. 1, doc. 96.

4 See E. Zaozerskii, 'K istorii Tul'skoi oruzhenoi slobody', *Voprosy voennyi istorii* (Moscow, 1969), 145–8, on arms manufacturing in Tula in this era.

5 A. V. Chernov, *Vooruzhennye sily Russkogo gosudarstva v XV–XVII vv. s obrazovaniia tsentralizovannogo gosudarstva do reform pri Petre I* (Moscow, 1954), 130–1, 166–7.

6 William M. Reger, 'In the Service of the Tsar: European mercenary officers and the reception of military reform in Russia, 1654–1667', (Ph.D. dissertation, University of Illinois at Urbana Champaign, 1997); Hellie points out that the translated military manual may not have sold in Muscovy because it was intended for older muskets.

7 S. Baron, 'The Origins of Moscow's Nemeckaja Sloboda', *California Slavic Studies*, vol. 5 (1970), 1–17. The Leslie case is described in Joseph T. Fuhrmann, *Tsar Alexis. His Reign and His Russia* (Gulf Breeze, Florida, 1981), 49–51.

8 Reger, 'In the Service', 159.

9 A. Z. Myshlaevskii, 'Ofitserskii vopros v XVII veke', *Voennyi sbornik* no. 5 (1899), 39–40; *PSZ*, vol. 1, doc. 529. There were bottlenecks in promotion after 1665. Russian officers were promoted by a slightly different process.

10 Richard Hellie, *Enserfment and Military Change in Muscovy* (Chicago, 1972), 189, 215; *AMG*, vol. 2, docs 482, 496, 539–42, 617; *AI*, vol. 4 no. 70; Chernov, *Vooruzhennye*, 139–40, 143.

11 RGADA f. 210 Smotr. Kn. 35, ll. 186–95; *AMG*, vol. 2, docs 540, 717; vol. 3, docs 49, 301; *PSZ*, vol. 1, doc. 261.

12 Chernov, *Vooruzhennye*, 146; Hellie, *Enserfment*, 198.

13 Hellie, *Enserfment*, 183–4; A. N. Mal'tsev, *Rossiia i Belorussiia v seredine XVII veka* (Moscow, 1974), 23.

14 K. V. Bazilevich, *Denezhnaia reforma Aleksei Mikhailovicha* (Moscow, 1936), 5; Philip Longworth, *Alexis Tsar of all the Russias* (New York, 1984), 89.

15 Hellie, *Enserfment*, 193–4; Mal'tsev, *Rossiia i Belorussia*, 29, 34–5.

16 For discussions of the Thirteen Years' War in English: Robert Frost, *The Northern Wars. War, State and Society in Northeastern Europe, 1558–1721* (Harlow, 1993), ch. 7; Orest Subtelny, *Ukraine. A History*, part III (Toronto, 1988); Longworth, *Alexis*, ch. 5ff; and the much older C. Bickford O'Brien, *Muscovy and the Ukraine* (Berkeley, California, 1963). See also A. N. Mal'tsev, *Rossiia i Belorussia*, esp. chs 2–6.

17 Frost, *Northern Wars*, 177; Mal'tsev, *Rossiia i Belorussia*, 111.

18 Mal'tsev, *Rossiia i Belorussia*, 112.

19 Peter B. Brown, 'Tsar Aleksei Mikhailovich as model military autocrat', in Marshall Poe and Eric Lohr, eds, *The Military and Society in Russia, 1450–1917* (Leiden, 2002), 121–3, 131. Later in his reign, Aleksei Mikhailovich provided some of the same coordinating effect with the notorious Chancellery of Secret Affairs; Mal'tsev, *Rossiia i Belorussia*, 61.

20 Cf. Frost, *Northern Wars* 169–83 for a succinct discussion of the Swedish war; his *After the Deluge* (Cambridge, 1993) for the political underpinnings of Commonwealth collapse and partial recovery.

21 I. N. Kushnerev and A. E. Pirogov, *Russkaia voennaia sila* (Moscow, 1892), 375–6; A. A. Novosel'skii, 'Bor'ba Moskovskogo gosudarstva s Tatarami vo vtoroi polovine XVII veka', *Issledovaniia po istorii epokhi feodalizma* (Moscow, 1994), 60–8.

22 A. Baiov, *Kurs istorii Russkogo voennogo isskustva*, vol. 1 *Ot nachala Rusi do Petra* (St Petersburg, 1909), 154–7; Novosel'skii, 'Bor'ba Moskovskogo' 70–1.

23 P. O. Bobrovskii, *Perekhod Rossii k reguliarnoi armii* (St Petersburg, 1885), 114; Novosel'skii, 'Bor'ba Moskovskogo' 75, 77ff.

24 *AMG*, vol. 2, doc. 1035.

25 Mal'tsev, *Rossiia i Belorussiia*, 39, 47, 53, 67.

26 Jan Chryzostom Pasek, *Memoirs of the Polish Baroque* (Berkeley, California, 1976), 39; Mal'tsev, *Rossiia i Belorussiia*, 49, 67.

27 Pasek, *Memoirs*, 75.

28 Novosel'skii, 'Bor'ba Moskovskogo' 66–8, 70, 71; Carol B. Stevens, *Soldiers on the Steppe* (Dekalb, Illinois, 1995), 68. Even early in the war, Russian losses were significant. Reger, 'In the Service', 88–92.

29 Hellie, *Enserfment*, 217, 269; *AMG*, vol. 2, docs 736, 768, 913–15, 933; vol. 3, docs 410, 524.

30 Hellie, *Enserfment*, 218–19, 269; Bobrovksii, *Perekhod*, 108, 117; *AMG*, vol. 3, docs 301, 336, 530.

31 Stevens, *Soldiers*, 69; Chernov, *Vooruzhennye*, 146.

32 Reger, 'In the Service', 168.

33 Bobrovskii, *Perekhod*, 81; Benjamin Philip Uroff, 'G. K. Kotoshikhin, *On Russia in the Reign of Alexis Mikhailovich*' (Ph.D. dissertation, Columbia University, 1970), vol. 2, 566 and G. K. Kotoshikhin, *O Rossii v carstvovanie Alekseja Mixajlovica*, ed. A. E. Pennington (Oxford, 1980), ch. 9, section 2. There were also contractors who operated through the market. *PSZ*, vol. 1, docs 132, 138.

34 Brian L. Davies, 'Village into Garrison', *Russian Review* (1992), 481–501; Uroff, 'G. K. Kotoshikhin', vol. 2, 570–1.

35 Hellie, *Enserfment*, 194–5.

36 I. D. Beliaev, *O Russkom voiske v tsarstvovanie Mikhaila Fedorovicha i posle ego* (Moscow, 1846), 59; Hellie, *Enserfment*, 196 n. 126–9.

37 RGADA, f. 210, Novgorodskii stolbets 293, ll. 326, 331.

38 Depriving approaching armies by destroying such sustenance was already a familiar tactic. Kotoshikhin describes looting during the Thirteen Years' War. Bobrovskii, *Perekhod*, 84.

39 E. Stashevskii, 'Budzhet i armiia', in M. Dovnar-Zapol'skii, *Russkaia istoriia v ocherkakh i stat'iakh* (Kiev, 1912), 416, 439; Richard Hellie, 'The costs of Muscovite military defence and expansion', in Eric Lohr and Marshall Poe, eds, *The Military and Society in Russia* (Leiden, 2002), Table 21. Hellie also calculates that 3 million rubles represented about an eighth of the Muscovite GNP.

40 Talk of the 'Russian budget' is largely symbolic, however, since a unified state budget was not produced until 1680; until then revenues were hypothecated.

41 Stevens, *Soldiers*, 58; Bazilevich, *Denezhnaia*, 10, 27, 32, 37; Uroff, 'G. K. Kotoshikhin', 486; A. C. Brueckner, *Miednyia dengi v Rossii, 1656–1663* (St Petersburg, 1864), 27, 28; Bobrovskii, *Perekhod*, 90. There was also a loan from England in the aftermath of the copper riots. *Idem*, n. 100.

42 Bobrovskii, *Perekhod*, 97; see *AIIuZR*, vol. 13 (St Petersburg, 1884) doc. 13 for a later example.

43 Stevens, *Soldiers*, 57–8.

44 Bobrovskii, *Perekhod*, 114; *DAI*, vol. 4, doc. 128.

45 Stevens, *Soldiers*, 58–9. Southern grain collections were not entirely devoted to front-line troops; an effort was made to provide for local military needs as well.

46 Uroff, 'G. K. Kotoshikhin', 451, 507; E. D. Stashevskii, *Smeta voennykh sil Moskovskago gosudarstva v 1663g.* (Kiev, 1910), 20ff.

47 Chernov, *Vooruzhennye*, 170–1; Stevens, *Soldiers*, Table 3, p. 167. See Uroff, 'G. K. Kotoshikhin', 561–2 on the army's field structure.

48 Myshlaevskii, 'Ofitserskii', 4–5; Stashevskii, *Smeta*, 50–7.

49 Reger, 'In the Service', 150–1; Chernov, *Vooruzhennye*, 103–4.

50 Reger, 'In the Service', 112–27.

51 Brian L. Davies, 'Revolt in Ukraine', unpublished typescript, 70, 81–2.

52 F. I. Kalinychev, *Pravovye voprosy* (Moscow, 1954), 95ff; A. V. Chernov, 'TsGADA kak istochnik po voennoi istorii Russogo gosudarstva do XVIII v', *Trudy MGIAI* (1948), 119–20, 140.

53 Davies, 'Revolt', 93.

54 For detail, see Davies, 'Revolt' and N. I. Kostomarov, 'Ruina', *Viestnik Evropy*, vol. 14 no. 4–no. 6 (1879).

55 Peter B. Brown, 'Early Modern Russian Bureaucracy: the evolution of the chancellery system from Ivan III to Peter the Great, 1478–1718' (Ph.D. dissertation, University of Chicago, 1978), 476–7.

56 Longworth, *Alexis*, 197.

57 N. A. Smirnov, *Rossiia i Turtsiia*, vol. 2 (Moscow, 1946), 116ff.

58 For example, D. I. Bagalei, *Materialy dila istorii kolonizatsii i byta stepnoi okrainy Moskovskogo gosudarstva* (Khar'kov, 1886), doc. 14; (1890) doc. 8; *AIIuZR*, vol. 13 no. 42; Kostomarov, 'Ruina', *Viestnik Evropy*, vol. 14 no. 5 (May 1879), 8.

59 Hellie, *Enserfment*, 191.

60 So one can deduce from the total numbers of troops present and the number of officers still drawing their payments in the south. C. B. Stevens, 'Belgorod: notes on literacy and language in the 17th century', *Russian History*, vol. 7 (1980) parts 1–2, 116 n. 10; Bobrovskii, *Perekhod*, 77.

61 I. Ivanov, 'Siabry-pomeshchiki', *ZhMNP* (Dec. 1903), 409 and elsewhere.

62 Bobrovskii, *Perekhod*, 117; Stevens, *Soldiers*, 67–8; *AIIuZR*, vol. 9, docs 2, 5, 75, 131.

63 Hereditary servicemen in the rest of Muscovy did experience close to universal mobilization however.

64 L. J. D. Collins, 'Military organization and tactics of the Crimean Tatars in the sixteenth and seventeenth centuries', in V. J. Perry and M. Yapp, eds, *War, Technology, and Society in the Middle East* (Oxford, 1975), 275.

65 Victor Ostapchuk, 'The Human Legacy of the Ottoman Black Sea', *Oriente Moderno*, vol. 20 no. 1 (2001), 60–1; V. P. Zagorovskii, *Belgorodskaia cherta* (Voronezh, 1969), 281–2.

66 Khodarkovsky, *Russia's Steppe Frontier*, 138.

67 M. B. Mikhailova and A. P. Ostiatinskii, 'Goroda srednego i nizhnego Povolozh'ia', in N. F. Gulianitskii, *Gradostroite'lstvo Moskovskogo gosudarstva XVI–XVII vekov* (Moscow, 1994), 101–2.

68 James Gibson, *Feeding the Russian Fur Trade* (Madison, Wisconsin, 1969), 3–9; N. I. Nikitin, *Sluzhilye liudi v zapadnoi Sibiri* (Novosibirsk, 1988), 28–30, 42–3. The use of these tactics was not necessarily more efficiently handled, however.

69 Lindsey A. Hughes, *Sophia, Regent of Russia* (New Haven, 1990), 210.

70 See Khodarkovskii, *Russia's Steppe Frontier*, 147–8; T. S. Proskuriakova, 'Goroda Sibiri i Priural'ia', in N. F. Gulianitskii, *Gradostroitel'stva*, 103–40; Gibson, *Feeding*, 4–8.

71 N. V. Gorban, 'The New Ishim Fortified Line', *Soviet Geography*, vol. 25 no. 3 (1984), 177–8.

72 Peter Purdue, 'China, Inner Asia and imperial expansion, 1500–1800', lecture at Colgate University, 27 Sept. 2002.

73 *PSZ*, doc. 1346. When the Treaty of Nerchinsk was signed, 1689, special maps of the frontier were signed by Golovin. Detailed account in N. S. Demidova, 'Iz istorii zakliucheniia Nerchinskogo dogovora 1689g', *Rossiia v period reform Petra I* (Moscow, 1973), 289–310.

74 For a detailed account in English, see Paul Avrich, *Russian Rebels 1600–1800* (New York, 1976) and, more recently, Michael Khodorkovsky, 'The Stepan Razin uprising: was it a peasant war?' *Jarbücher für Geschichte Osteuropas*, vol. 42 no. 1 (1994), 1–19.

75 *Kest'ianskaia voina pod predvoditel'stvom Stepana Razina* (Moscow, 1976), vol. 4 no. 11.

76 E. V. Chistiakova, 'Volneniia sluzhilykh liudei v iuzhnykh gorodov Rossii v seredine XVII v.' in *Russkoe gosudarstvo v XVII veke. Sbornik statei* (Moscow, 1961), 254–5.

77 AN SSSR II *Zapiski inostrantsev o vosstanie Stepana Razina*, 122–4.

78 Robert O. Crummey, 'Old Belief as Popular Religion: new approaches', *Slavic Review*, vol. 52 no. 4 (Winter, 1993), 704–6; G. B. Michels, *At Won With the Church* (Stanford, California, 1999), 182–4.

79 L. V. Cherepnin and A. G. Man'kov, eds, *Krestianskaia voina pod predvoditel'stvom Stepana Razina* vol. 1, docs 4, 8, 16, 18, 48, 56, 113; vol. 2 part I, docs 21, 106.

80 *AIIuZR*, vol. 9 no. 68.

81 It is worth pointing out that provincial elites had few ways of expressing themselves collectively about any of these issues, since the service city was one of the few organizations they shared. A. A. Novosel'skii, 'Praviashchie gruppy', *Uchenye zapiski RANIONa*, vol. 5 (1928), 315.

CHAPTER 6

The steppe frontier after Razin, 1672–97

Overview

When Tsar Aleksei Mikhailovich died in January 1676 he left behind a son both sickly and young, a volatile international situation and domestic political uncertainty. During the 20 years that followed, Muscovy experienced persistent political weakness and disunity at the centres of power. *Boiar* disputes swirled frequently first around Tsar Fedor (r. 1676–82), then around his sister, Sophia (regent to her younger brothers Ivan and Peter from 1682 to 1689), and lastly around the young Peter himself.

These disputes did not significantly alter the focus of Muscovite foreign policy and military activity in the waning years of the seventeenth century. With a wavering if interested eye on the Baltic, Muscovy concentrated on events to its south and south-west. Its efforts in opposing the Ottoman Empire and its clients on Crimea took two distinguishable but interdependent forms – the defence of its recent acquisitions in Ukraine, and the extension of its claims to steppe land through settlement, negotiation and warfare. On the one hand Muscovy had to deal with the aftermath of the Razin rebellion and the shifting loyalties on the southern frontier. It responded with the provocative and brutal sponsorship of agricultural colonization southward into the Pontic steppe. Between 1679 and 1681 the construction and garrisoning of the 'new' or Izium fortified line protected such colonization as far south as Tsarev-Borisov, only 450 km (280 miles) from Crimea. Thereafter, Muscovy restricted expansion by settlement in the European south-southwest, continuing such efforts only along the Volga and further east. Nonetheless, all along the southern frontier an important goad to Russo-Ottoman competition was the steppe and

Caucasian peoples – the Cossacks, Kalmyks, Tatars and others trying to negotiate a space for themselves between the encroaching empires.

At exactly the same time Moscow was engaging in full-scale battlefield confrontations with the Ottoman Empire. Military engagements between the two began in the early 1670s, erupted into a Russo-Ottoman war, 1678–81, and ended only after the turn of the eighteenth century. These military events ensured Muscovy's continued involvement in European diplomatic affairs, as it attempted to negotiate a broad anti-Ottoman coalition to defend its new claims against that formidable empire and its clients.

On the face of it, the net result of Muscovy's military engagements was discouraging. Skirmishes on the Don in the 1670s were inconclusive. Fighting in Ukraine in 1678 seemed at first to go Moscow's way. Indeed, Moscow's ability to deliver armies nearly comparable in size to the massive Ottoman forces represented a new achievement. But it was difficult to sustain. Muscovy proved unable to enlist a supporting coalition of forces, and the Russo-Ottoman War (1678–81) ended in the reinforcement of the gains of the Thirteen Years' War by the Turks at the Treaty of Bakhchisarai.

The complexities of its military commitments spurred the government in Moscow to launch a platform of military reforms. The new changes helped to create a simpler, more uniform and more effectively administered army. The battlefield army that emerged over the following decades was almost entirely composed of new formation regiments; it boasted a unified command, more predictable recruitment and improved resource mobilization. The reforms did not, however, move the army in the direction of more permanent, year-round forces. Nor, as the army converted wholesale to the new formations, did the reforms continue to disengage social status from military service. Instead, the 1678–82 reforms somewhat redefined and explicitly renewed the fundamentals of elite military service. This collection of outcomes was perhaps a result of domestic political weakness combined with the practical consequences of confronting the sizeable and well-supplied Ottoman forces.

Whatever the setbacks, Muscovy's foreign policy and military establishments remained focused nearly exclusively on the Russo-Ottoman competition until the end of the century. The Crimean campaigns of 1687 and 1689 were expensive, full-scale field-army attacks on an Ottoman client. These encounters tightened Muscovy's negotiated ties with Poland and other European allies, but they ended in military ignominy and a change of government. Tsar Peter's attack on the Ottoman fortress of

Azov in 1695 and his conquest of much of the Ottoman Black Sea littoral in 1696 briefly reversed Muscovy's situation. Although Muscovy retained its foothold on the Black Sea coast only until 1711, Peter's conquests profoundly altered relationships on and across the steppe by breaking through the northern ring of Ottoman fortresses and inducing serious changes in steppe politics.

The Russo-Turkish War

The exercise of political power at the Muscovite court underwent a significant shift with the death of Aleksei Mikhailovich in 1676. The change was instigated at least in part by the position of Aleksei Mikhailovich's favourite, Artamon Segeevich Matveev, in the waning years of the reign (1671–6). Matveev was unusually powerful, in part because he had personal access to the Tsar, and in part because he held leadership posts in certain key chancelleries. This situation was thoroughly detested by a number of old *boiar* families. Not only was a commoner-favourite close to their prince, but sensitive policy matters could be referred directly to the Tsar, more or less bypassing leading *boiars* in the Duma or Council. Predictably, Matveev was disgraced soon after Aleksei Mikhailovich died. It was an indicator of the growing importance of administrative posts to court politics that the next step was the appointment of new chancellery heads. Acrimonious disputes at court followed. The Miloslavskii clan and its supporters succeeded in gaining ascendancy over the Naryshkin clan, the family of Tsar Aleksei Mikhailovich's second wife. This configuration persisted for most of Tsar Fedor's reign (1676–82). Young and plagued by ill health, the Tsar himself exercised personal control over policy only occasionally.

Muscovy's international position during the mid-1670s continued to be quite tense. Muscovy maintained a precarious hold on its Andrusovo gains against many rivals: the Commonwealth, a resurgent Ottoman Empire, its Crimean ally and, less directly, the peoples of the easterly steppe. It was broadly successful in shoring up its southern defences, re-establishing and then tightening its control over the Don Cossacks and the southern military districts. As a result, although Crimean raids persisted throughout 1673–6, they devastated Ukraine and the extreme Muscovite south; that is, lands lying outside the protection of the extended Belgorod fortified line. The one time that raiders crossed the defences in 1673, their impact was contained – a clear but by no means unique testimony to the continuing effectiveness of the southern defence system.[1]

In an effort to distract the Ottomans from Ukrainian affairs after 1672 (and to exercise some control over the Don Cossacks), Muscovy supported the Cossacks' anti-Ottoman activities in the south-east. While Muscovy was preoccupied by the Razin rebellion of 1670–1, the Ottoman Empire had taken the opportunity to reinforce its garrisons and fortifications on the lower Don, especially at and around Azov. This represented a northward shift in the Ottoman defence perimeter, and it was a significant loss to the Don Cossacks, since it blocked their mobility to the south. After 1672 Muscovy supported Cossack counter-attacks against the Ottomans. Large grain shipments to the Cossack encampment resumed.[2] And, for the next four years, two Muscovite infantry regiments and eight musketeer units remained on the lower Don. As far as possible, their activities were used as a counterweight to events in western Ukraine, where Ottoman armies battled the Commonwealth. Meanwhile, Muscovy attempted to negotiate a supportive international coalition against the Ottomans. It also attempted to build its own fortress on the Don narrows as a challenge to the stronghold at Azov; this effort had to be relinquished, since the Cossacks were as hostile to Muscovite as to Turkish encroachment.[3] An unsuccessful attack on Azov in 1675 led to a reduction in number of Muscovite troops on the Don. By 1677, given a growing need for men on the western front, they were withdrawn altogether.[4]

Undeterred, Ottoman attention in Ukraine focused more and more on Muscovy. Ottoman troops under Mehmed IV were quite successful between 1672 and 1675. By the Truce of Zhuravno in 1676, the Turks gained parts of western Ukraine and Podol'ia. The other Ottoman endeavour in Ukraine, and its support of Hetman Petro Doroshenko, was not as effective. The Hetman's gamble on Turkish and Tatar aide helped to erode his local support and popularity; disaffection was inspired in particular by the presence of Tatar forces in the already devastated territories of the Right Bank. Doroshenko was replaced as hetman in 1674, although he did not abandon the field.[5] In 1676 Muscovy supported an attack by the Right Bank Hetman, Ivan Samoylovych, on Petro Doroshenko's Right Bank fortress town, Chyhyryn. Although Samoylovych's victory did not eliminate all rivals to Cossack leadership, it reinforced his position as effective Hetman of all Ukraine. The reunification of Ukraine under Muscovite auspices was particularly undesirable to the Turks, since it placed Muscovy on the borders of their newly conquered province of Podol'ia. As the Polish conflict concluded, the Ottoman Empire focused more exclusively on Muscovy, gathering its forces for a summer campaign.

This situation quickly resolved indecision among the new policy makers at the Muscovite court. They had been unsure where to concentrate their attentions. Matveev had been associated with Muscovy's engagement in Ukraine. A concurrent war between Sweden, on one side, and Denmark and Brandenburg-Prussia on the other, had attracted the new Tsar's interest. Court factions debated the advisability of entering the northern conflict.[6] In preparation for the 1677 campaign season, Moscow irresolutely distributed its forces along its south-western frontier and also reinforced its Baltic frontier. Debate about changing the direction of Muscovy's foreign policy was arrested by the belated news that a massive Ottoman Imperial army under Ibrahim Shaitan Pasha was moving toward Chyhyryn and Kiev.

The Ottoman Empire was a formidable enemy, at this time in an expansionist phase. It remained virtually invulnerable to full-scale military attack from any single European power. Much has been written about the size of Ottoman forces in relation to individual European armies in the seventeenth century. For its campaigns in Ukraine and the Polish–Lithuanian Commonwealth, the Ottomans fielded armies in excess of 70,000 men. Tatar cavalry from Crimea further swelled their numbers.[7] The Ottoman armies also remained exceptional in their ability to support their forces with food, matériel and weapons, even at a distance from their own frontiers. The Empire's evolving siege techniques, equipment, and trained miners and sappers made its army more formidable still.[8] Muscovy's long-standing reluctance to confront it, even indirectly, was understandable.[9]

By 1677 military change made it more plausible for Muscovy to engage the Porte over Right Bank Ukraine. Muscovy had demonstrated its ability to put a large army and competent artillery in the field. The capacity of its military administration to extract and deliver resources was much improved. The presence of Turkish and Turkish-trained officers in the Muscovite army suggests that Muscovy was informed about recent technological and organizational changes to the Ottoman army.[10]

The Russo-Turkish war (1678–81) began well for Muscovy with a successful defence of its presence in Ukraine. Its troops, led by a foreign commander, joined Cossack forces at the Cossack fortress-capital of Chyhyryn. The Muscovite presence reinforced the loyalty of the Left Bank, restrained Zaporozhian autonomy, protected nearby timber reserves and defended access to the major fortress of Kiev.[11] Another force of about 48,000 Muscovites gathered quickly. Two-thirds of these men were new formation troops; more than half of the total were from the

Belgorod and Sevsk districts, and many had fought in earlier campaigns in Ukraine. Russian commander Romodanovskii's forces were bolstered by Samoylorych's Cossacks, under the Hetman's personal leadership. Muscovite reserve troops stood at Putivl, Mtsensk and Rylsk. Special taxes and in-kind collections paid and prepared the forces.[12]

In 1677 the combined Cossack–Muscovite forces successfully defended Chyhyryn. The natural advantages of the town helped the garrison to withstand an initial Ottoman attack. Sandy soil slowed the Ottoman sappers as they attempted to undermine Chyhyryn's rather flimsy defences, recently 'refortified' by wooden walls packed with earth.[13] Romodanovskii's troops arrived quickly to lift the siege; they were both numerous and the new formation troops manoeuvred effectively on the battlefield. The Ottoman forces pulled back forthwith, although major Crimean attacks on the southern fortified lines continued.[14] The campaigning season over, the Muscovite field army was dismissed to return home.

The Ottomans were not so easily discouraged. Led by the Grand Vezir himself, they returned in major battle array to renew the siege of Chyhyryn the following year with some 70,000 Ottoman troops and supporting Tatar cavalry. Muscovy had not prepared well for a return engagement. Fewer troops were assigned to defend the fortress than in the preceding year, and they were less well supplied. However, a large Muscovite army had been gathered to relieve the defenders of Chyhyryn. Commander Prince Romodanovskii again advanced to meet the Ottomans and break the siege. On this occasion, however, Romodanovskii made the curious, if not fatal, mistake of halting east of Chyhyryn to await further troops; his request to use the nearby reserves commanded by his political rival, Golitsyn, was denied. Despite a spirited if rather disorganized defence led by Patrick Gordon from within the fortress, Muscovite activities around Chyhyryn generally lacked the previous year's commitment and effectiveness. Eventually, Romodanovskii ordered the evacuation and destruction of the Chyhyryn fortress without engaging the main Ottoman forces. His decision was and is the subject of some controversy. The decision to abandon Chyhyryn may have been made in Moscow, choosing to protect Kiev and the borders rather than continuing the costly defence of the Hetman's capital.[15] At the time, however, Romodanovskii bore the blame for the surrender; he lost his command and the court cast about for new leadership for the southern armies.

Despite this important loss, the war was far from over. In 1679 Muscovy again assembled a large force; for the third consecutive year, it included men from central Muscovy, regiments from the southern districts' field troops and garrisons, and Don Cossacks. A sizeable field army moved westward towards Kiev, while other troops were disposed along the defensive line. However, the main Ottoman forces did not conduct a campaign that year. And although Tatar attacks did considerable damage south of the defensive fortifications, they did not cross them.

By 1680–1 neither the Ottomans nor the Muscovites evinced much interest in further battles over Ukraine. In the Treaty of Bakhchisarai, signed in 1681, the Ottoman Empire recognized Muscovite possession of Left Bank Ukraine and Kiev; Muscovy was forced to drop its claim to Chyhyryn and the Right Bank.

Settlement and migration as a wartime strategy

An aggressive policy of colonization and fortification supplemented Moscow's battlefield confrontations with the Ottoman Empire on the lower Don or in Ukraine. Between 1679 and 1681 – that is, during the Russo-Turkish War – Muscovy launched the construction and arming of another defensive line on its European steppe frontier. The Izium line enclosed a V-shaped area south of the older Belgorod fortifications. The top of the triangle was a piece of the old Belgorod line. One arm of the V stretched southward from Userd on the older line; another began at Vol'nyi. These two arms met forming a triangle with its southernmost point near Izium and Tsarev-Borisev. Like its predecessors, its line of wooden palisades, dense forests, ditches and earthworks, interrupted by numerous small fortress-towns, was primarily intended to prevent cavalry attack. The new line protected further Muscovite colonization of the steppe between Belgorod and the Ottoman client state of Crimea.

Construction on the line was directed by the Military Chancellery, at this point led by Duma Secretary Semenev, a career administrator with more than a decade's experience in that chancellery. The construction of the Izium line was coordinated with the fighting of the war and was one of its less obvious but important victories.[16]

Muscovy's battlefield forces were not the primary soldiers in this part of the war. Initially, in 1679, the Izium line defences were built by the field regiments, local garrisons and Cossacks assembled to fight the Ottoman army; they were joined by those few serfs who could be found in the southern regions. The following year, however, it was primarily southern garrison forces that built and guarded the new wall – often as many as 20,000 of them at a time.[17] Even more than the battlefield regiments of the previous year, these troops were profoundly disinclined for any military service that took them away from their own homes and garrisons. Poor men with few resources, they appeared at muster points with little food and few weapons; the small cash supplements they received hardly remedied their problems. When faced with hard labour for a season, desertion rates rose to 50 per cent. Throughout the process, Muscovy's mobilization of resources ranged from barely adequate to impressive. Taxes, for example, were habitually in arrears, often in significant amounts. Repeat or emergency collections and the regular hoarding of large reserves was required to offset the resulting shortfalls, whose existence, but not volume, could be foreseen.[18] Allowances for unpredictability and lack of speed were in this way partially built into the system. However, these men and their fellows remained effective garrison troops in their local fortresses. As the war continued in the west in 1680–1, massive Tatar attacks were again successfully repulsed at the Belgorod defensive line, providing Muscovite leadership with the incentive to persist with its newest, southernmost segment.[19]

Population of the newly opened regions was reinforced by migration from Right Bank Ukraine. In 1679 there were new Muscovite attacks on the Right Bank. Muscovite and Cossack troops burnt villages and drove out their residents, creating a depopulated zone on the Right Bank.[20] With the prolonged fighting after 1654, these new events drove as many as 20,000 Right Bank Cossack families to flee parts of the Right Bank; a few resettled on the Left Bank, but more moved south of the Belgorod defensive line into Muscovy proper. The influx from the Great Expulsion into Muscovy was carefully negotiated. Regiments of newly arrived Ukrainians were offered collective rights to land and some independence of jurisdiction. Their military settlements were then appended to the Belgorod military-administrative district. Some of the settlers from Ukraine helped build the Izium line and a small later extension. Gradually, over the next decades, the 'newly built' line became a more imposing and permanent barrier, more densely settled by migrants, its fortifications expanded and provided with artillery, its leadership largely given over to Ukrainian governors.[21] As a result, the westward-facing Sevsk military-administrative district lost the primacy it had acquired during the wars over Ukraine, and the larger, older, southward-oriented district centred at Belgorod regained importance.[22] In the light of this large population transfer and the defence of its new borders against the Ottoman Empire, Moscow's abdication of claims to Right Bank territory in 1681 hardly seems a failure.

Once building on the Izium line was complete, Muscovy halted its sponsorship of southward colonization into the western Pontic steppe for at least the next 30 years. In fact, in the years following the completion of the Izium line, Muscovy made strenuous efforts to restrict settlement and colonization. It did little to help Ukrainians who lived beyond the defensive line to repel Tatar attacks. Formerly routine offers of loans or support payments to colonizers were no longer forthcoming, and expansion further south was discouraged. Additional defensive lines and sponsored settlement resumed only late in the reign of Peter I.[23]

The hiatus in state-sponsored colonization to the south helped to create and sustain a fragile stability along the southern frontier. With Muscovite southward expansion, the proximity of Muscovite settlement to the Crimean Khanate had already pressured the nomadic peoples of the steppe, provoking and exacerbating open warfare between the empires. As noted in the previous chapter, the Razin rebellion had briefly turned the Cossacks northward, before the Cossacks were themselves gradually incorporated into the Muscovite borderlands. The Great Expulsion and the Izium line consolidated Muscovy's southern frontier after Razin, but as events in Ukraine had already demonstrated, movement into the steppe could go only so far before rousing the Ottoman Empire itself. Indeed, for the rest of the century, it was the battlefield, rather than colonization, that dominated Muscovy's confrontations with the Ottomans and their clients on Crimea. Meanwhile, the narrowing of the steppe set off internecine rivalries among Kalmyk, Nogai and Bashkir, instigating renegotiation of border alliances to the east. The focus of Muscovite settlement shifted eastward – to the Volga, the Trans-Caucasus and western Siberia.[24]

The events of 1677–81 vindicated much of Muscovy's mid-century military reform, confirming the efficacy of Muscovy's evolving military administration and the battlefield superiority of new formation troops. Brian Davies has argued that the battle of Strel'nikov Hill, near Chyhyryn, displayed Muscovy's new troops, their discipline and fighting capability in the open field to advantage. Ottoman and Tatar troops fled in disarray from troops led by two regiments of Moscow Select Infantry whose soldiers remained under arms year-round. More generally, the organization of weapons' use and sorties had been improved, and improved troop discipline was evident in the orderly retreat from Chyhyryn in 1678 with relatively few losses of life and little in matériel. The best of the new formation troops also revealed a new kind of durability and usefulness on the field and, when necessary, new formation troops were still more reliably mustered and replaced.[25] After two campaigns into Right Bank Ukraine, for example, the regional garrison forces and the field army still mustered 100,000 men along the borders for 1679 and 1680.

The war also vindicated (and indeed made excellent use of) jurisdictional expansion of the new military-administrative districts centred at Belgorod and Sevsk. In the latter part of the seventeenth century each of these territories continued to add to its unusually comprehensive regional control over military and civilian affairs.[26] At the same time, technological substitution received some new emphasis. In southern garrison fortresses, artillery was deployed during the Russo-Ottoman War to substitute for garrison troops withdrawn for other purposes; this strategy was fraught with complexities, not least since the artillery in question was not yet standardized. The state began providing weapons for some poor cavalrymen, as well as its continuing provision of arms to the infantry.[27] Shortcomings were equally evident: for example, the elaborate administrative and economic mechanisms devised to diffuse mounting pressures in the southern districts continued to threaten their efficacy, even as they reinforced the homogeneity and relative poverty of district residents.

Finally, a key issue was the important and highly successful coordination of garrison and settlement, on the one hand, with foreign policy and campaign armies on the other. At least in the context of nearly 30 years of conflict over Ukraine and on the steppe, there was remarkable fluidity across that boundary. At its simplest, there was little hard-and-fast separation between garrison and campaign personnel. A variety of personal and policy factors might make a garrison soldier into an infantryman at the next military inspection. In a much broader sense, construction of the Izium line and population transfer directly offset the enormity of the Ottoman military threat and Muscovy's inability definitively to confront it on its own or with a coalition of forces.

These achievements notwithstanding, the disappointments of the war reinforced the need for further change.

Reform?

Between 1678 and 1682 the government of Tsar Fedor Alekseevich instituted a broad set of reforms. Institutionally and politically these changes clearly responded to the ongoing conflict with the Ottoman Empire. Their timing also coincided closely with the period of Tsar Fedor's most independent personal rule. Reforms were still underway when he died in 1682, and some of these were never completely implemented.

Military reform was a key element of, perhaps even the spur to, this effort to standardize and regularize the Muscovite government of the era. A primary goal of military change clearly was to support a sizeable

new formation army. After a half-century of trial and error, a commitment was made to the eventual creation of an army entirely composed of
such units. There were several important components to this effort that
required resolution as part of the standardization process. From a political
perspective, the most complex of these was to redefine clearly and satis-
factorily the future of the service state. In particular, how might the status
concerns of Muscovy's landholding elite, its hereditary servicemen, be balanced with the new kind of military service? In addition to the ordinary
cavalryman, the status and precedence concerns of court and *boiar* families
had to be accommodated within the command structure of a fully new
formation army. The fate of the musketeers (*streltsy*), Cossack and other
contract servicemen in a new formation army clearly involved similar
issues, but they were less politically sensitive. Complex, but quite different, was the need to build upon recent improvements to create a well-
coordinated military administration, supported by regular financial and
other bureaucratic institutions.

Reform began with the milestone decree of December 1678,[28] which
clearly established the standards for elite military service. Notably, these
standards did not abandon social status as a fundamental category.
Rather, elite social status was defined explicitly to include landed wealth,
as well as traditional understandings of hereditary rank and personal
achievement. That social status then became the basis of a new, socially
exclusive vision of military service. Thus membership in the prestigious,
traditional cavalry hundreds (*sotnia*) was reserved for hereditary servicemen of metropolitan rank who owned 24 or more serf households – a
relatively small and select group. All other hereditary elites, the vast
majority, would serve in the new formations. Those assigned to the new
formation cavalry (*reitary*) had not only to demonstrate hereditary status,
they too had to meet a (lower) standard of wealth and offer a record of
loyal and persistent service to the Crown. Meanwhile, regardless of past
position or lineage, hereditary servicemen who were very poor, or those
who had previously shirked their military obligations, served henceforth
in the infantry regiments (*soldaty*) with the commoners.

Appointments based upon this system linked socio-economic position
to military service much more rigidly and explicitly than the more flexible
existing understandings and accommodations.[29] For example, prior to
1678, it was still theoretically possible for provincial noblemen to advance
up the provincial ranks of socio-political and military prominence until
they were appointed to metropolitan rank – serving in the capital city – and
thence to court. In practice, such advancement was virtually unheard of

by the late seventeenth century.[30] In part this was because many provincial servicemen were quite poor; the family lineage of others, particularly those from frontier districts, was questionable. On the other hand, numerous promotions to the capital earlier in the century, the inflation of favours at court in the last years of Aleksei Mikhailovich and the early years of Fedor's reign, and the gradual movement of the uppermost elite into administration, had also clogged the promotion process from above.[31] The reforms formalized the implications of this bottleneck. Servicemen alive in 1678 had to attain metropolitan rank within their lifetimes. Otherwise, access to the metropolis, and to service in the prestigious cavalry hundreds, was forever closed to their descendants. A closed aristocracy of military service would exist within a generation. The implication of the new formation cavalry service was similar – that is, it would remain exclusive to the elites (as defined by the decree). Finally, 'elites' who served in the infantry would quickly lose many traditional markers of their status.

These changes unquestionably assured the eventual dominance of the new formation regiments in the Muscovite army. Beyond that, however, it is clear that Fedor's government could not or did not wish to disassociate socio-political status from military service. Rather, the 1678 decree reinforced those connections: it rigidified and standardized the service state, changes taking place more at its margins than at its core. It reinforced an aristocracy and nobility of service. At the same time, by consigning the bottom echelons of hereditary service to the infantry, the decree distanced them from elite status and its perquisites. It was a politically shrewd reformulation of developing practice, which fulfilled the expectations of those with greatest political clout. It also fit equally with the concurrent effort at rationalizing and standardizing the Muscovite government.

This had important (negative) implications for military performance. Clearly, it made the entire Muscovite cavalry synonymous with a prosperous, landed elite, which was capable of partly or completely supporting itself while on military duty, by drawing on its landed wealth for food, arms and supplies. This was unlikely to produce trained, professional cavalry units, or to improve cavalry manoeuvrability and effectiveness on the field of battle. Trained professional units remained unlikely, if the cavalrymen envisioned by the reform had also to supervise the estates that yielded their private income. Further, the reform assumed in familiar fashion that prosperous landed nobles did not suffer from the general reluctance to serve that had plagued the Muscovite cavalry for nearly a century.

It is not difficult to suggest pragmatic reasons for such a militarily inconsistent result. The 1678 decree provided the Muscovite army with a numerous cavalry without much investment of cash or subsidies, during a period of great financial pressure. War in the south, with numerous Cossack and Tatar forces in addition to trained Ottoman units, included large-scale skirmishing as well as battlefield encounters; perhaps such encounters reinforced different perspectives on cavalry warfare than fighting the Polish hussars or Swedish cavalry units. But it is difficult to escape the conclusion that a vulnerable leadership in 1678 found it politically expedient to meet the social and military expectations of its elite.

The military reforms also had an immediate impact on the status and service of commoners, but showed little regard for their aspirations. As a part of the general effort at standardization, the reform phased out infantry units that did not conform to the new formation model; some older regimental forms were quite abruptly terminated. Various categories of contract service were consolidated to form new formation regiments. Thus Cossacks, artillerymen and others with special landholding or other privileges were assigned to new formation regiments in 1679; alternatively, more numerous officers and the new organizational structures were unceremoniously imposed on existing units. In 1681, for example, numerous provincial musketeer units (*pribory*) were reorganized in conformity with the hierarchical structures of new formation regiments. Their heads (*golova*) became colonels, and any shortage of men was made up with recruits and 'wanderers'. Once Muscovy's prized standing regiments, some musketeers were thus merged into new formation infantry units that did not, for the most part, even pretend to permanence. Infantrymen in other units were impoverished elites or even serfs. Other musketeers, particularly in the capital, retained their older form.[32]

At the same time, nationwide conscription of the peasantry remained the mainstay of new formation infantry regiments. Standardization rather than transformation appears to have been the goal. Although reform gave all infantry units the same structure and command, devices for further professionalization of the infantry were ignored in favour of older methods and greater numbers. The demands for more men to serve in the infantry intensified.[33]

Implementation of the reforms began with a military muster and review throughout Muscovy in 1680. This revealed some important if unexpressed results of reform. The first of these was army size. Muster-reviews typically resulted in an accounting of how many men in Muscovy could be called upon to serve in the army. The number of availables, which had numbered about 50,000 men – excluding slaves – at the end of the sixteenth century, was approximately 100,000 for most of the seventeenth century up to the

1660s. New accounts produced in 1681, however, record more than 200,000 military men available for service. From the time Turkish armies appeared in western Ukraine in the late 1660s, the Muscovite leadership tried to assemble campaign armies of 100,000 or more.[34] Standardization, recounts and more draconian service requirements stemming from the reform clearly made that an easier task.

The muster also produced a different kind of army, with the expected preponderance of new formation troops, but also with a significant increase in the proportions of infantry to cavalry. Availables, as recorded in the 1681 records, were approximately half infantry and half cavalry (49/51 per cent), including remaining musketeers, Cossacks and a few cavalry hundreds. Armies leaving on campaign were for the first time slightly more than half infantry soldiers from 1680 on.[35] Despite the emphasis on new formations and infantry, however, it is notable that the Muscovite armies retained much larger proportions of cavalry than was characteristic for armies further west. Robert Frost has recently argued that, far from being an indicator of 'backwardness', a large cavalry was necessary in east European terrain into the eighteenth century. His contention is supported by the deliberation with which the Muscovite government ensured itself a large cavalry, evidently for military reasons but certainly not for political convenience. That is, the central government explicitly specified the size of the cavalry for campaigns in 1680 and after. By contrast, it did not 'dump' poor or unwanted cavalry into its garrisons – in the southern provinces at least, the numbers of hereditary and retired cavalrymen in garrison towns remained quite consistent before and after the reform.[36]

Practical problems arising during the 1680 muster made the central government's fundamental military interests very clear, even as they augured poorly for the implementation of the reforms themselves. For example, garrison forces were identified as an absolute military necessity, whatever the socio-economic standing of their members. A variety of cash-free, militia-like arrangements were officially sanctioned for the support of restored garrison units. More significantly, the Muscovite elite proved inadequate in size and prosperity to meet the need for cavalry. Given the new army's size and proportions, this was predictable. Even if every one of the 38,000 hereditary service families recorded in 1672 had proven prosperous enough to support cavalry service in 1680, they could not have met regular demands for 50,000 or so cavalrymen. The size of the cavalry in the 1680s took precedence over most other considerations, as clearly demonstrated by Moscow's willingness to stretch and renegotiate its new standards in their first application. When Muscovy announced the number of horsemen it needed, district by district, officials in some districts were unable to identify enough hereditary servicemen who met the standards for cavalry service. With the tacit agreement of the centre, they bent the standards. In the south, men with only a few peasant households were enrolled in the cavalry hundreds (*sotni*); cavalrymen manifestly unable to support themselves were enlisted in the new formation cavalry. But by the end of the muster there were the required 20 regiments, supported by another 10,000 recruits. A total of 16,000 *sotni* remained on the books.[37]

Standardization of elite service, however, continued with a final, dramatic step after the 1680 muster. The remaining cavalry hundreds (*sotni*) were divided into new formation companies, their first officers to be chosen by merit. But this change threatened the status of honour-conscious members of the court. A young courtier of appropriate age and talent might quickly rise in these conditions to a command position over men whose families were of greater status, but who enrolled later because the men of their family were younger or inexperienced. In 1682, by general consensus, the old precedence-ranking system (*mestnichestvo*) for court elite was abolished as part of the drive for greater efficiency and standardization.[38] The political and precedence rivalry that hampered command decisions during the second siege of Chyhyryn can only have urged such a decision. The abolition of *mestnichestvo* was among other things a final element in the military reforms; it reinforced the court's agreement to the consolidation of the new forces and its own integration into the new system.[39] No alternative to precedence could be agreed upon, despite lengthy discussions. Once the abolition was accomplished, however, all Muscovite troops had a common hierarchical command structure.

The problematic, even contradictory, nature of these reforms to the armed forces did not escape contemporary notice. Patrick Gordon, the Scots officer who commanded at Chyhyryn in 1678, lamented the lack of military skill characteristic of the Muscovite cavalry, while conceding that increased emphasis on recruitment and training of the infantry had led to their more disciplined and efficient battlefield behaviour.[40] Foreign officers like him, who had for some time been principal agents of change within the army, were apparently severely disgruntled by reforms to regimental composition and support – and, perhaps, by the introduction of elite young Muscovites into the officer corps. On a significant scale, they objected to the changes, complained about the reform, and applied for permission to leave the country.[41]

Meanwhile, the standardization of military service, status and command was complemented by institutional change. Nine military-administrative districts were put in place across the country, extending those four that worked so well along the Muscovite borderlands: Belgorod, Sevsk, Smolensk and Novgorod. The Tambov district, briefly created in the aftermath of the Razin rebellion, was folded back into the Belgorod military district in 1681. A new and more complete system of military-administrative districts offered a new degree of permanence to army administration across the country. Each district mustered its own troops, with their own cavalry, infantry and artillery. Regional bases for army units represented a new degree of flexibility and army preparedness. Muscovy now knew (fairly) accurately how many men it could muster from each district and with what support. Such useful characteristics of the southern military-administrative districts were quite successfully extended to other parts of the country.[42]

At the centre, three military chancelleries now controlled most military affairs: The Foreign (*Inozemskii*) and Cavalry (*Reitar*) Chancelleries controlled the central regions' infantry and cavalry, respectively, while the Military Chancellery (*Razriad*) governed the various military-administrative districts, primarily along the frontiers. As larger chancelleries consolidated their functions, some smaller ones were eliminated: the Grain Chancellery of the Thirteen Years' War was abolished, for example.[43]

The administrative changes included a serious effort to confront the constantly growing financial demands resulting from Muscovy's larger army. In the last years of Aleksei Mikhailovich's reign, the bureaucracy had already studied Moscow's finances quite carefully. For example, the musketeers' tax was still one of the largest single military taxes, although it was no longer used for its original purpose; its records were reviewed with an eye to recouping arrears. Fedor's reforms simplified financial institutions, and some of the numerous older taxes were united into a new musketeers' tax. The consolidated tax was levied by household in cash. The government also ordered a new census to enumerate and assess the taxable population.[44] Although a multitude of extraordinary, indirect and in-kind taxes persisted, these financial reforms broadly speaking redefined the major tax base and took measures to improve the accuracy of its assessment and the predictability of its collection.[45] As an element of financial reform, Muscovy produced a unified state budget, establishing expected levels of income and expenditure overall for the first time. Military taxation (that is, collections intended explicitly for military use) yielded revenues that paid for approximately half of military expenditures.[46]

A transformation of the fiscal system that might have supported a significant shift to salaried troops was not envisioned.

Rationalization and the creation of a unified budget by all accounts resulted in a general decline in the major taxes. Calculating tax burdens in late seventeenth-century Muscovy is a considerable challenge, but there are some revealing indicators. Taxes still assessed on cultivated land dropped sharply after 1675, as household assessments were introduced. Household taxes, such as the new musketeers' tax, gradually declined soon after their general introduction in 1680.[47] Military rationalization and off-market provisioning had perhaps in a small way reduced the pressure on the state budget. But declining, if more efficiently collected, taxes are also consistent with a relatively weak central government and the end of the Russo-Ottoman War.[48]

Military change under Tsar Fedor Alekseevich produced a very large army of new formation forces supported by a growing permanent military administration. Within the army, the proportions of infantry to cavalry were nearly equal. The reforms also explicitly reinforced the semi-permanent nature of nearly all of Muscovy's (numerous) forces. Financial support for the army concentrated on existing salaries, as well as supply, firearms and matériel for a larger army, rather than upon the creation of more permanent and professional troops.[49] At the same time, the connection between social status and elite military service was standardized and reinforced. While these last two characteristics are perhaps redolent of Muscovy's former army, standardization and new military realities had changed them significantly.[50] These changes as a group apparently responded to Muscovy's ongoing engagement with the Ottoman Empire along its southern and south-western borders; the mixed character of reform also seems understandable in the context of relatively weak political leadership and the complexity of the financial and social questions involved.

Military backlash

The military changes of Fedor's and Aleksei's reigns took place in the context of significant shifts of cultural, social, and political norms – gradually away from personal and clan relationships towards a more bureaucratic state, for example; military change was often directly and causally associated with these shifts. But their relatively piecemeal introduction had not necessarily made them any more palatable.

In 1682 rebellion broke out among the Moscow musketeers, including the Kremlin's palace guard. Some of the musketeers' concerns connected directly to recent reforms. Military change in the seventeenth century had not been kind to the musketeers, and little effort had been made to placate them. Their original character as elite military forces (trained, paid soldiers) had long since eroded into a more relaxed order, in which they received some pay, but trained less assiduously and were reimbursed in part through trading and tax concessions. Not unnaturally, these developments undermined their military usefulness and with it some of their military cachet. The most recent reforms under Fedor had (humiliatingly) converted numerous units of provincial musketeers into ordinary infantrymen of the new formation.[51] Consequently, many musketeers viewed older cultural tropes and military styles more positively than those currently propounded at court. Towards the end of the seventeenth century this inclination was compounded by the presence among them of Old Believers, whose religious concerns included some similar socio-cultural elements.[52] These beliefs and preferences were fanned by immediate complaints. Musketeers were inappropriately treated by their commanding officers, unpaid, and they complained that they were forced to work on their colonels' estates on religious holidays. A complaisant government disregarded their complaints.

Political uncertainty in the capital amplified the importance of the musketeers' discontent. Tsar Fedor died in 1682 without a clearly designated heir, just as their complaints and petitions began to surface. Faced with a choice between Fedor's 15-year old brother Ivan – nearly blind and with inhibited speech – and Fedor's healthy 10-year-old half-brother, Peter, the *boiars* selected Peter, and supported their choice 'by popular acclamation'. But this also meant a political shift at court, away from the Miloslavskii and their supporters, and back to the Naryshkins (relatives of Peter's mother) and their ally, Aleksei's former favourite Matveev.

Conciliatory behaviour toward rebellious musketeers did not defuse the situation. The musketeers persisted. The Miloslavskiis convinced them also to express the fear that some at court were prepared to assassinate Ivan to make way for his brother, Peter, and Peter's reform-minded relatives, the Naryshkins.[53] Several musketeer units and an infantry regiment appeared in the Kremlin, demanding to see Ivan. This sparked a rampage through the capital city, during which musketeers hunted down and killed their political enemies: Romodanovskii, Dolgorukii father and son, a Naryshkin and others.

The rampage brought about immediate political changes. The rebellion itself ended with the surrender of the musketeers, the execution of Prince Khovanskii, popular head of the Musketeer Chancellery, and the restoration of order. The Patriarch staged a public debate over the Old Belief.

Ivan and Peter jointly became tsar. Many of the great families were divided in their support, and government appointments were shared between political opponents. In the aftermath, Peter's eldest half-sister, Sophia, emerged as the dominant figure in a regency government, supported by Prince V. V. Golitsyn. Their political alliance, although it lasted until Sophia's overthrow in 1689, was persistently threatened by rivals, particularly supporters of Peter.[54]

Despite political uncertainty and acrimony in the capital, the new government continued a broadly anti-Ottoman policy. Notably, it scored a major success in completing a network of international alliances for this orientation – the product, in part, of nearly three decades of more intensive Muscovite involvement in east European diplomatic endeavours. In 1682 the Ottomans invaded Hungary with a large force; within the year they were at the gates of Vienna. A Habsburg alliance with the Polish–Lithuanian Commonwealth, Saxony and Bavaria successfully lifted the siege. From 1684 the Holy League united these states in anti-Ottoman crusade with the blessing of the Pope. The allies sought Muscovite support. Sophia and Golitsyn negotiated the domestic and international prerequisites to agreement. In the Treaty of Moscow of 1686, Poland formally relinquished its claim to Kiev, which became part of Muscovy, as did Zaporozhe with its Cossack forces. It was a political highpoint of Sophia's regency, clearing the way for Moscow's cooperation with the Commonwealth in the Holy League.[55] According to the terms of the agreement, Sophia was to help the Holy League in seeking new members and launch a campaign against the Crimean Tatars.

With the agreement in hand, the government undertook two major campaigns against Crimea, one in 1687 and the second in 1689. These offer an excellent opportunity for assessing the state and condition of the Muscovite military at the turn of the seventeenth century.

The first campaign in many respects offered few surprises. The principal command necessarily went to Prince Golitsyn. He was one of a number of leading *boiars* with military experience in the south; he had commanded armies there for two years, before returning to Moscow to claim political leadership.[56] That experience does not necessarily connote skill or involvement in military affairs for their own sake. Elite Muscovites continued to associate socio-political status with military position, choosing its commanders from among families of high standing at court and assuming that these members of the traditional military elite remained the best sources of military leadership; inversely, the political leadership assumed its prerogative (and responsibility) to lead major campaigns.[57] Golitsyn himself was a cultured man with Europeanized taste and the wealth to indulge it; he was also a politician and statesman of considerable skill and standing in the west European communities. He does not appear, however, to have been at all anxious to assume the command of the Crimean campaign, not only because of the political stakes involved but also, perhaps, because of relative personal indifference to battlefield matters.[58]

The army that Golitsyn was to lead began mustering in the south in the spring of 1687. In its *causus belli*, Muscovy made little mention of its European alliance, focusing rather on traditional complaints about raids, slaving and the destruction of property.[59] The gathering army conformed to the 1680 reforms: it was large, numbering more than 100,000 men; two-thirds of them were in the new formation services and the troops were just over half infantrymen. Immediate administrative tasks – mustering the troops, providing food rations, gunpowder and shot as appropriate, standardizing the army's weaponry, and organizing the shipment of these and the cavalry's private supplies – were familiar tasks to the Muscovite bureaucracy, eased by the recent reforms.[60] There were some problems and delays in mobilization; manpower fell short, as reluctant servitors appeared late or not at all. Supplies, too, arrived slowly. The army departed later than expected.

An attack on Crimea through the isthmus at Perekop posed formidable problems. The army had to cross 500–650 kilometres (300–400 miles) of open, in some places nearly uninhabited, steppe. This landscape offered fodder for horses, but next to nothing for human consumption; there were no forward supply depots nor the opportunity of moving additional men and supplies by river. Thus, when the army finally set out, it was a formidable assemblage. The 20,000 carts of the baggage train surrounded the infantry, marching on foot. The next layer of this bulky rectangle was artillery, protected on the exterior by the cavalry forces – the whole measuring approximately one kilometre by two (3/4 by 1¼ miles).[61] The army moved slowly and unwieldly across the steppe. The huge, but very necessary, baggage train slowed the pace of march. The army further devoted every fourth or fifth day to gathering fodder and other necessaries. After more than a month, the army – now joined by Hetman Samoylovych's 50,000-man supporting army – had only reached Konskie Vody (a tributary of the Dniepr above the Zaporozhian Sech).

Steppe-grass fires were sighted south of the army in mid-June. First the Tatars, then Muscovy's Cossack allies, were suspected of setting them. The fires deprived the troops of water and fodder, the two items they were not carrying; these became the deciding factors. The infantry, whose supplies were still more than adequate, advanced to inflict what damage it could, while the cavalry turned back 200 kilometres (130 miles) from Perekop.[62] Whatever the sanguine prognostications about Crimea's vulnerability,[63] the army had little opportunity of demonstrating its battlefield worthiness. There was some irony in this, since it was assumed by all that the Crimean Khanate was unable to withstand battlefield confrontation with Muscovite forces.

Despite the investment of men and resources on a grand scale, the campaign ended in failure. It has been attributed to inappropriate and poor leadership; Golitsyn's pace may indeed have been unwise. Still, it seems obvious that the failure was primarily due to logistical shortcomings. And it was fodder that ran out, rather than the supplies the army undertook to provide. This particular piece of steppe territory offered Crimea serious protection against incursion from the north, and it remained difficult for large Muscovite armies to cross it for another 40 years, at least.[64] The suggestion that the campaign was never meant to succeed seems somewhat implausible, given the scale of the effort. In one way, however, the campaign succeeded. It partly fulfilled Moscow's treaty obligations; Crimea had not sent Tatar cavalry to support the Ottoman army. Muscovy's foreign allies were nonetheless offered an explanation. Hetman Samoylovych was accused of setting the steppe fires to undermine Muscovy's military obligations to the Holy League. Surrounded by Muscovite troops to encourage a proper outcome, the Cossacks replaced him with Ivan Mazeppa.[65]

A second campaign against Crimea in 1689 learned from the first. It was launched amid more explicit references to the Holy League and its goals; Muscovy offered assurances to Wallachia and Serbia of its intention to attack, and consulted the Commonwealth about its military plans. A fortress was built at Novobogoroditsa, at the confluence of the Samara and the Dneipr Rivers, over the intervening period; Muscovite troops met the forces of the Hetmanate there. More importantly, more than 6,000 tons of supplies waiting at Novobogoroditsa replenished the baggage trains. Despite delays in mustering and supply,[66] the Muscovite troops left their base camp much earlier in the year, in a determined effort to avoid extremes of heat and possible steppe fires.

These additional preparations did not prevent a second debacle. By mid May more than 100,000 Muscovite troops were approaching Perekop.[67] Tatar attacks, reportedly with firearms and artillery, were repulsed by massed Muscovite troops and weaponry in *Wagenburg* formation until the armies reached the isthmus. Golitsyn and his subordinate, Gordon, reported that the environs of Perekop had been reduced to burnt out remains, and that the Khan sued for peace. However, fodder and water again ran short. Golitsyn reported that he refused Crimea's terms, allegedly because they were contrary to the Muscovite agreement with the Commonwealth; certainly, he turned his forces homeward. Harassed in retreat by Tatar detachments, water shortage and illness, the army regained Novobogoroditsa in early June. Although less than 500 men had been lost in battle, European mercenary officers estimated that some 20,000 Muscovites had died and another 15,000 had been captured.[68] Crimea remained firmly out of Muscovite reach, independent, and Golitsyn had neither prisoners nor treaty to show for his efforts. Again, neither training, technology, nor even generalship was alone responsible for the defeats; apparently insuperable logistics problems were. Nonetheless, it is difficult to interpret this second Crimean campaign as anything other than a serious political, international relations and military misjudgement.

Despite the attempt to promote the campaign as a victory, the political storm clouds gathered quickly. Political hostility between Peter and Sophia's supporters rose; Golitsyn's control at court slipped, as the Naryshkins moved into greater political prominence. Tsar Peter, now 16, made little effort to assume greater personal power until he was warned of a plot against his life. The Tsar's personal regiments then rallied to him; musketeer regiments were commanded to join him, as were the officers of the Foreign Suburb. After a brief period of hesitation, Sophia ceded power, entering the Novodevichii Convent where she would spend the rest of her life, leaving full personal control to Peter.

Neither the failure of the Crimean campaigns, nor their momentous domestic political consequences, changed the focus of Muscovite policy. Abruptly, in late 1694, Peter, too, turned his forces southward.[69] Although the Crimean campaigns won Muscovy a place in European affairs, interest in the anti-Ottoman alliance had declined by the mid-1690s. Peter persisted, driven by his desire to support the Don Cossacks against Tatar raids, the encouragement of the Church and his own desire for glory.

This first Muscovite attack was simultaneously launched in the west, against the mouth of the Dniepr, and in the east, against Azov. The intention of the two-pronged attack was to limit accessibility from the Ottoman Balkans and block Nogai access to the Crimea. The main attack against Azov allowed the Muscovites to move supplies and men downriver easily, in dramatic contrast to the Crimean campaigns. The 30,000 men in the Azov force included not only Peter's former 'play' regiments, the Preobrazhenskii and Semenovskii Guards regiments, but musketeers

and new formation servicemen still mustered on the regional basis promoted by the 1680 reforms.[70] Peter shared the command with two foreign
officers, Lefort and Gordon, as well as with Artomon Golovin; command
qualifications for these forces differed noticeably from its predecessors.
Nonetheless, the command was disunited and circumstances did not
favour the Muscovite forces. The Empire easily maintained supplies and
reinforcements to the garrison from the sea, and the Tatars effectively
coordinated their efforts with the Ottomans. The first Azov campaign was
a failure.

Muscovite troops withdrew to build and launch a supporting fleet. A
major organizational effort produced warships, galleys and riverboats on
the river docks at Voronezh in a few short months, using local labour and
timber. Both resources and labour were mustered using fairly traditional
Military Chancellery means; the direction of foreign experts and Peter's
personal involvement in naval affairs were new elements. The results were
remarkable for the speed with which they were produced, if not for their
quality. As subsequent events demonstrated, however, the southern fleet
was adequate to its first task.[71]

The second campaign quickly established that the Muscovites had
learned both technique and tactics since the previous year's events. The
army approached the fortress directly, without a parallel attack on the
Dniepr (46,000 Muscovites, again including musketeers, select infantry
regiment and regionally mustered infantry; 20,000 Cossacks and 3,000
Kalmyks). A rolling earthen rampart gave Muscovite artillery, restored to
prominence in part by expert foreign advice, access from above to targets
in town, and Ottoman supply ships were prevented from delivering men
or goods. Muscovite command was united under A. S. Shein, and the
Guards in particular proved flexible and highly mobile. The Cossack
presence proved useful in a variety of ways, especially their small boats'
facility in approaching the fortress. The musketeers, many of whom had
wintered locally, were excoriated by Gordon as unwilling and unskillful.
They would revolt once more in 1698 as a result of the unaccustomed
demands placed upon them and their tsar's apparent preference for the
foreign' troops. Peter's personal and reform-oriented military enthusiasms
were clearly to be seen in these events, although exercised in the context of
earlier policy and administrative orientations. Azov surrendered in June.[72]

The European diplomatic community was indifferent to Peter's victory.
While the Holy League had weakened the Ottomans overall, the conquest
of Azov conveyed no particular immediate advantage to the allies (or the
Muscovites). The Habsburgs withdrew from the Alliance in 1699, signing

the Treaty of Karlowitz. A Muscovite attempt on the Straits of Kerch, to gain access to the Black Sea, was undercut by the news. Muscovite negotiations with the Ottoman Empire began immediately. Azov was ceded to Muscovy for 30 years in return for the destruction of the new Dniepr forts; a number of other Muscovite military and religious requests were denied.

Along the steppe frontier, however, the conquest of Azov by the Muscovites had a different effect. First, the safety of the cities and villages on the new Izium line increased. The Ukrainian population in particular expanded to more than 100,000;[73] only a few of the towns even had Muscovite governors. Shortly, however, the lure of protected and secure lands drew more Muscovites into the region. A new resident regiment was formed towards the turn of the century to the accompaniment of prohibitions against the enrolment of fugitive serfs from Muscovy. After 1692, furthermore, regiments of the Belgorod army formed in this area and prepared for the Azov campaigns.

Even more importantly, 1696 was followed by some accommodation with the Kalmyks; not only did the Kalmyks acknowledge the relative permanence of the Muscovite presence, but the Muscovites judged it to their advantage to negotiate an agreement with them. The Kalmyks had Muscovite help against Kazakh and Karakalpak raiders, while the Kalmyks helped control raids on Muscovy and acted as Muscovite army auxiliaries. The borderlands between the Muscovite and the Ottoman Empires narrowed again, this time north of the Caucasus. The Kalmyks retained a certain freedom of action, but intense pressure on their pasturelands by Muscovite settlement was not many generations away. Muscovite officials vigilantly tried to promote a similar situation still further east as their control shifted. Increasing demands on the Bashkirs for tribute and compliance would shortly pit them against the Kazakhs moving east.[74] The configuration of the steppe politics altered as the steppe frontier zone continued to narrow.

With this background of apparent stability in the south and east, Muscovy's interests under its new tsar turned westward once more. Notwithstanding his reputation for introducing radical change, it is important to remember that Peter I had well-established military traditions behind him as he launched the Russo-Swedish War in 1700. Muscovy could reliably muster the large and replaceable armies it needed to hold off the Ottoman Empire and protect its southern border – using national conscription and an expectation of elite service to produce numerous forces. Its settlement and colonization practices on the steppe were successful if brutal. Muscovy was developing experience with the European diplomatic community. It reliably produced and skilfully used artillery. Its army shared throughout the structure and shape of European forces, and it had a tradition (more than a century old) of professionally trained forces that made abundant use of foreign technology, military advice and culture.

Equally importantly, Muscovy had developed a stable, loyal bureaucracy, able to collect usable resources with some efficacy; bureaucratic coordination and oversight were improving. The seemingly endless years of war during the seventeenth century developed a broad institutional and personal familiarity with the discipline, support and social implications of new formation troops. Decades of incremental change had also pushed to the brink the relationship of the socio-political elite to the new military that had grown under its tutelage. The fortunes of war and military change were fickle at the turn of the eighteenth century, as the Commonwealth's experience made clear. Much would depend upon Peter.

Notes

1 V. P. Zagorovskii, *Belgorodskaia cherta* (Voronezh, 1969), 286.

2 RGADA f. 210, Belgorodskii kn. 81 ll. 1, 3–4; kn. 89 l. 436. Some of this grain was used to feed the Muscovite troops in the area.

3 N. A. Smirnov, *Rossiia i Turtsiia* (Moscow, 1946), vol. 2, 122, 127–9; Zagorovskii, *Belgorodskaia*, 285, n. 14.

4 V. P. Zagorovskii, *Iziumskaia cherta* (Voronezh, 1980), 81–6. Arguably, their efforts had drawn some Ottoman and Tatar resources away from the confrontations in Ukraine; it had also stirred existing steppe relationships. The Russians, however, had reserved both their better troops and their greater numbers for the Ukrainian fighting, and it is difficult to imagine the Ottomans doing otherwise themselves.

5 V. P. Zagorovskii, *Iziumskaia cherta* (Voronezh, 1980), 80; Smirnov, *Rossiia*, 130–2.

6 Paul Bushkovich, *Peter the Great. The Struggle for Power, 1671–1725* (Cambridge, 2001), 86; Muscovy moved more than 45,000 men closer to the border at Narva.

7 Gabor Agoston, 'Ottoman warfare in Europe, 1453–1826', in J. Black, ed., *European Warfare, 1453–1815* (New York, 1999), 132, 136, points out that fiscal and manpower limits to the Ottoman military became apparent in the seventeenth century, as Europeans were increasingly able to match Ottoman

army size. Nonetheless, Ottoman numbers remained high, and difficult for many individual European countries to match. (F. G. Agoston, *Guns for the Sultan* (Cambridge, UK, 2005); A. Corvisier, *Armies and Societies in Europe, 1494–1789*, trans. A. T. Siddall (Bloomington Indiana, 1979), 112.

8 Rhoads Murphey, *Ottoman Warfare, 1500–1700* (Brunswick, New Jersey, 1999), 86, 100–1, 114. With respect to supply, Muscovy would be unable to match its southern opponent well into the next century.

9 In particular, Muscovy refused to support the Cossack conquest of Azov in the 1640s. Smirnov, *Rossiia*, vol. 2, 38, 41–2.

10 Presumably, officers signing south Russian military registers in Arabic rather than in a Slavic or west European language were Turkish or Crimean in training or origin. RGADA f. 210, Belgorod kn. 95 and 100.

11 Smirnov, *Rossiia*, vol. 2, 125; Brian L. Davies, 'The Second Chigirin Campaign, 1678: late Muscovite military power in transition', in Eric Lohr and Marshall Poe, eds, *The Military and Society in Russia, 1450–1917* (Leiden, 2002), 98.

12 *AIIuZR*, vol. 13 (St Petersburg, 1884), docs 21, 33, 63, 69; Zagorovskii, *Iziumskaia*, 92. The Russian commander at Chigirin was Trauernicht.

13 Murphey, *Ottoman*, 113, refers to F. Silahdar, *Tarih* (Istanbul, 1928), vol. 1, 68; also see Smirnov, *Rossiia*, vol. 2, 141.

14 Zagorovskii, *Iziumskaia*, 92–3.

15 *Tagesbuch von Generalen Patrick Gordon*, 3 vols (Moscow, 1849–52), vol. 2, 35–40, 170; Davies, 'The Second Chigirin Campaign', 100–5, 108–11; Zagorovskii, *Belgorodskaia*, 101.

16 Semenov's promotion and title were connected to the power shifts of 1676. See Bushkovich, *Peter*, 84, citing S. K. Bogoiavlenskii, *Prikaznye sud'i XVII veka* (Moscow, 1946), 148–9.

17 Zagorovskii, *Iziumskaia*, 107, 126; A. A. Novosel'skii, *Bor'ba Moskovskogo gosudarstva s Tatarami v pervoi polovine XVII veka* (Moscow, 1948), 116.

18 RGADA f. 210 Belgorod kn. 78, ll. 315–17; Belgorod stlbts. 643, ll. 388–433.

19 Zagorovskii, *Iziumskaia*, 109, 119.

20 When a number of Right Bank cities were recaptured during a brief campaign by Iurii Khmelnytsky, Bohdan's son whom the Ottomans raised in Doroshenko's place.

21 C. B. Stevens, *Soldiers on the Steppe* (Dekalb, Illinois, 1995), 172–3.

22 D. I. Bagalei, *Ocherki po istorii kolonizatsii stepnoi okraine* (Moscow, 1887), 400–7, also cited in Davies, 'The Second Chigirin Campaign', 117; Stevens, *Soldiers*, 172–3; Zagorosvskii, *Iziumskaia*, 213.

23 Novosel'skii, 'Bor'ba', 116; Zagorovskii, *Iziumskaia*, 120–2.

24 Michael Khodarkovsky, *Russia's Steppe Frontier* (Bloomington, 2002), 136–9, 201.

25 Davies, 'The Second Chigirin Campaign', 110–11; Zagorovskii, *Belgorodskaia*, 101; P. O. Bobrovskii, *Perekhod Rossii k reguliarnoi armii* (St Petersburg, 1885), 77ff.

26 A. V. Chernov, 'TsGADA kak istochnik po voennoi istorii Russogo gosudarstva do XVIII v', *Trudy MGIAI* (1948), 118.

27 Stevens, *Soldiers*, Table 5, 172–3; Bobrovskii, *Perekhod*, 78. Cavalry weapons, when provided, were sold as well as given to the men who appeared without appropriate weaponry.

28 *PSZ*, doc. 744.

29 Landed infantrymen who were not of elite status (as well as conscripted serfs, of course) further confused the social implications of military service.

30 A. V. Pavlov, 'Gosudarev dvor v istorii Rossii XVII veka', *FzOG*, vol. 56, 230.

31 See Robert O. Crummey, *Aristocrats and Servitors* (Princeton, NJ, 1983), 177, for example.

32 P. P. Epifanov, 'Oruzhie i snariazheni', *Ocherki Russkoi kul'tury XVI veka* (Moscow, 1977), 128; Stevens, *Soldiers*, 81; A. V. Chernov, *Vooruzhennye sily Russkogo gosudarstva v XV–XVII vv. s obrazovaniia tsentralizovannogo gosudarstva do reform pri Petre I* (Moscow, 1954), 187–90.

33 V. M. Vazhinskii, 'Usilenie soldatskoi povinnosti v Rossi v XVII veka', *Izvestiia Voronezhskogo edinstituta*, vol. 157 (1976), 52–68; Vazhinskii, *Zemlevladenie i skladyvanie obshchiny odnodvortsev* (Voronezh, 1974), 117 n. 102.

34 Richard Hellie, *Enserfment and Military Change in Muscovy* (Chicago, 1972), 269, 272.

35 Infantry were 51 per cent of Golitsyn's army in 1680 and 49 per cent of the total of available men at approximately the same time. P. Ivanov, *Opisanie gosudarstvennago razriadnogo arkhiva* (Moscow, 1842), 71–92; Hellie, *Enserfment*, 269, 272; Chernov, *Vooruzhennye*, 189.

36 Robert Frost, *Northern Wars. War, State and Society in Northeastern Europe, 1558–1721* (Harlow, 1993), 16–18 and elsewhere; Stevens, *Soldiers*, 169–70; cavalry registers in RGADA f. 210 Belgorod kn. 100.

37 RGADA f. 210, Belgorod stolbets 1000, ll. 108–11; Sevsk kn. 18, ll. 70–85; Stevens, *Soldiers*, 169–70; Ivanov, 'Rospis' ratnym liudiam, 1681', in

Opisanie, appendix 10. The same happened in Novgorod. RGADA f. 210 Novgorod stlb. 293, ll. 606–18.

38 The literature discussing the abolition of *mestnichestvo* is quite prolific, including: J. H. L. Keep, 'The Muscovite elite and the approach to pluralism', *Slavonic and East Europan Review*, 48/111 (1970), 201–31; R. O. Crummey, 'Reflections on *mestnichestvo*', *FzOG*, vol. 27 (1980), 269–81; B. I. Buganov, ' "Vrazhdotvornoe" mestnichestvo', *Voprosy istroii* (Nov. 1974), 1118–33; A. I. Markevich, *Istoiia mestnichestva v Moskovskom gosudarstve v XV–XVII veke* (Odesssa: 1888); M. Ia. Volkhov, 'Ob otmene mestnichetsva v Rossii', *Istoriia SSSR* no. 2 (1977) 53–67; V. Nikol'skii, 'Boiarskaia popytka', *Istoricheskaia izvestiia* vol. 2 (1917), 57–87; and Nancy Shields Kollmann, *By Honor Bound: State and Society in Early Modern Russia* (Ithaca, 1999), ch. 6 esp. 226ff.

39 *PSZ*, vol. 2, doc. 905 and the comments of Kollmann, *By Honor Bound*, 227–8.

40 *Tagesbuch des Generalen Patrick Gordon*, vol. 2, 35; *AIIuZR*, vol. 13 no. 152.

41 They were presumably objecting to the dilution of professionalism. See, for example, *Opisanie dokumentov i bumag*, vol. 11, stlb. Belgorodskogo stola, 1680.

42 Chernov, *Vooruzhennye*, 190; Bobrovskii, *Perekhod*, 66. Other, well-entrenched chancelleries in older parts of the country were not easy to override, however.

43 Peter B. Brown, 'Early Modern Russian Bureaucracy: the evolution of the chancellery system from Ivan III to Peter the Great, 1478–1718' (Ph.D. dissertation, University of Chicago, 1978), 485–500; S. K. Bogoiavlenskii, 'O pushkarskom prikaze', in *Sbornik statei v chest' M. K. Liubovskogo* (1917, reprint Dusseldorf, 1970), 367–8; Chernov, *Vooruzhennye*, 188. Siberia was not included in the military districts but had an older, if similarly territorial, jurisdiction.

44 The census was not completed under Fedor; Sophia's government tried unsuccessfully to complete it. A. A. Novosel'skii, 'Kollektivnye dvorianskie chelobit'ia po voprosam mezhevaniia i opisaniia zemel' v 80-kh godakh XVII v.', *Uchenye Zapiski RANIONa*, no. 4 (1929), 107.

45 E. V. Anisimov, *Podatnaia reforma Petra I* (Leningrad, 1982), 34.

46 P. Miliukov, *Gosudarstvennoe khoziaistvo Rossii* (St Petersburg, 1905), 62–7.

47 Richard Hellie, *The Economy and Material Culture of Russia, 1600–1725* (Chicago, 1999), 537, 544, 547. This description applies to assessment rates, of course, not actual rates of collection, which were lower, given some wholesale forgiveness of arrears in this era.

48 See *AAE*, vol. 4, doc. 250 on tax complaints; see Miliukov, *Gosudarsvtennoe khoziaistvo*, 85–92 on 1682 reforms.

49 Bobrovskii, *Perekhod*, 108–9, argues that Muscovy could not in any case have afforded this large a standing army.

50 P. V. Sedov, 'Rossiia na poroge', *FzOG*, vol. 56, 300 describes this as a reluctance to break with 'Old Muscovite principles', which does not take into account either standardization or the development of greater social exclusivity.

51 *Strelets* salaries had also dropped in 1681. Bobrovskii, *Perekhod*, 99 n. 126.

52 Robert O. Crummey, 'Old Belief as Popular Religion: new approaches', *Slavic Review*, vol. 52 no. 4 (Winter, 1993), 700–12.

53 Broadly on the events of 1682: V. I. Buganov, *Moskovskie vosstanie* (Moscow, 1969), 170–90 and the accounts in N. G. Ustrialov, *Istoriia tsarstvovanie Petra velikogo* (St Petersburg, 1858–63), I, 330–46, and Lindsey A. Hughes, *Sophia, Regent of Russia, 1657–1704* (New Haven, 1990), 52–88.

54 Bushkovich, *Peter*, 125–38; N. N. Danilov, 'V. V. Golicyn', *JGOE*, Old Series 2 (1937), 543–8.

55 The Treaty was concluded with broad support. Novosel'skii, 'Kollektivnye', 107.

56 Lindsey A. Hughes, *Russia and the West. The Life of Prince V. V. Golitsyn, 1643–1714* (Newtonville, MA, 1984), 8–14; Zagorovskii, *Iziumskaia*, 213, 218–19. The recent literature on Golitsyn includes Hellie, *Economy*, ch. 24.

57 Crummey, *Aristocrats and Servitors*, 46.

58 Foy de la Neuville, *A New and Curious Account of Muscovy* ed. and intro. Lindsey A. Hughes, trans J. A. Cutshall (London, 1994), 34–5. Golitsyn notably did not manoeuvre himself into the military limelight during the Russo-Turkish War, despite his presence near the front and his undoubted political significance.

59 *PSZ*, doc. 1204.

60 Stevens, *Soldiers*, 89; N. I. Novombergskii, ed., *Ocherki vnutrennego upravleniia . . . : Prodovol'stvennoe stroenie* (Tomsk, 1914), vol. 1, 316–17; Bobrovskii, *Perekhod*, 77.

61 Chernov, *Vooruzhennye*, 197; C. B. Stevens, 'Why Muscovite Campaigns Against Crimea Fell Short of What Counted', *Russian History*, 1–4 (1992), 503. I. N. Kushnerev and A. E. Pirogov, *Russkaia voennaia sila* (Moscow, 1892), vol. 2, 416, Plan 9, offers a drawing of the marching order.

62 Bobrovskii, *Perekhod*, 79; Ustrialov, *Istoriia*, I, 191–211; *Tagesbuch*, vol. 2, 174–5. Gordon reports that water and wood were in short supply even before the fires were sighted.

63 By Patrick Gordon, among others.

64 Stevens, 'Why Muscovite Campaigns'. Initial shortfalls in wages were still large. Bobrovskii, *Perekhod*, 85 n. 98.

65 A. S. Lavrov, 'Novyi istochnik o pervom Krymskom pokhode', *Vestnik SPbGU*, series 2, no. 23 (1994), 14–19; Poland was dissatisfied with Muscovy's performance.

66 Hughes, *Sophia*, 204–5; Chernov, *Vooruzhennye*, 196–8; Ustrialov, *Istoriia*, IV, ii, 487, lists 'failures to appear' for the campaign.

67 Hughes, *Sophia*, 214; Chernov, *Vooruzhennye*, 198.

68 Ustrialov, *Istoriia*, I, 373–4; *Tagebuch*, 1689 *passim*.

69 Supply and other administrative systems remained as before. Novombergskii, *Prodovol'stvennoe*, vol. 2, 322; V. M. Vazhinskii, 'Vvedenie podushnogo oblozheniia na iuge Rossii v 90-khgodov XVII veka', *Izvestiia Voronezhskogo gospedinstituta*, vol. 127 (1973), 90, indicates procedural changes were made largely after the 1696 Azov campaign.

70 Not until 1707–8, in RGADA f. 210 Belgorod kn. 201, does the Belgorod military district record mustering for new, Petrine kinds of forces.

71 Edward J. Phillips, *The Founding of Russia's Navy. Peter the Great and the Azov Fleet, 1688–1714* (Westport, Conn., 1995), 59–70, 85–99; John Perry, *The State of Russia under the Present Tsar* (New York reprint, 1968), 7–11; cf. V. P. Zagorovskii, 'Vopros o russkom morskom flote na Donu', *Trudy Voronezhskogo universiteta*, vol. 53 no. 1 (1960), 163–4.

72 G. P. Herd, 'The Azov Campaigns, 1695–1969', (unpubl. 2001) has translated Patrick Gordon/Charles Whitworth's description of the siege.

73 Orest Subtelny cites 86,000 males in his *Ukraine* (Toronto, 1988), 153.

74 Michael Khodarkovsky, *Where Two Worlds Met: the Russian State and the Kalmyk Nomads, 1600–1771* (Ithaca, NY, 1992), chs 3–4.

PART III

1698–1730

CHAPTER 7

Peter the Great and the beginning of the Great Northern War

There was an affair near Poltava
A glorious affair, my friends
Then, we were fighting the Swedes
Under Peter's banners
Our mighty Emperor
(Everlasting glory be his)
Himself commanded the regiments
Himself charged our cannon[1]

Overview

As Peter Alekseevich Romanov and his co-tsar and half-brother, Ivan, began their personal rule in 1689, the reputation of Russian arms did not stand high either at home or abroad. Incomplete reform under Tsar Fedor, followed by two ignominious retreats from Crimea (1687 and 1689), deflected attention from hard-earned skills and battle-experienced men. The Crimean expeditions were also closely connected to the just-deposed Regent Sophia, which compounded distaste for the military. The army was not recalled to action for six years, one of the longer battlefield lulls in the Russian seventeenth century.

The road back to a major military victory at Poltava in 1709 is the topic of this chapter. As with many a transformative battle, Poltava was won for a variety of reasons. The victory was partly due to Swedish miscalculation, international coalition politics well managed by the Russians, and excellent Russian leadership, but it also resulted from broad changes to the Russian military. Before 1710, however, that process of change was uneven, frequently interrupted, and fraught with political and financial crises.

At first, there was little to distinguish the military policy and activities of the new tsars from their predecessors, except for the personal interest and involvement of the younger man; Peter turned 17 in 1689. He instituted some military changes during the attacks on the Ottoman fortress at Azov in 1695 and 1696, but an acceleration of these efforts became more pronounced with Peter's return from a European trip in 1698 and with the opening of war against Sweden in 1699–1700. At once, the requirements of a war in progress overshadowed all else, as the army took the field against Sweden in its Baltic provinces. Mass military conscription, numerous cavalry regiments, a professional officer corps and manufacturing for military consumption were reinstituted, using seventeenth-century Russian methods. Changes in tactics, structure and a more permanent military force followed from the experiences of war against Sweden. The Tsar and his advisers also proved keen strategists. The administrative elements of building an army were less tractable, despite the relative efficiency of the seventeenth-century chancelleries. Bureaucratic bottlenecks attended some Petrine efforts; financial and political resistance to military needs was disruptive and sometimes dangerous. Successful outcomes depended often on the Tsar's personal attention and on draconian policing. Nevertheless, after the initial defeat at Narva in 1700, the Russian armies gradually captured much of Sweden's Baltic empire. When Russia's Polish–Lithuanian ally was eventually eliminated from the field, Charles XII of Sweden at last turned his forces against Russia proper. The campaign of 1707–9 ended at Poltava in Swedish defeat and Russian celebration.

Beginnings

Peter the Great's personal interest in military affairs was so crucial to Russia's military achievements that even his childhood activities are often heavily emphasized by historians. Two pursuits are typically seen as formative. First, in the 1680s, young Peter created a real infantry unit (called his 'play' regiment), enlisting young courtiers (among others) and making up regimental numbers with men from standing new formation infantry regiments, drilling and even staging real battles with them under the leadership of expert, foreign officers. Such activities, though perhaps not unusual elsewhere in Europe, were unheard of in Muscovy.[2] From the beginning, these soldiers acted as a healthy disincentive to Peter's political enemies, but some of their importance also lies in what they became: a military and social elite, the Guards regiments of the Russian Imperial army. Still later they were key political actors and kingmakers. Second, in addition to his broad, if somewhat unfocused royal education, Peter was a regular visitor to Moscow's Foreign Quarter during his youth and early adulthood. In the Foreign Quarter, he developed firm friendships (with officers Patrick Gordon and François Lefort, for example), an appreciation of things foreign, and an enjoyment of a much freer and more open life than was practical at the royal palaces.[3] The Foreign Quarter was relevant not only because it acquainted Peter with European innovations and practices; by the 1690s there were a number of Muscovites who shared his interest in European culture and practices, although not necessarily with the same focus or to the same degree. Peter's absence from court, however, meant less direct contact with his mother's relatives, the Naryshkins, and with complex court politics. Foreign officers, military favourites and technicians moved into Peter's inner circle; Russian men whose place near the Tsar might have followed directly from their family and heritage were distanced from him.[4] At the same time as Peter's military intentions alienated some, Peter's personal behaviour increased his metaphorical, political and physical distance from kinship politics. Opposition to Peter was therefore but partially based on specific military or policy matters.

Peter and Ivan's joint reign (1689–96) initially followed politically accustomed paths. Of chief foreign concern was the Ottoman Empire. Russia was still a member of the Holy League, an alliance of the Habsburg Monarchy, Russia, the Polish–Lithuanian Commonwealth and Venice, with papal backing, against the Porte. As described in the preceding chapter, Russian forces gathered to attack the Ottoman Empire on the Black Sea coast to besiege Azov in 1695 and again in 1696. The first campaign failed. The second campaign introduced some military changes in the context of familiar Muscovite institutions and practices. Peter's newborn enthusiasm for ships and the sea led Russia to build seagoing ships for use against Azov. Broadly speaking, the labour, resources and skills used to build the new vessels were gathered by established methods. In 1696 technical advice about mining and tactics was offered by European officers in Russian employ. Nevertheless, allied Cossack forces in small traditional boats made a decisive contribution to the conquest of Azov. The successful conquest of Azov and other Ottoman holdings on the Black Sea coast in 1696 was followed by Peter's famous and unprecedented journey, supposedly incognito, to western Europe (1697–8). There he learned practical military skills first-hand and was initiated into the complexities of European diplomacy, as he vainly tried to resurrect the anti-Ottoman coalition.

As these events were taking place, Peter's personal ties to the court, its style of governance and politics eroded further with the death of his mother, Natalia Naryshkina, in 1694 and his half-brother, Ivan, early in 1696. Peter's own style of rule – through a trusted coterie of friends and favourites, and through practical and persistent personal involvement – was clearly established. This new approach was to have significant implications for military affairs.

Russian monarchs had certainly previously demonstrated an interest in military events. Ivan IV, for example, superintended military reform after his army's first defeat at Kazan. Most recently, Peter's father, Aleksei Mikhailovich, had attended Russian armies at the front for several years at the start of the Thirteen Years' War from mobile field headquarters; he had dictated strategy along the Russo-Polish front, exhorted and commanded his generals, managed the complex chancellery machinery in its support of the largest army Muscovy had ever fielded, and very occasionally emerged on the battlefield in person.[5] By the late seventeenth century the military had even become part of the ceremonial representation of the tsar.[6] But Peter changed the kind of attention paid to the military, while raising its intensity to new heights.

Peter's personal style and interests in most things were more practical and participatory than his predecessors'. The military elements of this are part of the Petrine legend: the Tsar earned his promotion up the ranks of his own army (even while he was commander-in-chief), personally worked on the Dutch docks as a shipwright, tested his own military equipment, led his men into battle at Poltava, and got a bullet through his hat for his pains. The young Tsar's relentless energy and assiduous personal attention to details were important elements of his leadership, and his close attention to military and diplomatic affairs was lifelong. As a result, he developed an impressive grasp and expertise in both areas.

His personal involvement carried a political importance beyond his unusual degree of application and knowledge. In particular, after absenting himself from his throne to visit Europe, Peter severely limited his contact with the formal court; he avoided consultation with his central consultative body, the Boiar Duma, and made few appointments to the ranks that comprised it. Instead he invested his great symbolic power as tsar in accomplishing his goals by using very different means. One of these was the heavy reliance upon himself and his inner coterie as present agents and enforcers of the Tsar's will. Thus, Peter not only led the troops at the great battles of Poltava and on the Pruth River. He appeared at otherwise commonplace events to ensure by his presence that his wishes were speedily executed. In the early 1700s the awe-inspiring personal vigilance of the Tsar monitored ordinary musters of hereditary servicemen, to guarantee that young men of high rank did not shirk their military responsibilities because of favouritism or malfeasance.[7] It was a particularly pragmatic and secular display of symbolic power, firmly within the hierarchical context of the military.

Over the next decade, when the Tsar himself was not present to ensure that his will was carried out, a member of his often overworked[8] inner coterie frequently was: Apraksin, Golitsyn, Sheremetev, Lefort, Gordon, Bruce, the great favourite Menshikov, Romodanovskii and others. Many, like his closest associate Menshikov, developed unenviable reputations as a result. This was, in many respects, a version of 'rule by favourites,' which had upset Russia's political balance beginning late in Aleksei Mikhailovich's reign. Peter's avoidance of ranking *boiar* factions helped to shape who supported him and who carried out his commands. Peter certainly did not reject the elite or the aristocracy per se. Many of his inner coterie were themselves members of powerful families, or related by marriage to the Tsar, although a few – notably Menshikov – were not. Still more members of elite families held high military office, despite an initial decline in their numbers in the army.[9] But these men were limited in total number, and their importance by no means automatic because of their social position. Further, the Boiar Duma, its attendant ranks, and its connections to the administrative system were increasingly shunted aside.[10] Thus Peter's inner circle often functioned outside the much-tried political framework of Muscovite Russia, a fact that augured poorly for its survival.

It is perhaps for this reason that Peter's personal power was also charged with a new harshness, even brutality. His political experience began with a musketeer rebellion in 1682; the Tsykler affair uncovered discontent against Peter prior to his departure for Europe. Then, another musketeer (*strelets*) rebellion against new changes and unwelcome responsibilities brought Peter back from his European tour in 1698. The revolt was both suppressed and investigated prior to the Tsar's return. Peter insisted on a new investigation and trial, followed by harsh and public punishment that Peter attended. This demonstration of Peter's determination as well as his brutality was by no means unique. On the most mundane level, the tone of his orders and the retribution invoked for failure to follow them took on a new level of ruthlessness.[11] Prince Romodanovskii became head of the Preobrazhenskii Office, where the 'pretend' tsar was charged with investigating political crimes against the reigning monarch.[12] Later, a network of direct agents of the Tsar appeared, ruthlessly extending Peter's personal oversight. Throughout his reign, there were new institutions and officers for oversight and enforcement; threats, informers, and heavy policing became a constant element in running the Russian state.[13]

The shift in the focus and style of Peter's rule, very marked in the period 1700–9, bore attendant risks. Peter's personal isolation from court politics seemed to require that he and his favourites succeed in their endeavours, so as to justify his avoidance of traditional politics. Elaborate rituals helped to sustain this inside group in their connections to and support of Peter.[14] Still, insistence on compliance with his orders, even brutality toward those suspected of undermining him, became an integral element of Peter's practical personal involvement in reform.

The opening salvos

Despite Peter's best efforts, his European embassy in 1698 revived neither anti-Ottoman sentiment nor enthusiasm for the Holy League among his fellow monarchs. Instead, Russia's perennial concerns about access to the Baltic led Peter to join a fledgling anti-Swedish coalition. He was much encouraged in this by his personal compatibility with Augustus II, Elector of Saxony and newly elected King of the Polish–Lithuanian Common-wealth. Russia's future allies in the anti-Swedish endeavour (Saxony, the Commonwealth and Denmark) had new monarchs, who, like Peter, had not experienced the last round of northern conflict. They also suspected that, despite its high military reputation, Sweden was as overextended as its new monarch, Charles XII, was young and untested.[15] When Russia's Holy League ally, the Habsburg Monarchy, signed a unilateral peace with the Ottomans in 1699, Russia quickly negotiated its own 30-year peace with the Ottoman Empire, to free itself for war against Sweden. Peter took a hand in parts of these negotiations himself.

The Sweden that Russia would fight in the Great Northern War had made important military changes since its glory days in the Thirty Years' War. Although Gustavus Adolphus's army essentially remained, Charles XI had refined it towards the end of the seventeenth century. The core regiments of the Swedish army were still mustered from the central pro-vinces of the Swedish peninsula. There, an army of landless men was sup-ported from their home provinces, where they were also given allotments for peacetime use. Swedes who maintained cavalrymen enjoyed special tax exemptions. The system efficiently maintained an army of defence from a poor agricultural economy. Putting an army in the field for a long time, however, represented exceptional expense, as did the military staffing of the Empire's outposts. These problems were offset by the development of exceedingly aggressive field tactics to hasten the progress of war and by the hiring of mercenaries to supplement the regular army. Towards the end of the seventeenth century, the army was frequently drilled and its techniques updated, but the army was rarely used, while its resources accumulated. Even so, defending the Empire required (and received) some foreign support. Sweden's eastern outposts were the least well defended as Charles XII took power.[16]

As conflict in the north began in 1700, the allies might have expected a short, successful war. Sweden, under its teenage king, was fighting on three fronts simultaneously. But Charles XII, far from the helpless youth his antagonists had hoped, proved a formidable military opponent, and Swedish political and administrative arrangements were both durable and effective. Swedish forces immediately drove the Danes out of the war, even as Russia mustered its opening attack on the Swedish fortress of Narva (on the south Baltic coast at the extreme eastern edge of Estonia/ Estland). Within two weeks, a small Swedish force of 9,000 men under Charles's personal leadership appeared suddenly before Narva to relieve the Russian siege. Europe was unsurprised to learn of the Swedish victory in November 1700; Peter blamed the defeat on raw, untrained troops and outdated tactics. Russian troops blamed their foreign commanders.[17] Charles withdrew through Livonia, relieved the town of Riga of an ineffectual siege by Augustus, annexed Courland, crossed Lithuania, and moved to the western side of Poland proper, into the centre of Augustus's kingdom. To defend Sweden's Baltic possessions, he left behind small Swedish garrisons in a number of fortress towns and General Schlippenbach's army of about 7,000 men.[18]

Even during Great Northern War, observers characterized this withdrawal as rash, if not contemptuous of the Russians.[19] Recent Swedish experience, however, justified Charles's concern with the Commonwealth, given its location and military potential. There were other advantages to locating the main Swedish army in western Poland. It would be near some of Augustus's Polish opponents; Augustus' chief opponents in the Lithuanian part of the Commonwealth, the Sapieha family, were under attack by their fellow Lithuanians. Swedish troops in western Poland also kept watch over the nearby Electorate of Saxony, Augustus's inherited lands. The Saxon army, which Augustus freely used both in Commonwealth conflicts and in the Northern War, was a well-regarded, experienced force of about 25,000 men. Furthermore, while they were in Poland, Swedish troops were richly provided with local food and forage, which was far from the case in their own Baltic provinces. So, Charles remained in Poland, encouraged by deep disagreement and distrust among Commonwealth magnates in both Poland and Lithuania over their king, Augustus II.

For the next five years (1701–6), the Swedes struggled to dethrone Augustus and replace him with a more compliant king who would take the Commonwealth out of the war. Despite numerous, sometimes brilliant, military victories, the process was slow and ineffective. Some credit for this should go to Peter's skilled coordination of Russian military and diplomatic goals. He assiduously bolstered Augustus with troops and cash, which helped keep the Commonwealth conflict alive. His careful treatment of Augustus's supporters, especially in Lithuania, was rewarded, while the Swedes' somewhat dismissive and incautious behaviour toward Polish magnates and institutions did not win reliable allies. In any case, the political conquest of a decentralized, divided and contentious Commonwealth was not at all simple. In so far as the Swedes accomplished it, they did so only by leaving Poland and invading Saxony proper in 1706. The Electorate of Saxony then withdrew from the war, and Augustus was forced to abdicate the Commonwealth throne. Stanislaw Leszczynski, long since tapped as Augustus's pro-Swedish replacement, was left in charge, but he had little real control over Commonwealth affairs.[20]

Reforming the army of the Baltic

While the main contingents of the Swedish army were fighting in Poland, Russian troops remained active in Sweden's Baltic provinces after Narva. They raided Swedish Livonia from their headquarters at Pskov and engaged particular Swedish fortresses. General B. P. Sheremetev, an experienced military officer and an aristocratic cohort of Peter's, won a battle against the Swedes at Erestfer in December 1701. By the summer of 1702 there were more victories at Hummelsdorf, Marienburg in Livonia, and Noteburg on Lake Ladoga.[21] These early victories in and near Ingria (also known as Izhora or Ingermanland, at the eastern end of the Baltic) were often achieved by numerically superior Russian troops attacking relatively isolated fortresses with limited manpower; Russian forces notably avoided larger fortresses. In this process, the Russian cavalry, including dragoons, Cossacks from the Ukrainian Hetmanate and horsemen from Russia's Kalmyk ally, proved tactically and strategically important – something that might not have been expected in warfare further west.[22] While the main

forces of the formidable Swedish army remained enmeshed in Commonwealth affairs, the Russian military continued to make substantial Baltic
gains. Once the mouth of the Neva River had been captured with aid from
a newly created Baltic Russian navy, the foundations of St Petersburg,
famously called Russia's 'window on the west', were laid in 1703. In 1704
Russian troops once again besieged Narva, this time successfully. By 1706,
as Swedish troops finally entered the Electorate of Saxony, Russian forces
had moved across Estland/Estonia, Livonia and even Courland, leaving
only a few major towns and fortresses in Swedish hands.[23]

Russian victories in Sweden's Baltic provinces between 1700 and 1706
have suggested to many that Peter, spurred by the humiliating defeat at
Narva, dramatically reconstructed the Russian military, bringing his army
out of the 'middle ages' into the modern world. This frequently repeated
tale is one that Peter himself promoted. However, it is seriously misleading.
First, of course, Russian troops at Narva were neither 'medieval hordes',
nor undiluted light, mobile cavalry. There had been additions to that
cavalry in the sixteenth century; major institutional, tactical and technological changes in the seventeenth century were followed by Peter's own
early efforts at military reform. In addition to Russian accomplishments
at the sieges of Azov and during Peter's European trip, his preparations
for the Swedish war included calling for volunteer regiments, promising
them year-round pay and supply, as well as dismissing and making new
appointments to the officer corps (certainly, military 'modernization' as
it was then understood).[24] Second, Russia already had four established,
well-trained and well-equipped regiments at Narva, who should have been
unsurprised by the military manoeuvres of most European battlefields.
Peter's two 'play' regiments, now the Semenovskii and Preobrazhenskii
Guards, and two older select infantry regiments numbered some 4,500
men. Since some of these men had served at Azov, and even Crimea, they
were also experienced in battle. They were neither well deployed nor
cleverly used at Narva, but they were there. Disconcertingly, the Swedes
did not use conventional European tactics; their attack was so startlingly
unusual and risky that it surprised experienced western observers;[25] and
it succeeded. Narva, in short, may have inspired Peter's major military
reforms, but neither the battle itself nor the change it inspired were as
transformative as is sometimes suggested.

The pace of military reform did accelerate after 1700, however. Many
of Peter's most effective changes built directly on seventeenth-century
efforts – sometimes innovatively, other times destructively. The Russian
army, after a tentative step in another direction prior to 1704, resumed

the size and proportions of the seventeenth-century Russian military. In practice, this meant that the Russian army had about 100,000 actives, nearly half of whom were cavalry, supported by a growing navy. The size and configuration of the army had extremely important implications, although they may not be immediately obvious.

As in a slightly earlier era, western European armies of the early eighteenth century were predominantly composed of infantrymen. Typically, 75 per cent of an army was foot soldiers, and in individual cases the proportions could be considerably higher.[26] Manoeuvres of well-trained, professional soldiers were increasingly important to strategy and tactics. The great expense of producing such infantry might limit the number of troops a particular state fielded. Cavalry forces, in this model, remained relatively small, playing a supportive role on the battlefield. Since cavalry units were even more expensive to create and maintain than foot, there was little incentive to alter these proportions. In fact, this characteristic distribution of land forces is sometimes used by historians as an indicator of political will, administrative skill and successful military reform in early modern Europe.[27]

In preparing for war against Sweden, Peter appeared to be headed in this same direction. Twenty-seven new infantry regiments were organized in 1699, but only two dragoon units. Three divisions, comprised largely of these new regiments, were sent to Narva, supported by an artillery train. Infantry volunteers in these units were promised year-round support, as mentioned above, while the cavalry was mustered in the old, seasonal style. The army as a whole contained other older-style units, which were half cavalry, as well as auxiliary Cossack and Kalmyk horsemen. Thus the infantry numbers overall were not quite so overwhelming as it appeared during the recruitment process.[28] Nevertheless, Peter's intention of greatly increasing the proportion and training of his infantry seems clear enough.

Within four or five years, however, this goal was deliberately rejected and replaced by another. As Russian successes in the Baltic mounted in 1704–5, the future of the Russian army was under discussion. Russian Field-Marshal Oglivy, hired from the Habsburg Imperial forces for his foreign military expertise, contributed his *Plan and Arrangement for the Army According to Foreign Practice*. It made three important suggestions. First, it argued for consistent regimental size and organization across the army; this suggestion was adopted. Second and third, Oglivy proposed that the Russian army should be smaller overall than in the seventeenth century, with a higher proportion of infantry. This would allow Russia to pay a professional soldiery, creating a smaller but better trained infantry-army. *Foreign Practice* or no, the size and proportions of the army proposed in the plan were rejected.[29] The Russian field army, as of 1705–6, was intended to grow to 33 dragoon regiments, 47 units of foot, the Guards and an artillery train – a very large army with an important cavalry presence. These proportions were quite similar to the Muscovite army of the preceding century, and these proportions remained throughout Peter's reign and for some time after.

The reasons for such a final and durable change of heart were not far to seek. War with Sweden demanded abundant cavalry. That is, in the east European theatre, significant numbers of horsemen were more useful than an overwhelming preponderance of infantry. Cavalry was vital for flexibility and mobility across wide and unpopulated space, for reconnaissance and supply in areas of low population density. This was precisely Russia's experience in the Baltic in 1700–4.[30] Set-piece field battles were uncommon in these years; skirmishing sieges were more frequent. Horsemen protected the infantry lines in siege trenches, blockaded fortresses, scouted the expanses of Baltic territory in rapid raids, and not least secured supplies in relatively unpopulated and desolate lands. The lieutenant of dragoons who in 1703 raided villages for informers, guarded the approaches against enemy troops, attacked Swedish sorties and later protected standing crops in the field, all the while besieging a Swedish fortress, was in no way unusual.[31]

These activities were so valuable that all the major armies of eastern Europe had large cavalry contingents during the second half of the seventeenth century: the Ottomans, the Polish-Lithuanian Commonwealth and Sweden, not to mention Russia.[32] To repeat, this fact was not an outmoded military practice on Europe's eastern edge, but a response to specific local conditions in a wide stripe of eastern Europe; such conditions were infrequent in the more densely populated areas further west. All the above-mentioned armies retained high proportions of cavalry into the eighteenth century. In particular, the Swedish army, 'backward' by no one's definition, was more than half cavalry at the beginning of the Great Northern War.[33] Russia's decision to retain high proportions of cavalry after 1705 was practical. Strategically, it reflected the demands of the Northern War and its Swedish opponent. On the battlefield, cavalry was used for flank attacks and to respond to the Swedes' terrifying, and frequent, attacks with cold steel.[34] Arguably, this was a practical, immediate response to the exigencies of war, as much as a consciously selective approach to European military models.

The practical need for numerous cavalry once met, however, Peter remained very concerned with the demanding task of developing a large, well-trained, reliable infantry. Instructions and regulations for the army included Adam Weyde's Regulations of 1698, which drew on Austrian examples; Golovin's Artikuly of 1700; and Peter's own Rules of Combat of 1708, which later became the basis for tactical instructions in the Military Statute of 1716. They were all directed primarily, if not exclusively, to infantry usages. Indeed, infantry appeared sometimes to define the army: 'Soldier is defined as everyone who belongs to the army, from the highest general to the lowest man', state Weyde's Regulations.[35]

The overall size of the Russian military, itself, had important implications. Simply put, if Russia was to keep large numbers of men in arms, it had first to gather them somehow. As a result, persistent, permanent conscription into the rank-and-file of the army continued to be the bane of Russia's taxpaying population, which was made up overwhelmingly of serfs but also included townspeople, artisans and others. Pressure for more and more men started with Peter's desire for infantry in 1699 and persisted well past Poltava in 1709. Peter began by trying to draw volunteers into military service that first year. As in the seventeenth century, however, Russian society did not have many free men who could join the army, and volunteers never became a major source of the rank-and-file. Instead, conscription resumed in 1699 and continued throughout Peter's reign and after. As in the preceding era, conscription in 1699 took one man from every x households of a particular taxpaying category. For lack of better information, conscription was based on partially updated household lists from 1678. Conscription continued after 1699 in an ad hoc and unpredictable fashion. On one occasion a region's peasants might be quite systematically drafted. A conscription shortfall, military emergency, or vacancies due to desertion (a common problem) could lead to another conscription drive on an overlapping region or different social group. In 1704 disbanded musketeers and their relatives were re-enrolled into fortress garrisons. One man was conscripted from every two households in the Muscovite postal suburbs shortly thereafter.[36] The new Petrine chancelleries lacked both up-to-date information and administrative machinery, so these drafts were frequently less deliberate and more disorganized than those of the seventeenth century. An important difference, however, was that more of the men drafted in the early eighteenth century became permanent members of the military. Serfs taken from their fields, in other words, often remained in the military for a lifetime of service; fewer returned to their fields and families at the end of a season or a campaign, despite the absence of adequate military provisioning and billeting.[37]

Beginning in 1705, however, conscriptions became national and apparently more systematic, with every 20 households producing and, if need be, replacing a single recruit.[38] The principle that a group of households should not only provide recruits, feed and clothe them,[39] but also replace them at need, echoed the Swedish example. The Russians obviously intended to have a more regular and predictable force. However, the Russian national drafts were still not systematically organized. The old Estates Chancellery, where the clerks had previous experience with organizing national conscription, had been avoided as much as possible during Peter's earliest endeavours, but it had to be revived to take on this job. Conscripts (and their replacements) proved hard to track using outdated census materials. Emergencies, desertions and deaths still resulted in part-time, ad hoc and localized drafts, which co-existed with the national, nearly annual, levies.[40] In some cases, cash payments were acceptable substitutes for a recruit. The navy and the cavalry, each of which had other sources of men, also conscripted nationally, but on a different basis. It took 80 households to support a cavalryman, for example.[41] In short, the resumption of national-level conscription did not necessarily prove more equitable or more predictable than its predecessors. As in 1699, however, the men the national conscriptions drew into service were still more likely to serve for life and less likely to return to their farms and livelihoods after a military season or a campaign than their seventeenth-century counterparts.

The proliferation of levies and the welter of different records have left historians uncertain how many men were drawn into the military before Poltava, or during Peter's reign overall. Currently, historians estimate that about 140,000 men were drafted into all the military services before 1710.[42] Over Peter's whole reign some 250,000–300,000 men were drawn into the military from a population of more than 12 million; local and labour drafts may justify raising this estimate slightly.[43] By Euro-Ottoman standards, this was a high percentage. Russia's insistence on a large army thus had a direct social and economic cost: frequent and more permanent conscription of Russia's agricultural and commercial populations.

Whatever the precise numbers, conscription demands were heavy, and poorly received by Russian society. Peasants and townspeople concealed themselves when possible, and evaded what they could, sometimes by fleeing beyond the frontiers; once conscripted, many 'melted away' en route to their regiments or to the front. Serf owners' participation was almost as reluctant; they hid their agricultural labourers and cheated on their support of military men where they could. Desertion from front-line regiments only increased the demands for new conscripts. Estimates for the numbers of deserters varies widely, from 3 or 4 per cent of new conscripts to 20 per cent and higher.[44] As a result, one Petrine addition to the conscription system, besides greater permanence and the vulnerability to conscription of heretofore exempted population categories such as clerks' sons, was once again to increase vigilance and policing of the existing process: conscripts were branded or chained together to prevent their escape, groups of men were made collectively responsible for one another's continuing presence, and deserters were executed if found.[45]

The size of Russia's early eighteenth-century cavalry had very different implications. As in the seventeenth century, the Petrine cavalry continued to recruit men of the old landholding hereditary service class into its ranks through the old-style service muster. In the past, such men had received some cash payments but had also had to rely on their estates and peasants to support and arm themselves; these men and others had played a seasonal role in the armed forces and continued to do so, especially in the very early years of the Northern War.[46] No temporary arrangements, however, could make the elite large enough to fill and maintain 33 cavalry regiments (33,000+ men). Early in Peter's reign, even during the Baltic campaigns, Russia began filling its cavalry regiments with other servicemen (Cossacks and former soldiers) and then with peasant recruits.[47] This was not entirely new. Men who were not part of the hereditary service class also filled the numerous cavalry regiments of the late seventeenth century. After a particular war or campaign, however, at least a cosmetic effort was made to return these men to socially appropriate services. As long as this was so, men with continuous cavalry service could claim the right to service (*pomest'e*) land.[48] Such socially important window-dressing disappeared in the eighteenth century. Apparently, no attempt was made to isolate hereditary servicemen in their own cavalry regiments; nor were mixed cavalry regiments restored to social homogeneity after a campaign. Long years of service and campaigning, rather than a common social background, provided regimental cohesion.[49]

The recruitment and retention of Cossacks, infantrymen with military experience, peasants and urban conscripts in the cavalry ranks had two profound implications. First, the social exclusivity of the cavalry was gone forever. Russian hereditary servicemen still preferred cavalry service, if they had to serve. But the Russian government was unable to rely on them to fill the ranks of the cavalry and was unwilling to keep others out of the cavalry regiments on their behalf. Russia had definitively moved towards a mass army and navy.[50] Second, Petrine cavalrymen, whether hereditary servicemen or not, no longer received service estates or serfs in return for their service; like infantrymen, they were paid in cash. Their salaries were not always issued as promised, and many cavalrymen's salaries were pro-rated for lands they had inherited. Nonetheless, the *pomest'e* system, landholding guaranteed by seasonal cavalry service, whose military significance and economic viability had been in decline for more than a century, changed irrevocably, and with its alteration perforce came greater military permanence and professionalism.

The military, as well as the social, qualities of the Petrine cavalry were unusual. Peter's cavalry regiments were almost exclusively dragoons; a variety and diversity of horsemen remained only in the older-style troops. Russia was nearly unique among contemporary armies in its heavy reliance on dragoons. The dragoons did, however, offer advantages. They were exceptionally adaptable, since they normally acted as cavalry, but could also fight dismounted, as infantry. The Russian dragoon regiments were relatively inexpensive to maintain, because of their regiments' similarity to other parts of the army in size, organization and equipment. Nor did they require large, robust horses, which Russia would have found it most difficult to supply since Russian horses were overwhelmingly light and steppe-bred. Peter later experimented briefly with regular light cavalry forces, but they did not live up to expectations, and the so-called Serbian regiments were never numerous.[51]

As suggested above, Russian dragoons were most immediately effective in their off-battlefield role – as marauders, scouts, and suppliers. While important in the Baltic theatre, these skills were not new. Irregular Cossack and Kalmyk forces were also effective for this purpose.[52] In set battles, the Russian cavalry initially remained quite weak.[53] In part this was because the Northern War made stern demands on horsemen. For one thing, by 1700, the Swedish cavalry used exceedingly aggressive battle tactics. It charged enemy battle-lines at full speed, swords drawn, riding stirrup-to-stirrup in a wedge shape; this *gå-på* (or 'have at 'em') manoeuvre routinely broke attacking lines of infantry and could make slow-firing field artillery nearly useless. Resisting such a charge required considerable training; replicating it, still more. At least for a while, it was the speed, mobility and strategic importance of Russian dragoon units, rather than their tactical abilities on the battlefield, that proved most valuable. Peter and the army command made use of their existing qualities and turned concentrated attention to further improvements in the cavalry quite late in the reign.

Another parallel, most significant change to the Russian army after Narva lay in the officer corps. Here, Peter built on the growing professionalism of seventeenth-century officers, as well as the reorganization of the elite's military role at the end of the preceding century. Deliberate and intensive reform under Peter built on these seventeenth-century roots to yield a thoroughly transformed officer corps by the 1720s. In the late seventeenth century a significant number of new formation officers were professional military: they were salaried 'career' men with a knowledge of their craft. Their presence was partly a result of Aleksei Mikhailovich's hiring of foreign mercenary officers, who had the knowledge to direct military change, but whose social and political standing did not challenge the Muscovite elite. By the 1680s there were 47 foreign colonels in cavalry units and 77 in the infantry, and the political importance of favoured foreign officers was on the rise.[54]

Peter continued to use foreigners as a source of information and professional training for Russian officers and men alike. Their skills, and those of their second-generation descendants, were an important continuing source of informed military practice and policy. However, Russians were increasingly drawn into the command process. Likely candidates for junior officers' posts were unabashedly 'drafted' when hereditary servitors were reviewed at traditional musters. These men, as well as gifted commoners, were promoted up the command structure. Peter's personal insistence on the participation of hereditary servicemen built on seventeenth-century trends and helped to make officers into a social elite. Russians were sent abroad to gain military training and technical expertise. Special Russian schools trained engineers, artillery and naval officers, and a growing insistence on literacy for command posts touched many others. By the 1720s greater confidence in the Russian officers' proficiency and training limited foreign officers to one-third of a regimental command.[55]

Furthermore, a sense of professionalism and direct involvement in the Tsar's military plans was promoted among the highest-ranking Russian officers very early in the Northern War, despite the presence of prominent foreigners. For example, leading generals, senior military and diplomatic staff met together frequently in councils of war to discuss and coordinate both immediate tactics and long-term strategy, often with Peter in attendance. This might be equated with the creation of a general staff, with a written record of deliberations and disagreements. Initially, the senior Russian staff may have used it to overcome any shortcomings in their understanding of Swedish strategy; and Peter may have used it to balance personal jealousies and competition among his closest advisers.[56] In Peter's hands, however, councils of war proved truly remarkable institutional devices: collegial debates that often promoted not only successful but unconventional military planning.

Russian senior officers also oversaw, if they did not command, the activities of many high-ranking foreigners after Narva. For this reason, General Oglivy's dispute with Peter over the abandonment of Grodno in 1706 was conducted with the full knowledge of senior Russian staff. Not only were they present at council meetings but Oglivy communicated with Peter from the field only through Menshikov and Repnin. Sheremetev, in particular, already experienced in military and diplomatic life before Peter, blossomed with Peter's encouragement in the early years into a gifted commander.[57]

This group of changes to the officer corps had some immediate as well as long-term benefits. In tandem with the hiring of foreigners, Russia's immediate need for new officers was in part met by involving many more Russians, of both elite and more ordinary backgrounds. Russian officers developed new skills and an increasing sense of professionalism. Despite a significant shortage of officers at all ranks, the Russian officer corps developed a practical tactical and strategic acumen. This was most immediately reflected in successes in the Baltic to 1705, but it would stand the Russian war effort in good stead in the years immediately following. More significant still, in the long run, was Peter's success in making service in the officer corps a defining element of elite Russian social life, but this would not be evident for some time. Better-trained Russian officers serving year-round arguably had a positive impact on infantry. The highest number of officers was concentrated in this part of the army, where a high officer-to-enlisted ratio had the greatest impact on performance.

In other ways, Peter built well on established Russian strengths. Artillery, for example, had for some time been a Russian forte. Russia already had centres of arms and ammunition manufacture, a specialized artillery corps of *pushkarskie liudi*, and had sponsored some technological innovation.[58] Nevertheless, Russia still imported a substantial proportion of its arms, and it lacked internal standardization, which made the training of specialists and the manufacture of weaponry difficult. The first siege of Narva complicated matters seriously, since ignominious defeat had led to the loss of an entire artillery train of about 180 field and siege guns. Nevertheless, when an elderly Andreus Vinius was ordered to collect all available metal, including church bells if necessary, and provide new artillery for the army, the capacity, skilled labour and technical expertise were largely in place to do so. Urban artisans made the gun carriages, bells were hauled down, the foundries produced new cannon, and Vinius used all the power that his sovereign's personal decree and interest could command. Russian troops under Sheremetev had new ordnance at its disposal by the spring of 1701. This was far from the end of the matter. Jacob Bruce, a Scot whose family had been in Russian service for several generations, directed further improvements. Russian artillery was mobile and flexible. The invention of the horse-pack mortar and the creation of a separate artillery regiment for the army further promoted these qualities. The restored and improved Russian artillery was key to the 1704 Russian conquest of Narva. The metallurgy and arms manufacturing sector continued to produce under pressure, putting new (and increasingly standard) arms in the hands of Russian troops.[59] Although Russia purchased arms abroad until 1712, it became self-sufficient shortly thereafter. A generation later, Russian artillery, according to another observer, was (still) 'the one branch of the military art to which the Russians apply themselves industriously, and in which they have able native-born officers'.[60] Something similar might be argued about the exponential growth of Russia's tiny textile sector as Peter demanded native-made cloth for his army's uniforms.

Changes to the officer corps, adjustment to the size and proportions of the Russian military and even pressure on Russia's small manufacturing sector – these brought useful, even expeditious results, when enforced by the Tsar's personal attention and significant policing. These changes had well-established earlier efforts at their back. Where the groundwork was less thorough or where reform required large-scale institutional change, Peter's efforts in the pre-Poltava period moved fitfully or altogether inadequately. Particularly thorny problems were the financial and other support systems needed to sustain the standing military Peter (and his predecessors) so badly wanted to achieve.

A higher degree of permanence for the military was a new, Petrine phenomenon. Some of the men enrolled in the army in 1700 or 1701 served without interruption until 1721. Others boasted a single absence from the front; many who went home returned to the same units. Although it is difficult to say exactly how many men spent their years in continuous service, a reasonable degree of permanence still represented a major shift for Russians. More trained men remained in the army; more men gained and handed on battlefield experience. As always, this new characteristic did not apply universally to the Petrine military. Incomplete conscription numbers, and ranks thinned by desertion, disease or fighting were often filled by seasonal or temporary draftees.

Recruitment from an appropriate population is not, of course, the only requirement for a standing, permanent military. The men needed salaries, food, equipment and uniforms; and the cavalry required a regular supply of mounts and fodder; the more permanent the troops, the more persistent their needs in this regard. In the years before Poltava, Russia's ability to provide these things for the greater number of men in arms year-round was very much in doubt, and the fiscal and administrative constraints to its efforts severe.

The demands for more cash to pay for salaries, equipment and other military needs became more pressing as war demanded ever greater outlays. Under such pressure, unsurprisingly, little thought was given to expanding those resources, only to their improved extraction through taxation. The state imposed temporary ad hoc measures, as well as more predictable annual taxation, to pay for the army in the Baltic. New extractions were largely imposed in cash; older methods, which included direct collections in kind, were not heavily used. Household assessments on peasant and urban households remained very common until the 1720s. Regular annual payments, sometimes called *podat'*, rose quite abruptly in 1695–1703. In addition, 'companies' of wealthy landholders and churchmen paid collectively for the materials and expert labour to produce a single ship. Other taxes were levied on personal property, such as the collection of 1–5 kopeks per domestic farm animal in Astrakhan in 1704. Individuals were taxed, too, as in the levy on native Siberian populations, the ship tax to launch the navy in 1699, and the tenth tax. Taxes were imposed on letters written by a scribe. Special military taxes, alcohol taxes, customs duties, bridge and road tolls, and a new version of the salt tax were all levied by the Petrine government. Richard Hellie's monumental study lists 44 separate collections imposed on the Russian population by Peter's government during its early years.[61] The bewildering array of taxes, levies and duties was nothing new. Scrounging about to find new sources of surplus in an unproductive agricultural economy was, after all, a long-established way of raising cash and, if need be, goods in kind. Although administrative disarray and the variety of taxes again makes it difficult to calculate exactly the burden on individual households, it has long been believed that there was a broad, sharp, but uneven, increase in taxes levied on ordinary households in the period leading up to 1708–9. When there was still not enough, Peter raised more money by debasing the coinage.[62] This inflated prices, imposing another kind of charge on Russian households. There were still others: in addition to conscription, labour levies withdrew additional agricultural labour power. The first sea-going boats at Voronezh, for example, were built by a draft on the southern provinces; other labour levies built fortifications near Azov, the foundations of St Petersburg and the Ladoga canal. There were also some taxes in kind and requisitioning to feed the troops at the front.

Peter's changes to the bureaucracy that collected taxes or disbursed support to the military did not necessarily help matters. That is, the administrative problems of the early 1700s were not simply inherited with seventeenth-century institutions. In fact, the seventeenth-century chancelleries had generally performed their appointed tasks with some degree of reliability.[63] The organization of the older system as a whole and the limited nature of its abilities may have inherently presaged a kind of administrative crisis.[64] However, Peter's incomplete if frequent reforms to the earlier system generated their own problems. Thus a decree of February 1700 created the Provisioning Chancellery to collect and provide food for the infantry regiments that marched to Narva in September. A national-level provisioning organ was thus created, replacing the territorial organization of partial army supply by the Military Chancellery in the late seventeenth century. The new chancellery created a single provisioning standard for all the troops in its jurisdiction, while the old musketeers' grain collection provided the wherewithal. When this combination of older and newer military chancelleries failed, renewed centralization efforts created the War Chancellery, which after 1701 became responsible for more and more troops. By 1706 some 47 infantry and 15 dragoon troops were within its purview. The subsuming of the Provisions Chancellery into the War Chancellery in 1701 gave the former access to more cash (which was transferred from the municipalities to the War Chancellery), but some older regional grain collections remained untouched under the old Military Chancellery's jurisdiction. Meanwhile, General-Commissar Prince Iakov Fedorovich Dolgorukii, a key overseer of the provisioning process, was captured at Narva and remained a prisoner of war in Stockholm for a decade without being directly replaced; Romodanovskii probably took over many of his responsibilities. Furthermore, three different men held the office of provisioning chief between 1700 and 1708; the office also may have been vacant during that period for as much as a year. When the War Chancellery's efforts, too, proved unreliable, Peter decentralized provisioning in 1708.[65] Recentralization followed in 1711. Meanwhile, the old Military Chancellery and other once-powerful seventeenth-century chancelleries continued to function with diminished responsibilities.[66] As this tangled narrative suggests, Peter's administrative behaviour was of a piece with his political reactions. He was inclined to supersede or avoid the older chancelleries, rather than disbanding or replacing them.

These and similar developments appeared to rationalize and centralize the administration. However, crowding a variety of provisioning arrangements or financial responsibilities into a single institution did not necessarily improve the amount delivered or the process of delivery. Nor, in the early Petrine period, was the added burden of integrating and reconfiguring new institutions offset by the addition of new staff. Skilled clerks and secretaries were in very short supply and not necessarily sympathetic to the changes.[67] The shifting of chancelleries from Moscow to the new capital in St Petersburg may have circumvented administrative cliques who had dominated the older structures,[68] but it did not necessarily improve administrative efficiency. These were among a variety of ways in which the effective (as well as the ineffective) old routines of bureaucratic behaviour and established administrative efficiencies were disrupted. It was a result of such complications that the Estates Chancellery resumed control over conscription in 1705 when it became a country-wide enterprise, while the newer War Chancellery continued to deal predominantly with smaller, local drafts.[69] This transfer of responsibilities emphasizes the degree to which old procedures and separate hierarchies persisted. Continued hypothecation (the allocation of specific revenues to specific purposes) added to administrative complexity and significantly complicated other fiscal goals, such as the creation of a unified budget. The collection of most revenues in cash, while a few others remained in kind, did not improve the situation.[70] The political heads of the institutions handling such matters were frequently Peter's closest cohort, who were often also involved in direct military matters and over-burdened by multiple responsibilities.[71] Administrative chaos thus compounded shortages, and unpredictable resource extraction made it difficult to support a standing military. Policing, although useful in individual situations, did not provide a long-term solution.

It should be noted that administrative and fiscal restraints to military reform, at some level, were the norm rather than the exception for most early modern governments. The need for larger infantry forces that were well trained in the use of firepower placed financial strain even on the comparatively vast resources of the Ottoman Empire.[72] The fiscal constraints of developing a large standing army in the face of political opposition were circumvented in Britain by vigorous international borrowing. French revenue collection was limited by the administrative device of tax farming. The Swedes instituted a kind of local militia system to support their army from a limited agricultural base, but this device required that the army in action be dependent upon the field of action for a significant part of its support.[73] Russia had its own particular difficulties: low productivity, geographic expanse and a limited network of reliable professional administrators. Although the Tsar's court was not united in his support, very limited fiscal accountability served partially to offset these liabilities.

However, large-scale administrative change and new, ad hoc taxation early in Peter's reign probably made provisioning, supply and salary payment less effective than the partial but stable and realistic efforts of the seventeenth century.[74] Peter and others complained that the men were desperately hungry, ill-clothed and their weaponry was of uneven quality. Russian troops requisitioned food and fodder locally and otherwise supplemented state supplies when and how they could. For much of the early part of the war, this burden fell on populations living outside Russia or near its borders.

Russian administrative efforts to increase and stabilize the fisc did not lead to overt political counter-demands. They did demonstrably contribute to large-scale desertions from the army, to the failure to pay taxes and the growth of tax arrears, and to the creation of large, multi-generational households whose taxpaying ability more viably matched the demands made upon them. They also increased social tensions, in so far as they contributed to the flight of serf labour to the freer southern and eastern borderlands.

The southern borderlands

Russia's focus on the army and navy fighting Sweden bore high costs, even beyond the administrative and financial pressures just mentioned. Mass recruitment into the military, when military activity gave every sign of being prolonged or permanent, abruptly disturbed established economic habits and still powerful socio-military distinctions. Economic disequilibrium was felt at several levels of society when men were withdrawn from agricultural labour. Reactions against enforced, lengthy service were voiced immediately and persistently across Russia – in complaining petitions, in reluctance to serve and in outright desertion. Peasants and serf owners were not alone in feeling this change. The merchantry, whose cash reserves made them the targets of a cash-starved state, fared ill during Peter's reign. Nor was permanence appreciated by hereditary servicemen, whose care for their estates accorded ill with their absences at the front.

In the Russian context, military change ineluctably led to long-term alterations in socio-political as well as military status. The declining importance of provincial and low-ranking hereditary servicemen in the seventeenth century was reinforced in the eighteenth by the evisceration of the *pomest'e* system and the social dilution of the cavalry. The status of special contract servicemen also suffered; the musketeers were a case in point. In the aftermath of Azov, for example, the musketeers (*streltsy*) objected not only to continuing duty instead of recuperative winter months at home; they also objected to the gruelling and inappropriate military tasks they had been given at Azov.[75] Their characteristic involvement in the religious and familial politics of the court, where they were ceremonial guards, both emboldened them to use these matters as the standard of rebellion in 1698, and ensured their harsh suppression.

The negative socio-economic impacts of the Petrine military build-up were particularly strongly felt in one region of Russia. The southern and south-eastern frontiers of Russia had long held an economically vulnerable, mobile and volatile military population, which was only gradually being absorbed by the central government. The early Petrine era's economic pressure and standardization efforts, coupled with high manpower demands and declining military status for irregular and old-style troops, had particular impact in these southern borderlands. In 1705 musketeers stationed in the distant but important frontier town of Astrakhan rebelled against local guards and began a massacre of government officials. Rebellion spread; the enforcement of regulations against the wearing of old-style beards and long caftans was cited as a particular grievance. Religious and cultural issues, long the spur to rebellions in the region, were further fuelled by the heavy military taxation, an increase in trading duties and the exercise of monopolies on fish. Astrakhan was a border town. Nomadic, non-Russian and unsettled elements of the population as well as fugitives from both the social code and the legal code of Muscovite society were present in significant numbers there, where they swelled the trading population, disregarded by local authorities. Rebellion spread to similar populations in Cherny and Krasnyi Iar and among marginalized populations along the Terek River, although it was not supported by the large garrison town of Tsaritsyn or the nearby Don Cossacks. To control it, regular army troops were diverted from Courland with General Sheremetev at their head. Although conciliatory offers were made to the rebels of Astrakhan, pressure to return troops to the front quickly took precedence. The town was recaptured, and interrogations, trials and executions continued until 1707.[76]

Nor was the Astrakhan rebellion the only one in this era and region. As Swedish troops moved eastward across Poland in 1707, the Don Cossacks rose in serious rebellion under their hetman, Kondratii Bulavin. As in many previous eras, the Don Cossack lands were a desirable destination for fugitives from central Russia, and the Cossacks saw their lands as a legitimate refuge. Before Peter, Cossack independence was curbed only partly by the presence of registered Cossacks who received a stipend in return for their willingness to serve the Russian state as military auxiliaries. As an element in standardization, the Petrine government discontinued registration and insisted that any fugitives to the Cossack areas who had arrived since 1695 should be returned to Russia proper.[77] This action was bound to generate enthusiasm from central Russian landholders, who anticipated the return of runaway serfs. Any official Don Cossack compliance with these policies, however reluctant, aroused immense hostility among other Cossacks. As on several other occasions, internal Don Cossack disagreements were attached to other local disputes and even international concerns along the open steppe frontier. Bulavin and his supporters made common cause with other hard-pressed men of the borderlands, and the numbers of his supporters rapidly swelled to include Old Believers, shipyard and other labourers, and even sparked negotiations with the Nogai, Tatar and Kalmyk border peoples. There were outbreaks of rebellion as far into the interior as Tambov; Bulavin was elected ataman in Cherkassk and even the Zaporozhian Cossacks in south-west Ukraine made common cause. After one envoy was slaughtered and an army detachment defeated, Prince Vasiliy Dolgorukii (another experienced military aristocrat close to Peter) was dispatched southward with 32,000 regular troops, who were sorely needed elsewhere in the summer of 1708. Bulavin was assassinated shortly thereafter, a victim of internal Cossack politics rather than the Russian army.[78]

This general ferment in the southern borderlands under Peter from 1705 to 1707 was an indirect result of the intensified cultural and fiscal pressure attendant on the Swedish war. The ferment also had direct military causes and brought military consequences. These lands were of recent and almost exclusively military settlement. Petty servitors who aspired but could not quite attain the status of central Muscovites were dominant elements in the highly volatile and deracinated population in these regions. It is notable that the Muscovite government of the late seventeenth century had relied quite heavily on this population, not only as an element in the campaign army, but also as resident defenders against raids from the steppe. The irregulars beyond the border had formed another layer in this quite stable and effective pattern of defences. Because of their usefulness in the seventeenth century, the government had dealt with both these populations in a correspondingly cautious manner when issues of socio-economic and military status arose. By contrast, Peter's army between 1698 and 1709 aspired to be a uniform, permanent force, primarily with the capacity for fighting Sweden. Peter was also concerned with the Ottoman Empire and its armies, but in this early period he was dis-interested in the steppe frontier as such. The Russian army in the early 1700s designated no new forces for steppe defence. Instead all new field troops were uniform regiments who were pressed into service in a variety of ways, from dock building, manning garrisons, seconding to the fleet and front-line battle duties. As military concern with the steppe diminished, so too did the caution with which these border populations were treated.[79] This was not only a socio-political problem, however. Raids from the steppe became increasingly likely, greater volatility developed along the border, and the regular army had to be diverted from its campaign activity to suppress rebellion.

Confrontation

To Peter's dismay, Augustus of Saxony and the Commonwealth had been forced out of the war by the end of 1706. During 1707 the Swedish army under Charles XII moved eastward from Saxony across the Common-wealth toward the Russian border. It would be easy to misread Peter's nervousness as a purely military judgment about the relative quality of his own troops. In 1706 he was evidently even willing to return all his Baltic conquests to end the war, so long as he could retain St Petersburg. But the causes of his trepidation are clearer in a broader political and military context.

First, the instinct to avoid decisive battle was not Peter's alone. Armies all over Europe (and elsewhere) were still raised and put in the field at enormous cost, administrative strain and considerable political risk to the combatant governments.[80] In the event of an important loss, the replace-ment of supplies, matériel, equipment, ordnance and, most of all, skilled and experienced military men put great pressure on societies already at war. In Russia's particular case, a central core of the army had been trained and tested in the field. Russia certainly did not have an efficient system to replace these men in the event of serious failure, however. Creating just the army of 1706 had pushed Russia's administrative and financial systems hard, generating open hostility and serious rebellion. At the same time, Peter had invested much political capital in military success. Peter's reluctance to give battle without some kind of clear advantage was perhaps broadly understandable on these grounds alone.

There were however good things to be said about the Russian army by 1706–7. Russia certainly had battle-hardened troops; many of the officers and their troops had been in the field through several campaigns. The training of new recruits was somewhat more prolonged than a decade earlier, and more of the recruits had become permanent members of the armed forces. Officers' efforts to train their men were bolstered by increasingly precise regulations, even if training manuals were not standardized until 1709.[81] Turnover in the ranks, which could dilute the impact of training and battlefield experience, was muted by interspersing some experienced regiments among new troops.[82] Soviet historians have emphasized Russia's ability to improvise on standard west European battlefield tactics. The Swedes, however, were not known for their adherence to such standards themselves, and the Russian innovation may well have been partly a response to the Swedes. In the context, even had they been very familiar with them, standard west European practices may not have proven appropriate.[83] In any case, Peter, himself a severe critic, was increasingly confident of his army's quality. Foreign observers, too, remarked particularly on the increasing capabilities of the Russian infantry.[84]

It is especially noticeable to the modern-day observer that the Russian command was, by 1707–8, finely attuned to the particular military character and capacities of the Swedish army. Such awareness was particularly important in this case, since the Swedish military did not fight in a typical or predictable fashion. Sweden's army (like Russia's) had quite limited resources at its disposal, even if it was much more efficiently mobilized; it too was raised from a poor agricultural economy. It bears remembering, despite its exploits in Poland and Saxony, that the Swedish army after Charles XI was structured fundamentally to provide homeland defence. As a consequence, its organization and style retained its emphasis on flexibility, speed and mobility as a way of minimizing pressure on its resource base. Reliance on local food and forage was predictably important. The army was tactically unusually aggressive, despite variation among commanders. Under Charles's leadership, the *gå-på* (have at 'em) cavalry tactics already described reached an apogee; even the infantry was unusually likely to rely on speed and cold steel in the attack instead of firepower.[85] When these tactics were paired with the effective use of arms and artillery, they had the advantage of shock and surprise. More than one commander of a perfectly respectable European army was stunned to see Swedish forces appearing at a dead run (or gallop) directly in front of his lines, before a supposedly deadly hail of bullets from his own guns had had time to do its work. The Russian army by 1709 was in many respects honed to fight the Swedes, specifically. The Russian infantry, like the Swedes, kept their pikes and fought with swords as well as guns. Russians continued to emphasize battlefield entrenchments and redoubts as a way of breaking the shock of Swedish attack. The Russian cavalry was trained to use its firearms to that same purpose. As the Baltic campaigns had taught them, the Russians used their own unusual mobility as an important strategic element.[86] The improving quality of Russian troops and particularly their familiarity with Swedish affairs would prove key over the next few years.

As the Swedes crossed Poland, the Russian general staff met with Peter to determine their course of action.[87] A council of war in the village of Zholkiev in April 1707 decided to withdraw Russian troops from the Commonwealth and prepare to meet the Swedes in Russia proper. In so doing, Russia disregarded the desires of its own and Augustus's Polish supporters, the Sandomiercz Confederates, who wished to give battle in the Commonwealth. In addition to staying out of the Polish situation, the Russian army had other reasons to pull back; it planned to destroy crops, supplies and forage as it withdrew, using the Swedish army's reliance on local supplies against it. The council was a superb example of the specific ways in which Russian army reforms had succeeded. The Russian commanders, especially Sheremetev, played major roles in the discussions, although the final decision was clearly Peter's. The final plan made most effective use of the character of the Swedish army and its dependence on local food supplies. It also took advantage of the desolate terrain and underpopulated conditions of Lithuania and western Russia, conditions that made cavalry operations, mobility and flexibility key to the outcome. It made use of the political conditions of Petrine Russia, since it depended for its execution upon the ability of military commanders to enforce the Tsar's command over a wide swath of lands. William Fuller has argued that this plan was an efficient use of Russian geography, that is the wide expanses of empty territory that Charles would cross. Using the 'Russia factor' was not entirely a product of the terrain itself, of course, but also of the sophistication of Russian strategic thinking in exploiting their own military strengths and the weaknesses of their opponent.[88]

As Charles crossed the Russian border, the Swedes were in fighting trim, a force of approximately 30,000 men. Charles considered the battle of Holowczyn, won by the Swedes as they crossed the Vabich River, to be

MAP 9   *The Great Northern War* (adapted from Frost, Robert I., *The Northern Wars, 1558–1721* (Pearson Education, 2000))

militarily one of his best. As Charles approached Russia, however, he was crossing already-well-fought-over terrain, and the Russian forces melted away in front of him, destroying food and forage as they went. Charles had anticipated that supply might be a problem, and a major relief effort was planned. General Lewenhaupt was to join Charles with reinforcements of men and supplies from Sweden. As Charles entered Russia east of Grodno, he was therefore faced with at least two choices: to move directly eastward toward Pskov and thence directly on Moscow – unpromising from the perspective of supply; or to turn southward into richer territory to bring in supplies and possibly allies.

Charles's choice, to turn southward, was not as desperate as it may seem in retrospect. His troops turned south with palpable relief at not having to deal with desolate and empty expanses. Charles himself was confident enough that Lewenhaupt and the relief train would join him that he moved southward before the rendezvous was joined. Finally, along his southern route, Charles had the possibility of support from numerous allies: the Tatars, the Ottomans, the supporters of King Stanislaw in Poland and, most hopeful of all, the probable desertion of the Ukrainian Cossacks to his side.[89]

Russian activities almost immediately put paid to the most sanguine of these plans. At the village of Lesnaia a 'flying division' of the Russian army caught up with the Swedish relief army, while a larger force under Sheremetev shadowed the Swedes' movements. The *corps volant* attacked with nearly 8,000 dragoon and 5,000 mounted infantrymen. Relatively slow because of the need to protect the baggage train, the Swedes were nonetheless slightly more numerous that the Russians. Ironically, it was Russian speed and surprise that won the day as the Swedes circled to protect the all-important supplies. When the smoke cleared, nearly half of the supporting Swedish force was lost. Strategically important was the loss of the supply train, so sorely needed by the main army. It was a triumph for the mobility and flexibility of Russian arms.[90] Only half of Lewenhaupt's force joined Charles's army, and they brought few provisions for themselves or for the main army.

The second element of the Russian strategy did not involve any battlefield confrontations at all, so much as heavy use of their abundant (often irregular) cavalry. Even without Lewenhaupt's supply train, the Swedish army's position seemed quite positive as it turned south. Diarists and others recorded that the army was passing through rich lands. Although the Russians had tried to destroy food and supplies as they moved, the Swedes at first found buried supplies and materials within relatively easy reach. As one of the coldest winters of the eighteenth century set in, however, extreme cold exacerbated growing shortages. At the end of December, men froze to death in their saddles. The creative use of Cossack cavalry tactics by the Russians, at minimal risk to themselves, turned meteorological happenstance to strategic advantage.[91] Limited, Cossack-style raids harassed the Swedes as they ranged further and further from the path of direct march in search of supplies. These encounters were hardly sophisticated affairs, but depended for their effectiveness on speed and frequency. Cossacks' regular appearance not only limited foraging efforts, but also kept the Swedes constantly on alert and in the saddle. Local irregulars and garrison troops from the south-western border fortresses supported the army's efforts in terrain that was particularly familiar to them.

Charles, on the other hand, had had renewed promises of support from the Ukrainian Cossack Hetman, Mazepa, as well as from Leszczynski's forces in Poland. Mazepa may have negotiated an alliance with Sweden as early as March 1708; his defection became known in October and was followed by that of the Zaporozhian Cossack host early in 1709. Although Peter had supported Mazepa in 1703–4 as he occupied Right Bank Ukraine, the Cossack–Russian relationship had been deteriorating for some time over issues such as high Cossack casualties in allied military manoeuvres, Russian and allied treatment of Mazepa and his officers, and the rumoured Russian replacement of the Hetman. Charles had hopes not only of gaining manpower, but the supplies stored at Mazepa's capital, Baturyn.[92]

Hopes of both Cossack and Polish relief were quickly ended by Russia. Once Mazepa's defection was known, both Charles's and Russian troops raced for Baturyn. Russian troops arrived first, sacking the capital, destroying provisions and supplies, and with them much of Mazepa's value to the Swedes. Those Cossacks who joined Mazepa and the Swedes were neither numerous nor very helpful to Charles, who was perhaps less experienced in the use of irregulars than his opponent. Peter himself recovered quickly, turning to his Kalmyk allies for more cavalry. The Commonwealth also proved less helpful to Sweden than anticipated. Charles's already eroding support was dealt a further blow by a major defeat for Leszczynski at the battle of Koniecpol (November 1708). A final half-hearted effort by the Polish King to break through to Ukraine was blocked by Augustus's supporters. It appeared that Charles had not, after all, won the war in Poland. The Zholkiev strategy, backed by Peter's astute and knowledgeable coordination of military movements with diplomatic initiatives, was richly rewarded.

As the main Swedish force made its way southward in the winter of 1708–9, the supply situation, the weather and Russian harassment told heavily on the army's condition.[93] Swedish memoir and other materials record exhaustion, increasing hunger among the troops, death from cold and malnutrition, and declining military capability. Many of the men had not been home since the start of the war. Declining military capability was not exclusively the product of the men's condition, of course. Horses, too, needed fodder and suffered from the cold. Cavalry mounts were in short supply, and powder ran short for both cannon and firearms. To conserve both energy and horses, King Charles ordered cannon to be spiked and abandoned.[94] The Russians certainly did not have everything their way. Although it was easier for them to recoup their losses, the Russians too suffered from the weather, and from manpower and supply shortages. In May, Charles attempted to take the Russian garrison town of Poltava.[95] The Russian army hovered just across the Vorskla River until Peter himself arrived. Inspecting his outposts, King Charles was seriously wounded in the foot by a musket ball. The King did not recover quickly, depriving his troops of personal leadership. After one failed attempt, the Russian army crossed the river in mid-June. It built a fortified camp on the west bank, with little interference from the Swedes, who were concerned not only with Charles's health, but with establishing their own fortifications.

The Russian army, characteristically, immediately fortified its camp, surrounding it with a ditch and *chevaux de frize*. The perimeter of the fortifications had a rampart, with a step to support cannon. Beyond this, a strip of sandy soil about a kilometre (3/4 mile) wide surrounded the fortifications, except where it backed against the river. It was not only the bluffs that made it impossible to approach from the riverside; down-stream, the Vorskla had a marshy wooded bank, which made it difficult to move troops along the river bank to or from Poltava. The new Swedish camp was near the ruined village of Pavlenki, to the north-west of Poltava and to the south-west of the Russians. The only easy communication between the two armies was an open V-shape between two creeks; their banks were marshy and wooded. The Russians entangled nearby under-growth further, so that troops in formation could not pass through, and Cossacks were stationed at the edge of the wood to warn of any approach. Then the Russians built a row of redoubts across the opening between the camps. There were six of these about 150 metres (165 yards) apart. Each had a high earth parapet with a ditch, surrounded in front by *chevaux de frize*. The Russians also began building a second row of

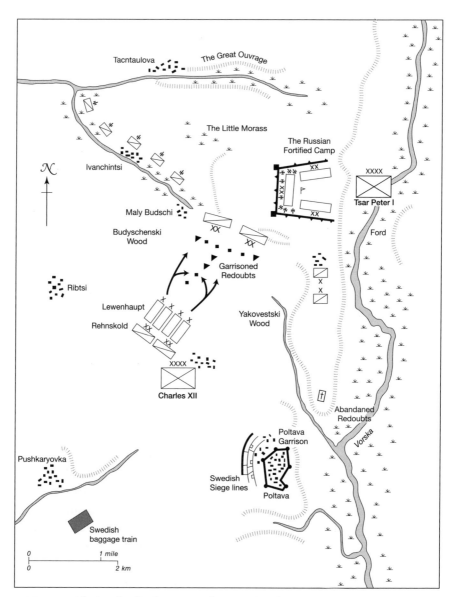

MAP 10   *The Battle of Poltava; initial positions* (adapted from Konstam, A., *Poltava, 1709: Russia Comes of Age* (Osprey, 1994))

redoubts perpendicular to the first, like the downstroke on a T facing the Swedish camp. These four additional redoubts were intended to provide crossfire, placing the Swedes in the uncomfortable position of having to stop to capture them or suffer the consequences of fire from the side or rear. Like the fortified camp, this arrangement was intended to forestall that most impressive and successful of Swedish tactics, attack at the double, and to provide protection for artillery to counteract it; it was also clear evidence of the Russians' tactical preparedness. Only two of these redoubts were complete by 28 June, however.

Although the Russians had chosen and fortified the battlefield, the Swedes had plans to circumvent at least some of the difficulties in their way. Under cover of night, they intended to surprise the redoubts, capture them, and then launch an attack on the Russian fortifications proper; Swedish cavalry was to go around the Russians and blockade them from the north, to prevent their fleeing the full force of Swedish attack. The execution of this plan began poorly. The infantry's night-time start was delayed by waiting for the cavalry to take up position. Belatedly, the infantry was ordered to proceed anyway. However, the redoubts afforded unexpected problems. While the inner columns of Swedish infantry took the first two (unfinished) redoubts while keeping pace with the outside columns, confusion ensued at the third redoubt. A separate battle developed there between Swedish Colonel Roos and the Russian defenders, while the rest of the Swedes moved forward against the final line of redoubts. Some of these were captured, and the attackers pursued the Russians through them towards their own camp. The Swedes reformed with cavalry and infantry to the west of the Russian fortifications, but waited behind a rise in the ground for Colonel Roos's infantry. These men had fared ill. Although the Swedes captured the third redoubt, the Russians quickly discovered that they had no support. Trapped between two large Russian forces, they were unable to break free. By 9.00 a.m., one-third of the Swedish infantry had surrendered without reaching the main battlefield.

In the final stages of battle, the remaining Swedish infantry in a long thin line charged the Russian fortifications in front of them. Encouraged by the news of Roos's surrender, the Russians emerged from behind their ramparts and used their left wing to separate the Swedish infantry from the cavalry that had been just behind it. The Swedish cavalry could not break through, nor could the Russians break them. Fresh Russian units broke the stalemate; they outflanked the Swedish troops and attacked the exhausted Swedes from the rear. The long march south had simply left the Swedes without the luxury of reserve forces. Charles XII was carried from the battlefield and rushed to the Ottoman border, as his troops tried to rally and follow. Even the direct route to their baggage train was blocked by the Russians, who had reoccupied the redoubts after Roos's surrender; the way through the marsh was hampered by Cossack harassment. The Swedes lost some 6,900 men on the field, and another 2,800 were taken prisoner immediately. The Russians had 1,345 killed and another 3,200 wounded.[96] As the Swedes fled, Russian mounted troops (similar to those used at Lesnaia) quickly followed them to Perevolochna on the Dniepr River. There, in the absence of any organized river crossing into Ottoman territory, the remainder of the Swedish army surrendered. At a festive banquet that evening, Tsar Peter toasted those who had so successfully taught him the art of contemporary warfare – the Swedish officers before him.

There was much truth in what he said. The Russians were certainly at considerable advantage at Poltava in numbers and morale. This was the result of deliberate strategy on the Russian side, taking advantage of ill luck and overextension on the Swedish side. Some advantage also lay in Peter's sophisticated grasp of Polish and Ukrainian political diplomatic situations. Peter's ability to head off any rapprochement between Ottomans and Cossacks, on the one hand, and Charles on the other, for example, should not be taken lightly. So much can perhaps be put to the personal credit of the Russian Tsar. Furthermore, Cossack cavalry and a well-trained artillery section had long been elements of Russian military power. Peter put them to good use at Poltava, while Charles lacked the ammunition to use his artillery effectively, and his commanders proved less adept in the use of defecting Cossack forces led by Mazepa. Russian military forces' behaviour on the field of battle against their Swedish enemy was much improved. The infantry stood and fought stolidly, even when faced with the formidable if depleted Swedish line. The Russian cavalry, commanded at Poltava by Sheremetev, acted independently and skilfully. Russian weaponry, especially by comparison with the Swedes', was in good shape. Perhaps most important was the improvement in battlefield discipline. After its victory, the army was still sufficiently well organized to mount the infantry on horses and pursue the fleeing Swedes,[97] demonstrating further the appropriateness and effectiveness of mobility on the east European front.

The Zholkeiv–Poltava campaign may have marked a major shift in Russian strategic thinking.[98] That is, early in the war, the Russian army's goals seem clearly and immediately based upon the conquest of the next fortress, the survival of the next siege. The war for territorial gain was cleverly supported not only by military, but by diplomatic manoeuvring – an element of strategy used by Peter more effectively than by Charles. By contrast, the Poltava campaign was more directly aimed at the destruction of the Swedish army than at the capture of specific territorial points.

The difficulties of any such strategy in early eighteenth-century eastern Europe were already clear to Charles, and undoubtedly became clearer to Peter. The battle of Poltava devastated the core of the Swedish army, since nearly half its soldiers, their families and servants were captured at the Dniepr crossing of Perevolochna. Their king escaped to spend the next five years as virtual prisoner of the Ottomans. One could easily speculate that such a catastrophe would have come close to annihilating the Russian army's ability to fight. Swedish military institutions, however, mustered Sweden's limited resources extraordinarily effectively and surprisingly straightforwardly. Sweden rallied and fought on in defence of its empire and then its heartland for more than a decade. The great battlefield encounter at Poltava put Russia on the European military map, but it did not end the fighting. The Great Northern War was entering a new phase.

Notes

1 My thanks to Zoia Pavlovskii Petit of SUNY Binghamton for bringing this traditional ballad to my attention. I am further indebted to Robert Frost and Paul Bushkovich whose recent works have contributed substantially to my understanding of the Petrine period and its military history.

2 *Vide* the efforts of Friedrich Wilhelm I of Prussia to 'encourage' just such activities in his sons.

3 See the discussion of both topics in N. I. Pavlenko, *Petr velikii* (Moscow, 1990). Of two recent English-language surveys of Peter's reign, Lindsey A. Hughes, *Russia in the Age of Peter the Great* (New Haven, Conn., 2002) explores these elements in greater detail than Paul Bushkovich, *Peter the Great* (Cambridge, 2001).

4 For example, Peter's personal letters as discussed in A. Borozdin, 'Petr Velikii po ego pi'smam v 1688–1703', *Petr velikii. Sbornik statei* (St Petersburg, 1903), 160.

5 Peter B. Brown, 'Tsar Aleksei Mikhailovich as Model Military Autocrat', in Marshall Poe and Eric Lohr, eds, *The Military and Society in Russia, 1450–1917* (Leiden, 2002), 126, 130–1, 136.

6 Richard S. Wortman, *Scenarios of Power. Myth and Ceremony in Russian Monarchy* (Princeton, NJ, 1995), 35, 40.

7 Ivan T. Pososhkov, *The Book of Poverty and Wealth*, trans. and intro. A. P. Vlasto and L. R. Lewitter (London, 1987), 200. Peter's most vehement insistence on noble service came later in his reign, however.

8 For example, Sheremetev's inability to devote time to estate management: E. Zaozerskii, 'Fel'dmarshal Sheremet'ev i pravitel'stvennaia sreda Petrovskogo vremeni,' in N. I. Pavlenko et al., eds, *Rossiia v period reform Petra I* (Moscow, 1973), 175.

9 Sheremetev, Dolgorukii, B. Golitsyn and Shein are obvious examples of early military leadership from members of *boiar* families. Lesser hereditary servicemen also joined the officer corps in large numbers. On the initial decline in their participation, see Richard Hellie, *Enserfment and Military Change in Muscovy* (Chicago, 1972), 369 n. 173.

10 The last meetings of the Duma were in approximately 1704; it was never formally abolished. E. V. Anisimov, *Gosudarstvennye preobrazovaniia i samoderzhavie Petra velikogo* (St Petersburg, 1997), 20–1.

11 RGADA f. 210 Belgorodskii kn. 192 (opis 6A ed. khran. 192, part 1), Smotrennyi spisok, 1705, ll. 21, 27.

12 There are some parallels to the reign of Khan Simeon Bekbulatovich at the behest of Ivan IV. On Romodanovskii's 'reign' see Hughes, *Russia*, 98 citing N. B. Golikova, *Politicheskie protsessy* (Moscow, 1957), 14–16.

13 Tsar Aleksei Mikhailovich had the Prikaz Tainykh Del, but the atmosphere of policing was hardly its exclusive purpose.

14 Ernest A. Zitser, *The Transfigured Kingdom: Sacred Parody and Charismatic Authority at the Court of Peter the Great* (Ithaca, NY, 2004).

15 It took some 18 months for Charles to take matters into his own hands after his father's death; he was also young. R. M. Hatton, *Charles XII of Sweden* (New York, 1968), 76–7, 84.

16 Alf Åberg, 'The Swedish Army from Lutzen to Narva', in M. Roberts, ed., *Sweden's Age of Greatness* (New York, 1973), 268–78.

17 L. G. Beskrovnyi, *Russkaia armiia i flot v XVIII veke* (Moscow, 1958), 188; according to some, the foreign officers still bear a share of the blame. For example, *VIO*, vol. 1, 253, points to Russian forces being drawn up in a single line, the absence of reserves, and the failures of the foreign officers.

18 I. I. Rastunov, ed., *Istoriia severnoi voiny 1700–1721 gg* (Moscow, 1987), 58–9; Åberg, 'The Swedish Army', 286.

19 John Perry, *The State of Russia under the Present Tsar* (London, 1716), 204: an Englishman briefly in Russian employ, commented after the Swedish loss at Poltava that 'the successes that the Czar has since had . . . may in great measure be ascribed to the rash conduct of the young king of Sweden and to his contempt of the Russ forces'.

20 Hughes, *Russia*, 30–1; Robert Frost, *The Northern Wars. War, State and Society in Northwestern Europe, 1558–1721* (Harlow, 1993), ch. 10.

21 *VIO*, 255.

22 Michael Khodarkovsky, *Where Two Worlds Met* (Ithaca, NY, 1992), 138, 141–3, 145.

23 Beskrovnyi, *Russkaia armiia i flot*, 184–200.

24 V. N. Avtokratov, 'Pervye komissariatskie organy Russkoi reguliarnoi armii, 1700–10 gg', *IZ*, vol. 68 (1961), 165; M. D. Rabinovich, 'Formirovanie reguliarnoi Russkoi armii nakanune Severnoi voiny', in V. I. Shunkov, ed., *Voprosy voennoi istorii Rossii XVIII* (Moscow, 1969), esp. 221–3.

25 DeCroys, a Frenchman in command of the Russian troops at Narva, was certainly surprised, as were observers on the Swedish side. Frost, *Northern Wars*, 277; N. G. Ustrialov, *Istoriia tsarstvovanie Petra velikogo* (St Petersburg, 1858–63), IV, ii, 50, 181.

26 Peter Wilson, 'Warfare in the old regime, 1648–1789', in Jeremy Black, ed., *European Warfare, 1453–1815* (New York, 1999), 85.

27 Geoffrey Parker, *The Military Revolution. Military Innovation and the Rise of the West, 1500–1800*, 2nd ed. (Cambridge, 1996), 27, 38, for example, provides one of the earlier discussions; others abound.

28 M. D. Rabinovich, *Polki Petrovskoi armii, 1689–1725. Kratkii spravochnik* (Moscow, 1977) individually lists the new infantry regiments formed before 1704 (80, some disbanded, reconstituted) and the same for dragoons (25 excluding 'irregulars' from the old forces).

29 Christopher Duffy, *Russia's Military Way to the West* (Routledge, 1982), 13, comments only on the change in overall size of the army from the plan, but does not mention the proportions of cavalry and infantry.

30 Porutchik Kartsov, *Voenno-istoricheskii obzor Severnoi voiny* (St Petersburg, 1848), 43–55.

31 RGVIA f. 489 opis 1 ed. khran. 2451, ll. 95–7ob; but see *Pisma i bumagi* vol. 8, 9, doc. 6 while in battle.

32 Angus Konstam, *Poltava, 1709. Russia Comes of Age* (London, 1994), 18; Frost, *Northern Wars*, 246; Rhoads Murphey, *Ottoman Warfare* (Brunswick, New Jersey), 35–49.

33 Frost, *Northern Wars*, 64, 147, 235. German armies followed suit: Ronald G. Asch, 'The Thirty Years' War', in Jeremy Black, ed., *European Warfare, 1453–1815* (New York, 1999), 57; Konstam, *Poltava*, 18; Jeremy Black, *European Warfare, 1660–1815* (New Haven, Conn., 1994), 104, 107.

34 Cf. William C. Fuller, *Strategy and Power in Russia, 1600–1914* (New York, 1992) ch. 2, which argues that Petrine army structure was an 'advantage of backwardness' – despite the similarities to the Swedish army.

35 Angus Konstam, *Peter the Great's Army* (London, 1993), 13; O. Leonov and I. Ul'ianov, *Reguliarnaia pekhota, 1698–1801* (Moscow, 1995), 15–16 and elsewhere.

36 *PSZ*, vol. 4, doc. 1979, (1704); doc. 1996 (1704), 217; John H. L. Keep, *Soldiers of the Tsar, Army and Society in Russia, 1462–1874* (Oxford, 1985), 105; Beskrovnyi, *Russkaia*, 25.

37 Rabinovich, *Formirovanie*, 231.

38 *PSZ*, vol. 4, doc. 2036 (1705), 296; doc. 2050 (1705), 306.

39 *PSZ*, vol. 4, doc. 2038 (1705), 298.

40 Keep, *Soldiers*, 105, points out that these smaller levies were carried out by the new *Voennyi Prikaz* for some years. Eventually, this chancellery absorbed national levies from the *Pomestnyi Prikaz*. A further complication was that Muscovy (and Peter) tended to levy by dividing the necessary number among the available households, with little regard for affordability or realism.

41 *PSZ*, vol. 4, doc. 2023 (1705), 285; doc. 2065 (1705), 313; doc. 2273 (1710), 497.

42 Keep, *Soldiers*, 106; V. N. Avtokratov, 'Voennyi prikaz', in L. G. Beskrovnyi, ed., *Poltava* (Moscow, 1959), 230–2; Beskrovnyi, *Russkaia*, 26.

43 Fuller, *Strategy*, 46; Keep, *Soldiers*, 107. Beskrovnyi, *Russkaia*, 23–9 lists the drafts and their uptake.

44 Keep, *Soldiers*, 114; Fuller, *Strategy*, 46–8. Of a single labour draft in southern Russia in 1705, about one-third fled or evaded. RGADA f. 210 Belgorodskii kn. 187. ll. 383ff.

45 *PSZ*, vol. 4, doc. 2271 (1710), 493; doc. 2281 (1710), 526–7; doc. 2456 art. 17 (1711), 765–71; doc. 2532 (1712), 837–8; Beskrovnyi, *Russkaia*, 30–1.

46 Richard Hellie, 'Petrine army', *CASS*, vol. 8 (1974), 246.

47 Rabinovich, *Polki*, docs 579–80, for example.

48 Cf. A. Tan'kov, ed., *Istoricheskaia letopis' Kurskago dvorianstva*, vol. 1 (Moscow, 1913), 42 which discusses *pomest'e* holding for the Cossack leadership.

49 I am indebted to Marshall Poe and Eric Lohr, the organizers of a conference: 'Military and Society in Russia', Harvard University, Sept. 2000, and my fellow participants for their comments in the course of a discussion of the social content of the Russian armed forces under Peter I. Also see

C. B. Stevens, 'Evaluating Peter's army', in Poe and Lohr, eds, *The Military and Society*, 147–75.

50 Ia. E. Vodarskii, 'Sluzhiloe dvorianstvo v Rossii v kontse XVII-nachale XVIII v.', *Voprosy voennoi istorii Rossii XVIII i pervaia polovina XIX vekov* (1969), 233.

51 Rabinovich, *Polki*, docs 535–8a.

52 The Kalmyks were the more disciplined horsemen. L. J. D. Collins, 'Military organization and tactics of the Crimean Tatars in the sixteenth and seventeenth centuries', in V. J. Perry and M. Yapp, eds, *War, Technology, and Society in the Middle East* (Oxford, 1975), 275. The Cossacks felt themselves ill used. Theodore Mackiw, *English Reports on Mazepa* (New York, 1983), 35.

53 L. G. Beskrovnyi, 'Strategiia i taktika', in L. G. Beskrovnyi, ed., *Poltava; sbornik statei. K 250-letiiu Poltavskogo srazheniia* (Moscow, 1959), 59, 61; Iu. R. Klokman, 'Severnaia voina, 1700–21', in L. G. Beskrovnyi, ed., *Stranitsy boevogo proshlogo* (Moscow, 1968), 73–114.

54 Frost, *Northern Wars*, 234; A. Z. Myshlaevskii, 'Ofitserskii vopros', *Voennyi sbornik*, vol. 247 (1899), 298–9.

55 P. O. Bobrovskii, *Perekhod Rossii k reguliarnoi armii* (St Petersburg, 1885), 166; *PSZ*, vol. 4, doc. 2319 (1711), 591–3; M. D. Rabinovich, 'Sotsial'noe proiskhozhdenie i imushchestvennoi plozhenie ofitserov reguliarnoi Russkoi armii v kontse severnoi voiny', in N. I. Pavlenko et al., eds, *Rossiia v period reform Petra I* (Moscow, 1973), 154.

56 Hellie 'Petrine army', 244–5; Fuller, *Strategy*, 71–3.

57 Zaozerskii, 'Fel'dmarshal Sheremet'ev', 189.

58 Hellie, *Enserfment*, 184–5.

59 *VIO*, 285; Baiov, *Istoriia Russkoi armii* (St Petersburg, 1912), ch. 1, 15.

60 C. H. von Manstein, *Contemporary Memoirs of Russia from the Year 1727 to 1744* (London, 1968), 44–7, 94–5.

61 Richard Hellie, *The Economy and Material Culture of Russia, 1600–1725* (Chicago, 1999), ch. 23.

62 Evgenii V. Anisimov, 'Remarks on the fiscal policy of Russian absolutism', *Soviet Studies in History* vol. 28 no. 1 (1989), 18.

63 Borivoj Plavsic, 'Seventeenth-century chancelleries', in W. Pintner and D. Rowney, eds, *Russian Officialdom. The Bureaucratization of Russian Society from the Seventeenth to the Twentieth Centuries* (Chapel Hill, NC, 1980), 44–5, and, on military supply matters, C. B. Stevens, 'Why Muscovite Campaigns Against Crimea Fell Short of What Counted', *Russian History*, 1–4 (1992), 487–504.

64 E. V. Anisimov, *Gosudarstvennye preobrazovaniia i samoderzhavie Petra velikogo* (St Petersburg, 1997), 86–9.

65 Avtokratov, 'Voennyi prikaz', 228–45; V. N. Avtokratov, 'Pervye komissariatskie organy Russkoi reguliarnoi armii, 1700–1710', *IZ*, vol. 68 (1961), 163–88; Bobrovskii, *Perekhod*, 141.

66 RGADA f. 210 Belgorod kn. 201 (1707–8).

67 A. N. Medushevskii, 'Petrovskaia reforma gosudarstvennogo apparata. Tseli, prevedenie, resul'taty', in F. Shelov-Kovediaev, ed., *Reformy vtoroi polovine XVII–XX vv* (Moscow, 1989), 64–70; A. N. Medushevskii, 'Reformy Petra Velikogo v sravnitel'no-istoricheskoi perspecktive', *Vestnik vysshei shkoly* (1990) no. 2, 79–83; no. 3, 70–93.

68 Medushevskii, 'Reformy', 70–1.

69 Beskrovnyi, *Russkaia*, 26; *PSZ*, vol. 4, doc. 2020, 284–285.

70 A comparative summary is offered in Simon Dixon, *The Modernization of Russia, 1676–1825* (Cambridge, 1999), 63–4.

71 Paul Bushkovich, *Peter the Great* (Cambridge, 2001), 252, 252 fn.73 notes problems caused by the absence of one individual holding many key posts; Golovin in this case.

72 Gabor Agoston, 'Ottoman warfare in Europe, 1453–1826', in Jeremy Black, ed., *European Warfare, 1453–1815* (New York, 1999), 135.

73 Peter Wilson, 'European warfare, 1450–1815', in Jeremy Black, ed., *War in the Early Modern World* (Boulder, Col., 1999), 177–206, provides an excellent overview of the problem.

74 Hellie, 'Petrine', 244.

75 Graeme P. Herd, 'The Azov campaigns' (unpubl. 2001).

76 Hughes, *Russia*, 454–7; A. V. Chernov, 'Astrakhanskoe vosstanie, 1705–1706', *IZ*, vol. 64 (1959), 186–216.

77 *Pisma i bumagi Imperatora Petra Velikago* (St Petersburg, 1887), vol. 6, 9–10.

78 Narratives in Hughes, *Russia*, 475–8; Paul Avrich, *Russian Rebels 1600–1800* (New York, 1976), part III; E. P. Podiapol'skaia, *Vosstanie Bulavina, 1707–1709* (Moscow, 1962).

79 C. B. Stevens, *Soldiers on the Steppe* (DeKalb, Illinois, 1995), ch. 4, conclusion, on seventeenth-century status and its accommodation.

80 That is, it required a major effort of political will to raise, for a second time, the relatively vast amounts of cash involved in creating an army of trained men or a seaborne navy.

81 P. P. Epifanov and A. A. Komarov, 'Voennoe delo', *Ocherki Russkoi kul'tury XVIII veka*, 3 vols (Moscow, 1987), vol. 2, 197–200; Beskrovnyi, *Russkaia*, 129–30.

82 Rabinovich, *Polki*, docs. 283, 300, for example; Stevens, 'Evaluating', 161.

83 Brian L. Davies, 'The Development of Russian Military Power', in Jeremy Black, ed., *European Warfare, 1453–1815* (New York, 1999), 170; Beskrovnyi, *Russkaia*, 130–5, 168–70; Zolotarev, *VIO*, and elsewhere.

84 Simon Dixon, ed. and trans., *Britain and Russia in the Age of Peter the Great* (London, 1998), doc. 263; Walter Pintner, 'Russia's Military Style. Russian society and Russian power in the eighteenth century', in Anthony Cross, ed., *Russia and the West in the Eighteenth Century* (Newtonville, Mass., 1983), 262–71.

85 Assessments of Charles XII as a strategist and tactician differ widely. See Knud J. V. Jespersen, 'Warfare in the Baltic, 1500–1800', in Jeremy Black, ed., *European Warfare, 1453–1815* (New York, 1999), 197; Hatton, *Charles XII*, 245, on the Russian campaign, and 511–22, esp. 521, more generally.

86 Fuller, *Strategy*, comments on the 'backwardness' of some of these tactics, 82–3. Cf. Leonov and Ul'ianov, *Regulairnaia pekhota*, 29, on the use of pikes against the Swedes after 1708.

87 There are many accounts of the Poltava campaign. For a short, reasonable English version, see Konstam, *Poltava, 1709* and Peter Englund, *The Battle of Poltava that Shook Europe* (London, 2003) for the Swedish perspective. A longer recent Russian account is in *VIO*, vol. 1, ch. 7, part 4. Also see Rostunov, I. I. et al., *Istoriia severnoi voiny, 1700–1721* (Moscow, 1987).

88 Fuller, *Strategy*, 79.

89 Hatton, *Charles XII*, 268–73.

90 Baiov, *Istoriia Russkoi armii*, 32–5.

91 A. A. Kernovskii, *Istoriia Russkoi armii* (Belgrad, 1933), ch. 1, 44, comments on Russia's skilful use of Cossack forces in other, perhaps more standard, circumstances.

92 Theodore Mackiw, *English Reports on Mazepa* (New York, Munich, Toronto, 1983), 31–7.

93 *VIO*, vol. 1, 258.

94 Englund, *The Battle that Shook Europe*, 49–50, 89, and following.

95 *VIO*, vol. 1, 262.

96 These disparate numbers, among other things, suggest that the battle of Poltava was not quite so closely matched as it is sometimes suggested. Personal communication, Paul Bushkovich, and subsequent survey of RGVIA f. 490.

97 Hellie, 'Petrine army', 241.

98 Pavlenko, *Petr*, 281.

CHAPTER 8

Military institutionalization after Poltava

Overview

The Russian victory at the battle of Poltava was celebrated with vigour, enthusiasm and relief. Public celebrations featured classical images of Peter as Hercules, triumphal arches and Roman historical references, fireworks and parades. The publication at home and abroad of engravings, maps and battle depictions trumpeted the news to those unable to attend.[1] Poltava was the end of an old era and the start of a new, self-consciously European one. Foreigners as well as Russians were quick to grasp the emergence of a newly confident north-European power. Less obvious after Poltava was Russia's move away from Peter's ad hoc military changes to the institutionalization of its new abilities.

Despite the victory at Poltava, the decades following proved militarily and politically trying for Peter's government. For one thing, bringing the Swedish war to a satisfactory close was a complex business, involving not only Russia's newly demonstrated military prowess, but also the negotiation of changing diplomatic configurations throughout north-eastern Europe. The institutional strengths of the Swedish military state, despite a major defeat and, until 1714, an absent king, contrasted favourably with uneven Russian efforts. The entry of the Ottoman Empire into the fray led to a profound and disturbing defeat for Russian arms in the campaign of 1710–11. The battle on the Pruth River revealed serious shortcomings in the Russian military, and it was an important catalyst of the military reorganizations that followed. The events of that brief Russo-Ottoman War forced the Russian government to reconsider military needs along its steppe frontier, rather than focusing so exclusively on its battle regiments near the heartland and in the north-west. After Poltava, permanent and stable Russian institutions developed gradually and unevenly to support the heretofore rather chaotic functioning of the Russian army and navy. Meanwhile, once the Swedish war was over in 1721, a new round of fighting erupted in Persia, 1722–4.

This chapter argues that the political and institutional adjustments being completed in the 1720s were crucial elements in Russia's eighteenth-century military transformation, since they solidified the economic and social framework within which the Russian army and navy acted. The social and fiscal transformations, in particular, are as important as the victory at Poltava in understanding the early eighteenth-century Russian military change and its survival after Peter. In some cases, these lasted until the Great Reforms of the 1860s and 1870s, when serfdom was abolished and Russian institutions were accordingly reconfigured.

Institutionalizing change

In the immediate aftermath of Poltava, Russian victories in the Baltic resumed. Augustus of Saxony returned to the throne of the Polish–Lithuanian Commonwealth, supported by a new Russian alliance. Denmark re-entered the war against Sweden. Russian troops took Elbing and cleared Karelia of Swedish regiments; Viborg was taken, ensuring the safety of the new Russian capital of St Petersburg. Riga fell in 1710. The rapid spread of plague through adjacent Baltic territories helped doom the remaining Swedish garrisons, which capitulated quickly to the Russians. By October, Reval had fallen, and Swedish troops left both Livonia and Estonia. Peter signed special agreements with large Baltic towns to consolidate Russian control. The towns and their surrounding provinces were depopulated, devastated by disease and years of war; Russia hoped to gain loyalty, as well as to encourage renewed trade and prosperity.[2]

Although these military activities were key to Sweden's ultimate defeat, Peter had other things on his mind in the years following Poltava. One persistent concern remained the administrative underpinnings of war: how to recruit, pay, feed and supply Russia's men at arms. Changes made to the administrative apparatus prior to Poltava had again failed to produce reliable institutions of military supply and support.

At first glance, more draconian and stringent enforcement seem to have been Russia's principal method for dealing with this problem. The military recruitment process, which remained essentially the same from 1705 to 1724, is a case in point. As before Poltava, conscription drives varied in scope and intensity: they might take one recruit from 20 urban households, or multiple conscriptions might gather men for specific purposes (grenadiers for the King of Prussia) or from particular regions (from around Moscow). The Russian government continued to tinker with recruitment norms, but the broad inequities and inconsistencies of conscription remain unresolved. In 1722 Peter exempted newly converted indigenous Siberians from service, so that it would not deter them from converting to Orthodoxy.[3] More and more conscripts were required to serve for life.[4] Meanwhile, it was hoped that fines, collective responsibility for recruits and the branding of conscripts would help in dealing with the chronic problem of desertion; local officials could be punished as traitors to the Empire if they failed to deliver the appropriate number of conscripts on time; and the roads where recruits passed were specially guarded.[5] The death penalty was invoked against those who harboured fugitives.[6] Meanwhile, free men (landholders and free servicemen) mustered for service in the established way; their service too became life long, and their participation was more stringently monitored.[7]

In fact, enforcement was not the only or even the principal change in this or other military support systems. Positive efforts were made to limit desertion by improving the treatment of recruits, for example, although these commitments were honoured only intermittently.[8] More profound was the prolonged, and eventually effective, attempt to address administrative ineffectiveness in the years after Poltava. Peter's impatient avoidance of established administrative procedures and institutions, during the military and political crises before Poltava, had not improved Russia's ability to support its military. Significant failures in supply and pay systems persisted; outright requisitioning transferred some of Russian troop maintenance to the localities where they fought; elsewhere, men went hungry. The need for more reliable and permanent arrangements was obvious.

Administrative consolidation and reform began shortly after Poltava. Initially, the central administrative apparatus itself remained untouched. Instead, between 1707 and 1710 some military administration was again relocated, moved out of the capitals and away from the purview of the central chancelleries. Russia was divided into large new territorial units, *gubernii*, under the leadership of governors. The new governors had civilian titles, but their responsibilities revolved heavily around the Empire's fiscal and military needs.[9] Each *guberniia* had army regiments directly assigned to it. (Confusingly, each regiment at the same time received a territorial name that did not correspond to its *guberniia* assignment.)[10] The *guberniia* to which a regiment was assigned then became responsible for providing it with new recruits, horses, salaries for men and officers, supplying uniforms and so on. A local war commissar, who collected the *guberniia*'s contributions, maintained contact with a *guberniia* representative who marched with the regiment. The head of the war commissariat, the local commissar's titular superior, supervised this system as he travelled with the army. In the same way, support for the artillery, navy and even the diplomatic apparatus was tied directly to the taxpayers.

These arrangements decentralized military administration dramatically. Decentralization allowed rapid local responses to internal threats, such as the Bulavin rebellion in 1708, as well as much more direct administrative supervision over the support of the field army. There were fewer opportunities for unnoticed malfeasance and misdirection. Decentralization, however, also undermined oversight and coordination by the central chancelleries. Governors were responsible directly to the Tsar and then to the Senate, created in 1711 during Peter's absence with the army, and these were the principal links between the *gubernii* and the centre. However, the Senate itself was neither permanent nor completely operational in 1711, but remained an institution in flux even after the events of that year.[11]

The *guberniia* reforms did, however, have one unusual new attribute. Military and fiscal decentralization did not themselves constitute an unusual or previously untried device for the support of Russia's armed forces.[12] Rather, the establishment of *gubernii* represented a significant political shift. When they were appointed, the new governors included not only Peter's established coterie (his favourites, such as Menshikov, Peter's relatives and friends), but also – in much greater numbers than previously – some men from aristocratic families. Such prominent representatives of old *boiar* families would, in the very recent past, have had every reason to expect automatic inclusion in the highest political affairs of the country through the now inactive Boiar Duma. In the latter part of the seventeenth century, depending upon the political configuration at court, high administrative office as a governor or chancellery head might have followed. Russian men of such standing were likely to be aware of, even partial to, contemporary European and other cultures, military events, and so on. That is, they were not inherently hostile to the content of some Petrine reforms. In avoiding the Duma and all it implied from the 1690s, however, Peter had disregarded many of their political expectations. Men of old and powerful families did, of course, serve close to Peter and had done so since his earliest years. Frequently, it was military action and loyalty to Peter's efforts that served to raise them, particularly among his coterie; one might describe these particular men as serving Peter largely on his terms. The inclusion of more men from aristocratic families into the administrative inner circle as governors in 1709 not only had the potential to broaden the political base of the Petrine court. Because it distributed important administrative tasks over a larger group, it also might have lessened some of the persistent administrative pressure on Peter's inner coterie.[13]

The revival and transformation of the Russian diplomatic service had some similar implications. As Russia gained in international stature, it resumed more formal use of diplomatic institutions. Ceremonial ambassadorial receptions reappeared at the Russian court. Russia appointed and used more formal overseas representatives: by the end of the reign, there were 23 men of experience, ability and often considerable social stature in European capitals, some of them with their own on-site networks of spies and informers. The days when Peter, with the help of his favourite Count Golovin and the state secretary P. P. Shafirov bore the brunt of diplomatic activity, were over, and the coordination of military and diplomatic events, which had worked to such advantage for the Russians, moved to a more institutional setting. To the personal attention of the Tsar and his immediate inner circle in diplomatic affairs were added broader, more formal controls. More men, many of them of old elite families, became a part of the process.[14] Such arrangements had a greater chance of survival and regular functioning even without Peter's hard hand on the reins. Peter had not mustered support to do this earlier, but now the country's political elite was participating in a formal structure.

The Ottoman catastrophe

As the *guberniia* reforms took shape, Charles XII of Sweden and his involuntary Ottoman hosts remained Peter's major military and diplomatic problem. The Ottoman Empire was a source of particular concern. Russian leadership had long been aware that it might become involved in the Swedish war. To forestall such an eventuality, Peter had visited Azov just before the battle of Poltava to demonstrate that he was not planning war against the Empire. A renewal in 1709 of the Russo-Ottoman treaty of 1700 seemed to reaffirm peaceful relations, but not for long. The Swedish King made every effort to involve the Porte in his war against Russia. He had the tacit support of the French and the British, and the open support of the Crimean Khan, Devlet Girey, who even offered to escort Charles back to Sweden. Ottoman distrust also grew with Russian power in Ukraine, associated with Peter's destruction of the independent (Mazepa's) Cossack presence there.[15]

Late in 1710 the Ottomans indicated that war against Russia was approaching; they formally declared their military intentions early in 1711. The Ottoman Empire remained a threatening and powerful military force, then engaged in a limited effort at military change and refortification of its borders.[16] Until 1699 European powers had defeated the Empire only in coalition – such as the Habsburg–Polish forces at Vienna in 1683. Even a decade after its battlefield defeat by Austria at Zenta (1697), the massed Ottoman cavalry and the Empire's overwhelming logistical and organizational capacity held important advantages.

Peter responded to the declaration of war with plans for a rapid, surprise attack into the Balkans, before the Ottoman army could reach its own north-eastern border. This effort represented a change in Russian strategy after Poltava; a move away from territorial warfare, the gradual seizure of fortress after fortress, aiming instead for the destruction of field armies.[17] The direction of his attack allowed Peter to intercept the Ottoman troops at some distance from their Swedish ally's forces in Pomerania. At the same time, Russia appealed to Moldavia and Wallachia for support, representing itself as the protector of Balkan Christians and hoping to generate Christian uprisings against the Porte. The Russians also brought to the field their recent prowess, new technological and tactical advantages, in that they fought in trained formations with flintlock muskets and bayonets.[18] If Peter saw war against the Ottomans as geopolitically different from war against the Swedes, he did little to insist on fighting them differently.[19]

Peter's plan was not successful. Militating against his efforts was the nature of recent Russian military activity. Its battlefield actions and sieges in the north-west had left relatively little attention for preparedness along the defensive perimeter in the south and south-west. And the Ottoman border was across open steppe to the south-southwest of Poltava. In fact, Russia could muster neither the resources nor the men speedily to muster and support a numerous Russian army for a march southward from the heartland nor westward from the defensive line. It tried. Recruits were called up from new communities: the postal suburbs, scribal families, even household servants. Shortfalls led to a new round of conscription. In exasperation, Peter ordered governors to check on new conscripts themselves, noting just before the battle at Pruth that some of the new arrivals were 'so bad, that they are unfit to be peasants, never mind soldiers'.[20] The court was reminded that courtiers too should constantly serve. The need for soldiers stretched Russian forces thin on several fronts: not only against the Ottomans, but along the southern defences, even reinforcements for the northern front after severe outbreaks of plague eroded the numbers there.[21] Supplies for the southern troops were another problem. There were shortages of food and matériel. When such items could be found, they were often far from the front, and their transfer to the southwest was time-consuming. The long years of war mercilessly exposed the inefficiencies and delays of Petrine recruitment and supply; the recent decentralization of the *guberniia* system complicated rather than resolved matters; the Russian war machine was overextended.[22]

Russian diplomatic efforts also reaped little reward. Wallachia had developed a relationship with Russia from 1709, but so had the Hospodar of nearby Moldavia. The long-standing rivalry between the two operated against Russian interests.

Peter left for the southern front in late March. He arrived only in June. Despite Russian efforts to mobilize the Cossacks and Kalmyks against them, Tatar irregulars raided the south Russian border so effectively that Tsar Peter himself had to reroute his southward path. It was an ominous display of the superior placement of Ottoman–Tatar forces. When Peter met Sheremetev's forces, the 38,000 men already lacked adequate food and matériel. Extreme heat deprived the troops of water and burned off grass that might have served as fodder for the army's mounts. Poor intelligence misdirected many of the Russian army's last-minute decisions. Russian advance guards and forward detachments captured the Ottoman supply station at Brailow, but the main forces remained unaware of it.

The Ottoman army, by contrast, quickly assembled and marched north toward the Pruth River with about 130,000 men. The early and overwhelming presence of their Ottoman overlords limited rebellion by Balkan Christians and undercut any uprisings supportive of Russia.

The encounter between the main Russian and Ottoman land forces along the Pruth River on 9 July 1711 was a major setback for Russia. Characteristically, the Russian army dug itself into a fortified encampment before joining battle. In the early fighting, Russian artillery was predictably effective against its Ottoman attackers. Long a Russian strength, Russian artillery had also been successful against the Swedes. The Russian infantry, its new tactical manoeuvrability proving irrelevant, was ineffective against such numerical odds, and the Ottoman army soon occupied the heights behind the Russian camp. On the second day the Ottoman

Janissaries were loath to face Russian artillery again, and the Ottomans learned that Brailow had fallen to the Russians. The Russians neither knew of the former, nor were able to take advantage of the latter, since their supplies were already running low. In a letter dated 10 July, Peter instructed the Senate that he expected to die or be taken prisoner, in which case he was not to be treated as their sovereign. The Ottomans, perhaps surprised by their inability to overwhelm the smaller Russian force, willingly opened negotiations.[23]

The demands made by the Ottoman Empire, whose European aims were evidently the maintenance and recapture of the fortresses lost in the 1680s and 1690s, have been represented by many historians as moderate. Azov and its environs (Kammenyi Zaton, Taganrog) were to be returned, and Peter's prized southern fleet was to be destroyed. Beyond this, Russia was not to interfere with merchants, in Polish politics, or in Charles's return to Sweden. There were rumours that Peter (or his new consort, Catherine) had bribed the Grand Vizier. Charles XII and Khan Devlet Girey were understandably furious.

But after Peter and Catherine returned to their capital, there was little indication that the Russian government found the terms moderate. Peter brazenly disregarded the treaty clauses about Charles XII, and he displayed an overwhelming reluctance to pull back from the Black Sea, destroying his Azov fleet. Such dallying led to a renewed declaration of war in 1712 and a new treaty of Adrianople in 1713 before peace was finally concluded. The battle on the Pruth continued to cast a long and lasting pall over the success of Russian arms, even beyond the loss of hard-won land and ships. Russian officers, when reporting on their personal exploits a decade later, did not harp on their presence or activities in south-east Europe, unanimously referring to Pruth briefly and obliquely as 'the Turkish action'.[24] Since the events on the Pruth accord ill with the theme of Peter's exploits as European reformer, Pruth is also often ignored by historians discussing his reign.[25]

Reintegrating the garrisons

The shock of Pruth generated at least one important military reconsideration. Until 1711, Peter and his supporters envisioned the Russian military primarily as a field army and navy active against Sweden. As regularization of that army took place after 1704, it boasted some 49 regiments of infantry (including Guards and grenadiers) and 33 dragoon regiments. Russia's open border to the south and east played a peripheral role in these arrangements. Frontier garrisons and southern outposts were also staffed by irregular troops whose loyalties were questionable; the Bulavin rebellion of 1707–8 was testimony to that fact. The consolidation and protection of Russia's steppe frontier had been neglected. It was not so much a base for action against the Ottomans, as a secondary nomadic-agricultural frontier.

As the Ottoman–Tatar threat reappeared in the south in 1710 and 1711, the Russian military perforce devoted a new kind of attention to these regions. Thirty-two regular garrison troops were formed; they were overwhelmingly infantry. The decree announcing their establishment followed hot on the heels of the declaration of war against the Ottomans; the text of the decree began with a discussion of the garrisons and proceeded only secondarily to the field forces.[26] The new troops served several purposes. First, they guarded frontiers and key cities throughout the Empire. New garrison forces on the Baltic, southern, and Siberian frontiers placed more Russian regulars outside the Russian heartland. As regular troops, these men were subject to the same training, standards and organization as the field army. *Streltsy* and other irregular units that had lingered in the garrisons were divided among the new regiments or disbanded. New garrison troops also helped train the field army and its officers. Both recruits and new officers now often served in a garrison before joining the field army; some garrisons were linked by geographic and territorial affiliation to particular field regiments, for whom they regularly fulfilled these functions. This pass-through population meant a declining number of local residents or affiliations among an increasingly permanent garrison soldiery. Thus the south and Siberia again shared military and political standards and institutions with the regular army, and a field-ready element joined the frontier dwellers on the southern and eastern frontiers.[27]

Garrison troops had other functions. Older or injured officers could pass on hard-won battle knowledge, while earning a small wage that did not throw them entirely on the charity of a miserly central state. The garrisons ran schools for the early training of garrison children for the army. (It was reported in the 1730s, however, that many of these children left the military life). Although some individuals rotated, the regiments themselves did not move, so that maintaining them in these functions cost less than for an equivalent field unit.[28] Here was the return, on the late seventeenth-century prototype, itself borrowed from early periods, of a rationalized intertwining of garrison and field forces. In tandem with *guberniia* reform, the decentralization of forces allowed the army to respond directly to external threats or even to frontier rebellion in particularly vulnerable areas.

The garrison troops of 1711 did not replace resident troops along the southern steppe frontier. The latter became regularized local troops in 1713, as war against the Tatar–Ottoman alliance loomed once more. The *landmilitsiia* regiments were made up of local military men whose lands and residences (as before) gave them a personal commitment to their region. As the threat of war passed in 1714, these troops were sent home to await developments and later disbanded.[29]

If this defence of Russia's steppe frontier seems to be based on an older approach, so too was Russia's further expansion to the south and south-east. A new defensive line was begun through Tsaritsyn in 1718.[30] With these protections in place, Russian agricultural settlement began to advance again over the next half century until Kalmyks and others were pushed away from the Russian borders.[31] Peter had not previously used defensive lines except in building the rather different fortress defences of Pskov, Smolensk, and Briansk between 1706 and 1708.

Later, in 1723, five and then six land militia (*landmilitsiia*) regiments appeared, as semi-permanent fixtures. Small landholders, called *odnod-vortsy*, staffed these units; some 90 per cent of *odnodvortsy* lived in the southern districts. In the preceding century they had formed the backbone of several southern regiments. By virtue of their landholding arrange-ments and service, they had some claim to old hereditary service status. However, their status was undermined by their inability to support them-selves while on campaign, except by the most arcane of arrangements. As a result, by century's end, many served locally and paid in-kind and cash dues, in lieu of the peasants they did not own. Theirs was only an extreme case in the general downward social pressure on the seventeenth-century provincial landholder. Petrine Russia imposed further burdens and then altogether disallowed the claims of the *odnodvortsy* to the new noble sta-tus. By the late 1720s they were registered straightforwardly as taxpayers. In particular *gubernii* their local knowledge and military expertise con-tin-ued to distinguish them, however, and kept them in military service as land militia (*landmilitsiia*). Members of the land militias trained and served during the summer, but rejoined their households for the winter. Where households were prosperous enough to support an adult male who was away from the fields for most of the agricultural season, this was very effective; Habsburg Colonel Manstein wholeheartedly admired the milit-ary prowess of the *landmilitsiia* in the late 1720s.[32]

The timely appearance of land militias, reorganized garrison troops and the new defensive line created military forces whose role was to defend the settled agricultural frontier against raiders (and insurrection), but who were also trained for the battlefield if necessary. Thus, by the 1720s, the Russian army had divided into several different groups for different kinds of military encounters. There were regular battlefield troops, regular defensive garrison troops and a few settled militia units. The latter two on the southern frontier essentially protected the peace and renewed Russian agricultural expansion against mobile steppe peoples. As this happened, the Russian establishment obliquely acknowledged the need for a multi-faceted military. Indeed, Peter initially created an army to fight one kind of European army in particular – the Swedish one. Only after Pruth did Russia formally acknowledge the effectiveness of a mixture of forces, with similar training and preparation, in confronting Russia's different foes.[33]

The Northern War ends on a naval note

Southern military reorganization did little to bring the Northern War to a close. With Russian conquests in the Baltic secure, fighting resumed in Swedish Pomerania. Britain and other combatants in the War of Spanish Succession, anxious to prevent the spread of hostilities into the Habsburg Monarchy, were alienated by Sweden's unwillingness to cooperate. Although the Swedish position did not look entirely hopeless in 1712, it grew steadily more ominous. Allied Russian, Danish and Saxon troops took Friedrichstadt, Stralsund and Stettin. Stenbock's army was forced to surrender in 1713. Meanwhile, Russian naval and land attacks against Finland captured Åbo, pushed the Swedes inland from the Baltic coast, won a naval victory at Hangø, and finally, by late 1714, nearly drove the Swedes from southern Finland.

The disintegration of the Swedish Empire was briefly delayed by the return of Charles XII from his five years in exile in 1714. The international situation at first appeared encouraging to him. The British Crown was again willing to support Sweden's interests, if not go to war on its behalf. Britain's King George (of Hanover) shared concerns with Prussia over the expansion of Russian interests in the Baltic – and the marriage of Peter's niece to the Duke of Courland and his negotiations with the Duke of Mecklenburg, in particular. These almost outweighed George's irritation with pro-Jacobite activity in Sweden. In the Polish–Lithuanian Commonwealth by 1715, not only Augustus of Saxony's opponents, but he himself, increasingly resented Russian domination and feared Russia's developing collaboration with Prussia. Sweden skilfully counterbalanced the opening of Swedish–Russian negotiations with discussions with Britain and a second diversionary attack on Norway.

Charles's XII death by a stray bullet at the siege of Fredricksten in 1718 complicated rather than improved the Russian position. By 1719 France was involved in negotiations on Sweden's behalf, a British squadron patrolled the Baltic, and Russia's erstwhile allies abandoned it. Sweden succeeded in negotiating separate treaties with each of the former allies. The new Swedish rulers, Ulrika Elonora and her spouse, Fredrich of Hesse, quite willingly relinquished most north German elements of their former empire in the Peace of Stockholm (February 1720). Denmark, unable to inflict lasting military damage on Sweden, relinquished many of its claims at Fredricksborg in June, 1720. Sweden, meanwhile, hoped that Russia's powerful presence might encourage the other powers to support Swedish retention of its Baltic provinces. In the end, however, French and British preoccupation with internal affairs and devastating Russian raids on the coast of Sweden proper eliminated this possibility. On 30 August 1721 the Peace of Nystadt awarded to Russia the provinces of Estonia, Livonia, Kexholm and most of Ingria (Izhora, Ingermanland), but returned to Sweden most of its Finnish lands.

The Northern War was over. There were huge public celebrations in St Petersburg, Moscow and other Russian cities; Peter was crowned Emperor of All the Russias. International worries over the changing regional balance of power had prolonged the war, but so too had the effectiveness and persistence of the small Swedish state in mobilizing men and resources for war. Russian victory led quite quickly to a profound reorganization of political power in Sweden, but the long years of war were less economically devastating to Sweden than might be imagined.[34]

The closing years of war saw the rapid development and use of the Russian navy. The first Petrine navy, developed to capture Azov, had been beset by complications. Not the least of these was the absence of a Russian seafaring population with an established interest in the fleet. This led to mistakes in constructing the southern fleet, as acidly described by Captain John Perry.[35] Other problems included inadequate supplies of appropriate materials, such as aged lumber, an absence of trained shipwrights, and the need for new revenues to pay for them. It has been observed that, for all Peter's pride in his Black Sea fleet, light older-style Cossack boats made major contributions to the taking of the fortress at Azov.[36]

The destruction of Russia's Azov fleet after 1711 brought the Baltic navy and its demands into sharper focus. Shipbuilding on Lake Ladoga and in the hinterland of St Petersburg had long since moved to the shores of the Baltic. The absence of a seafaring population was partly overcome by the drafting of men in the provinces closest to the Baltic and finally resolved with the regular conscription and training of men from all over the country. If Russian naval officers were not always willing or numerous, the expertise of British officers, shipbuilders, engineers and advisers played an important role in launching the Baltic navy.[37] And naval requirements, whether for officers, boats or technical-mathematical expertise, received persistent and enthusiastic attention from the Tsar. The Russian Baltic fleet was perhaps chiefly notable for the abruptness of its appearance, in the face of British and Dutch commercial and diplomatic interests in the Baltic. Its rapid growth was also surprising. Where there had been few Russian ships 15 years earlier, by 1720 Russia's 34 ships of the line, 15 frigates and large galley fleet outnumbered the Swedish and Danish fleets combined. Improvements in both supply and expertise, and in naval construction represented a considerable Russian achievement; a naval service ethos was enshrined in the Naval Statute (*Morskoi Ustav*) of 1720.[38]

The Russian fleet under Peter was used cleverly and effectively in support of land manoeuvres. In the south it had famously supported the capture of Azov and bombarded Bulavin's rebels. The Russian galley fleet provided invaluable support to the Russian troops in the Baltic, much as irregular cavalry had supported the Russian army in the early 1700s. As larger Russian ships guarded them from offshore, the galleys ferried soldiers in a series of persistent and devastating attacks on the Finnish shoreline in 1712–13, which forced the Swedes to abandon Helsinki and then Åbo. Galleys performed the same function in the attacks upon Sweden proper in the final years of the war (1719–21).[39]

Rarely, however, did Russia's navy operate independently against another navy. Peter was inordinately proud of the Russian victory at Hangø, one of the few such battles. As Sweden attempted to block Russian galleys moving down the coast in 1714, a becalmed Swedish fleet was outflanked by oared Russian galleys, which were dragged across a narrow peninsula finally to surround the larger Swedish vessels. Occasions like Osel (1719) and Hangø peninsula (Gangut, in Russian) were rarities, however, and for all the immense importance of its naval support, the Russian fleet captured just one Swedish ship of the line throughout the war.

Peter, his allies and his opponents were all well aware of the navy's key role in supporting Russia's move into the Baltic, especially after 1713. Peter gloated over his navy's size, and Britain bemoaned its own heedless role in earlier encouraging the growth of a Russian navy. Nevertheless, it is not difficult to understand why the continued building of costly ships-of-the-line, in particular, was quickly sacrificed in later, militarily more frugal times.[40]

A delicate balance

Further government change followed the *guberniia* reforms (1708–10) and the creation of the Senate in 1711. These eventually improved the character and consistency of administrative support offered to the military. However, initially, they probably compounded the disruptions caused by Peter's earlier administrative inconsistencies.

Problems with civilian administrative support for the military had both financial and educational roots. Moving the capital to St Petersburg had required many central chancelleries to coordinate activities in Moscow and St Petersburg; soon after, *guberniia* reform drew many clerks out of the capitals into provincial employment. A shortage of trained clerks made the situation worse. Part of the difficulty was that Peter's attention to technical and educational preparation had focused overwhelmingly on the military. The School of Mathematics and the Naval Academy enrolled noblemen. Cipher and garrison schools played a similar role for less exalted social groups. But the civil administration was not fed by similar institutions. Instead, the Russian clerkly class tended to replicate itself from within, while only a few men abandoned military careers and educations for civilian employment. The sons of churchmen, a possible source of more literate clerks, were drafted to fight during the Great Northern War. Only a few privately organized schools, including Jesuit and 'German' ones in Moscow, prepared literate graduates. The assignment of social status to the civilian administration complicated the problem. The nobility viewed work at the lower levels of civil administration with distaste. It was, however, equally unwilling to allow commoners, who had entered at the lowest ranks, to be promoted into the higher administrative positions.[41] The number of employees in the central governmental institutions actually declined from 1690 to 1715, surpassing the seventeenth-century numbers again only at the end of Peter's reign.[42]

Financial shortfalls did not encourage the dispassionate and hierarchical functioning of a rule-based bureaucracy. The move to St Petersburg was personally costly for staff, who lost local arrangements, lands and houses acquired through long service near Moscow. Salaries for clerks grew by as much as 50 per cent after 1710, but inflation and new foreign specialists consumed a great deal of money. There was simply not enough cash to pay clerks in the lower ranks. Under the circumstances, bribery, gifts and other irregular procedures certainly helped the system to function, but did little towards the goal of rule-based administration. The absence of the kind of committed, consistent leadership enjoyed by the army did little to improve the situation.[43]

These financial and educational problems were then complicated by the organizational shortcomings of the *guberniia* system. Demands on the various *gubernii* were uneven. Central oversight and control greatly diminished with the introduction of *guberniia* institutions. Indeed, some of the central chancelleries were subordinated to the governor of Moscow *guberniia*. Finally, below the governor and his immediate circle, the personnel and decision-making processes of local administration often remained unchanged. When local governors (*voevody*) were replaced by commandants, it was frequently only the title of the office, not the man holding it, that changed. The Belgorod military-administrative district retained some administrative viability as part of the Kiev *guberniia* even when the Military Chancellery of which it was a part joined the Senate Chancellery. Provisioning and troop supply within such units continued to depend heavily on local relations as well as on hierarchical institutional functioning.[44]

Some efforts to rebuke, police or alter administrative malfunctioning and malfeasance were institutionalized. Administrative posts of particular importance were sometimes simply transferred to the army and navy; or military men were seconded to the bureaucracy to take care of them.[45] In 1711 the *fiskaly*, or fiscal police, were introduced as administrative watchdogs, a layer above other Petrine institutions. They were charged with uncovering financial and administrative misappropriation, corruption and misdeeds, often through denunciation, while themselves remaining immune from retribution. Their powers to curb financial and other wrongdoing were later greatly expanded and much abused, particularly at the provincial level. The fiscal police first appeared with the creation of the Senate, but their numbers and importance continued to grow to the end of Peter's reign. Nearly 500 *fiskaly* existed by 1725.[46]

Nor did Peter fail personally and unstintingly to participate in administrative oversight himself. He kept continuous watch over the coordination and functioning of government through his Cabinet, formed in 1704. Admonitions swamped the Senate. In 1717 Peter ordered senators not to appoint their relatives and friends to lucrative posts; he complained of his administrators' lack of initiative, and of their insubordination when he perceived inappropriate initiative, and could penalize either. He punished corruption in numerous cases – most notably and belatedly in 1714 in his longtime favourite, A. D. Menshikov, whom he then reinstated two years later for loyalty and administrative decisiveness.

Peter's confrontations with the Senate and *gubernii* over administrative behaviour were complicated by national political issues. Peter's son by his first wife, Aleksei Petrovich, had never enjoyed a close or even satisfactory relationship with his father. The personal and political distance between them lengthened in 1715 with the birth of sons both to Catherine, Peter's second wife and then consort, and to Aleskei's wife, Charlotte. With the question of succession in the air, many high-born Russians responded to their relative loss of political power under Peter by implicitly or overtly offering support to Aleksei and his son (Peter's grandson). When Aleksei fled to Vienna in 1716, then returned to interrogation and subsequent death in prison, the fragility of Peter's support from the upper reaches of Russian society was made painfully clear. Although no actual plot was uncovered, Aleksei's supporters included not only aristocrats and recently made senators, but also some of Peter's own inner circle.

Major administrative restructuring followed on these events, and this institutional reconstruction of the upper levels of Russian government at last proved politically and institutionally more durable. Peter first spoke of borrowing Swedish institutions for Russian use in 1712, but it was 1717–20 before Russia introduced 'colleges' on the Swedish model. At first, nine colleges replaced all the chancelleries of the central Russian administration; all other administrative units were disbanded or subsumed into these new ones. The decision-making power of each college was vested in a group of ten individuals, one of whom (the vice-president) was to be a foreigner. The perhaps obvious goal was to limit the ability of any single man or family to dominate the new structure; inevitably, this did not always work. Initially, the president of each of nine colleges (a Russian) was also to be a senator; this would later be revised. Thus, the new colleges were formally linked by the Senate, the unifying central governmental body, now nearly a decade old. As colleges became the norm, the *gubernii* were sub-divided and much civil administration returned to the capitals. A procurator, appointed to keep watch over the Senate, and the General Regulation of 1720, which lay down formally the rules of administrative behaviour, were the watchdogs of the system.[47]

There were at least two notable elements in these arrangements. The first was the reshuffling and redistribution of politically powerful court figures with the proliferation of central government offices. New men appeared; the older and now diminished favourite, Menshikov, was restored. A more recent arrival, Iagushinskii, who had advanced first up the ranks of the military, was politically independent both of his fellow commoner, Menshikov, and of the older aristocratic factions. Men of foreign origin and long service, such as Iakov Bruce, balanced the old aristocratic families (of suspect allegiance) and the newer, less elite favourites in the central apparatus. This arrangement carefully balanced the capitals'

political factions in the central administration, although the older aristocratic clans remained entrenched in the provinces.[48] The result helped to
make the institutional framework more stable, by creating diverse groups
with a vested interest in its continuation. Notably, in the provinces, the
Petrine institutions were displaced soon after Peter's death; by contrast,
the carefully balanced Senate and the colleges were among the few institutions that persisted beyond the Petrine era.

Second, as E. V. Anisimov has argued, the broad outlines of this developing structure were more hierarchical and unified than the remnants
of the older chancelleries. Heavy-handed policing of the administration
perhaps pushed innovation and decision making to the top of the system,
where political power resided. Nevertheless, the shift also encouraged the
bureaucracy to acknowledge in new ways the existence of institutional
rules, to the extent that their manipulation became an overt element of
bureaucratic infighting and autocratic enforcement.[49]

These political and administrative adjustments did not diminish the
import of the military. Quite the contrary, the Colleges of War, Foreign
Affairs and the Admiralty were the most important of the colleges, and
operated quite independently of much of the rest of the system. Their
personnel took precedence over all other civil administrators, even over
the senators.[50] Minor complications resulted. In 1723, for example, the
Commissary was subordinated to the College of War, and its chief lost
his Senate seat. This was impractical because the chief supply officer
needed direct contact with the civil apparatus. In 1724 a new Provisioning
Chancellery appeared with the privileges of a college, under the Senate's
jurisdiction.[51] These travails refined the reintegration of a dominant military with the civilian hierarchy, both of which were increasingly regular
and institutionalized by the end of Peter's reign.

The social and fiscal bases of durable
military reform

The final balance of institutional power was not just the result of court
politics and administrative structures. Numerous other components
played key roles. Here, two major examples will be offered. First, the soul
tax and fiscal regularization perpetuated the Petrine military economically. Second, the nobility's acceptance of service in a reformed military,
which culminated in the Table of Ranks, provided its social basis.

The social adjustment of the lesser elite to Petrine demands is often,
and justifiably, seen as among the most perplexing issues of Peter's reign.

Why, after two relatively weak rulers, did the Russian nobility so docilely agree to the arduous compulsory service thrust upon it by the Russian throne under Peter? An answer is perhaps best begun by recalling the declining fortunes and mobility of the middle and lower levels of the Russian elite. By the late seventeenth century the political power and social prospects of this population were limited in important ways. No longer did cavalry service in the hundreds guarantee hereditary (elite) status and landholding, never mind the opportunity for upward mobility into the Moscow ranks and towards the court. Indeed, active cavalry hundreds were fewer and fewer as the century wore on, and places in them reserved for the most prosperous and best connected. Cavalrymen served reluctantly in the new formation cavalry (or even infantry) regiments. Here, their status might be acknowledged, even somewhat protected, but the opportunities for greater prosperity diminished with the decline in unoccupied land stock. The possibility of upward movement into metropolitan ranks was severely restricted and, then, with reform in 1678–82, stopped.[52] Only one pathway to advancement remained, and it was limited: meritorious service in the officer corps of the new formation army could bring military rewards and perhaps financial stability, but it did not convey social status. However, it required a certain readjustment of aspirations since, until 1682, such officers could serve only in the new formation troops. Between 1682 and the early 1700s, when the entire army used the new formation structure and further promotions became possible, service as an officer in the new formation regiments still did not convey the automatic political and social status the older system had offered. New obstacles stood in the way of any petty nobleman wishing to earn his way out of relative poverty and obscurity.

The Petrine era brought some radical change to the relationship of social status to the military. Cavalry service did not convey or protect the status of provincial landholders. The cost of service, often borne nearly exclusively by impoverished estates, undermined their economic standing. At the same time, the frequent creation, melding and disbanding of cavalry regiments in a measured but relentless way transformed the cavalry (like the infantry) into a mass-based, rather than an elite, service.[53] However, promotion into and up the ranks of the officer corps provided a rapid, if not an easy, substitute, especially for those whose service began before Poltava. Extended tours of service were transformative. Officers in the Petrine military enjoyed considerable group solidarity; regimental staffs became a kind of corporate association.[54] Officers shared a practical military education, revealed by a common, technical and Europeanized vocabulary

and growing literacy. They had clearly defined qualifications and responsibilities, and even a military ethos. Finally, they enjoyed the status and
cachet of a military lifestyle that could include recognition from the highest
political lights of the land.[55]

There were, however, numerous difficulties. Landholding was no
longer an inevitable result of military service. Other opportunities to buy
or receive land were severely limited by Peter, who wished to reserve
the Crown's lands. A traditional perquisite of hereditary service, land and
serf ownership, was thus denied to those young servicemen who did not
inherit family lands. Cash salary rates were generous after 1711,[56] although
for both fiscal and administrative reasons, they were not always paid or
paid on time. Elite servicemen spent long periods away from home and
family, often a decade or more. If service as an officer bore greater cachet
and rewards than as a rank-and-file dragoon, it too was less exclusive in
principle than seventeenth-century cavalry service. As is well known, Peter
quite consistently permitted, if he did not directly encourage, military
promotions for those who were able, but not well born. The obligation to
serve under such conditions was obviously not always enthusiastically
met, and Peter's reign is unsurprisingly characterized by the reluctance of
elite individuals to serve in the military.

The latter years of the reign changed, but did not necessarily improve,
the situation. For one thing, beginning in 1713–14, declining casualties,
better record keeping and other factors meant that there were more
officers than there were positions in the military to offer them; promotions
slowed proportionately. Primogeniture, mightily resisted by the Russian
nobility, became law in 1714 and may have aided the financial prospects
of the eldest son, but not those of his siblings. Considerable resentment
developed over the promotion and high standing of commoners.[57] Service
in the officer corps did, however, slowly become more exclusive towards
the end of the reign. With the imminence of peace, the military hierarchy
became more politicized, and Peter himself played a less intrusive role.
Entry into and promotion within the officer corps became more conservative, and the exceptional nature of non-noble appointments became
clearer.[58] The Table of Ranks, which appeared in January 1722, formally
acknowledged many aspects of a newly consolidating system.

The Table of Ranks[59] formally codified a definition of the Russian
nobility in service to the Russian Crown; in fact it reconstructed a system
for acknowledging (military) service, status and relative social standing.
Such a system had not formally existed in Russia since before the abolition
of precedence-ranking (*mestnichestvo*) nearly 40 years earlier. Peter had

early and persistently rejected attempts to move back toward *mestnichestvo*, but the emergence of an alternative system was a complex process, involving not only Peter's Europeanizing ambitions for his nobility, but the demands of military life, and the social and status aspirations of the nobility itself. The assumptions encoded in the resulting Table were almost as complex as the understood rules of *mestnichestvo*, if not as covert; they were the result of quite open bureaucratic and political manoeuvring.[60]

On the face of it, the Table named a series of positions at court, in the civil administration and in the military, awarding them grades or levels from 14 (the lowest) to 1 (the highest). The Table thus established equivalencies among positions in the three areas. An army colonel, for example, was equivalent in rank to a rear admiral in the navy, the president of a college, or the court's senior chamberlain as he advanced to more exalted levels, he earned first personal and then hereditary nobility. The Table thus sharply defined the line between nobility and non-noble.

That noble families serve the state predictably was required outright; state service was the only way of acquiring rank. There were penalties for not serving: a serving officer took precedence over a non-serving nobleman, for example. Financial incentive was provided in part by the requirement of entail, which prevented subdivision of estates and required younger siblings to earn their own salaries.

Unsurprisingly, the Table acknowledged both the nobility's and Peter's pre-eminent interest in the military. The military was so important that it was consulted as drafts of the Table were being drawn up. As a partial result, any officer in the military (grade 14 and up) automatically qualified for the nobility, while otherwise one had to advance much further, as high as grade 8, to qualify. Military officers, furthermore, took precedence over men of the same civil or court rank. The qualifications and requirements even for low military rank were laid out in considerable detail, emphasizing the relationship of merit and advancement.[61]

Despite the overwhelmingly bureaucratic tenor of the document, however, the Table of Ranks obliquely recognized noble concerns about family and heritage; the document also reflected Peter's belief that the talent and leadership of the state lay overwhelmingly with the nobility. For example, special individual merit (*zasluga*), as defined in the Table, was an element in promotion. *Zasluga* could include both genealogical merit and seniority. Other recognitions were more direct; rank and precedence, quite naturally, shifted in the presence of a prince of the blood, even of low rank.

A number of foreign examples were consulted in the construction of the Table of Ranks, including a Swedish one. Peter's interest in a European-style nobility is well known.[62] It is clear, however, that Russian practice and needs overrode the foreign models.[63] In many respects, the Table of Ranks acted as an official definition of the Petrine nobility and of access to it, and it relied substantially upon a pre-existing relationship between the Crown and its nobility. In the context of a general call-to-arms of the old hereditary service class and often rapid social mobility within the officer corps, the Table of Ranks also acknowledged the loss of old social distinctions and the formation of a more broadly defined 'nobility' (*shliakhetstvo*), encompassing many older service and status categories. While the relationship between the Crown and this nobility had important new characteristics, the relationship itself was not only a hard-won triumph of royal absolutism, but also the (dramatic) evolution of an older Muscovite relationship.[64]

The old *boiarstvo*, although integrated with this nobility, retained its distinctiveness both formally and informally. The well-born remained prominent in the court firmament. The court-ranked (*tsaredvortsy*) continued to demand, and often got, special treatment from the Crown and in the bureaucracy. The Guards units, initially drawn from among *tsaredvortsy*, gradually also became a refuge for aristocrats who did not win officers' commissions, their status preserved by their Guards' appointments. A Heroldmeister recorded and acknowledged family standing, and bureaucratic procedure took different account of regiments containing an aristocratic membership. On the other hand, such men were not exempt from the educational and other requirements of their offices, and *mestnichestvo*-like disputes were brusquely rejected. The Procuracy General, created to oversee the Senate, later provided the mechanism for clan and family domination of high office throughout the eighteenth century.[65]

If the Table reconstructed old definitions of noble service, it also recognized a newer reality. Seniority and eligibility requirements applied to civil posts, not just to military ones, in order not to offend men who had worked hard to advance up the parallel military scale. Noblemen continued to prefer army service. However, these provisions firmly attached administrative reform (not just military change) to the ideas of noble service and responsibility. The inclusion of the civil administrative hierarchy, even if as a poor relation, contributed to the unification and integration of noble service across the upper reaches of government. In the process, the Table openly recognized administrative power as no earlier system had. For the willing, the recognition of civil service rank provided venues for further promotion and mobility. As military officers transferred into administrative roles, military discipline and hierarchy sometimes went with them.[66] A highly politicized, but relatively stable, central administration rapidly emerged.

It is difficult to exaggerate the significance of the Table of Ranks and its corollaries as social legislation. They codified key mutual adjustments between the society and the military as envisioned by Peter and as led by a Russian nobility. Most importantly, they were the outcome of a new relationship between the nobility and the Crown, acknowledging the nobility's distinction without guaranteeing its social exclusivity.

If the codification of the nobility's relationship to the Crown was a key element in defining the Petrine military legacy, so too was a partial resolution of Russia's fiscal problems. The severity of these problems in the Petrine era was similar only to the financial pressure Russia experienced during the Thirteen Years' War. The Russian state budget during the Petrine era was largely consumed by military expenditures, with peaks of 80 per cent and higher.[67] In fact, it was not unusual for other states within the Euro-Ottoman zone of military parity to spend similar percentages of their state incomes for this purpose (70–90 per cent of income).[68] As in the mid-seventeenth century, a key eighteenth-century expense in Russia and elsewhere lay in putting the army in the field, if ships, uniforms, arms, cannon, horses and supplies were all purchased within a very limited time period. Greater administrative coherence and the easing of this particular fiscal burden after Poltava were almost simultaneous. At that point, new taxes and dues had already been added to the myriad in existence; currency devaluation was another favoured way of paying the bills in the early Petrine era. The collection and payment of some of these dues is often credited with the undermining of the urban commercial sector.[69]

In the second half of Peter's reign, excepting ongoing construction on the Baltic fleet, it was the maintenance of the military, rather than its furnishing and reconstruction that was the principal expense. When peace arrived late in the reign, it might have been expected to diminish the costs of the military establishment; this expectation should be balanced by the recognition that Russia, for much of the Northern War, had fed its troops partly at the expense of its enemies and allies, on whose territory they foraged. The return home of large numbers of permanent standing troops that required payment, housing and food from Russian resources alone represented an increase, rather than a decrease in expense; salaries, food, fodder, supply and systematic replacement of men and their supplies did not come cheap.[70]

Limited resources remained a chief and ongoing problem in supporting the permanent army and navy. Russia still had neither a robust commercial economy nor prosperous agriculture upon which to draw. Its economy was cash-short, and the state's purposeful move toward cash payments instead of in-kind payments or arrangements only exacerbated the problem. The government could not depend upon international borrowing. There were also administrative problems: despite Peter's efforts, the generation and consolidation of chancellery budgets even after Poltava into a unified state summary was far from automatic or reliable. Administratively, taxes were comparatively simple to assess; collecting cash and distributing it appropriately posed more severe challenges.

Several devices were adopted to stabilize and manage military expenditure. First, the *guberniia* reforms of 1708–10 had provided a more direct route from the taxpayer to the regiments, a fiscal advantage. Nonetheless, a financial review in 1710 produced the unpleasant conclusion that army expenditures exceeded total revenue. Another household census, like that of 1710, was taken in 1716, in the hopes that a growing population could be identified and made to pay the permanent costs of the army and navy. It was a thoroughgoing failure, since it recorded an actual decline in the number of taxable households. What this result demonstrated with clarity was the futility of a household basis for the census: more generations crowded into fewer households to manage the tax burden better.

New arrangements to deal with this complex of fiscal problems were not long in forthcoming. As soldiers began to return from campaigning in Europe as early as 1717, the problem of peacetime living quarters, food and salaries loomed. The army and navy did not decline to a smaller size; on the contrary their numbers grew after 1711, with 121,000 men in the field army and another 74,000 in the garrison troops. Initially, the returning men were paid to work on large building projects: bridges, the defensive line and fortresses, and, famously, canals. Shortly, however, the fiscal problem implied by maintenance was resolved; the men were quartered on the population, more frequently than not in the countryside.[71] Except for the summer months (when there were training manoeuvres if not short campaigns), the cost of housing and feeding the military thus became a particular form of taxation 'in kind,' although its cost was calculated in cash equivalents. There were specific instructions about the ways in which battalions and companies could be distributed, but only where there were major fortresses or other accommodation could the population substitute cash for this responsibility.[72] The American public sufficiently disliked this practice that it would write freedom from billeting into the Constitution. There is little indication that Russians felt differently; all who could quickly made themselves exempt from the burden.[73] Overwhelmingly, it was urban taxpayers and the peasantry who bore this expense as the Russian army 'occupied' the Russian countryside. This very large contribution was neither uniform nor equitable. The billets were concentrated in the central regions, for example, where most troops were still stationed around Moscow. However, billeting did support a large Russian army in peacetime. Similarly to its Swedish prototype, it did so without draining the countryside of cash reserves or creating another bureaucracy. The result emphasized the military esprit of the army, but also the social milieu so many of the soldiers knew best. The hiring out of the rank-and-file to work on local estates and for their own officers was a simple extension of this, if one extraordinarily open to abuse.

In the countryside the army did play one new role, that of a more general and widely available policing against violent crime than had previously existed. The local regiment oversaw bandit control, as well as preventing vagrancy and detaining fugitives, in an extension of its role as general enforcer. Since the eighteenth-century countryside boasted a number of spectacular popular bandits, it would be difficult to claim any great success. Policing in the cities, by contrast, was not through the military, but through separate municipal institutions, whose duties included not only the suppression of violent behaviour, but also broader controls over cleanliness, trading stalls, dress and other matters.[74]

A fiscal adjustment intimately connected with army billeting was the move to the 'soul tax', which largely replaced the household tax after the failed census of 1716. In essence, the tax assessed an equal payment on each and every male of the taxpaying population in Russia, regardless of age or occupation. The tax was to be a replacement for some, but not all, older taxes and duties. Its purpose was exclusively military; other state expenses continued to be met as before. A new census, required by a tax based for the first time on individual taxpayers, began in 1718. The count was carried out by the military; so many officers undertook the job that commanders complained that the troops lacked adequate officers.[75] When the census was completed in 1724, it showed some 5.4 million male 'souls'. The first tax rate (74 kopeks per soul) was derived by dividing the 4 million rubles in cash required to maintain 73 regiments by 5.4 million souls. This calculation was clearly notional in almost every important way. The census had counted every male, including the young, the old and the infirm. Some households, however many males they contained, were also a great deal more prosperous than others. Furthermore, the process by which the tax was collected was not specified. In practice, the appropriate sum was simply handed over by local estate holders to the resident regimental officers. The individual tax rate thus bore little relationship to the number of those who really paid or to their ability to pay. In reality, the soul tax was a simple, if very effective, extension of the household tax of the 1670s; that is, villages or households were the actual units of payment.[76]

There were numerous technical difficulties in the collection: tax districts were not necessarily coterminus with provinces; civilian officials were left with the unenviable task of extracting other revenues after the poll tax had been collected and dispatched; and the tax collections were enforced by the army, even occasionally by the Guards. Tales of their terrorizing of rural districts were rife.[77]

The soul tax was notorious both for the burden which it imposed on the peasantry and for the brutality with which it was collected. Its ill effects may have been due in part to the excessively cold winters (the Little Ice Age continued) and the agricultural depression with which its introduction coincided. The soul tax, coupled with billeting, did not eliminate many other taxes and dues. It did, however, provide directly for military maintenance, and it became the prop and mainstay of the military budget into the nineteenth century.

The social implications of the soul tax were bound up with the reinforcement and occasional adjustment of the great divide between taxpayers and the nobility. Serfs and peasants were not the only ones who paid taxes. As in 1679, townsmen also paid, now at a higher rate. The rigidity of larger, starker social and fiscal categories imposed in the name of the soul tax is legendary, but on occasion those categories could be applied in a misleading fashion. In their haste to enrol numerous urban taxpayers, census-takers included vagrants and itinerants; a category of 'trading peasants' came into being. *Odnodvortsy* and other former military men became state peasants, while other socio-legal categories, such as slaves, became indistinguishable from other taxpayers. Taxpaying, or not, continued as an element in defining social status. Nobility was associated as much with freedom from taxation, as it was linked to service.[78]

The outcome of fiscal reform, then, was to create a basis for military permanence, while minimizing its costs. The militia style of the new army was hard on the peasants, but largely successful if unpopular in maintaining the army. The new system allowed for greater speed, but functioned harshly on all concerned. With it, the last institutional vestiges of a part-time army disappeared. The army and the navy were shifting inexorably to a cash basis.[79]

Altogether, the Table of Ranks, billeting, the soul tax and the college system created a stable social and institutional context for Peter's military, just as Russia went to war again, in the distant south-east against Persia.

The Persian finale

An incident involving the destruction of merchants' stalls in Shemakha (130 kilometres, or 80 miles, west of Baku in Azerbaijan) provided the pretext for war against Persia to begin in 1722. Trading interests only partially motivated Peter's move against Persia, however. The old Volga–Caspian trade route, though still lucrative, was in decline.[80] The Russian campaign was also instigated in part by a desire for imperial expansion, linked to recent Ottoman-Russian competition in the borderlands. Missions to Persia and central Asia in 1714 and 1716 surveyed the natural territory; in a parallel fashion, Peter also supported Bering's maritime explorations off Kamchatka in 1724–5. The reports on political conditions in central Asia led to a repeat mission in 1718 bolstered by several thousand armed men, nearly all of whom died in an engagement against Khiva. Peter also dreamt of ports in Madagascar and India, envisioning himself as the monarch of a European empire.[81]

Preparations for war were not complex. In addition to regular cavalry and auxiliary irregulars, like the Kalmyk, a special new southern infantry corps (called the Nizovoi Korpus) was created for the Persian campaigns. Naval support on the Volga and the Caspian extended the reach of the army's supply lines. The steppe border garrisons were alerted in expectation of Ottoman–Tatar reaction. The taking of Gilian, Derbent and Baku by Russian troops from Persia was not militarily difficult, but operations in considerable heat amongst a hostile population made campaigning both wearing and costly in men, equipment and supplies.

The situation became more complex with Ottoman counter-attacks on the Persian trans-Caucasus from the west. Unwilling to reopen hostilities with the Ottomans and their Crimean clients, Peter opened peace negotiations.[82] A treaty with Persia in 1723 was followed by a treaty with the Ottomans in 1724; these acknowledged both Russian and Ottoman conquests. Russian forces garrisoned their new forts, and planned for settlement in their vicinity by Armenians and Russians. The Nizovoi Korpus continued in existence, supported by local dues and payments, in anticipation of Russia's future role in the area. Tatar raids on the Russian south persisted.

Military activity in the final full year of Peter's reign was otherwise minimal. He died in late January 1725, apparently from a disease of the urinary tract and bladder. He left Russia in mourning and without a clearly appointed successor.

The Petrine army

When Peter died, the military establishment was clearly in better condition than it had been for many years. Its army was large, numbering some 200,000 men; its size depended upon national service by the population, a condition Russia shared to some degree with many central and east European states. This army was more than half infantry, but also contained numerous cavalry units, an artillery-engineering corps and a large navy, many of whose ships were designed for coastal and shallow waters. The infantry was drawn almost exclusively from the enserfed population, but included other members of the taxed population and some nobleman and free servitors. The conscription process, which filled the infantry, had numerous drawbacks. Its manpower yield was unpredictable, given high rates of desertion and escape from both army and navy. In the context of wartime, this could lead to emergency measures that drew recruits from unexpected parts of the population. The exceptions were three high-profile regiments: the two Guards units and the Ingermanland regiment, each of which was larger than an ordinary regiment and fit into the Table of Ranks two ranks higher than ordinary military service. They drew their recruits respectively from the nobility and from the best performing soldiery. The cavalry by contrast was drawn predominantly, but far from exclusively, from the free population. At military inspections and noble musters, free men were enrolled overwhelmingly into cavalry regiments; in smaller numbers, conscripts from the taxable population were included; military men could also be transferred into the battlefield cavalry regiments from the infantry and the garrisons.

The army was surprisingly homogeneous. That is, its regiments were overwhelmingly fusiliers and dragoons. These men trained in the garrison units, which served at once as reserves, police and defence units along the borders north-west and south and in the largest Siberian outposts. Regular garrison troops were somewhat different from the field units, especially when stationed in Siberia and the south-east, where they dealt with different military architecture, different supply systems, and were required to carry out slightly different duties as the colonial forces of an eastward-expanding Russian Empire. All these troops, but most particularly the

288 RUSSIA'S WARS OF EMERGENCE

field regiments, were trained aggressively and to rely quite heavily on cold steel rather than firepower. There were indications that this rather Swedish-style of fighting was undergoing some changes in the final years of Peter's life.

There were in essence two supporting arms to this army. The first was artillery and engineering; the former represented a relatively long-standing Russian strength. It was a branch of the military requiring considerable education and technical expertise. The enclave of producers and practitioners that had existed in the seventeenth century was expanded by Peter, who placed greater emphasis on the development of Russian mathematical and engineering expertise, but its format and even some of its manufacturing establishment (if not its educational one) were seventeenth-century survivors. This arm was dominated by men from outside the nobility. Europeans (and the Ottomans) recognized its high quality as early as the second siege of Narva.

The second supporting arm was the navy, which, although large, operated most successfully in conjunction with the land army. Although the navy was an important element of Russia's victory over Sweden, it was also exceedingly expensive in proportion to its size and its successes. The navy was supported until 1725 in part by the enthusiasm and propaganda efforts of the Tsar. With his encouragement, the metaphor of the ship of state and naval and nautical terminology became the prevailing mode at court, and books, engravings and other cultural products repeated the theme. The involvement of the population in and successes of the navy were, however, comparatively restricted.

The manufacturing and techno-educational elements of the army and navy were restricted to carefully limited economic and educational sectors. Artillery, for example, or uniforms, were enormously expensive to provide to the entire army in the short run. However, the technical expertise and manufacturing plant required could quite feasibly be reproduced within a small economic and educational enclave.

Despite the enormous reach of the Russian Empire and its pursuit of expansionist aims in the Caucasus, Siberia and elsewhere, Peter had clearly absorbed a cardinal geopolitical lesson of eastern Europe. Muscovy was vulnerable because it operated from a depopulated expansive core. The main deployment of troops during peacetime therefore protected a limited central area: Moscow, St Petersburg, the Golden Ring and other nearby areas. While the army could make deep strategic strikes into Persia, Central Asia and the Ottoman Balkans, it was primarily defensive forces that permanently guarded the distant and far-flung perimeters. The Empire's principal troops guarded its heartland proper. In some respects, this represented a retrenchment and redirection of military force since Aleksei Mikhailovich's time.

It was the ability to sustain this military machine not for a season, a campaign, or even a war, but permanently and more or less regularly that was the product of the era after Poltava. Towards the end of Peter's reign, more of Russia's elite at all levels was acquiring a vested interest in the Petrine military system, now 25 years in the making. Aristocratic families, whose scions had so recently operated in alien if not hostile fashion vis-à-vis the Petrine state, now more obviously shared in central administrative and court power. A perpetuation of Petrine policies seemed likely. Aristocrats inimical to reforms were balanced at the centre by Peter's old favourites (Menshikov, for example) and new men, both commoners and nobles (Iagushinskii). The Table of Ranks institutionalized a reorganized service and status system for a new nobility. Merit promotions up the ranks had long since diluted the numbers of foreigners in Russian service, and renewed and redefined hereditary service, creating a body of men with a vested interest in the continuation of the Petrine system in some form. These arrangements partially protected the position of hereditary noblemen, while the military part of the system, at least, appeared durable, flexible and stable.[83]

To greater social and political reliability and balance was added greater fiscal predictability. The revised *guberniia* system, supplemented by billeting and the soul tax, was nearly adequate to sustain the military. If taxes and other arrangements fell short, then the methods of their collection and enforcement provided licence enough to sustain officers and men alike.

This framework, although it offered stability and permanence to many, was still at great risk as Peter's reign ended. Despite the balance and relative longevity of most service-status provisions in the Table of Ranks, its conditions did not guarantee the support of some disgruntled hereditary service families. The most recent readjustment of administrative and political power in the Senate and colleges was unproven and of very recent vintage. The soul tax and allied financial mechanisms were profoundly hated not only by the peasantry, who paid its exorbitant demands, but by serfholders, who were hostile to its cost and to the petty tyranny of its military collectors. Fiscal and other pressures led to banditry and to flight, with so-called atamans leading peasants in a Cossack-like, internal resistance. The survival of the military system would depend as much upon political as upon the military events of the next reigns.

Notes

1 A. G. Ageeva, 'Severnaia voina i isskustvo graviury', in *Russkaia kul'tura v usloviiakh inozemnykh nashestvii* (Moscow, 1990) vol. 2, 157, 173–4.

2 I. I. Rastunov, ed., *Istoriia severnoi voiny, 1700–1721* (Moscow, 1987); L. G. Beskrovnyi, *Russkaia armiia i flot v XVIII veke* (Moscow, 1958), 217–18.

3 Lindsey A. Hughes, *Russia in the Age of Peter the Great* (New Haven, Conn., 2002), 353.

4 Beskrovnyi, *Russkaia*, 26–30.

5 *PSZ*, vol. 4, doc. 2315 (Feb. 1711), 588–9; doc. 2374 (14 June 1711), 595–6; doc. 2467 (Jan 1712), 776–9.

6 *PSZ*, vol. 4, doc. 2499 (11 March 1712), 818.

7 See RGVIA f. 490 op. 32 and op. 49, officers' insistence on their having been present with the regiment.

8 Beskrovnyi, *Russkaia*, 30–1.

9 E. V. Anisimov, *Podatnaia reforma Petra I* (Leningrad, 1982), 23, 35, discusses the wave of fiscal reforms that accompanied the establishment of *gubernii*; see V. N. Avtokratov, 'Pervye komissariatskie organy Russkoi reguliarnoi armii, 1700–1710 gg', *IZ*, vol. 68 (1961), 167, on the shift of military fiscal responsibilities from the centre to the *gubernii*.

10 N. K. Zeziulinskii, *K rodosloviiu 34-kh pekhotnykh polkov Petra I* (Petrograd, 1915), 10.

11 *PSZ*, vol. 4, doc. 2443 (Oct. 1711), 799. A general description of the *guberniia* reform is in E. V. Anisimov, *The Reforms of Peter the Great* trans. J. T. Alexander, (Armonk, New York, 1993), 89–92; E. V. Anisimov, *Gosudarstvennye preobrazovaniia i samoderzhavie Petra velikogo* (St Petersburg, 1997), 25–7, points out that the *boiar* commission (1701–10) within Peter's Secret Chancellery was made up of members of the former Duma, whose commitment to his cause he tried to foster.

12 Peter B. Brown, 'The pre-1700 origins of Peter the Great's provincial-administrative (*guberniia*) reform', typescript.

13 Above ch. 7, 4, 7 fn. 9; see Paul Bushkovich, *Peter the Great* (Cambridge, 2001), 215, 229 about Peter's difficulties in finding *boiar* help in his endeavours, both military and foreign policy.

14 Bushkovich, *Peter the Great* 215; Hughes, *Russia*, 61. Anisimov, *Gosudarstvennye*, 119, points out the practical similarities of the pre-1710 institutions to their seventeenth-century predecessors. The close personal

participation of the Tsar certainly persisted. See Simon Dixon, ed., *Britain and Russia in the Age of Peter the Great. Historical Documents* (London, 1998), docs 230–41, for example.

15 T. K. Krylov, 'Russko-Turetskie otnoshenie vo vremia Severnoi Voiny', *IZ*, vol. 10 (1941), 268, 271–2. After Mazepa's defection in Ukraine and the Bulavin rebellion on the Don, the Cossack host was subsumed into the Russian military establishment.

16 A. Levy, 'Military Reform in the Ottoman Empire', *Middle Eastern Studies*, vol. 18 no. 3 (1982), 229, 231; Gabor Agoston, 'Ottoman warfare in Europe', in Jeremy Black, ed., *European Warfare, 1453–1815* (New York, 1999), 140.

17 A. Z. Myshlaevskii, 'Voina s Turtsieiu 1711 goda: Prutskaia operatsiia: materialy, izvlechennye iz arkhivov', *Voennyi sbornik* (St Petersburg, 1892–1904), 3.

18 Jeremy Black *European Warfare, 1660–1815* (New Haven, Conn., 1994), 13; Levy, 'Military', 230.

19 Beskrovnyi, *Rossiia*, 291–220; Anisimov, *Reforms*, 129.

20 *PSZ*, vol. 4, doc. 2377 (19 June 1711), 699.

21 Russia stationed pickets to prevent the plague's spread. *PSZ*, vol. 4, doc. 2340 (March 1711), 649.

22 Myshlaevskii, 'Voina', docs 16–18, 24, 28–9, 34; Avtokratov, 'Pervye komissariatskie', 188.

23 *Pis'ma i Bumagi* vol. 11 part 1 (Moscow, 1962), docs 4566, 4567, 314–16; Beskrovnyi, *Russkaia*, 218–22. Shafirov was again in charge of direct negotiations in this case.

24 See RGVIA f. 490 op. 2 no. 32, l.3, for one among many such examples.

25 For example, Zolotarev, *VIO*, 266; a poem on Pruth by Feofan Prokopovich emphasizes the numerical superiority of the Ottomans and the participation of Cossacks and Kalmyks in the fighting. A. Borodulin and Iu. Kashtanov, eds., *Armiia Petra I* (Moscow, 1994), 20.

26 *PSZ*, vol. 4, doc. 2319 (Feb. 1711), 590–614, 627; N. I. Solov'ev, *Istoricheskie ocherki ustroistva i dovol'stva Russkaikh reguliarnykh voisk, 1700–1761*, Vyp 1 (St Petersburg, 1900), 45.

27 O. Leonov and I. Ul'ianov, *Reguliarnaia pekhota* (Moscow, 1995), 18. Irregulars and local residents were dispersed through other troops or disbanded. Solov'ev, *Istoricheskie*, 46. The reconfiguration of garrison forces also increased the structural similarity of the Russian armed forces to those of seventeenth-century France, Spain and the Netherlands. Geoffrey Parker, *The Military Revolution* (Cambridge, 1996), 40–1.

28 Elise Kimerling-(Wirtschafter), 'Soldiers' Children, 1719–1856', *Forschungen zur Osteuropäischen Geschichte*, vol. 30 (1982), 64, 70, 90; *PSZ*, vol. 4, doc. 2319 (Feb. 1711), 590–614, 627; N. Solov'ev, 'Kratkii istoricheskii ocherk raskhodov na armiiu', *Voennyi sbornik*, vol. 214 no. 12 (1893), 227.

29 M. D. Rabinovich, *Polki Petrovskoi armii, 1689–1725. Kratkii spravochnik* (Moscow, 1977), docs. 340–3 and others.

30 I. L. Busev-Davidov and H. L. Krasheninnikov, 'Goroda kreposti', in N. F. Gulianitskii, ed., *Peterburg i drugie novye Rossiiskie goroda XVIII-pervoi polovine XIX vekov* (Moscow, 1995), 282. Interest in frontier fortification in the south is clear from a 1718 survey of the condition of the southern fortresses, published in its entirety in A. Z. Myshlaevskii, ed., *Kreposti i garnizony iuzhnoi Rossii v 1718. Izvlechenie iz sovremennago otcheta Kievskoi gubernii* (St Petersburg, 1897).

31 Michael Khodarkovsky, *Where Two Worlds Met* (Ithaca, NY, 1992), 215–16, 219, 229–35.

32 C. H. von Manstein, *Contemporary Memoirs of Russia from the Year 1727 to 1744* (London, 1968), 44–7, 94–5; M. T. Beliavskii, *Odnodvortsy chernozem'ia* (Moscow, 1984), 17–19; T. Esper, 'The Odnodvortsy and the Russian Nobility', *SEER*, vol. 14 (1967), 127; M. D. Rabinovich, 'Odnodvortsy v pervoi polovine XVIII v.', *Ezhegodnik po agrarnoi istorii vostochnoi Evropy* (1971), 138–41. Eleven of the *landmilitsiia* troops were disbanded in 1741.

33 Peter later urged that his men 'be taught to use their guns as the Habsburgs do'; the Habsburgs apparently had some identifiable Eurasian and west European techniques. Black, *European Warfare*, 105.

34 David Kirby, *Northern Europe in the Early Modern Period. The Baltic World, 1492–1772* (Harlow, 1990), 318; R. M. Hatton, *Charles XII of Sweden* (New York, 1969), 516–18.

35 John Perry, *The State of Russia under the Present Czar* (London, 1716), 11.

36 Philip Longworth, 'Transformations in Cossackdom', in G. Rothenberg et al., eds, *East Central European Society and War* (Boulder, Col., 1982), 456–7; Graeme Herde, 'The Azov Campaigns', (unpubl. 2001), 39.

37 Anthony Cross, *By the Banks of the Neva* (Cambridge, 1997), 160–8, among others, names two British admirals and five more Britons commanding Russian ships in 1721.

38 Beskrovnyi, *Russkaia* 49–50; Claes Peterson, 'Der Morskoj Ustav Peter des Grossen', *JfGO* vol. 24 (1976), 345–56 on the Ustav's origins; Cross, *By the Banks*, 167, gives the fleet 29 battleships.

39 J. Kipp, 'Peter the Great. A naval perspective', *Records of the International Colloquy on Military History* (Manhattan, Kansas, 1984), 121, argues that the galley fleet was decisive to Russian victory.

40 P. A. Krotov, 'Sozdanie lineinogo flota na Baltike pri Petre I', *IZ*, vol. 116 (1988); N. N. Petrukhintsev, *Tsarstovanie Anny Ioannovny* (St Petersburg, 2001), 213–14.

41 *PSZ*, vol. 4, doc. 4449 (1724); John LeDonne, *Absolutism and the Ruling Class: The Formation of the Russian Political Order, 1700–1825* (Oxford, 1991), 13–14; Kimerling-(Wirtschafter), 'Soldiers' children', 90. Also see Hughes, *Russia in the Age*, 299–307.

42 A. N. Medushevskii *Reformy Petra I i sud'by Rossii* (Moscow, 1994), 76.

43 Medushevskii, 77–81; P. Sedov, 'Podnosheniia v Moskovskikh prikazakh XVII veka', *Otechestvennaia istoriia*, no. 1 (1996), 139–150, points out that this, too, was something the Petrine administration shared with its late seventeenth-century predecessors.

44 Peter Brown, 'The pre-1700 origins', 19; LeDonne, *Absolutism*, 78–9; Hughes, *Russia*, 115.

45 Anisimov, *Gosudarstvennye*, 259–60 and Appendix I, 293–8.

46 *PSZ*, vol. 4, doc. 2230; vol. 7, doc. 4484. The *fiskaly* were eventually subordinated to the Procuracy. See Anisimov, *Gosudarstvennye*, 37–8.

47 Ibid., 108, 260–1.

48 See Bushkovich, *Peter the Great*, 'Epilogue', on the political restructuring.

49 Anisimov, *Gosudarstvennye*, 92, 291–2; John H. L. Keep, *Soldiers of the Tsar* (Oxford, 1985), 128. There were still 'remnants' of older administrative forms even in 1720 (Anisimov, *Gosudarstvennye*, 145.)

50 Anisimov, *Gosudarstvennye*, 118–19, 121–2.

51 LeDonne, *Absolutism*, 72, 77–8. He cites *PSZ*, vol. 4, docs 4257, 4430, 4621; F. P. Shelekhov, 'Glavnoe intendantskoe pravlenie: istoricheskii ocherk', *Stoletie voennago ministerstva* (St Petersburg, 1903), vol. 5 part 1, 24–6, 31–2.

52 C. B. Stevens, *Soldiers on the Steppe* (DeKalb, Illinois, 1995); A. V. Pavlov, 'Gosudarev dvor v istorii Rossii XVII veka', *Forschungen zur osteuropaischen Geschichte*, vol. 56, 227–42.

53 Carol B. Stevens, 'Evaluating Peter's army: the impact of internal reform', in Eric Lohr and Marshall Poe, eds, *The Military and Society in Russia, 1450–1917* (Leiden, 2002), 165–8.

54 See RGVIA f. 490 op. 2 delo 49, 114 as an example of corporate loyalty. Service promotions charted from f. 490 op. 2 dela 3, 4, 14, 32, 48, 49, 54 and f. 489 op. 1 ed. khr. 2451; LeDonne, *Absolutism*, 25.

55 RGVIA f. 490 op. 2; most officers clearly recollected which individuals had promoted them.

56 *PSZ,* vol. 4, doc. 2319, 599–602.

57 LeDonne, *Absolutism,* 12; RGVIA f. 490, op. 2: 'dates of officers' promotions'.

58 S. M. Troitskii, *Russkii absoliutizm i dvoriantsvo* (Moscow, 1974), 124.

59 Troitskii, *Russkii absoliutizm* contains a frequently cited discussion; for recent English accounts see Keep, *Soldiers of the Tsar,* 120–9 and Hughes, *Russia,* 180–5. The decree is *PSZ,* vol. 6, doc. 3890 (1722).

60 Troitskii, *Russkii absoliutizm,* 47–118.

61 Peter's first thoughts on this topic seem to have applied only to the military. *Pis'ma i bumagi* vol. 13 part 2, doc. 6361, 207 and 49, notes.

62 Isabel DeMadariaga, 'The Russian nobility, 1600–1800', in H. M. Scott, ed., *The European Nobilities in the Seventeenth and Eighteenth Centuries* (Harlow, 1995), 244.

63 Troitskii *Absoliutizm,* to 118.

64 Keep, *Soldiers of the Tsar,* 128; Anisimov, *Gosudarstvennye,* 265–7. The *Heroldmeister* often acted as record keeper.

65 *Idem*; RGVIA f. 490 op. 2, delo 3 offers an example of the different treatment afforded rank-and-file military who were also *tsaredvortsy.*

66 Anisimov, *Gosudarstvennye,* Appendix I; Troitskii, *Absoliutizm,* 105–7.

67 P. N. Miliukov, *Gosudarstvennoe khoziaistvo v pervoi chetverti XVII stolietiia i reforma Petra Velikago* (St Petersburg, 1905), 115–21, cites 62–87 per cent between 1680 and 1701; Keep, *Soldiers of the Tsar,* 137, and Solov'ev *Istoricheskie ocherki,* 75, offer re-examinations and calculations for later years.

68 Parker, *The Military Revolution,* 62–3.

69 S. H. Baron, 'The Fate of the *gosti*', *CMRS,* vol. 14 no. 4 (1973); Miliukov, *Gos. Khoz.,* 89–90.

70 Arcadius Kahan, *The Plow, the Hammer, and the Knout* (Chicago, 1985), 330; Anisimov, *Reforms,* 160, and his *Podatnaia reforma,* 35; Solov'ev, *Istoricheskie ocherki,* 88.

71 See Anisimov, *Gosudarstvennye,* 163, and his *Podatnaia,* ch. 7, on billeting.

72 This amount counted on 47 males to support each infantryman, 57 for each dragoon, and 40 more for each dragoon's horse.

73 LeDonne, *Absolutism* 274.

74 Op. cit., 128, 133.

75 Anisimov, *Reforms*, 162.

76 Anisimov, *Podatnaia reforma*, 103, 233; see Richard Hellie, *The Economy and Material Culture of Russia, 1600–1725* (Chicago, 1999), 548–9, on 'notional' taxation.

77 Keep, *Soldiers of the Tsar*, 133–4.

78 Anisimov, *Podatnaia reforma*, 135–232.

79 Anisimov, *Podatnaia reforma*, 258.

80 V. P. Lystsov, *Persidskii pokhod Petra I, 1722–1723* (Moscow, 1951), 97–101, 107–9, 119.

81 Hughes, *Russia*, 59.

82 See *Armiia Petra I*, which minimizes the Pruth defeat, and also recounts the Persian campaign without mention of the significant role played by the Ottoman presence and threat, 18–20.

83 M. D. Rabinovich, 'Sotsial'noe proizkhozhdenie i imushchestvennoi plozhenie ofitserov reguliarnoi Russkoi armii v kontse severnoi voiny', in N. I. Pavlenko et al., eds, *Rossiia v period reform Petra I* (Moscow, 1973); Nancy Shields Kollmann, *By Honor Bound* (Ithaca, 1999), 224, 233.

Russia without Peter[1]

When Peter died in January 1725 he had asserted his right to select the next Russian sovereign, rather than leaving it to chance and primogeniture. He had not, however, actually chosen the next Emperor or Empress. The selection of Peter's second wife, Empress Catherine I, was far from automatic. Peter's own inner coterie was divided, with a number of its more aristocratic members expressing a preference for Peter's grandson, Petr Alekseevich. As it turned out, however, Catherine succeeded to the throne the morning following Peter's death, supported by Menshikov and less directly by those around the Duke of Holstein, Catherine's future son-in-law. Although Catherine proved quite adept at balancing rival factions, she not surprisingly lacked the command and legitimacy of her late spouse. Her death in 1727 was shortly followed by the removal from power of Menshikov, and the aristocratic Dolgorukii family dominated the brief reign of the young Peter II, r. 1727–30. Peter I's great reforms to the military (and elsewhere) thus lacked a stable and committed hand at the political tiller for at least five years following his death.[2]

On the face of it, the Russian military after Peter's death continued much as it had under Peter. That is, for the next five years the army's size, composition and distribution remained similar to 1724–5. A field army with a large dragoon contingent remained in quarters in the *gubernii* as they had since the end of the Northern War (or since 1723 in some cases). These regiments defended the Muscovite heartland, while the special Nizovoi Infantry Corps staffed newly conquered Persian fortresses on the Caspian. Garrison forces and cavalry land militia completed the battle-ready regiments; 40 per cent of the garrisons faced the Baltic, while the land militia was distributed along the southern frontier. Most field and garrison regiments were supported by billeting and by the regular soul tax; Siberian taxes paid for the Guards, the Persian provinces paid for the Nizovoi Infantry, and the state-peasants' tax (a special variant of the soul tax) for the land militia. The navy, superficially, remained approximately the same size. National conscription maintained military manpower at the level of the late Petrine years with a draft about every 1.7 years. The 1726 recruitment drew more recruits than ever gathered to date in the Russian Empire.[3] The size of the army was thus retained in the face of clear evidence (in desertions and failures to appear) of the population's reluctance and inability to sustain it. A large army was an inviolable inheritance from Petrine, and earlier, times.[4]

Nevertheless, a gradual retreat from the most onerous burdens of the Petrine system soon began. In an effort to ease tensions building around the soul tax and its collection, the assessment was lowered to 70 kopeks immediately following Peter's death. The new assessment, never mind the yield, fell below demand. Expenditure on the navy and, in particular, on ship construction dropped quite sharply, as did other kinds of military payments. At first the army was immune to such cuts, since it continued to collect the soul tax itself. Under Peter II, however, the military was eased out of tax collection. Available cash even for the army thus declined during Peter II's reign. The resulting financial cuts were absorbed in an unplanned and rather ad hoc way. The drop in both assessments and collections relieved pressure on the country's new leaders and allowed some relaxation after the continuous high demands of the Petrine era. Nevertheless, the system of taxation and recruitment nonetheless remained burdensome, despite (and sometimes because of) succeeding governments' half-hearted efforts to limit its impact.[5]

Russia's post-Petrine rulers were unwilling to relinquish Russia's military system or its fledgling stature. In fact there were minor institutional changes, such as the separation of engineering sections from the artillery units. The land militia of the southern frontier, rather than retrenching, grew by one regiment.[6]

Perhaps fortunately for Russian aspirations, this was neither a period of great technical and military change, nor a period of intense military activity. Russian foreign policy was quiescent. After some initial concerns over the throne of Holstein-Gottorp, the Baltic area remained relatively peaceful despite Swedish revanchism. A Russo-Austrian alliance was signed in 1726. Russia thus recuperated from the Northern War without withdrawing from the international system and without returning to war. Russia's forces occupied the Caspian ports until 1732 at considerable expense and little gain. Russian expansion into Siberia continued, although an expedition into the Chukchi peninsula pulled back in the late 1720s. The great European wars of the second quarter of the eighteenth century were yet to come (War of Polish Succession, the Russo-Ottoman War of 1735). Russia's southern neighbours on the steppe, especially Crimea, found themselves increasingly pressured and even impoverished by Russian agricultural colonization of the steppe. The military strengths of their Ottoman overlords declined by comparison with the newly institutionalized Russian army. However, Russia's defensive frontiers were not extended by additional fortified lines until the reign of Anna Ioannovna.[7]

Although contemporaries bewailed military decline and underpreparedness, the character and seriousness of Russian military retreat should not be overstated. Much of the Petrine system continued to function as before. Decline, from one perspective, was accommodation to the most significant demands of the political elites, from another. Foreign experts continued, predictably, to be promoted to occupy positions of importance. Count Burkhard Christoph von Munnich, who had entered Russian service under Peter, rose to prominence first as Ober-Direktor of Fortifications (1727) and then Master General of Ordinance (1729). His efforts to renew and refurbish the army in the Empress Anna's reign were concomitant with harsher tax collection by the military, but they were balanced by an increasingly high valuation of Russian officers and conditions of increasing ease and privilege for the nobility. An ever-growing number of Russian officers and bureaucrats were directly and indirectly committed to working within the Petrine (military) system. By 1730 Russia's military and political disputes took place within that system, rather than in opposition to it.

In the final analysis, achieving such commitment was one of the great triumphs of the Petrine, and immediately post-Petrine, eras. Referring to the result as 'the Petrine system' risks adding to all-too familiar over-attribution to the great Emperor. In practice the new military culture and its appurtenances were in significant part an evolution of seventeenth-century Muscovite behaviour, albeit with an admixture of contemporary Euro-Swedish institutions and culture. And the sources of the transformation hardly derived from the Emperor and his institutions alone, drawing as they did upon the individual and diverse Europeanization of the Russian elite, the presence of a diverse group of foreigners in many walks of Russian life, and the deracination of military life.

One fundamental result was the acceptance by the Russian elite of a self-definition that reaffirmed, while reconfiguring, its basis in military service. Although the Russian nobility may have shared its preference for military careers with other European elites, the Russians' obligation to serve was less typical. Their responsibilities partially embodied in the Table of Ranks were even more stringent and demanding than their seventeenth-century predecessors. They did however carry benefits. From the perspective of the lesser nobility, the new status arrangements were less exclusive and more stable than the *cursus honorum* of the preceding century. Furthermore, they recognized, as never before, bureaucratic and administrative power. The institutional definition of the new status-service system, as it appeared in the Table of Ranks, may have been borrowed from Sweden and Denmark; its success was linked to its Muscovite past. A relationship of the military-service nobility to the state and its institutions was thus solidly reaffirmed in the early eighteenth century.

The significance of the military within the state apparatus flowed directly from that relationship. The army and navy dominated the fiscal and financial concerns of the state. Not only did most of the state budget go to military concerns, the military was deeply involved in the collection of funds (its collection of the soul tax was reinstated in 1730), and in the enforcement of fiscal regularity. In policy and administration, the concerns of the military remained a top priority; at all levels, the institutions of policy making and administration contained many men whose first loyalties and training were military. The rise of Count Burkhard Christoph von Munnich to the heights of power by the reign of the Empress Anna only re-emphasized its obvious importance.

Several of the elements of this new military culture had a far-reaching impact on the lives of those Russians involved. Service for a cash salary rather than a land grant gave solid economic basis, as well as legal obligation, to service. The nobility needed salaries to sustain their lifestyles. At all levels of military service, salaries opened up the possibilities for a permanent and professional military. A clearly defined hierarchy of military and civilian offices operated on the basis of written rules, a window on social as well as professional advancement.

Such characteristics of eighteenth-century military life should not be idealized. Salaries were often underpaid or even unpaid, especially at the lowest ranks, jeopardizing survival and encouraging bribery and corruption. Promotions were unjustifiably confirmed for reasons of favouritism and patronage. The brutality of a socio-political system which gave the nobility life-or-death power over their serfs was replicated in military arrangements: in conscription, in soul tax collection, and typically reproduced in the relationship between officers and men. A new brutality of military relationships was a predictable sequel of seventeenth and eighteenth-century political and legal reorganization.

Nevertheless, an institutionalized military culture emerged. The army and navy became more permanent and regular; they were increasingly supported by persistent governmental structures and rules. Many generations and individuals contributed to identifying and attaining this goal. It also required over a century's socio-cultural and political adjustment. In comparison, the technological and internal organization of an effective military had been quite easily achieved. Its culture and achievements were embodied in the Russian defeat of the Ottomans at Stavuchany, Khotin and Jassy in the 1735–9 war – even without Peter.

Although the fundamentals of this military system remained in place for more than a century, however, the system itself was not static, as the next reigns would show.

Summary

How can the broad transformations of Russia's military forces over the centuries before 1730 best be understood? The nature of change within the military proper is relatively easily categorized. Succinctly, Russia's army in 1460 was a growing force of archer-cavalry men that mobilized around the Muscovite Grand Prince. Nearly three centuries later, a vast Russian Empire had a trained, regular, standing military, with all the attendant changes that that implied. Shifts of this nature have been characterized as part of an early modern military revolution. It encompassed the tactical and technological shifts associated with the use of gunpowder and firearms; bureaucratic change for resource and manpower mobilization; social changes that permitted different recruitment; and above all the political will to identify and implement military change on a grand scale. In Muscovy in the late sixteenth century this process created only a small contingent of free, trained and salaried infantrymen – a social anomaly among nobles, and a military anomaly on the steppe. After the Time of Troubles, the advantages of the different military style were clear; as the century wore on, so were the advantages of numbers. More of Muscovy's large army became trained infantrymen and cavalry. The political and social toll of the transition was enormous and lasting – the final legal enserfment of the Russian peasantry and the destruction of traditional social and economic status for hereditary serviceman. Despite near financial collapse, ingenious administrative expedients and the significant importation of foreign expertise, furthermore, the late seventeenth-century army was only a semi-standing and semi-permanent one. Peter the Great, however, built on its framework to create an increasingly permanent and professional military without abandoning its particular eastern European characteristics. More noble officers made a lifelong career of the military, depending for their promotions on knowledge and merit, as well as social relationships. For the rank-and-file, a different military life perforce became a primary and lasting identity.

Greater permanence and professionalism did not come easily. Russia had first to undergo some dramatic transitions in political structure and noble culture. These processes had, of course been underway for a considerable time and the military had been key to the process of their transformation. Extending the effectiveness of Muscovy's administrative bodies and integrating them with the political system were key to military transformation. The Muscovite bureaucracy grew out of the household of the monarch, with servants fulfilling skilled administrative functions, while the court resolved political issues. As the chancelleries expanded in number and function, they demanded, and got, knowledgeable, professional staff who were largely independent of the court. By the late seventeenth century, the chancelleries were numerous, their staffs skilled and able, and their leaders were important in the political realm. Peter and his predecessors attempted to revamp areas of governmental practice for the benefit of the military, but initially saw no need to tamper with the *prikaz* system itself. Significantly, institutional coordination and direction for the chancelleries was slow to arrive. Central coordination was formally exercised only by the Tsar's Secret Chancellery and the Tsar himself. Only with the Senate in 1711 did Russia acquire a formal institution for political and administrative coordination.

A more formal political process was finalized at about the same time. Until quite late, the court remained a rather informal series of concentric rings of consultative political patronage and power, with the Tsar at its centre surrounded by the Boair Duma and Assembly of the Land. The assumption of administrative power at the chancelleries by powerful families was an expression of a newer form of political power. But the informal consultative organizations were undercut by the growing size of the court, by the Tsar's favourites, and by bureaucratization in the seventeenth century. The old system was moribund before the end of the seventeenth century with the recognition, in the abolition of *mestnichestvo*, that the old method of linking service to family status no longer worked.

A new system was longer in the making. Peter the Great first ignored and then dismissed the Boair Duma, just as his father had ignored the Assembly of the Land a half century earlier. The power of aristocratic clans, however, was not just wielded through the Duma, and both the bureaucracy and dynastic politics were tools in the reconfiguration of political power. A resolution seems to have been attained by Peter and his immediate successors, not by the brutal disregard of political rivals, as is often suggested, but rather by the careful balancing of rival political powers through the court and into the institutions of the new bureaucracy. A Swedish model may have lain at the base of the final reconfiguration and the desire to balance different political factions. All the way down the line, however, traditional Muscovite concerns illuminated the final answers. The result (a Senate with a Privy Council presiding over colleges with hierarchically organized bureaucratic systems) was a Muscovite political creation as well as a Swedish administrative idea. The Senate ruled over the new Swedish colleges; regional administrations drew upon *gubernii* and their subsidiary provinces and districts. The Emperor in his Supreme Privy Council oversaw all. The Procuracy and its subsidiaries observed the entire system policing it for compliance and cooperation. This system did not, however, function just on abstract bureaucratic principles. The Table of Ranks was a renegotiated understanding of the nobility's role in power. The major political families of the Empire continued to dominate the administrative and political processes, now through the Procurator General and aristocratic appointments. On the local level, dignitaries governed through delicately balanced arrangements based on family rela-tionships, bureaucratic rules and *kormlenie*. The new balance generated political and social commitment to the new arrangements, and it proved finely enough calibrated to carry the country through more than five years without a strong monarch.

The role of the military in this transformation was a cardinal, if not a causal, one. It was the army that generated the largest chancelleries (Estate, Military); it was the army that demanded new revenues, new resources and new efficiencies in extracting resources. More than 70 per cent of Russian imperial moneys went to the military (not at all an unusual per-centage by the standards of the time). Russian elite status, as it was debated from the mid-seventeenth-century onwards, was debated in largely milit-ary terms. And it was the military that helped to instigate the new struc-tures of Petrine Russia, whether literally (the Senate was formed to govern Russia while Peter was at the Ottoman front) or practically (the army needed new revenues as it returned home after the Northern Wars). It was the army that required the consolidation of command and budgetary pro-cesses, and military bureaucracies that needed consolidation to produce reasonably predictable results. Peter's personal involvement with the milit-ary and its appurtenances made proximity to the Tsar a military matter, a transformation of the traditional association of status and military rank. The early eighteenth century marked the final element in the shift of the Emperor and his elite to a new mode: a military court surrounded by the structures of a bureaucratic Empire.

The cultural transformation of Russia was at least, if not more, profound as the bureaucratic one. The Europeanization (or more accurately de-isolation) of the Russian elite was well underway after the middle of the seventeenth century. Men of elite status read and spoke other languages, espoused European ideas, admired technology, literature and styles coming across Russia's borders. Outside the capitals, the exposure of men and women to such ideas came in large part through the army where foreign doctors, officers and technicians plied their trades, leaving contact with new assumptions and aspirations in their wake. These contacts were not all deeply appreciated. Serious cultural movements rejected the impact of Europeans living in Russia. With Peter, however, cultural change accelerated. All Russian officers were trained in and expected to teach European military science. While the Tsar's court reflected his appreciation of European styles, manners and the arts, army officers demonstrated a different familiarity with European practices. Officers in the 1720s universally discussed military science using European (usually German) terms; the language of their discourse, moulded by years at the front and minimal contact with civilian society, took on the shape of Europe and professionalism. It was a sea change, and, as it proved, a more-or-less irreversible one, spread by garrison schools and Guards regiments alike.

Military change by the eighteenth century thus instigated and indeed represented a prototype of political-administrative and elite cultural change. In this context, the events of the second half of Peter's reign were by far the more important, more important than the more obvious victory at Poltava, although they are rarely so characterized and infrequently studied.

The unsteady but persistent changes to the Russian military, tied to the cultural, economic and administrative structures that supported it, were key underpinnings to Russia's emergence as a European – indeed a world – power by the middle of the eighteenth century. The triumphal tone of this asseveration may not, however, have been felt or echoed by the Russian soldier who fought for it, nor the Russian peasant who supported him. The Russian military offered as its Petrine legacy a brutal and exploitative life; the successes of the Russian administration translated into the necessities of life, not its luxuries; the relationship between officers and men was a harsh echo of that between serf and master. For the peasantry, the costs of supporting the military machine consumed men, labour and money, imposing such burdens as to threaten both stability and prosperity. From the political perspective, however, the achievements of the military were reflected in the growing role that the Russian Empire would play on the European stage for the rest of the eighteenth century.

Notes

1 This title repeats that of E. V. Anisimov's 1994 monograph.

2 See E. V. Anisimov, *Rossiia bez Petra* (Leningrad, 1994), esp. chs 2, 6 for details.

3 N. N. Petrukhintsev, *Tsarstvovanie Anny Ioannovny. Formirovanie vnutripoliticheskogo kursa i sud'ba armii i flota, 1730–1735* (St Petersburg, 2001), 104–7, 314–315; *PSZ*, vol. 7, doc. 4859 (26 March 1726).

4 L. G. Beskrovnyi, *Russkaia armiia i flot v XVIII veke* (Moscow, 1958), 34–5, 55.

5 John H. L. Keep, *Soldiers of the Tsar* (Oxford, 1985), 144; Petrukhintsev, 109–10; E. V. Anisimov, *Podatnaia reforma Petra I* (Leningrad, 1982), 281.

6 Beskrovnyi, *Russkaia*, 58–60.

7 I. L. Busev-Davidov and H. L. Krashennikov, 'Novye goroda na reguliarnoi osnove; Goroda kreposti', in N. F. Gulianitskii, ed., *Peterburg i drugie novye Rossiiskie goroda XVIII-pervoi polovine XIX vekov* (Moscow, 1995), 275–301.

Bibliographic notes

The study of Russian military history in the early modern period is hampered by the many things that we do not yet know. As Paul Bushkovich has recently noted, almost all areas of Russian military history are in need of further research for the period 1613–1725, and, broadly speaking, that period is better studied than the century and a half that precedes it. For example, there are surprisingly few detailed studies of individual campaigns for the entire period under consideration in this book, up to and including those of Peter the Great. We have a better – if still intermittent – understanding of how military life was supposed to work (laws, orders, and intentions) than of military practice on the ground. The fundamental state and social structures underpinning the operation of the army, including finances, recruitment, promotion, provisioning and training, are still unevenly understood. As a consequence, what follows primarily describes the variety of topics and themes dealt with by historians writing in English.

For the reader's convenience, a full bibliography of works is available on the Worldwide Web at http://people.colgate.edu/kstevens/WarsBiblio.

Overviews

However great the opportunities for future study, Russian military history has also recently undergone a renaissance, which will offer the English-speaking reader some options for further reading and study. There is no single book-length overview for the early modern period, however. For the fifteenth to seventeenth centuries, an important introduction is the seminal work of Richard Hellie (*Enserfment and Military Change in Muscovy* (Chicago, 1972)). John L. H. Keep's *Soldiers of the Tsar. The Army and Society in Russia, 1462–1874* (Oxford, 1985) is another seminal contribution; where he can, Keep offers the soldiers' eye perspective in a field where the state's perspective is the most common. A volume in the

'Modern Wars in Perspective' series, Robert Frost's *The Northern Wars. War, State and Society in Northeastern Europe, 1558–1721* (Harlow, 1993), brings insight to the conditions of war on Russia's north-western front for an extended period, as well as providing an exceptionally international perspective on the contest for the eastern Baltic. William C. Fuller's *Strategy and Power in Russia, 1600–1914* (New York, 1992) offers a two-chapter overview of the Petrine period, while Brian J. Taylor's *Politics and the Russian Army, 1689–2000* (Cambridge, 2003) offers only introductory comments on the early period.

A number of articles offer very useful summaries on military history. These include articles by Brian Davies, with a broadly early focus ('The development of Russian military power, 1453–1815', in Jeremy Black, ed., *European Warfare, 1453–1815* (London, 1999), 145–179 and 'The foundations of Muscovite military power, 1453–1615', in Fredrich W. Kagan and Robin Higham, eds, *The Military History of Tsarist Russia* (New York, 2002), 10–30) and one by Paul Bushkovich on a slightly later period ('The Romanov transition', in Fredrich W. Kagan and Robin Higham, eds, *The Military History of Tsarist Russia* (New York, 2002), 31–45). Richard Hellie, 'Warfare, changing military technology, and the evolution of Muscovite society', in John A. Lynn, ed., *The Tools of War* (Urbana, Illinois, 1990) should also be mentioned. A broad comparative outlook is to be found in Marshall Poe's 'The consequences of the military revolution in Muscovy', *CSSH* (1996), 603–18. A collection of articles – Eric Lohr and Marshall Poe, eds, *The Military and Society in Russia, 1450–1917* (Leiden, 2002) – offers no overview, but largely research pieces, mentioned in the appropriate sections below.

Some comprehensive overviews of this period's military history are available in Russian only. Some key works are A. V. Chernov, *Vooruzhennye sily Russkogo gosudarstva v XV–XVII vv.* (Moscow, 1954); P. O. Bobrovskii, *Perekhod Rossii k reguliarnoi armii* (St Petersburg, 1885); E. A. Razin, *Istoriia voennogo iskusstva*, 3 vols (Moscow, 1955–61); A. S. Grishinkii et al., eds, *Istoriia russkoi armii i flota*, 15 vols (Moscow, 1911–13) and L. G. Beskrovnyi, *Russkaia armiia i flot v XVII veke* (Moscow, 1958). The new three-volume *Voennaia istoriia otechestva s drevnykh vremen do nashikh dnei* (Moscow, 1995) offers some helpful information, but also has notable lacunae.

Comparisons with Russia's foes and allies provide valuable context for Russian events. Footnote citations throughout the text mention some of them. The lasting debate over the 'military revolution' provides another important background.

Part I: 1450–1600

Research monographs and articles in English are the sparsest for the period before 1600. Thematically scattered but notable are: the work of Gustave Alef, especially 'Muscovite Military Reforms in the second half of the fifteenth century', *FzOG*, vol. 18 (1973), 73–108; articles by Thomas Esper, including 'Military Self Sufficiency and Weapons Technology in Muscovite Russia', *SR*, vol. 28 no. 2 (1969), 185–208. Lohr and Poe, eds, *The Military and Society in Russia* – contains an article by Janet Martin on the Tatar military role during the Livonian Wars, 365–88; Don Ostrowski's 'Troop mobilization by the Grand Princes, 1313–1533', 19–40 and Sergei Bogatyrev on Ivan IV's campaigns against Novgorod and Pskov, 325–64. Also see Marshall Poe's 'Muscovite Personnel Records, 1475–1550', *JfGO*, 45 (1997), 361–78; and the work of Dianne L. Smith: 'The Muscovite Officer Corps, 1475–1598' (Ph.D. dissertation, University of California, Davis, 1989) and 'Muscovite Logistics, 1642–1598, *SEER*, 71/1, 35–65.

Studies of Russia's expansion eastward necessarily include military elements: Matthew P. Romaniello, 'Controlling the Frontier: monasteries and infrastructure in the Volga region, 1552–1682', *Central Asian Survey*, 19, 3–4 (2000), 429–43, as well as his thesis; Henry Huttenbach in two summary articles on Kazan and Siberia in Michael Rywkin, ed., *Russian Colonial Expansion to 1917* (London, 1988); and Halil Inalchik in English and Turkish, 'The Origin of Ottoman–Russian rivalry and the Don-Volga Canal (1569)' *Ankara Üniversitesi Yilligi*, vol. 1 (1946–7), 47–111. L. J. D. Collins, 'Military Organization and Tactics of the Crimean Tatars in the 16th and 17th centuries', in V. J. Perry and M. Yapp, eds, *War, Technology and Society in the Middle East* (Oxford, 1975) provides a nearly unique perspective.

A variety of excellent articles and monographs deal with matters of key importance to military development without themselves focusing on the military. Where possible and appropriate, I have cited English-language work of this kind in the footnotes to help identify them to the interested reader. For this early period, the work of Ann Kleimola, Nancy Kollmann, Janet Martin, Donald Ostrowski and Jaroslaw Pelenski are particularly useful to the military historian. Biographies of Ivan IV perforce deal with military matters to some extent. Isabel de Madariaga's has recently appeared (New Haven, 2005) and one from Charles Halperin is expected.

English-language primary sources with material on the army include R. M. Croskey and E. C. Ronquist, trans. and eds, 'George Trakhaniot's description of Russia in 1486', *Russian History/Histoire Russe* (spring

1990) 55–64; the acid early sixteenth-century observations of Austrian
envoy Sigismund von Herberstein, *Notes Upon Russia*; the accounts of
sixteenth-century English travellers in L. E. Berry and R. O. Crummey,
eds, *Rude and Barbarous Kingdom* (Madison, Wisc., 1968); and Heinrich
von Staden on Ivan IV.

Part II: 1600–1700

Recent work discussing the seventeenth-century military in some detail
includes Chester Dunning's new *Russia's First Civil War: The Time of
Troubles and the Founding of the Romanov Dynasty* (University Park,
Penn., 2001); it disputes the standard interpretation of the Time of
Troubles as discussed in Sergei Platonov, *The Time of Troubles*, ed. and
trans. J. T. Alexander (Lawrence, Kansas, 1970) and others. Brian Davies'
examination of the garrison town of Kozlov in the 1630s and 1640s,
State, Power, and Community in Early Modern Russia (Palgrave, 2004)
and Carol Belkin Stevens' late seventeenth-century *Soldiers on the Steppe*
(DeKalb, Illinois, 1995) both focus on military mobilizations on the
southern steppe. William Reger's work on European mercenaries includes
'In the Service of the Tsar' (Ph.D. dissertation, University of Illinois, 1997)
and 'Baptising Mars', in Lohr and Poe, eds, *The Military and Society in
Russia*, 389–412. Chapter 6 of Geraldine Phipps's Ph.D. dissertation,
'Britons in seventeenth-century Russia' (University of Pennsylvania, 1971)
focuses on such men in the army.

  Robert I. Frost's work (*After the Deluge: Poland-Lithuania and the
Second Northern War, 1655–1660* (Cambridge, 1993) and *Northern
Wars*) provides nearly the only detailed overview of the Thirteen Years'
War in English since Carl Bickford O'Brien's *Muscovy and the Ukraine
. . . 1654–1667* (Berkeley, 1963); the latter is not particularly military
in orientation. Readers are urged to consult the works of Frank Sysyn,
Serhi Plohy and Myhailo Hrushevskyi for context on Ukraine. Michael
Khodarkovsky's *Russia's Steppe Frontier* (Bloomington, 2002) is not mil-
itary in its perspective, but provides a broad overview of otherwise little
discussed events on the eastern steppe from 1600 onwards; similarly,
Alton Donnelly's *The Russian Conquest of Bashkiria, 1552–1740* (New
Haven, Conn., 1968). Robert O. Crummey's *Aristocrats and Servitors*
(Princeton, 1983) includes a view of the Muscovite elite in the army; further background for military change is to be found in Lindsey Hughes'
biographies: *Russia and the West: V. V. Golitsyn* (Newtonville, Mass.,
1984) and *Sophia: Regent of Russia* (New Haven, Conn., 1990).

Among shorter pieces, the collection edited by Jarmo Kotilaine and Marshall Poe, *Modernizing Muscovy. Reform and Social Change in Seventeenth Century Russia* (London, 2004) contains articles on the Thirty Years' War (Paul Dukes), European mercenaries and the reception of reform in the seventeenth century (Reger), and musketeer rebellions in the late seventeenth century (Graeme Herd); the Lohr and Poe collection, *The Military and Society in Russia*, mentioned above, has another five articles on the seventeenth-century military: Richard Hellie offers another of his very useful and revealing numerical analyses – here a broad picture of the costs of defence and expansion; Jarmo Kotilaine's overview of the arms trade and production is followed by two analyses of the late seventeenth century – Brian Davies on the failure of the second Chigirin campaign (1678) and Peter B. Brown on Tsar Aleksei Mikhailovich's command style. The last of the five is John Le Donne's overview of the Russian grand strategy during the seventeenth and eighteenth centuries.

Visitors to Russia wrote memoirs, some of which are available as original sources in English; particularly interesting from a military perspective are Jacques Margeret (a French mercenary for Boris Godunov), a group of Poles (Zolkiewski, Maskiewicz, Pasek) and General Patrick Gordon, who began working for the Russian crown in the 1660s and eventually became one of Peter I's chief advisers. The Russian Law Code or *Ulozhenie* of 1649 (Richard Hellie, trans. and ed. (Chicago, 1988), contains several key articles on military service and related subjects.

Part III: 1700–30

For the early eighteenth century, there are some richer offerings. Recent overviews of Peter's reign offer particular information about his military endeavours. Lindsey Hughes' *Russia in the Age of Peter the Great* (New Haven, 2002) includes a chapter specifically on military affairs. Although Paul Bushkovich's *Peter the Great: the Struggle for Power* (Cambridge, 2001) focuses on political matters, his 'The politics of command in the army of Peter the Great' in David Schimmpelpennink van der Oye and Bruce Menning, eds., *Reforming the Tsar's Army* (Cambridge, 2004), 253–72, focuses some of those themes on the military. Evgenii Anisimov's *The Reforms of Peter the Great: Progress through Coercion* (New York, 1993) offers a chapter's overview of military events. Richard Hellie also has an overview of the Petrine army in an article in *CASS*, vol. 8 (1974). Christopher Duffy's *Russia's Military Way to the West* (London, 1985) treats Peter's reign as part of an eighteenth-century whole, as does Bruce

Menning's 'Russia and the West: the problem of 18th century military models', in A. C. Cross, ed., *Russia and the West in the 18th Century* (Newtonville, Mass., 1983).

There are a several more specific studies. Carol B. Stevens examines the social implications of military reform and the impact of the frontier after Pruth (1711) in articles in Lohr and Poe, eds, *The Military and Society in Russia*, 147–74 and Kotilaine and Poe, eds, *Modernizing Muscovy*, 247–63, respectively. M. S. Anderson adds 'British Officers in the Russian Army in the 18th and early 19th centuries', *Journal for the Society for Army Historical Research*, vol. 38 (1960). The collection, *Russia and the West*, edited by Lindsey Hughes, contains articles in both military and diplomatic history; in particular, note Graeme Herd's 'Peter the Great and the Conquest of Azov', 161–76. On a different note is Peter Petschauer's 'In Search of Competent Aides,' *JfGO*, vol. 26 (1987), 481–502. Alan Ferguson compares the Russian frontier forces with Austrian in 'Russian Landmilitia and Austrian Militårgrenze', *SudOst Forschungen*, vol. 13 (1954), 139–58. John Bushnell's 'The Russian Soldiers' Artel', 1700–1900', in Roger P. Bartlett, ed., *Land, Commune, and Peasant Community in Russia* (New York, 1900), 376–95, speculates about the life of the Petrine soldier.

The Poltava campaign has drawn particular attention: a significant element of R. M. Hatton's classic *Charles XII of Sweden* (New York, 1969) is military in content; also from the Swedish perspective is Peter Englund's *The Battle that Shook Europe. Poltava and the Birth of the Russian Empire* (London, 2003). A Ukrainain perspective is offered by Theodore Mackiw, 'Swedish invasion into Ukraine in 1708', *Ukrainian Quarterly* 43/3–4 (1981), 210–24. In a more popular vein are Angus Konstam's *Poltava, 1709* (London, 1994) and *Peter the Great's Army* (1993). The English-language literature deals poorly with the Russo-Ottoman confrontation in 1711 and army affairs generally after 1710. There are, however, a number of printed document collections in Russian. A recent exception is J. R. Moulton's *Peter the Great and the Russian Military Campaigns During the Final Years of the Geat Northern War, 1719–1721* (Lanham, Boulder, 2005).

Works on Peter's navy include Edward Philips, *The Founding of Russia's Navy: Peter the Great and the Azov Fleet, 1688–1714* (Westport, 1995); various pieces by Jacob W. Kipp; Anthony Cross, *By the Banks of the Neva* (Cambridge, 1997), esp. 159–223; and the much older Cyprian Bridge, *The History of the Russian Fleet during the reign of Peter the Great* (London, 1899). Lindsey Hughes, ed. *Peter the Great and the West*

(Basingstoke, 2001) includes two naval pieces by A. Karimov on forest regulation and Richard Warner on the role of British merchants in the Russian navy.

Source materials in English include Simon Dixon et al., eds and trans, *Britain and Russia in the Age of Peter the Great. Historical Documents* (London, 1998); C. H. von Manstein, *Contemporary Memoirs of Russia from the year 1727 to 1744* (London, 1968); Peter Henry Bruce, *Memoirs of . . . A Military Officer in the Services of Prussia, Russia, and Great Britain* (New York, 1970) and John Perry, *The State of Russia under the Present Tsar* (New York reprint, 1968).

For the interested reader, there is much research that remains to be done.

Glossary

Appanage/udel Term used here to describe territory bequeathed by the Grand Prince to his younger sons, where they ruled with nearly complete autonomy, although the land itself remained a part of the patrimony. The practice was gradually eliminated in the fifteenth and sixteenth centuries.

Bey Leaders of prominent Crimeans clans.

Bez mest A campaign bez mest was one on which assignments did not count toward precedence ranking.

Boiar Duma Boiar Council; appointed advisers to the Tsar or Grand Prince.

Boiar(s) or **Boiar(y)** The highest rank at the Muscovite court. *Boiars* were selected by the Prince from ranking male members of leading court families.

Capitaine d'armes (kapiten darmus) Officer in European-style military regiments who was in charge of firearms, seventeenth century.

Cherkassy Ukrainian Cossacks, term used by Muscovites.

Cherta Earthen and wooden defence line, abattis line.

Chetvert(i) Muscovite dry measure.

Chevaux de frize A piece of wood with projecting spikes, used as battlefield obstacles especially against cavalry; first used by the Prince of Orange during the siege of Groningen, Friesland, against the Spaniards.

Contract service/contract servicemen Non-elite military service in Moscow's army: musketeers, Cossacks and artillerymen. They gained importance under Ivan IV.

Corps Volant Light, mobile military units used by Peter I at Battle of Lesnaia in 1708, discussed in his 1716 Military Regulations.

Deti boiarskie Literally, sons of *boiars*; clients and lower ranking members of a service nobility, often serving from provincial lands.

Diaki State secretaries, scribes.

Duma   Council; the Boiar Duma customarily offered advice to the Tsar and consent to his activities. Under certain circumstances the Duma is understood to have held considerable power to limit the Tsar's actions.

Dumnye dvoriane, dumnye d'iaki   Elite military men and state secretaries with Duma rank, new in Ivan IV's time.

Dvor   The royal court (also household or courtyard).

Dvoriane   Lower-ranking courtiers. In the early sixteenth century they ranked below *deti boiarskie*; by the seventeenth century they were above.

Dvorianstvo   The eighteenth and nineteenth-century term for the Russian nobility.

Fiskaly   Fiscal police introduced by Peter I in 1711.

Gå-på   Have at 'em; refers to the aggressive cavalry tactics of the Swedish army.

Guberniia/gubernii   Territorial units of government introduced by Peter I, 1707–10; provinces.

Guliai gorod   'Mobile fortress' or system of interlocking wooden walls that served as protection for infantry on the battlefield.

Hereditary servicemen   Military man who held the hereditary right to serve in army, at court; collectively, they comprise a Muscovite nobility.

Hetman   Cossack military leader.

Iama, iamskie dengi   Pony-express style postal system on the Mongol model; a general tax that was levied to support it.

Khan   Title of Crimean and Kazan'ian rulers.

Konniushnia   Horse stable.

Kormlenie   'Feeding': maintenance and fees offered to a *namestnik* or viceregent in lieu of salary.

Landmilitsiia   Literally, land militias; locally resident, self-supporting troops introduced in 1713.

Mestnichestvo   Precedence-ranking system that institutionalized inter-clan competition at the Muscovite court, ended in 1682.

Mesto   Place in the ranking system.

Namestnik(i)   Viceregents or governors chosen from high-ranking, but not local, servicemen; remunerated by *kormlenie* or feeding. This system of local government was phased out in the sixteenth century.

Nizovoi Korpus   A corps, largely of infantry, formed for fighting in the war against Persia, 1722–4.

Odnodvortsy   Holders of small, often peasantless, lands.

Okol'nich'e Elite court rank below *boiar* and above *dumnyi dvorianin*.

Oprichnina Ivan IV's personal kingdom-within-a-kingdom, created in 1565 and largely disbanded in 1572.

Pishchal'niki Arquebusiers, early Russian infantry with firearms.

Podat' Tax.

Polki novogo stroia New style or new formation troops (1632–), this refers to hierarchically organized regiments in a European style.

Pomest'e, pomeshchik(i) The Muscovite system of offering men of hereditary service rank (noble, gentry) the temporary use of land in return for their service in the military; person(s) holding service land. Largely men of the middle service class.

Pomestnyi prikaz Service Land Chancellery.

Prikaz Chancellery, seventeenth century and earlier.

Pushechnaia izba; pushechnyi dvor; pushkarskie hudi State cannon manufactury; artillery specialists.

Razriad(y); Razriadnaia Izba; Razriadnyi Prikaz Military service lists, Military Chancellery.

Redoubt Temporary outlying fortification.

Reitar(y) The mid-weight cavalry of the seventeenth-century new style troops.

Shliakhy Tatar approach tracks where horsemen crossed the Oka and Ugra Rivers approaching European Russia from the south for trade, military and political purposes.

Sluzhilye liudi po otechestvu Military servicemen of hereditary (noble) rank; landholders and cavalrymen.

Sluzhilye liudi po priboru Non-elite, military men, including Cossacks, musketeers, artillerymen and others. Contract servicemen.

Soldat(y) Infantry, new-style troops.

Sotnia, sotni Cavalry hundred(s), steppe formation.

Strelets, streltsy Paid musketeer regiments introduced by Ivan IV.

Sudebnik Law code.

Tsaredvortsy Courtiers.

Udel/appanage Territory bequeathed by the Grand Prince to his younger sons, where they ruled with considerable autonomy, although the land itself remained a part of the patrimony.

Ulozhenie Law Code of 1649.

Voevoda Military commander; in the seventeenth century particularly, also a local military governor until 1710 or so.

Votchina As compared to *pomest'e* land, *votchina* belonged to a family; inherited land; patrimony.

Wagenburg A military safe haven created by circling the baggage carts and wagons, for protection against cavalry; also called *tabor* and used by Ottoman, Mongol, Hungarian and Bohemian forces.

Zasluga Individual merit counting toward promotion on the Table of Ranks.

Zemshchina The administrative entity remaining after Ivan IV carved out the territory of the *oprichnina*.

Zemskii sobor Assembly of the Land, national advisory assembly, first convened under Ivan IV.

Index

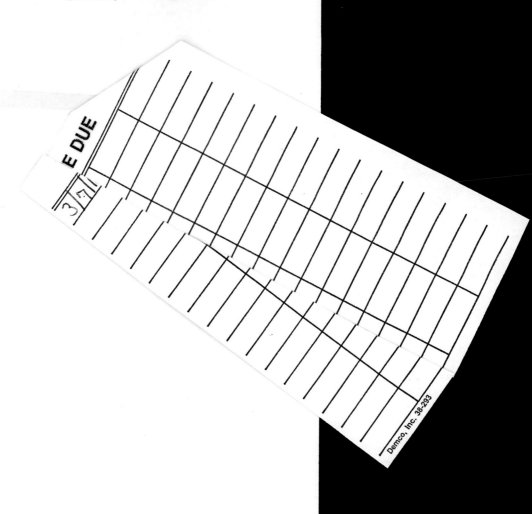